D1548570

VERGIL IN THE MIDDLE AGES

VERGIL
IN THE MIDDLE AGES

DOMENICO COMPARETTI

TRANSLATED BY
E. F. M. BENECKE

With a new introduction by
JAN M. ZIOLKOWSKI

PRINCETON UNIVERSITY PRESS
PRINCETON, NEW JERSEY

Library of Congress Cataloging-in-Publication Data
Comparetti, Domenico, 1835–1927.
[Virgilio nel medio evo.   English]
Vergil in the Middle Ages / by Domenico Comparetti ; with a new
introduction by Jan M. Ziolkowski.
p.   cm.
Originally published: 1885.
Includes bibliographical references.
ISBN 0-691-02678-5 (pb : alk. paper)
1. Virgil—Criticism and interpretation—History.   2. Latin
poetry—Appreciation—Europe—History.   3. Literature,
Medieval—Roman influences.   4. Rome—In literature.   I. Title.
PA6961.C63   1996
873'.01—dc20   96-34031

First Princeton Paperback printing, 1997

Printed in the United States of America by Princeton Academic
Press

1   3   5   7   9   10   8   6   4   2

TABLE OF CONTENTS

PART I

THE VERGIL OF LITERARY TRADITION

INTRODUCTION

The Making of Domenico Comparetti's
Vergil in the Middle Ages

Because in English the name of the great Roman poet *Vergil* is spelled far more routinely with an *i* (*Virgil*) than with an *e*, the very orthography of the first word in the title of Domenico Comparetti's (1835–1927) *Vergil in the Middle Ages* (henceforth designated *VMA*) highlights the utility of studying Vergil's fate in earlier times as an aid to comprehending his nature in our own day. Upon inquiry, we discover the spelling of Vergil with an *i* to be a corruption that had become entrenched in Latin already by the fourth or fifth century and that passed subsequently into the modern European languages.[1] In other words, even to fathom why we call Vergil what we do, we must pay attention to what has been loosely tagged "the Vergilian tradition"—the corpus of scholarship and stories, learned lore and folklore, that has taken shape around Vergil and his poetry during the past two thousand years.

The success of Vergil's *Aeneid* was so much greater than that of other poems for so long a time that to describe the epic as a bestseller would make sense only if the customary noun were "betterseller." The *Aeneid* was not just an epic but *the* epic, even *the* poem, the most enduring of schoolbooks, a repository of pure speech, history, and mythology. Revered in tandem with his poem, Vergil was not just the master of Latin poetic style but also the poet whose creation at once described and enacted the founding of a nation and dynasty. He was a culture hero, the cynosure of a cult that sometimes bordered on a mania—Vergiliomania. Not surprisingly, an extensive scholarly—or *scholastic*—equipment of biographies, commentaries, glosses, and the like was elaborated by ancient and medieval teachers to assist their charges in the mandatory reading of *the* preeminent

[1] Hardie, p. 1123.

poet, to identify whom referring to "the *poeta*" sufficed. Over the centuries the schoolmasters and clerics remade this poet in their own image, as a cleric, an author of a celebrated textbook and a schoolmaster, a sage and a seer, the wisest man of antiquity and the type of the universal philosopher, and even a Christian poet and a guide of a Christian poet. This portion of the medieval Vergilian tradition—which bestowed upon us the Vergil who escorted Dante through the Inferno and beyond—has its undeniable oddities, but it is the legends of Vergil that have earned a richly deserved reputation for their flamboyance. The legends, which first surfaced around the middle of the twelfth century, converted Vergil into a magician, endowed him with supernatural powers, and attributed to him characteristics that had been ascribed to the other prophet-sages and magicians whom he soon overshadowed.

Delving into the legends can become a psychotropic experience, not to be undertaken by anyone without a stout appetite or at least a strong stomach for the bizarre, a sense of humor, and a keen realization of the differences between fiction and reality. In investigating the legends we learn that Vergil cherished especially tender feelings toward Naples. To take three examples that have nothing in common except Naples and a very literal brazenness, the poet is reputed to have given the Neapolitans a bronze horse, which prevented horses from breaking their backs; a bronze fly, which repelled flies from the city; and a bronze statue of an archer, which kept Mount Vesuvius from erupting (*VMA*, p. 259). All we would need to round out the picture would be Vergil's appropriately bronzed baby shoes.

Predictably, Vergil was also associated with Rome in numerous colorful anecdotes. According to the famous escapade of "Vergil in the Basket," the poet becomes enamored of a daughter of the emperor. Although the feeling is not mutual, the young woman pretends to love him so that she can make a fool of him. She proposes to infiltrate him into her room by a Rapunzel-like ruse: by drawing him up in a basket to the window of her tower. Vergil arrives, notices the hamper, clambers into it, and is overjoyed to observe it moving upward according to plan. But suddenly the ascent stops when the young woman leaves the basket dangling only halfway up the tower. Vergil is left stranded until daybreak, whereupon he becomes a source of ridicule to the common people and of fury to the emperor. Consequently the poet-sage resolves to avenge himself. Through his craft as a necromancer he causes all the fires in Rome to be extinguished and arranges matters so that the only way they can be rekindled is for torches to be lit from a particularly private part on the person of the emperor's daughter (*VMA*, pp. 326–27)—an episode that gives radically new meaning to the concept of inflammation!

Such tales represent one wild extreme of Vergil in medieval legend. Other notions—e.g., that Vergil prophesied the nativity of Christ in the fourth bucolic (the "messianic" eclogue) and that he had a magic tome that contained all wisdom—were also widespread. Yet the oddity of these narratives should not make us forget that serious study of Vergil in the commentary tradition proceeded ceaselessly, and that the poet and his poems were never suppressed altogether by the legends. In fact, one of Comparetti's signal achievements in *VMA* was integrating into a single book and train of thought the dual aspects of Vergil in the Middle Ages—the literary reputation and the legends. Although the magical Vergil has tended to stand out in the minds of those concerned with the fate of the poet in the Middle Ages, Comparetti devoted more pages of *VMA* to the learned or literary tradition (pp. 1–238) than to the popular or folkloric Vergil (pp. 239–376). Most notably, he presented a tripartite classification of the main interpretative tacks taken toward the *Aeneid* in the Middle Ages: grammatical, philosophical or allegorical, and historical interpretation.

After the publication of *VMA*, a few major studies of the legends were composed, but they have by no means dislodged Comparetti's book.[2] The real advances have come in our appreciation of Vergil as a literary or textual phenomenon—and in our heightened awareness of the fine distinctions to be drawn between one phase in late antiquity or the Middle Ages and

[2] Alongside the minor contribution of Graf is the larger one of Tunison and the massive work of Spargo. Bronzini provides the most thorough reassessment of *VMA* from the point of view of its folkloristics.

another. Our comprehension of classrooms and schoolmasters has deepened remarkably. Ever closer attention has been paid to the ways in which Vergil's poems interact with late antique and medieval texts. Sometimes this scrutiny has focused upon verbal borrowings or allusions;[3] occasionally upon characters in the *Aeneid* who led unusual lives in medieval literature;[4] and often upon methods of allegorical reading practiced in the Middle Ages.[5] Despite the nearly unanimous praise for Comparetti's approach to the question (*VMA*, pp. 195–231), the complexities of Dante's outlook upon Vergil and upon the classical antiquity Vergil embodied have impelled *Dantisti* to release an incessant flood of chapters, articles, and monographs.[6] Of late most of the research into "the Medieval Vergil" has gone into manuscripts: how many survive, which of them were glossed or commentated and how, which contain musical notation, which have illuminations or drawings, and so forth.[7] Much more is now known than a century ago about the spectrum of interpretations that the *Aeneid* elicited.[8] Finally, laborers in the vineyard of Humanist and Renaissance literature have applied themselves to the enormous task of sorting out how the treatment of Vergil in their period differed from that of Vergil in the Middle Ages.[9] What has been lacking is an effort to consolidate all the new findings into a coherent unit—in other words, what has been and will probably always be missing is a new *VMA* on the scale of Comparetti's book.[10] All the centuries of reading

[3] Courcelle; Hagendahl.

[4] For example, Desmond.

[5] See Lubac; Jones, "Allegorical Interpretation" and "Allegorical Traditions."

[6] Three entire pages of references will be found in Suerbaum (pp. 346–48).

[7] For information on MSS, see Munk Olsen and Kaster. The next major repertory of information about MSS will be the entry on Vergil in the *Catalogus*. An outstanding recent book on Vergil in medieval literature with an emphasis on manuscripts is Baswell.

[8] For instance, Comparetti had little to say about the commentary on the *Aeneid* that is often attributed to Bernardus Silvestris; and unfortunately he confuses Bernardus Silvestris with Bernard of Chartres (Padoan, p. 227, n. 4).

[9] Early work was done by Zabughin. More recently the most active scholars have been Kallendorf and Stok.

[10] Baswell's fine monograph is the closest that we are likely to come, although as its title signals, this work is delimited more narrowly than Comparetti's, both geographically and chronologically.

and explication that have been devoted to Vergil have not exhausted the need for more to be said, but they have made it ever more arduous for anyone to achieve the overarching command of previous work that must precede any practical attempt to synthesize; and the lofty reputation of *VMA* has intimidated its readers and deterred them from the risk of trying to transcend it.[11]

As these remarks about *VMA* suggest, one intellectual of extraordinary range and versatility helped more than anyone else in the nineteenth century to blaze a trail through the phantasmagorically tangled jungle of lore about Vergil in the Middle Ages—and indeed he accomplished his pathfinding so effectively and so visibly that his name fused with that of the Latin poet as soon as his study appeared and remains so today: it is rare to encounter any substantial discussion of Vergil in the Middle Ages that does not begin with or at least include mention of Domenico Comparetti.

But Comparetti was hardly a one-project scholar. His more than one hundred articles and books pursue such diverse enterprises as editions of papyri and inscriptions, dialectology, textual criticism, prosopography, folklore, comparative mythology, Renaissance novellas, literary criticism, and literary history. His book on the Kalevala—which in recent years has continued to garner praise from Albert Bates Lord (1912–1991) and other American scholars of oral literature—was put into English early (1898) and has been reprinted more than once in Italian. Also translated into English (1881) soon after publication was his monograph on *The Book of Sindibad*. Yet among his many writings the work on Vergil is universally recognized as his masterpiece, partly because the topic enabled him to draw together so much of his knowledge and so many of his skills, partly because Comparetti's handling of the topic responded so powerfully (both knowingly and unwittingly) to preoccupations of his day that abide with us even today.

To identify the early 1870s as a time of unusual intellectual foment would be an amusing understatement. The book des-

---

[11] Rossi, p. 281; Graf, quoted by De Liguori, p. 163; Croce, vol. 2, p. 86.

tined to have the greatest impact on both science and society was Charles Darwin's (1809–1882) *The Descent of Man*, which appeared in 1871. In the realm of classical studies, the *annus mirabilis* was 1872, since it saw the publication of two books that have exercised enormous influence for more than a century. One was an investigation of Greek tragedy written by a prodigy who occupied the chair of classical philology at Basel University from 1869 to 1879. I refer of course to Friedrich Nietzsche's *The Birth of Tragedy*, which emphasized the Dionysiac constituent in Greek civilization and especially in Greek Tragedy—and which paid tribute to the *oeuvre* of Richard Wagner. The other marvel of 1872 was Comparetti's *VMA*, the two volumes of which culminated research that had started coming into print in 1866.[12]

Like both *The Descent of Man* and *The Birth of Tragedy*, *VMA* has been acknowledged continuously as a magnum opus by many who have perused it, from its first printing down to the present day. Again and again it has been labeled *magisterial*, *indispensable*, and *fundamental*: it is a *classic* about a classic.[13] In a preamble to the English translation that appeared in 1895, Robinson Ellis (1834–1913) referred to *VMA* as "already a world-famed book." At that point *VMA* had long since been translated into German (1875), was on the verge of seeing the second of its three Italian editions (1872, 1896, 1937–1941), and was poised for the first of several editions in English (1895, 1908, 1929, 1966). Ellis also prophesied rightly that the book seemed "hardly likely to be superseded." When in 1985—nearly a century later—the French school of Rome issued a collection of essays on "Medieval Readings of Vergil," the very first page of the general editor's preface contained the following profession:

> The learned bibliography pertaining to the medieval Vergil is naturally considerable and there can be no question of my providing a detailed critique. However, the afterlife of Vergil continues to

[12] Comparetti, "Virgilio nella tradizione," followed by Comparetti, "Virgilio mago."

[13] For "magisterial," see Ziolkowski, p. 217; for "indispensable," Ogle, p. 63, n. 1; for "fundamental," Rostagni, p. 346; for "classic," see Ogle, p. 63, n. 1; Hardie, p. 1127; Courcelle, vol. 1, p. 9; Jones, "Allegorical Traditions," p. 129, n. 1; Schnapp, p. 131, n. 69.

offer researchers a worksite which is far from being conclusively organized. Yet one thing is striking on first approach: it is the absence of a synthetic work devoted to the problem which occupies us. With one exception, granted, and it is appreciable: the great book of Domenico Comparetti, *VMA*, which, in many regards, is still authoritative . . . Doubtless "Comparetti" has taken on a few wrinkles . . . but it remains that, on a good number of points, his analyses have not been superseded.[14]

Among all the products of nineteeth-century Italian classical studies—and even of Italian historical and literary scholarship as a whole—*VMA* has been singled out as uniquely deserving of continuing to be consulted.[15] The final paragraph on Comparetti in the *Enciclopedia virgiliana* declares: "One hundred years after its appearance, Comparetti's *VMA*, written in an academic prose of rare intensity and beauty, remains a great book, still readable, the masterwork not only of nineteenth-century classical philology but also the best Italian preamble to Medieval Latin studies."[16]

In addition to its canonicity, another quality bonds *VMA* to both *The Descent of Man* and *The Birth of Tragedy*. Darwin attempted nothing less than to account for the origins of homo sapiens, while Nietzsche strove to explain the genesis of an entire literary genre. Like these other two books, *VMA* represents a quest for origins—a pursuit that typified much philology in the nineteenth century.[17] In it Comparetti undertook to demonstrate a continuity and a growth in literary consciousness in classical and medieval western Europe. His book has been called "a true and proper history of European consciousness from antiquity up through Dante."[18] Whether or not it achieved a breadth sufficient to warrant such a global—or, to be more precise, *continental*—tribute, it certainly probed the extent and meaning of Latinity by anatomizing the destiny of its most important poet. Nor did it stop there, since it delved into the rich

[14] Tilliette, p. 2 (my translation).
[15] Chiappelli, "La mente," p. 242; Rostagni, p. 346; Treves, *Lo studio*, p. 1065; Leonardi, p. 860.
[16] Leonardi, p. 860 (my translation).
[17] For this argument in relation to the study of Old English in the nineteenth century, see Frantzen.
[18] Leonardi, p. 860.

relationship between Latinity and what we could call "Italianity" by elucidating the context around Dante's choice of Vergil as his guide. To judge by the continued obeisance done to him in footnotes, Comparetti's achievement in this last regard endures.

It is a truism that most stemmata—"family trees" of manuscripts—generated according to the principles of Karl Lachmann's (1793–1851) genealogical filiation are bipartite; that is, they lead back to one common ancestor but show an almost immediate split into two principal families.[19] If we apply terminology of the "Lachmannian method" to *VMA*, we find that Comparetti identifies two "branches" in the family tree of Vergilian influences. Indeed, one of the few criticisms leveled against the book in the first round of reviews—and one to which he replied in the second edition, although only fleetingly—was that he drew an excessively rigid dividing line between the learned and popular (and, by implication, between the written and oral as well as between the clerical and lay). Comparetti's boldly stated endeavor "to give a complete history of the medieval conception of Vergil" (p. ix) led him to conclude that the Roman poet had two distinct but interrelated destinies, the one in the literary heritage culminating in Dante (the first volume of the original Italian edition) and the other in the popular legend (the second of the two volumes). The literary tradition was argued to be broadly European, whereas according to Comparetti the popular was more parochially Neapolitan—a viewpoint that has been contested by most of his successors.[20] In the case of Vergil, both the literary and the popular traditions could be traced back to brief biographies related in late antiquity and the Middle Ages. These concise "lives" had been streamlined to

---

[19] Timpanaro, *La genesi.*

[20] Vietor, Tunison, Stecher, and Graf denied at least partially the popularity of the legend. In the revised edition Comparetti limits explicit polemic with them to two notes (*VMA*, pp. 255–56, n. 21, and 262, n. 4). But a comparison between the first and second edition shows that in the initial chapters of the second part he was preoccupied with justifying and attenuating the disjunction between the two chief threads of the Virgilian tradition, although he never overcame it. The criticism continues to the present day: see Bronzini, p. 80.

serve the relatively narrow purposes of the schools. At the same time, they contained rudiments that were later extended as Vergil gained renown as a prophet-sage and magician.

Although Comparetti may be remembered most often in conjunction with the fantastic legends of the magician Vergil, he expended just as much effort in satisfying the need for "an adequate history of the classical studies of the middle ages" (p. xi). His compass is truly astounding. He begins his overview with the period in which Vergil himself lived (p. xiii) and moves steadily forward, always seeking to evaluate how the later images of Vergil—the later legends—dovetail with the more scholarly *vitae* of the poet. To bring out these interpenetrations, he presents a far-reaching survey of Vergil's success and influence from the poet's own day to the beginning of the Renaissance. Thus his book covers a grand sweep from the first century B.C.E. through the end of the Middle Ages, with implications even into the nineteenth century.

Authors who aspire to formulate general truths about much more than a millennium of European cultural history cannot do so meaningfully without having first acquired extensive knowledge about the natures of Roman antiquity and the Christian Middle Ages and a conceptual framework into which to fit that knowledge. Like both *The Descent of Man* and *The Birth of Tragedy*, Comparetti's book at once reflects its times and transcends them in its author's basic outlook. To attune ourselves to his attitudes—and in this case the most relevant ones are those concerning antiquity and the Middle Ages—necessitates uncovering and synthesizing what we can about his own early intellectual formation and milieu.

Domenico Comparetti was born in Rome on July 7, 1835, into a family of modest means and background. At first the plan was for him to follow in his father's footsteps by becoming a pharmacist. Accordingly, he took his diploma (*laurea*) in pharmaceutics from the University of Rome (Sapienza romana) in 1855 and practiced as a druggist in a shop that belonged to his maternal uncle.[21] But all along his thoughts and ambitions seem to

[21] Treves, *Lo studio,* p. 1051, states that Comparetti was one of only nine people who before 1859 received their laurea in *farmacia.*

have gravitated elsewhere—toward the study of languages and literatures.[22] As much time as he could, he spent not in the pharmacy but in a nearby library.

Already at a young age he evidenced a strong attraction and aptitude for philology and history, especially involving Greek, Latin, and Romance languages. He received his early training in Classics at the Collegio Romano, a Jesuit institution. Later he frequented lectures and meetings at the German archaeological institute in Rome. Yet of formal higher learning in Classics, medieval and modern languages and literatures, or any other discipline except pharmacology he had no part.

Like virtually all Italian historians and philologists of his generation, Comparetti may be regarded accurately as an autodidact.[23] He had nothing corresponding to postgraduate studies in the humanities of the sort that have become conventional in Europe or North America today—and not even anything equivalent to a present-day Italian *laurea* in Classics. His detachment from the foremost institutions—both Italian and German—in the Rome of his youth was an advantage intellectually, since a stale classicism which is sometimes labeled "antiquarianism" held sway there.[24] Whatever name we attach to the approach to antiquity that dominated in Rome, it was based on Latin epigraphy, and its practitioners rarely ventured beyond the narrowest of prosopographic and topographic concerns.

Comparetti was the first Roman of his century to evince an interest in a philology applied to historicist aims.[25] In addition, he exhibited an exceptional gift for foreign languages and be-

[22] The liveliest picture of this phase in Comparetti's life comes from his own correspondence in Italian and Latin with Gherardo Nerucci, a representative sampling of which can be found in De Gubernatis, p. 306.

[23] Carratelli, p. 672; Chiappelli, "Per Domenico Comparetti," p. 361; De Liguori, p. 195; Pasquali, "Domenico Comparetti," p. 4; Pasquali, "Prefazione," p. xix; Timpanaro, "Domenico Comparetti," p. 349; Treves, *Lo studio*, p. 1051.

[24] The standard study of this antiquarianism is that of Momigliano. The most distinguished of the antiquarians at the time would have been Giovanni Battista De Rossi (1822–1894), for Comparetti's attitude toward whom see Milani, p. 208.

[25] Gigante, p. 160, describes Comparetti as "pursu[ing] historicist goals along the lines of Boeckh's *Methodenlehre*."

came an adept conversationalist in a gamut that eventually included Russian and even Finnish. In his case the taste for foreign languages came with an appetite for travel abroad; at a time when relatively few Italians made a habit of crossing the Alps except when constrained to do so, Comparetti was by choice a frequent traveler on the Continent.[26]

More important for our purposes, he read voraciously in a variety of languages. Although to determine precisely all the books that he perused in his youth lies beyond the grasp of anyone today, he would surely have been acquainted with works of prominent figures such as, among others, the French historian Jules Michelet (1798–1874), the Swiss French historian and economist Jean Charles Léonard de Sismondi (1773–1842), and the Italian philosopher Giambattista Vico (1668–1774).[27] Of these three, Michelet would have provided a particularly inspirational model. None of the Frenchman's trips to Italy could have brought him face to face with Comparetti before 1870–1871;[28] but Michelet's writings would have found in Comparetti a responsive reader, since the older Frenchman and the younger Italian shared several important convictions. In the 1840s Michelet became outspoken in attacks against both Catholicism and the Middle Ages; his criticisms of the two were interwoven, since he saw the Catholic Church as having nurtured passivity and the Middle Ages as having been "barbarous" and "a world of illusion."[29] Like Michelet, Comparetti tended to view the Middle Ages reductively as a monolith, without recognizing many of the gradations between one medieval time and place and another that have become apparent to twentieth-century medievalists.

Because Comparetti's life centered upon Rome until 1859, his receptiveness to contacts with scholars abroad and with foreigners in Rome (especially those affiliated with the German archaeological institute) was indispensable for his intellectual matura-

---

[26] Pais, p. 385.

[27] Comparetti's indebtedness to Vico can be seen in the polemic with Lambruschini: G. Landucci, p. 64.

[28] Scharten, p. 162, quotes a letter from Pasquale Villari (March 5, 1871), which was sent to Michelet together with a letter for Comparetti.

[29] Kippur, p. 85, and Mitzman, p. 30.

tion; many of the most illustrious Italian intellectuals had fled Italy into exile after 1849.[30] During his Roman years Comparetti produced three articles, which showed him already equipped in his early twenties to engage as a peer with the greatest foreign philologists. Each of the three items was prompted by the publication of a document, but only this feature connected him with the antiquarians.[31] This triad of articles also provided a measure of the virtuosic scope that he would later display: his first article, written in Latin and published in a German periodical in 1858, identified a papyrus as a funeral oration by Hyperides; his second, also in Latin and in the same journal in 1858, was based on a freshly discovered palimpsest of a Late Latin text of the annalist Granius Licinianus; and his third reviewed an edition of the *Composizione del mondo* of Ristoro di Arezzo; in it Comparetti revealed that he had already constructed his own conception of the cultural history of the Middle Ages.[32] His interests continued to span these two eras, antiquity and the Middle Ages, and often guided him to the confluences of different disciplines and fields.

Exactly one decade before the *Wunderkind*—or *enfant terrible* —Nietzsche was elected at the age of twenty-five to a chair of classical philology at Basel University, Comparetti was nominated at the even more precocious age of twenty-four to be professor of Greek literature at the University of Pisa. He received his appointment in 1859 and stayed there until 1872, when he transferred to Florence—and when the first edition of *VMA* was printed.

Comparetti had formed himself very rapidly. At thirty he had already sketched out the basic contours of *VMA*; by thirty-seven he had published it in substantially its definitive outlines.[33] But

---

[30] Timparano, "Domenico Comparetti," p. 349.

[31] Pasquali, "Domenico Comparetti," pp. 6–8.

[32] "Observationes in Hyperidis orationem funebrem," *Rheinisches Museum* N.F. 13 (1858); "Epistula ad Fridericum Ritschelium de Liciniani annalium scriptoris aetate," *Rheinisches Museum* N.F. 13 (1858), reprinted in an expanded Italian version in *Archivio storico italiano* N.S. 10 (1859); and "Intorno all'opera sulla composizione del Mondo di Ristoro d'Arezzo, pubblicata da E. Narducci," *Giornale Arcadico* aprile 1859. See Pasquali, "Domenico Comparetti," p. 7.

[33] Pasquali, "Domenico Comparetti," p. 5

his intellectual energies and creativities were in no way depleted. Nietzsche, who was born in 1844 (nearly a decade after Comparetti), died in 1900. Comparetti lived on to become the Nestor of philologists in Italy, leading a highly active or even *hyperactive* career of research and publishing to the ripe old age of ninety-two: he died on January 20, 1927, with the proofs of his final book on his desk.[34]

Comparetti's academic appointment may have been as a classicist, but in terms of the profile that he has left in his writings, such a designation is inaccurate solely through being partial. He was a classicist, both Hellenist and Latinist, equally epigrapher, papyrologist, and archaeologist. By the same token he was a folklorist and comparative mythographer.

Comparetti also had ample justification to be called a medievalist, even though often he was far less complimentary about the Middle Ages than most medievalists are prone to be. Three examples will confirm his capacity for voicing the harshest judgments of medieval intellectuals and their writings. First is his assessment of the writer Fulgentius, who flourished around 500 c.e. (*VMA*, p. 112):

> But the process of Fulgentius is so violent and incoherent, it disregards every law of common sense in such a patent and well-nigh brutal manner, that it is hard to conceive how any sane man can seriously have undertaken such a work, and harder still to believe that other sane men should have accepted it as an object for serious consideration.

However fierce that quotation may seem, it pales beside Comparetti's verdict on the infamous seventh-century Virgilius Maro Grammaticus (*VMA*, p. 124):

> To attempt to follow the processes of these minds would be at once a wasted endeavour and an outrage on common sense. . . . [Vergil of Toulouse] is perhaps the only medieval grammarian who deserves to be called original, but his originality takes a strange turn. . . . This strange writer . . . reminds one irresistibly in the squalor of his time (6th–7th century) of those hideous and putrid fungi which are generated in the rotting leaves of autumn.

[34] For the likening of Comparetti to Nestor, see Pais, p. 385; for the description of his deskwork at death, see Milani, p. 203.

Nor are these passages on individual authors isolated aberrations. Rather, they reflect a viewpoint pervasive in his book that is sharply dismissive of medieval clerical culture (*VMA*, pp. 171–72):

> The culture of the middle ages, in everything concerned with secular matters, was too poor and feeble a thing to raise the mind far above the common level. Humanism was essentially foreign to this period; the most worldly monk, the most passionate admirer of the ancient writers, is yet infinitely more Philistine than the worst Latinist of the Renaissance could possibly be.

Such intemperate generalizations occur too abundantly in *VMA* to be overlooked. Yet unless they are put in the context of late-nineteenth-century attitudes, any condemnation of them runs the risk of being just as rash and simplistic as they seem to be themselves.

A good way to begin sizing up Comparetti's conception of the Middle Ages is to explore his notions of antiquity and the Classics. In the range of his interests and researches, Comparetti bears a resemblance to at least two other classicists of the nineteenth century: Karl Lachmann and Moriz Haupt (1808–1874), both of whom demonstrated comparable mastery of classical and medieval studies (in their cases, as classical philologists and Germanists).[35] Part of what motivated and enabled Lachmann and Haupt to attain this dual competence was perhaps the very fact that they did not regard it as dual at all. In the case of Comparetti the answer for his receptivity to both antiquity and the Middle Ages seems to be that he wedded elements of two major cultural movements that would have been current in his youth, namely, classicism and Romanticism. Even though he professed in the diary he kept in his early twenties "to be antiromantic in body and soul,"[36] his intellect was still largely Romantic in some regards—for instance, in his desire to achieve a panoptic view and in his fascination with the vitality of traditions.[37]

---

[35] Pasquali, "Domenico Comparetti," pp. 7–8, drew this comparison.

[36] Milani, p. 207 (later quoted by Timpanaro, "Domenico Comparetti," p. 356).

[37] Pasquali, "Domenico Comparetti," p. 12.

What unites him with the most brilliant of Romantics is that he did not dichotomize too starkly between popular and literary or popular and learned. He recognized that in coming to grips with almost all earlier periods the popular can be apprehended only with the help of texts that are anything but popular in their basic assumptions (*VMA*, pp. 253–54).[38] Yet at the same time he is a classicist, not just professionally but also in his admiration of classicism—and of the Classics.

To Italian scholars who have sought to devise a term that encompasses all the methods Comparetti deployed in his polymathic researches and writings, the one that has been used most often—by Benedetto Croce (1866–1952) and Giorgio Pasquali (1885–1952), among others—is *philology*. In the annals of Italian humanistic scholarship, Comparetti is credited with having created or founded modern philology—as having been the first "master" of what was in Italy in the second half of the nineteenth century "the new philology."[39] And what was this philology? It was not confined to such technical matters as grammar, textual criticism, and prosody—in all of which (by the bye) Comparetti showed scant interest. Formal philology was not his forte. As has been seen, Comparetti's definition of philology pushed him to ask big questions that held interest to classicists, medievalists, and comparatists alike. And, in good humanistic style, these questions were ones that pertained to the human condition as evidenced in texts. Every chapter of *VMA* attests that Comparetti saw the study of a textual tradition as inevitably entailing the examination of both national tradition and a human event in its public dimension. Finally, Comparetti's philology required a comprehensive knowledge of the period under analysis—a knowledge that was grounded in history as well as in a faith in historicism.[40] Although his method has been dubbed cultural history, it is propelled by a zeal for contextualizing texts that separates it from much of what pass-

---

[38] Leonardi, p. 859.
[39] Croce, vol. 2, p. 76; Pasquali, "Domenico Comparetti," p. 9; Timpanaro, "Comparetti, Vitelli, Hemmerdinger."
[40] Pasquali, "Domenico Comparetti," p. 9 (quoted by Leonardi, p. 859).

es under the name of cultural studies today.[41] It is philology, a historical or rather a historicist philology.[42]

What spurred Comparetti's choice of topic? Because Comparetti produced the first edition of *VMA* in 1872 and the second in 1896, it would appear superficially that he made no gesture to capitalize upon the swell of interest in Vergil that coincided with the nineteenth centenary of Vergil's death in 1882. As the author of a recent book on the Vergilian tradition put it, "The 1882 commemorations would seem to bear out Robert Graves's thesis that 'whenever a golden age of stable government, full churches, and expanding wealth dawns among the Western nations, Virgil always returns to supreme favour.'"[43] Did Comparetti distance himself deliberately from the festivities of 1882? Or was the political and social climate that made Vergil so logical a point of orientation—or, as the case may be, *occidentation*—already present in the 1860s and early 1870s?

Much support can be adduced for the latter view. Although sometimes Comparetti has been cast as apolitical or politically detached, his book betrays signs, hardly hidden, of certain political opinions he held. In particular, *VMA* cries out to be situated in the public and intellectual life of Italy in the third quarter of the nineteenth century; for Comparetti was assembling his insights into the afterlife of Vergil just as the establishment of modern Italy—the *Risorgimento*—was taking place. The Kingdom of United Italy under King Victor Emmanuel II (1820–1878) was recognized in 1861, and Rome was made the capital in 1872—which, at the risk of being very tedious, I will point out again was the very year in which *VMA* appeared.[44] Setting the book against the backdrop of Italian history may make it easier to determine why Comparetti chose to see Vergil as the supporting structure of Latinity's own self-consciousness and of the new nations that arose out of the Roman Empire and its

[41] Croce, vol. 2, pp. 77–78 (drawing a parallel to Burckhardt's book on the Renaissance); Leonardi, p. 859, following Timpanaro; Treves, *Lo Studio*, pp. 1051 and 1059; De Liguori, pp. 170–71.

[42] Timpanaro, "Comparetti, Vitelli, Hemmerdinger," p. 699.

[43] Ziolkowski, p. 6

[44] Ziolkowski, p. 4.

heirs—among which nations we would have to number the Italy of his day.

Once reconstituted (and it bears noting that the process was regarded as a *re*constitution), Italy quickly took measures to revitalize its culture. Many fine minds had been distracted or diverted from artistic creation and intellectual endeavor while the *Risorgimento* was being prepared. Afterward creative energies poured forth suddenly, at both personal and collective levels. The government set up universities and, in so doing, accorded central importance to classical philology and stimulated it by appointing professors of Classics. The year 1859 marked the turning point in this process from political resurgence to cultural rebirth, as can be documented very neatly in letters to Comparetti from one of his mentors—and subsequently the posthumous dedicatee of *VMA*—Gian Pietro Vieusseux (1779–1863).[45] In the summer of that year Vieusseux sent a letter in which he exhorted Comparetti to hold off on scholarship and publication projects because people owed their all to the cause of Italian independence.[46] But circumstances changed swiftly. In mid November Vieusseux wrote to the minister of public instruction to nominate Comparetti for a chair at Florence or Pisa.[47]

A decree of December 22, 1859, inaugurated what would ultimately become the University of Florence, with the explicit aim of making Florence the cultural capital of Italy. As it turned out, Comparetti would not assume a position there until 1872. Instead, he played a pivotal role in creating the so-called school of Pisa, together with the Romance philologist Alessandro D'Ancona (1835–1914), the Semiticist Fausto Lasinio (1831–

---

[45] Vieusseux is best known for having founded a series of Florentine cultural and political journals: see Mori, pp. 266–67. For Comparetti he would have exemplified ways to be receptive to Europe beyond the Alps and yet to be attentive to Italian and Tuscan traditions, to be politically engaged and yet to be committed to culture, to be open to both a controlled Romanticism and an enlightened Classicism, and to be alert to the past and yet wary of a Romantic nostalgia for the Middle Ages: see Spadolini, *L'Idea*, and Timpanaro, *Classicismo*, p. 21.

[46] Garin, pp. 30–31, n. 2 (June 11, 1859), and Conti, p. 17, n. 43.

[47] Garin, p. 41, n. 16 (November 11, 1859).

1914), and the Sanskritist Emilio Teza (1831–1912).[48] Comparetti himself gives a glimpse of this circle in his memoir of D'Ancona.[49]

Intellectually, D'Ancona was probably the most intimate of Comparetti's colleagues in this cohort; the same age, appointed to a chair at Pisa very soon after Comparetti, D'Ancona had also been a protégé of Vieusseux.[50] A few years before coming to Pisa, D'Ancona had attended the acclaimed series of lectures on the *Divine Comedy* by Francesco De Sanctis (1817–1883) in Turin in 1854–1855; in fact, D'Ancona even transcribed and published the lecture on Pier delle Vigne in a Florentine newspaper.[51] Relations between D'Ancona and De Sanctis remained close over the next two decades; De Sanctis referred laudatorily to articles written by D'Ancona, and even in his old age D'Ancona professed admiration for De Sanctis.[52]

But D'Ancona was not just a bridge between De Sanctis and Comparetti. More significantly, he was a colleague and collaborator of Comparetti's.[53] While Comparetti mapped the legends that grew up in the Middle Ages around Vergil, D'Ancona followed sacred legends and novelistic legends that could be found in both popular literature and artistic literature.[54] Both men, like many of their contemporaries in Tuscany at this time, forged enduring links with European culture outside Italy and manifested an impatience with abstraction when it was not firmly based in history and texts.[55] As a team D'Ancona and Comparetti edited the oldest and richest collection of Italian lyric literature, the *rime*.[56] The two also attracted many students who had successful careers as professors of Classics and

---

[48] Chiappelli, "La mente," p. 245; Leonardi; Milani, pp. 206–7.

[49] Comparetti's memoir was published first in the *Giornale d'Italia*, December 12, 1914, and later reprinted by Treves, *Lo Studio*.

[50] Pais, p. 388; Cocchiara, pp. 376–77.

[51] Muscetta, p. 31.

[52] S. Landucci, p. 245.

[53] On the intellectual influence of D'Ancona on Comparetti, see Pasquali, "Prefazione," pp. xx–xxi.

[54] Levi, pp. 3–4.

[55] S. Landucci, p. 242.

[56] Mazzoni, p. 528.

Romance Languages.[57] Comparetti continued to foster such renewal when he transferred to the chair of Greek literature in Florence in 1872, where he remained until his retirement (apart from a short stint of teaching at the University of Rome in 1882). There he influenced many students, among whom the classicist Giorgio Pasquali has had the greatest renown in the twentieth century.

Thanks to his activities in both Pisa and Florence, Comparetti established classical philology on a solid footing in Italy; but although Comparetti was important in the intellectual development and careers of students from both Pisa and Florence, there was never a "school of Comparetti." One reason is that Comparetti taught for much less than half of his life; another is that because his own interests were so far-flung, it would have been proper to speak of *schools* of Comparetti in the plural: his students went in as many directions as he did himself, but none managed to replicate anything approaching the entire span of his achievements.

No one would question the value of analyzing the interplay between cultural concerns and ideology in the literary-historical and aesthetic writings of Comparetti's contemporary, De Sanctis (who served as minister of education in 1861–1862 before becoming professor at the University of Naples in 1871);[58] but would many people perceive the prospect of similar benefits from subjecting the works of Comparetti to the same type of analysis? After all, throughout his career Comparetti gave the impression of being aloof from political concerns.[59] Even after becoming a senator, Comparetti never participated actively in politics as did De Sanctis. Yet however little engaged he was personally in public politics, it would be mistaken to believe either that his

[57] To name only three, Pio Rajna (1847–1930), Francesco D'Ovidio (1849–1925), and Girolamo Vitelli (1849–1935), who succeeded Comparetti in the chair of Greek literature at Florence.

[58] See S. Landucci and Cione (with section headings such as "Esperienze culturali e politiche durante l'esilio" and "L'armonia fra pensiero ed azione").

[59] On Comparetti's apoliticism and "natural inclination to *ataraxia*," see Carratelli, p. 674; Treves, *Lo Studio*, p. 1052; Vitelli, p. 222.

university appointments had no political dimensions or that his research lacked them. His step of writing a book on Vergil was also to some extent ideologically implicated.

Most of the faults that have been found in Comparetti's *VMA* can be explained—and *not* explained *away*—by the specific climate in which he conceived and composed it. Chief among these failings would be its anticlericalism and distrust of Catholicism (and even of Christianity in general?) as well as its pro-Italian nationalism and its anti-Germanicism.[60]

Let us inspect these flaws more closely. To start with anticlericalism, we find Comparetti stating of Dante (*VMA*, p. 199): "With him there is not only an absence of that hatred of the pagans which inspired so many of the early monks and ascetics, but also of that doubt and suspicion, that feeling of restriction in dealing with secular studies, which characterises so many of the more enlightened men of the Church." If this declaration does not seem forceful enough to prove the point, then we can turn to a note at the end of the same chapter in which, mincing no words, Comparetti underlines the differences in view between the fifth-century ecclesiastic writers Augustine and Orosius, on the one hand, and the early fourteenth-century Dante Alighieri, on the other (*VMA*, p. 231 n.): "Pagan Rome was still too near them, and they had not seen Christianity grown a persecutor in its turn and the history of the Church changed into a chronicle of obscenities."

Finally, there is Comparetti's introspection about his appraisal of Charlemagne's role in European history.[61] With candid self-awareness, Comparetti concedes that his judgment may be colored by an anticlericalism that derives from Italy's political circumstances (*VMA*, p. 185): "I do not know whether my judgment of this prince is prejudiced by that repugnance which an Italian cannot fail to feel towards one who did such harm to all Europe and has been till recently the curse of our unfortunate country. It certainly seems to me as if about his historical per-

---

[60] On these biases, see Rand, pp. 420–21; Pasquali, "Prefazione," p. xviii; Timpanaro, "Domenico Comparetti," p. 358.
[61] Boissier, p. 526.

sonality of prince, legislator and warrior there hung an unpleasant odour of sanctity. He was the 'homo Papae' *par excellence.*" As this little editorial and others (e.g., *VMA*, p. 177)
make crystal clear, Comparetti felt depressed as an Italian at
the political ramifications, throughout and even beyond the
Middle Ages, of a papacy that partook in secular affairs.

But Comparetti's dissatisfaction with the Church surpassed
mere distrust of the papacy's involvement in worldly politics.
One aspect of Comparetti's conflicted outlook on Christianity
has been called "rationalist laicism": a predisposition to accen-
tuate those beliefs and practices of medieval Christianity that
appeared to be adaptations of paganism.[62] Elsewhere in *VMA*
Comparetti makes asides that are caustically dismissive of
Catholic doctrines. For instance, at one juncture he brands the
Catholic promotion of celibacy as "a doctrine not only absurd,
but also immoral, in that it is egotistical, is contrary to the first
principles of human society, and places human perfection in
direct opposition to natural laws and the continued existence of
the human race" (*VMA*, p. 325).

Catholicism collides with Darwinism more than once in *VMA*.
Even though Darwinism had not been fully elaborated when
Comparetti wrote the heart of his book—a few more years
would pass before Florence's society would be thrown into up-
heaval by bitter debate over the relationship between man and
monkeys—the first shock-waves of evolutionary thinking had
already struck.[63] Indeed, in 1862 Comparetti had fought a skir-
mish about linguistics (was it a science comparable to the natural sciences? what did it reveal about the origins and interrela-
tions of man and races?) which took place on the outskirts of
this battlefield.[64]

If anticlericalism and distrust of Catholicism were one pole
toward which the political climate pressed Comparetti, another
was the passionate nationalism that obtrudes at many points in

[62] Treves, *Lo Studio*, p. 1059; De Liguori 199–200.
[63] Mori, pp. 267–68.
[64] On Comparetti's contention on behalf of his friend Gherardo Nerucci
with Raffaello Lambruschini (1788–1873), see Gentile, pp. 343–47; G. Landucci, pp. 56–75; Timpanaro, "Antileopardiani," p. 416, n. 37.

VMA.[65] Comparetti admitted to his pro-Italian sentiments already in the closing paragraph of the preface to the first edition (*VMA*, p. xiv):

> As an Italian, I have never been able to forget how thoroughly Italian are the nature and the interest of my subject; but I have endeavoured to write calmly, and to eliminate as far as might be any subjective cause of prejudice. If any such feeling has in any place warped my judgment, I can only regret it; but at the same time I would ask any one who feels tempted to condemn me for this to look carefully in his own conscience whether it be in his place to cast the first stone at me.

A more acute or honest estimation of the struggles that take place within a person who is simultaneously a scholar and a political animal—as all academics are to varying degrees—would be hard to imagine.

For better or for worse, Comparetti was not always able to filter out his patriotic spirit. Thus he professed to take pride in the continuing classicism of medieval Italians—in their classicizing distrust of the irrational. Take, for example, the observation (*VMA*, pp. 250–51): "One of the points in which the Italians, even in the middle ages, gave proof of their superiority to the other nations of Europe, was the small share which they took in the phantastic productions of that period." The same national pride, which in his case was very much a *Latin* pride, accounts for the force and beauty of the passages about Dante, who represented to Comparetti a last, unique exponent of Latin universality.[66]

Pro-Italian sometimes meant anti-German. Although Comparetti had close ties with German scholarship,[67] he built them before the creed took hold among Italians that what had been achieved in their own scholarship during the *Risorgimento* was worthless and that the one means of escaping from amateurish

---

[65] Remarked upon early and intelligently by Boissier.

[66] The final phrase is translated directly from Chiappelli, "Per Domenico Comparetti," p. 377.

[67] Early in his career he received support from Heinrich Brunn (1822–1894), who headed the German archaeological institute in Rome: Chiappelli, "Per Domenico Comparetti," p. 361; Pasquali, "Domenico Comparetti," pp. 3 and 9, n. 3; Treves, *Lo Studio*, p. 1054.

antiquarianism was to resort to the German philological method in its most positivist guise.[68] In other words, he came into his
own as an intellect before it became conventional for aspiring
scholars to go to Germany as a finishing school, even when their
subject was Italian literature.[69] Comparetti and the other leading lights of his generation in Italian higher learning may have
inclined toward positivism, but not yet toward a typically German positivism.[70]

As a consequence of the political climate that enveloped Italy
during the *Risorgimento*, Comparetti had developed propensities that would have to be called antiteutonic. Since Italians of
his generation had witnessed decades of struggle to free their
lands of German-speaking occupiers so that Italy could become
one country, it is to be expected that they should feel a certain
ambivalence toward German-speaking nations. Look at the ve-
hement judgment of non-Italians to which he gives vent in
verses written in 1853 or thereabouts, when he would have been
around eighteen years old: "To the foreigners who visit the monuments of Italy, an epigram. These monuments admired by you
still show you the Latin might, but the deep ruins which cover
them show you of whom you are the descendants."[71] It takes
little acuity to discern the criticism of Germanic peoples im-
plicit in these lines.

The understandable political suspicions of Italians toward the
Austro-Hungarian empire were imposed retrospectively upon
the Middle Ages. Most broadly, Comparetti's deep *Risorgimento*
anticlericalism—or was it an Enlightenment anticlericalism
that could be traced back to Voltaire (1694–1778)?—led him to
distrust the clericization of Europe that had been advanced
through the policies of Charlemagne.[72] It also prompted him to

[68] Gigante, p. 198; Timpanaro, "Comparetti, Vitelli, Hemmerdinger,"
p. 702.
[69] De Lollis, p. 132.
[70] Treves, *Lo Studio*, p. 1058, and De Liguori, pp. 199–200. Pais, pp. 387–
88, documents the increasingly German tilt of Italian scholarship and even
tries wrongly to associate Comparetti with it.
[71] Milani, p. 204, n. 1: "Agli stranieri che visitano/ i monumenti d'Italia/
Epigramma. Questi da voi ammirati monumenti/ Ancor vi mostran la virtú
latina/ Ma quella che li copre alta rovina/ Vi mostra di chi siate discendenti."
[72] On the Voltairean element, see Pasquali, "Prefazione," p. XVIII.

generalizations about Teutonic or Germanic races and cultures that were (if we were inclined to impose present-day standards with the same mirthless and remorseless anachronism) decidedly politically incorrect. My first two examples make sweeping assertions about antithetical traits of the Teutonic and Latin races:

> The Teutonic and Latin races were diametrically opposed to one another and separated by lively antipathies, for which there was every historical justification; the Germans, though quickly corrupted themselves, yet retained certain ideas which they had inherited from those barbarous ancestors of theirs whom Tacitus had contrasted with the Romans. (*VMA*, pp. 178–79)

> Moreover, the German races, whom the weakness of their superiors had suffered to gain the upper hand, were incapable, as may still be seen at the present day, of assimilation, and thus, so far from assimilating others, great masses of them were themselves assimilated when brought into contact with various of the neo-Latin nationalities. (*VMA*, p. 180)

Not unforeseeably, races as different in Comparetti's eyes as the Teutons and Latins produced art forms of their own sorts. Here too Comparetti makes no bones about his prejudice in favor of the Romans and their descendants: "It is a mere misuse of the word 'classic' to apply it, as is done in Germany, to Wolfram von Eschenbach, Gottfried von Strassburg and the other writers of the Mittel-Hoch-Deutsch, who hardly deserve such a title for that period of literature to which they belong" (*VMA*, p. 194).

These observations furnish proof that Vergil constituted a flashpoint in cultural tensions—in what we could call anachronistically the culture wars—between Germans and Italians in the nineteenth century. It is a truism that until 1903, which saw not only the advent of both Richard Heinze's (1867–1929) book on Vergil's epic technique and Eduard Norden's (1858–1941) edition of *Aeneid* Book 6 but also the death of an even more eminent German classicist, Germans had tended to turn much more enthusiastically to Greece than to Rome.[73] For all of their services to the study of Latinity, many German scholars ex-

[73] Hardie, p. 1128.

pressed a distinct lack of admiration for Roman writers, such as Cicero, Horace . . . and Vergil.[74] Thus when Comparetti undertook his toils on Vergil, all the elements were in place to guarantee that there would be a Germano-Italian conflict over Vergil: questions of Vergil's worth in comparison with Homer's, of the fitness of Italian scholars to embark upon classical studies without having first received tutelage in Germany, and of Vergil's contribution to Romance versus Germanic civilization. These issues took many decades to be settled (if indeed they have been resolved yet!), and well into the twentieth century we happen upon authors writing in Romance languages who feel obliged to rehabilitate Vergil after the assaults against him from German scholars.[75]

The tensions came to the fore in a coolness between Comparetti and Theodor Mommsen (1817–1903) that can be tracked in the actions and written words of both men, even before the publication of *VMA*.[76] Comparetti had none of the insecurity toward foreign scholars that became endemic in Italy not even a generation after him, when (partly out of the inferiority complex vis-à-vis the experimental sciences that ensued after Darwin) philology turned more positivist and less historicist and humanist.[77] Other Italian intellectuals of his day, such as De Sanctis, were able without contradiction to express admiration for Mommsen and pride in Italian achievements in ancient historiography.[78] Comparetti was unable or unwilling to strike such a balance. Although (or because?) younger than Mommsen by close to twenty years, he felt qualified already in the opening pages of *VMA* to react against Mommsen and against Mommsen's less than fervent embrace of Vergil, and in so doing perhaps to exaggerate Vergil's Romanness.[79] Perhaps he was egged

[74] Boissier, p. 517.
[75] On Espinosa Pólit's *Virgilio*, see Ziolkowski, p. 52.
[76] See Domenico Comparetti, "Sull'amovibilità dei manoscritti dalle pubbliche biblioteche," with a letter of Theodor Mommsen, *Giornale di Pisa*, March 27, 1864.
[77] Gigante, pp. 198–99.
[78] Cagnetta, p. 134.
[79] Pasquali, "Domenico Comparetti," p. 16; Timpanaro, "Domenico Comparetti," p. 353; Treves, "Ciceronianismo," p. 452 and notes.

on by his patrons, such as the antimommsenian Duke Michelangelo Caetani di Sermoneta (1804–1882).[80] In any case, Mommsen apparently responded to the criticism by preventing Comparetti from being named a fellow of the Berlin academy; and students in Italy were keenly aware that Mommsen and other Germans held *VMA* in low esteem.[81]

Questions about Comparetti's book linger—and not only in Germany. A book that unfolds a structure in which to view almost fifteen hundred years in the reception of a great poet and that lays claim to him as a national poet cannot help but stir controversy: Vergil is a poet whose interpreters have always been possessive. But even those people who criticize *VMA* for its shortcomings—and I have made no effort to conceal any of its drawbacks—grant that it is unmatched and utterly unsupplanted in its synthesis of ideas and information about Vergil and his *Aeneid* in both learned and popular culture in the Middle Ages. Of the much that has been written about Vergil since Comparetti and of the much more that will be written, not all will be mere marginalia to *VMA*;[82] but Comparetti's book will continue to be the starting point for those curious about the poet's *Nachleben*—not only about Vergil the magician but also about Vergil the poet-sage, about Dante's Vergil. Moreover, despite any and all of its defects, *VMA* stands as a monument of nineteenth-century thought about the place of the greatest Roman poet in European civilization.

Because Comparetti's *VMA* has been widely read for a century in the English translation by E. F. M. Benecke, retranslating it and bringing it up-to-date in its annotation would pose messy problems for readers who wished to find in it pages or passages cited in earlier scholarship. This is to say nothing of the expenses that the publisher would incur, and the labor that the redactor would face. Accordingly, this edition has been left just as it was when first printed in 1895, except that the brief

---

[80] Treves, *Lo Studio*, p. 1053.
[81] Treves, *Lo Studio*, p. 1051; De Lollis, p. 132.
[82] The final clause alludes equally to Ussani, "In margine," and to Tilliette, p. 2.

introduction by Robinson Ellis has been omitted. Readers who wish to consult a version in which the notes have been improved slightly and which contains the medieval texts that Comparetti incorporated as appendices in the two-volume Italian printings should refer to Pasquali's excellent edition; but even Pasquali refrained from tampering with Comparetti's style or from undertaking a thoroughgoing recasting of the notes. As Pasquali put it, "From the very beginning I have had no doubt that the text would have to be treated like that of a classic."[83] As the book is now reprinted in English exactly a hundred years after Comparetti's second edition, *VMA* deserves more than ever to be called a classic.

Jan M. Ziolkowski

WORKS CITED

The following bibliography includes all works on Comparetti and Vergil cited in the introduction. Although it makes no pretense to being comprehensive (to identify one area of omission, it features only a few of the many necrologies that appeared in the late 1920s), the bibliography lists most of the major secondary writings that have been devoted to Comparetti and especially to his *VMA* since his death. For a bibliography of Comparetti's writings, see his *Poesia e pensiero del mondo antico*, ed. Carratelli, pp. xi–xvi.

Baswell, Christopher. *Virgil in Medieval England: Figuring the Aeneid from the Twelfth Century to Chaucer.* Cambridge Studies in Medieval Literature 24. Cambridge: Cambridge University Press, 1995.

Boissier, Gaston. "Virgile au moyen âge." *Revue des Deux Mondes* XLVIIe année, Troisième période, 19 (1877): 515–36.

Bronzini, G. B. "Tradizione culturale e contesto sociale delle leggende virgiliane nell'Italia meridionale." *Cultura e scuola* 21, no. 82 (1982): 67–93.

Cagnetta, Mariella. *Antichità classiche nell'Enciclopedia italiana.* Biblioteca di cultura moderna 987. Roma: Laterza, 1990.

Carratelli, G. Pugliese. "Comparetti, Domenico." In *Dizionario biografico degli Italiani.* Ed. Albert M. Ghisalberti. Rome: Istituto della Enciclopedia italiana, 1960–. Vol. 27 (1982), pp. 672–76.

Catalogus translationum et commentariorum: Mediaeval and Renaissance Latin Translations and Commentaries. Ed. Paul Oskar Kristeller and

---

[83] "Prefazione," p. xxxiii.

others. Vol. 1–. Washington, D.C.: Catholic University of America Press, 1960–.

Chiappelli, Alessandro. "La mente di Domenico Comparetti." *Nuova rivista storica* 2 (1918): 239–52.

———. "Per Domenico Comparetti." *Rendiconti dell'Accademia dei Lincei* 3 (1927): 357–78.

Cione, Edmondo. *Francesco de Sanctis ed i suoi tempi.* Naples: Montanino, 1960.

Cocchiara, Giuseppe. *Storia del folklore in Europa.* Turin: Edizioni Scientifiche Einaudi, 1952. Pp. 376–78 and 389–93.

Comparetti, Domenico. *Il Kalevala: o, La poesia tradizionale dei Finni: Studio storico critico sulle origini delle grandi epopee nazionali.* Ritorni 3. Repr. Milan: Guerini, 1989. Trans. Isabella M. Anderton. *The Traditional Poetry of the Finns.* London and New York: Longmans, Green and Co., 1898.

———. Memoir of Alessandro D'Ancona. *Giornale d'Italia* 12 December 1914. Repr. in Treves, *Lo Studio.*

———. *Poesia e pensiero del mondo antico.* Ed. Giovanni Pugliese Carratelli. Napoli: R. Ricciardi, 1944.

———. "Ricerche intorno al libro di Sindibâd." *Memorie dell'Istituto Lombardo* 3rd series, 2 (1870). Trans. Coote. *Researches respecting the Book of Sindibad.* Folk-lore Soceity Publications 9. London: Pub. for the Folklore Society, by E. Stock, 1882.

———. *Virgilio nel medio evo,* 2 vols. Livorno: F. Vigo, 1872. 2d ed. Florence: Sansone, 1896. 3d ed. by Giorgio Pasquali. Florence: Nuova Italia, 1937–1941. German trans. Hans Dütschke. *Virgil im Mittelalter; aus dem Italienischen übersetzt.* Leipzig: Teubner, 1875. English trans. E. F. M. Benecke, with an intro. by Robinson Ellis. *Vergil in the Middle Ages.* London: S. Sonnenschein; New York: Macmillan, 1895 and 1908. New York: G. E. Stechert, 1929. Hamden, Conn.: Archon Books, 1966.

———. "Virgilio nella tradizione letteraria fino a Dante." *Nuova antologia* 1 (1866): 1–55.

———. "Virgilio mago e innamorato." 4 (1867): 605–647, and 5 (1867): 659–703.

Conti, Rita Peca. Ed. *Carteggio G. I. Ascoli-E. Teza.* Orientamenti linguistici 6. Pisa: Giardini, 1978.

Courcelle, Pierre. *Lecteurs païens et lecteurs chrétiens de l'Éneide.* 2 vols. Institut de France, Mémoires de l'académie des inscriptions et belles-lettres, Nouvelle série, Tome 4. Paris: Imprimerie Gauthier-Villars and Diffusion de Boccard, 1984.

Croce, Benedetto. *Storia della storiografia italiana nel secolo decimonono.* 3d ed. Bari: Gius. Laterza & figli, 1947. Vol. 2, passim.

De Gubernatis, Angelo. *Dizionario biografico degli scrittori contemporanei.* Florence: Coi tipi dei successori Le Monnier, 1879. Pp. 305–7.

De Liguori, Girolamo. *I "Baratri della ragione": Arturo Graf e la cultura del secondo Ottocento.* Manduria: Piero Lacaita, 1986.

De Lollis, Cesare. *Reisebilder e altri scritti.* Bari: Gius. Laterza & Figli, 1929.

Desmond, Marilynn. *Reading Dido. Gender, Textuality, and the Medieval "Aeneid."* Medieval Cultures 8. Minneapolis: University of Minnesota Press, 1994.

Espinoza Pólit, Aurelio. *Virgilio. El poeta y su misión providencial.* Quito: Editorial Ecuadoriana, 1932.

Frantzen, Allen. *Desire for Origins: New Language, Old English, and Teaching the Tradition.* New Brunswick: Rutgers University Press, 1990.

Garin, Eugenio. *La cultura italiana tra '800 e '900. Studi e ricerche.* Bari: Laterza, 1962.

Gentile, Giovanni. *Gino Capponi e la cultura toscana nel secolo decimonono.* 3rd ed. Florence: Sansoni, 1942.

Gigante, Marcello. *Classico e mediazione. Contributi alla Storia della filologia antica.* Studi superiori NIS 70 (Lettere). Roma: Nuova Italia Scientifica, 1989.

Graf, Arturo. *Roma nella memoria e nelle immaginazioni del Medio Evo.* 2 vols. Turin: Giovanni Chiantore, 1923. Pp. 520–66.

Hagendahl, Harald. *Augustine and the Latin Classics.* Studia graeca et latina Gothoburgensia 20, parts 1–2. Göteburg: Universitetet; Stockholm: Almqvist & Wiksell, 1967.

Hardie, Colin Graham. "Virgil." In: *The Oxford Classical Dictionary.* Ed. N. G. L. Hammond and H. H. Scullard. 2d ed. Oxford: Clarendon Press, 1970. Pp. 1123–28.

Heinze, Richard. *Virgil's Epic Technique.* Trans. Hazel and David Harvey and Fred Robertson. Berkeley: University of California Press, 1993.

Jones, J. W., Jr. "Allegorical Interpretation in Servius." *Classical Journal* 56 (1961): 217–26.

———. "The Allegorical Traditions of the *Aeneid.*" In *Vergil at 2000. Commemorative Essays on the Poet and His Influence.* Ed. John D. Bernard. New York: AMS Press, 1986. AMS Ars Poetica: No. 3. Pp. 107–32.

Kallendorf, Craig. Editor. *The Classical Heritage: Vergil.* New York: Garland, 1993.

———. *In praise of Aeneas: Virgil and epideictic rhetoric in the early Italian Renaissance.* Hanover, N.H.: University Press of New England, 1989.

Kaster, Robert A. *The Tradition of the Text of the "Aeneid" in the Ninth Century.* Harvard University, Ph.D. diss., 1975. New York: Garland Press, 1990.

Kippur, Stephen A. *Jules Michelet, a Study of Mind and Sensibility.* Albany, N.Y.: State University of New York Press, 1981.

Landucci, Giovanni. *Darwinismo a Firenze. Tra scienza e ideologia (1860–1900).* Florence: Leo Olschki, 1977.

Landucci, Sergio. *Cultura e ideologia in Francesco De Sanctis.* Milan: Feltrinelli, 1964. Repr. I fatti e le idee: Saggi e biografie 106. Milan: Feltrinelli Economica, 1977.

Lectures médiévales de Virgile. Actes du Colloque organisé par l'École française de Rome (Rome, 25–28 octobre 1982). Collection de l'École française de Rome 80. Rome: École française de Rome, Palais Farnèse, 1985.

Leonardi, Claudio. "Comparetti, Domenico." In *Enciclopedia virgiliana.* 5

vols. in 6. Rome: Istituto della Enciclopedia italiana, 1984–1991. Vol. 1 (1984), pp. 859–60.

Levi, Ezio. "Commemorazione di Pio Rajna letta all'accademia pontaniana il 10 gennaio 1931." *Atti dell'Accademia Pontaniana* 61 (1931).

Lord, Albert Bates. *Epic Singers and Oral Tradition*. Myth and Poetics. Ithaca: Cornell University Press, 1991.

Lubac, Henri de. "Virgile philosophe et prophète." In: *Exégèse médiévale. Les quatre sens de l'écriture*. Théologie 59. Paris: Aubier, 1964. Vol. 2, part 2, pp. 233–62.

Mazzoni, Guido. *L'Ottocento*. Vol. 2. In Storia letteraria d'Italia. 2d ed. Ed. Aldo Vallone. Milan: Casa Editrice Dr. Francesco Vallardi, 1973.

Milani, Elisa Frontali. "Gli anni giovanili di Domenico Comparetti, 1848–1859 (Dai suoi taccuini e da altri inediti)." *Belfagor* 24 (1969): 203–17.

Mitzman, Arthur. *Michelet, Historian: Rebirth and Romanticism in Nineteenth-Century France*. New Haven: Yale University Press, 1990.

Momigliano, Arnaldo. "Ancient History and the Antiquarian." In *Contributo alla storia degli studi classici*. Rome: Edizioni di storia e letteratura, 1955. Pp. 67–106.

Mori, Giorgio. Editor. *La Toscana*. Storia d'Italia: Le regioni dall'Unità a oggi. Turin: Giulio Einaudi editore, 1986.

Munk Olsen, Birger. *L'Étude des auteurs classiques latins aux XIe et XIIe siècles*. 3 vols. (with vol. 3 in two parts). Paris: Éditions du Centre national de la recherche scientifique, 1982–1989.

Muscetta, Carlo. *Francesco De Sanctis*. Letteratura italiana Laterza 51/8, Il secondo Ottocento. 2d ed. Roma: Laterza, 1990.

Ogle, Marbury B. "The Later Tradition of Vergil." *Classical Journal* 26 (1930): 63–73.

Padoan, Giorgio. "Tradizione e fortuna del commento all'*Eneide* di Bernardo Silvestre." *Italia medioevale e umanistica* 3 (1960): 227–40.

Pais, Ettore. "Domenico Comparetti." *Nuova Antologia* 16 febbraio 1927, pp. 385–91.

Pasquali, Giorgio. "Domenico Comparetti e la filologia del secolo XIX." *Aegyptus* 8 (1927): 117–. Repr. Quaderni critici 8. Rieti: Bibliotheca editrice, 1929. Pp. 7–46. Repr. in Pasquali, *Pagine stravaganti di un filologo*. Lanciano, Carabba, 1933. Repr. in Pasquali, *Vecchie e nuova pagine stravaganti di un filologo*. Turin: De Silva, 1952. Repr. in Pasquali, *Pagine stravaganti*. Florence: Sansoni, 1968. Vol. 1, pp. 3–25.

———. "Prefazione dell'Editore." Ed. Domenico Comparetti. *Virgilio nel medio evo*. Florence: La Nuova Italia Editrice, 1937–1941. Vol. 1, pp. xiii–xxxiv. Repr. in Pasquali, *Terze pagine stravaganti*. Florence: Sansoni, 1942. Pp. 167–86. Repr. Pasquali, *Pagine stravaganti*. Florence: Sansoni, 1968. Vol. 2, pp. 119–32.

Rand, E. K. "The Mediaeval Virgil." *Studi Medievali* N.S. 5 (1932): 418–42.

Rossi, Vittorio. Review of 2d edition of Comparetti. *Rassegna bibliografica della letteratura italiana* 4 (1896): 174–81. Repr. in Pasquali, ed. Domenico Comparetti. Vol. 2, pp. 274–81.

Rostagni, Augusto. Review of repr. *Virgilio nel Medio Evo. Nuova antologia* 73, fasc. 1601, 1 dicembre 1938, pp. 346–48.

Scharten, Théodora. *Les voyages et séjours de Michelet en Italie; amitiés italiennes.* Paris: E. Droz, 1934.

Schnapp, Jeffrey T. *The Transfiguration of History at the Center of Dante's "Paradise."* Princeton, N.J.: Princeton University Press, 1986.

Spadolini, Giovanni. *L'idea d'Europa fra illuminismo e romanticismo: la stagione dell'Antologia di Vieusseux.* Firenze: Le Monnier, 1985.

Spargo, John Webster. *Virgil the Necromancer. Studies in Virgilian Legends.* Harvard Studies in Comparative Literature 10. Cambridge: Harvard University Press, 1934.

Stecher, J. "La légende de Virgile en Belgique." *Bulletin de l'Academie Royale de Belgique-Cl. des sciences,* 3a série, 19 (1890): 585–632.

Stok, Fabio. "Virgil between the Middle Ages and the Renaissance." *International Journal of the Classical Tradition* 1 (1994): 15–22.

Suerbaum, Werner. "Vergil-Forschung/Aeneis: F VI 1." In: *Aufstieg und Niedergang der römischen Welt.* Ed. Wolfgang Haase. Volume 31.1. Berlin and New York: Walter de Gruyter, 1980. Pp. 337–48.

Tilliette, Jean-Yves. "Introduction." In *Lectures médiévales de Virgile.* Pp. 1–8.

Timpanaro, Sebastiano. "Antileopardiani e neomoderati nella sinistra italiana." *Belfagor* 30 (1975): 395–428.

———. *Classicismo e illuminismo nell'Ottocento italiano.* Saggi di varia umanità 2. Pisa: Nistri-Lischi Editori, 1965.

———. "Comparetti, Vitelli, Hemmerdinger." *Belfagor* 33 (1978): 697–704.

———. "Domenico Comparetti." In *Letteratura italiana: I critici. Per la storia della filologia e della critica moderna in Italia.* Ed. Gianni Grana. Milan: Marzorati, 1970. Vol. 1, pp. 491–504. Repr. in Timpanaro, *Aspetti e figure della cultura ottocentesca.* Pisa: Nistri-Lischi, 1980. Pp. 349–70.

———. *La genesi del metodo del Lachmann.* Padova: Liviana Editrice, 1985.

Treves, Piero, ed. *Lo studio dell'antichità classica nell'Ottocento.* Letteratura Italiana, Storia e testi, 72. Milan and Naples: Riccardo Ricciardi editore, 1962. Pp. 1051–63.

———. "Ciceronianismo e anticiceronianismo nella cultura italiana del secolo XIX." *Rendiconti dell'Istituto Lombardo* 92 (1958): 403–64.

Tunison, Joseph Salathiel, 1849–1916. *Master Virgil: the author of the Aeneid as he seemed in the middle ages: a series of studies.* Cincinnati: R. Clarke, 1890.

Ussani, Vincenzo. "In margine al Comparetti." *Studi medievali* 5 (1932): 1–42.

Vietor, Wilhelm. "Der Ursprung der Virgilsage." *Zeitschrift für romanische Philologie* 1 (1877): 165–78.

Vitelli, G. Letter on the death of Comparetti. *Rendiconti dell'Accademia dei Lincei* 3 (1927): 221–22.

Zabughin, Vladimiro. *Vergilio nel Rinascimento italiano da Dante a Torquato Tasso.* 2 vols. Bologna: N. Zanichelli, 1921–1923.

Ziolkowski, Theodore. *Virgil and the Moderns.* Princeton: Princeton University Press, 1993.

AUTHOR'S PREFACE TO THE FIRST EDITION

THE object of this work is to give a complete history of the medieval conception of Vergil, to follow its various evolutions and vicissitudes, and to determine the nature and causes of these and their connection with the general history of European thought. Such a history has never yet been written, though the Vergil of medieval thought has been made the subject of a few monographs. The short pamphlets of Siebenhaar [1] and Schwubbe [2] mention only a few of the best-known facts, while the works of Piper [3] and Creizenach, [4] though more profound and learned, consider but one aspect of the subject. Michel, [5] Genthe, [6] and Milberg [7] have endeavoured to discuss the whole question, but their works are far too brief for this purpose, and do not display any deep scientific or critical insight. The most

---

[1] *De fabulis quae media aetate de Publio Virgilio Marone circumferebantur.* Berlin, 1837, 8 pp.

[2] *P. Virgilius per mediam aetatem gratia atque auctoritate florentissimus.* Paderborn, 1852, 18 pp.

[3] *Virgilius als Theolog und Prophet des Heidenthums in der Kirche,* in the *Evangelischer Kalender.* Berlin, 1862, pp. 17–82.

[4] *Die Aeneis, die vierte Ecloge und die Pharsalia im Mittelalter.* Frankf. a. M., 1864, 37 pp.

[5] *Quae vices quaeque mutationes et Virgilium ipsum et eius carmina per mediam aetatem exceperint.* Lut. Par., 1846, 75 pp.

[6] *Leben und Fortleben des Publius Virgilius Maro als Dichter und Zauberer.* Leipz., 1857, 85 pp., in 16mo.

[7] *Memorabilia Vergiliana,* Misenae, 1857, 38 pp. *Memorabilia Vergiliana,* Misenae, 1867, 40 pp.

striking feature of the medieval Vergil, and that most generally known, is the legend which attributes to him magical
powers, and this feature has been commented upon by various
writers from the seventeenth century onwards ; but these
writers have generally looked upon it merely as a curiosity,
and have never made any close study of the subject.[8] The first
to undertake a detailed investigation of this matter was Du
Méril,[9] whose work is, however, more remarkable for the
quantity and novelty of the materials collected in it than for
method or critical insight. The real history of this legend was
first written by Roth,[10] whose work is beyond question the best
and the most important which has hitherto appeared on the
subject. But Vergil as magician is only a single feature in the
medieval idea of him, and cannot be properly understood without the rest. It is a notion which had its rise among the
common people, and from thence invaded literature, but this
invasion would never have been successful had it not found
congenial elements already awaiting it there. I have therefore
divided my work into two parts, the first of which studies the
vicissitudes of Vergil's fame in the medium of the literary
tradition during the whole period prior to the Renaissance—a
period which closes gloriously with the Vergil of Dante—while
the second examines the aspect which this fame assumes, after
the appearance in it of the popular legends, in the medium of
the new popular literature, which was independent of the

[8] The most important of these are V. D. HAGEN, *Gesammtabenteuer*, iii.
pp. cxxix.–cxlvii., and MASSMANN, *Kaiserchronik*, iii. p. 421–460.

[9] *De Virgile l'enchanteur*, in his *Mélanges archéologiques et littéraires*
Paris, 1850, pp. 424–478.

[10] *Ueber den Zauberer Virgilius* in the *Germania* of PFEIFFER, iv. pp.
257–298.

classical tradition. In the first of these two parts, which is at once the more essential and the more difficult, I have found the ground practically virgin. The only assistance of which I was at all able to avail myself was a work by Zappert,[11] which is, however, for the most part devoted by its author to the illustration, with a very large number of examples, of a fact which I have studied and formulated in an entirely different manner.[12] Above all, I have felt the want of an adequate history of the classical studies of the middle ages. The recent advances of knowledge have made the work of Heeren far too elementary; at any rate it is quite incompetent to give any proper idea of the medieval conception of the ancient writers and of antiquity generally. The commentators of Dante who have been led by the Vergil of the *Divina Commedia* to study the nature of the Vergil of the medieval literary tradition have been too ready to content themselves in this matter with generalities; so that the path by which I have arrived at the study of this character, a study which is important for many reasons, has been one hitherto untrodden; and yet it is, I am convinced, the right one. And here I must not be misunderstood. I merely claim that I am not doing over again what has been done already; I am very far from wishing to ignore the merits of those who have in any way gone before me in work of this nature. My method of treatment is new and entirely original, and is the result of ideas and facts collected for the most part in the course of my own studies and researches; but yet in certain cases I have been able to make good use of materials already amassed

[11] *Virgil's Fortleben im Mittelalter.* Wien. (Akad. d. Wiss.), 1851, 54 pp. in fol.

[12] *Vide* my notes, p. 159, and p. 240.

by various previous scholars, to whom due acknowledgment
is made in the proper place, and I should be the last to wish to
detract from the honour which their labours and their learning
deserve.

What renders the adequate treatment of this subject particularly difficult, and has perhaps been the reason why it has
never been properly taken in hand hitherto, is the rarity of
scholars who have studied both classical and romantic literature. In the history of Vergil in the middle ages, these two
are so closely combined that it is impossible for those whose
studies have been limited to one of them to form a true conception of the subject in its entirety or of the real relations
of its several parts. My own tendencies and the consequently
widened horizon of my studies have led. me to cultivate both
these branches of knowledge equally, and I have not found
them so irreconcileable with one another as many would seem
to think. I have cultivated both with interest and pleasure,
and have endeavoured in each to rise above the level of a mere
dilettante. And hence it seemed to me that my acquaintance
with both these departments of modern investigation could be
well employed in such a work as the present one, though I did
not conceal from myself the arduous nature of the task. A
first sketch of it appeared some years ago in the *Nuova
Antologia*,[13] but in this the more important part was only indicated in a very rudimentary manner. Further time and
study were necessary to fill in the outlines there suggested, and
to give the work that completed form in which it is now presented to the reader.

[13] Vol. i. (1866), pp. 1–55; vol. iv. (1867), pp. 605–647; vol. v. (1867),
pp. 659–703.

It may appear strange to some that my work should contain
more than its title professes, and that instead of confining
myself to the middle ages, I should commence my history with
the period in which Vergil himself lived.   But this was necessary in order to render the medieval idea intelligible in its
causes and its precedents.   Everything, however, which is
prior to the middle ages has been treated solely with this
explanatory purpose, and hence the history of Vergil's fame
during the earlier centuries has been confined to the barest and
most essential outlines.   I could have treated this part of the
subject with more depth if my intention had been to examine
the influence of Vergil on the literature of this period; but as
this was not the case, I did not feel called upon to devote more
space to what was after all but a side-issue.   This can still be
done by the scholar who undertakes to write the history of the
style and language of the empire, or the history of the grammatical studies of the Romans, works which have yet to be
accomplished, and for which even the materials can hardly as
yet be said to have been sufficiently collected.

The wish to make my work as complete as possible, has led
me to add at the end of the second volume the principal texts
which deal with the Vergilian legends, some of which are there
published for the first time, while others have been collected
from the various publications—not always easy to obtain—in
which they are scattered.   To have given all such texts would
have been too much, but I have included all the most important, which belong chiefly to the three literatures in which
the legends themselves are most prominent, viz., French,
German and Italian.   I have further thought it worth while
to add the popular Italian poem on the subject of the magician

Pietro Barliario, to which occasional reference is made in these pages, as the book in question is in Italy better known to the populace than to scholars, while out of Italy it is not known at all.

The reader will readily understand why in a book of this kind several of the chapters have but little obvious connection with Vergil. It must not be supposed that my object is merely to surprise and amuse by narrating a series of curious facts and follies. What led me to interest myself in these studies, and to devote much time and labour to them, was the consideration of how noteworthy a part of the history of the human mind was reflected in the varied and various phenomena of which the subject is composed. The reader must judge whether I have been mistaken in thinking that this is a theme on which a work may be written which will satisfy some higher feeling than that of mere erudite curiosity.

As an Italian, I have never been able to forget how thoroughly Italian are the nature and the interest of my subject; but I have endeavoured to write calmly, and to eliminate as far as might be any subjective cause of prejudice. If any such feeling has in any place warped my judgment, I can only regret it; but at the same time I would ask any one who feels tempted to condemn me for this to look carefully in his own conscience whether it be in his place to cast the first stone at me.

D. C.

VERGIL IN THE MIDDLE AGES

Tityrus et fruges Aeneiaque arma legentur
Roma triumphati dum caput orbis erit.
OVID, *Am.*, I. 15. 25,

O anima cortese mantovana
Di cui la fama ancor nel mondo dura
E durerà quanto 'l mondo lontana.
DANTE, *Inf.*, 2. 28.

INTRODUCTION

VERGIL is the chief representative of those poets whom their
contemporaries called the 'new poets'; and new poets they
were, living in times that were new. The Augustan age was
an epoch in which novelty was a general fact and a general
need of the Roman world. The Roman people, that had
striven through so many years of self-denial to attain such
greatness, was anxious now to enjoy the greatness to which it
had attained, to live in a way becoming to that greatness, to
expand in a thousand directions, to embellish and refine its
life, intellectual no less than material. The old life of the
Republic seemed crude and mean to this newer generation; it
was a thing to be admired from a distance, no doubt, but its
realization was no longer impossible, for it was no longer in
proportion to their ways of life and thought. And however
severely this great renewal, this breaking away from the stern

B

traditions of antiquity, may be judged from a political stand-
point or in the light of after events, there can be no doubt that
it was the new condition of things which gave birth in the
regions of science and art to those tendencies and those aims
to which are due the most lofty productions of Roman literature
and thought.

It is not our object here to study the growth of this new
school of poets, to discuss the causes of their greatness and success, or to describe the opposition which they encountered at
the hands of those champions of conservatism who are invari-
ably to be found in all periods of progress.   The nature of the
present work will compel us to direct our attention solely upon
Vergil, the greatest poet of that school, and at the same time
the greatest poet of all Latin literature.   Nor, again, is this
the place for a discussion as to the true position which the
poetry of Vergil deserves to occupy; it is our business here
to show, not what Vergil was, but what he seemed to be,
not what the judgment passed on him should be now, but
what it in former times actually was.   Had I not been myself
thoroughly convinced of the real value of the poetry of Vergil,
I should, doubtless never have undertaken this work, but, after
all, such a conviction is not so exclusively my own that I need
argue in its favour here; I trust therefore that I shall be
allowed to commence these investigations, in themselves sufficiently lengthy, without further comment, at a point more
intimately associated with their immediate subject, namely, the
first impression which the poetry of Vergil made upon the
Roman world.

The contemporary fame of Vergil reached its highest point
in connection with the Aeneid, and it is with the Aeneid that
it has been most closely associated in later times; for, however
great may be the poetical value of his Bucolics and Georgics,
there can be no doubt that it was in the Aeneid that his
powers were most conspicuously displayed, and it is by virtue
of the Aeneid that he takes rank not only as the greatest, but
also as the most essentially national of Roman poets.   It will
be upon the Aeneid, therefore, that our attention will be
chiefly fixed in the following pages.

CHAPTER I

THE supreme ideal of epic poetry, in ancient as in modern times, was always the Epic of Homer; it was to this that poet and public alike looked for a criterion; and so lofty was this ideal that while, on the one hand, the possibility of attaining to it was excluded, on the other hand those who failed to attain to it might yet reach to a great and imposing elevation. In their judgment of Vergil the Romans were met with this inevitable comparison, and, in distinguishing between the divine power of the creator and the arduous and wearisome labour of the imitator, they admitted, in fact, the inferiority of their own poet to the Greek.[1] But at the same time they recognised that of all other epic attempts in either language, that of Vergil had been the most successful. This judgment, when confined to a simply superficial comparison of the two poems, was doubtless correct; but when the comparison extended further to the nature and causes of the two works, the ancients, not having any clear idea, such as we at present possess, of the true nature of the Homeric Epic, and regarding Homer and Vergil as two individuals separated merely by distance of time and degree of genius, were compelled to judge less favourably of the younger writer than we should be disposed to do at the present day. We have learnt to distinguish between the primitive epic, which is spontaneous and national, not indi-

---

[1] The exaggerations of a few enthusiasts must not be reckoned at more than their real value. How great a part of the "Nescio quid maius nascitur Iliade" of Propertius was due to his friendship with Vergil becomes clear when we compare with it the praises he lavishes on the Thebaid o another friend, Ponticus:

"dum tibi Cadmeae dicuntur, Pontice, Thebae,
armaque fraternae tristia militiae,
atque, ita sim felix, primo contendis Homero," etc. (i. 7. 1–3).

vidual, in origin, and the artificial imitative epic, which is the
work of a single individual and the result of reflexion in an
age when history renders the production of the former class of
poem impossible; and hence, while assigning the first place
among the primitive epics of the world to the Greek, we are
able to recognise that in the imitative class, including modern
no less than ancient works, the poem of Vergil is equally pre-
eminent. We can thus allot to Vergil his true position, and
if we compare him with Homer, we do so with such a knowledge of the essential differences between the two authors as
will enable us in many cases to explain or excuse any inferiority of the Latin writer in a way which was not possible for
the Romans. But if, on the one hand, this knowledge permits
us at the present day to form a more favourable estimate of
Vergil than his contemporaries were able to do, it must be
admitted on the other that this is more than counterbalanced
by the harmony which existed between his poem and the feelings and desires of the age in which he lived. It has often
been said that the Vergilian epic was gratifying to the national
vanity, and that it was hence inevitably destined to succeed;
but this idea, though doubtless to a certain extent true, is yet
hardly so as commonly understood. The Roman people, or
rather, the Roman world, was so entirely unique in nature, in
growth, and in composition, that any judgment of it by ordinary standards cannot fail to be false. Its whole being was
essentially historical; its life had been one of continuous
growth from the smallest beginnings to gigantic proportions—
a growth dominated by an irresistible impulse, which commenced from the first moment of its existence, the historical
fact of the founding of Rome. This furthest limit of Roman
national records formed the nucleus of a development so constant and so closely connected with the subsequent national
life that even the legends of the origin of Rome and the
events which followed it obtained therefrom a practical and
political character.[2] A record of an heroic age divorced from
political activity, in which the national elements were scat-

[2] German scholars are guilty of a grave error, the effects of which are
visible in various parts of many of their works, when they insist upon

tered and not concentrated upon the one idea of the future greatness of the nation, does not exist among the Romans. The little Latin race, from which these germs of greatness were derived, was never, it is true, forgotten; but it and Rome retained always distinct individualities, the cognate yet distinct individualities of the mother and the child.

This historical being, which from the first moment of its life had felt the consciousness of itself and of its mission, which through all the vicissitudes of its history had marched with its eyes steadily fixed upon a real and definite goal, which owed to its own energies and resources all its greatness and success, could not fail to find in the contemplation of itself and its own marvellous development a powerful poetical inspiration. This was a feeling of a quite peculiar kind, to which we may give the name historical, in that it had its origin in the idea of a great historical activity; it was a feeling not limited to the confines of any one special country, but common to all the diverse nationalities which Rome had succeeded not only in subduing, but also in assimilating; and hence it differed from ordinary national feeling in its abstract nature and its universality,—qualities which enabled it to survive the downfall of actual Roman dominion. It was an enthusiasm which filled conquerors and conquered alike, and in the innumerable expressions of it which characterize—one may almost say constitute —Latin literature, it is impossible to find any distinction between writers of the most diverse nationalities, whether Roman, Greek, Etruscan, Gallic, African, or Iberian.[3]

To return to the epic, it is clear that the Romans would have

regarding the Romans from the same point of view as they do the Greeks. The Roman imagination was chiefly concerned with those κτίσεις πόλεων which did not to the Greeks constitute the most inspiring subject for national legend; but if the Roman legends give clear proof of the practical nature of their authors, they are not for that reason the less poetical. We may quote in this connection a writer who certainly cannot be accused of any partiality for the Romans, who concludes an article on the story of Coriolanus with these words: "Wer in diesen Erzählungen nach einem sogenannten geschichtlichen Kern sucht, wird allerdings die Nuss taub finden; aber von der Grösse und dem Schwung der Zeit zeugt die Gewalt und der Adel dieser Dichtungen, insbesondere derjenigen von Coriolanus, die nicht erst Shakspeare geschaffen hat." Mommsen, in *Hermes*, iv. p. 26.

[3] Cp. the numerous passages collected by Lasaulx, *Zur Philosophie der*

a natural tendency towards the historical epic; and a proof of this may be found in the number of historical epics actually composed from the time of Naevius to that of Claudian, a number with which Greek literature, for good reasons, can offer no comparison.[4] But the feeling which animated the whole Roman world and had such need of expression was of such a kind, both in nature and origin, that it had particular difficulty in finding utterance in epic poetry. Regarded from an abstract point of view, the feeling would seem as if it tended very readily to this form of expression; but no sooner did a writer discover a subject to which he could give the necessary concentrated form, than the historical idea at once presented itself, and this was fatal to his success; for historical facts, regarded as such, cannot in any way furnish the materials for an epic. Before actual events can form the subject of epic poetry, they must be elaborated by the imagination, not of an individual, but of the nation; and this is an achievement of which the national mind is no longer capable in an epoch of historical maturity. The Greeks had contributed nothing to the solution of this difficult problem, because their national character was so entirely different that no such problem had ever presented itself to them. The most important attempt at the historical epic among them was the poem of Choerilus of Samos on the war with Persia; but as this war, however glorious, was nothing but an incident in the national life, the success of the poem could only be a temporary one. Greek national feeling, moreover, had always found expression in other and more suitable forms. But the national feeling of the Romans was so intense, and their character as a historical nation so pronounced, that not only were their historical epics very numerous, but they were also successful to a degree which one would hardly have expected of the best works of this class. It was, in fact, the warmth of this feeling which compensated for the frigidity of its expression, just as it is in

römischen Geschichte, p. 6 seqq., to which, moreover, many others might be added, while the entire tendency of certain authors, such as Livy, is in this direction.

[4] *Vide* the list in Teuffel, *Gesch. d. röm. Lit.*, p. 27.

modern times the absence of any such feeling which causes even the best epics to be neglected. But however great might be the success both of the purely historical epics and also of those, such as the works of Naevius and Ennius, in which, for the sake of the form and owing to the unpoetical nature of the subject, legend and history consorted strangely together, yet the national need was by no means completely satisfied. The difficult problem remained until Vergil solved it, and this solution is alike one of his chief merits and one of the chief causes of the great enthusiasm with which his work was received—an enthusiasm which continued unabated as long as there remained alive any of the feeling of which that work was at once the most noble and the most faithful poetical expression.

The national aims of Vergil, as of the other Augustan poets, are always very evident; they do not come to the front, as in so many other Roman writers, unexpectedly, and as it were instinctively, but are always deliberately calculated with a view to artistic effect. Vergil did not wish to compose an epic which should be simply literary and learned, like those of the Alexandrians, and hence he did not, like so many before and after him, seek a subject in the rich storehouse of Greek mythology, such as the Little Iliad, or the ʼThebaid, or the Achilleid, or anything of that kind, which would have had no special national interest for the Romans. Guided by an artistic instinct simply marvellous in a writer of his age, he rejected all those subjects which so greatly tempted other poets, and had, in earlier days, also tempted him, and lighted upon the only one among the Roman legends which, while furnishing that ideal heroic character which is indispensable for an epic, was at the same time entirely national, if not in origin, at least in significance.[5] The way in which he

---

[5] " Novissimum Aeneidem inchoavit, argumentum varium et multiplex, et quasi amborum Homeri carminum instar, praeterea nominibus ac rebus Graecis Latinisque commune, et in quo, *quod maxime studebat*, Romanae simul urbis et Augusti origo contineretur." DONAT., *Vit. Verg.* (in REIFFER-SCHEID, *Suetonii praeter Caesarum libros reliquiae.* Lips., 1860), p. 59. (This edition will always be used in giving references in these pages to the Life of Vergil which bears the name of Donatus.)

arrived at this point by simple force of genius, modifying
gradually the original idea of his work, is made clear by various
evidence, and must not be disregarded by any who would form
a true conception of him.   He too, for the general reasons we
have already stated, when about to undertake a national poem,
turned instinctively for a subject to Latin or Roman history.
Before writing the Bucolics, he had projected a poem on the
kings of Alba, though he soon abandoned the idea, ' offensus
materia,' as his biographer says.[6]   Later on, when his connection with Augustus led him once more to contemplate seriously
the composition of a national poem, the first subject which
suggested itself to his mind was an historical one.   The importance of contemporary events and his friendship with the
prince who had taken such a leading part in them prompted
him naturally to consider as his theme the Deeds of Octavian.[7]
Such he himself declared to be the nature of the work he was
contemplating when, in the year 29, he read at Atella[8] his
Georgics to Augustus, on the latter's return from Asia.[9]   Starting with this idea, and modifying his first plan in accordance
with the requirements of his artistic feeling, he came, in the
course of eleven years,—from the year 29 to his death,—to
compose the Aeneid.   In the year 26 already Propertius was
acquainted with some part of the work, and speaks of it
enthusiastically as of a something great which was in course of
construction, though he praises in greater detail the Bucolics
and Georgics, on which up to that time the poet's fame
rested.   From the words of Propertius,[10] as well as from what

[6] DONAT., *Vit. Verg.*, p. 58 ; SERV., *ad Bucol.*, vi. 3.
[7] This was the original subject of the Aeneid as suggested by Augustus
himself.   This is what Servius means when he says, " postea *ab Augusto
Aeneidem propositam* scripsit."
[8] DONAT., *Vit. Verg.*, p. 61.
[9] " mox tamen ardentes accingar dicere pugnas
   Caesaris et nomen fama tot ferre per annos
   Tithoni prima quot abest ab origine Caesar.'·
          Georg., iii. 46.
[10] " Actia Vergilium custodis litora Phoebi
   Caesaris et fortes dicere posse rates,
  qui nunc Aeneae Troiani suscitat arma
   iactaque Lavinis moenia litoribus.
  cedite Romani scriptores, cedite Grai
   nescio quid maius nascitur Iliade."
         PROPERT., ii. 34, 61.

Vergil himself wrote to Augustus,[11] it is clear that the passages then composed belonged to what was subsequently the Aeneid, though the poet was still intending to work up from Aeneas to Augustus. But his poetical taste, as is now apparent from the complete work, led him eventually to abandon the idea of treating at length any actual historical facts. By occasional allusions to them on such occasions as artistic propriety would permit, he fulfilled his design, and at the same time did not in any way injure the heroic and poetical narrative which formed the basis of his subject.[12] The artistic value of this method of procedure was apparent already to the ancient critics, who point out the great inferiority of Lucan in this respect.[13]

Thus we may see in what manner the Aeneid came into being; and the process shows us clearly how superior was its author's feeling for poetry to that of the best of his contemporaries in an epoch which, with the exception of the period of the great Greek creations, is the most splendid of all in the history of art.

Modern criticism has succeeded in overturning certain ideas formerly held as to the historical value of the story of Aeneas and as to its origin; [14] but it cannot deny the indisputable fact that, from the time of the First Punic War onwards, this story had been current among the Romans, had been popularised by poets, historians, painters and playwrights, and had been acknowledged by religion and the state, till it had, by the time of Vergil, acquired the character of a national legend wholly sympathetic to every mind imbued with the spirit of Roman culture, and in perfect harmony with true Roman poetical feeling.[15] Had it been Vergil's intention to compose an epic

[11] "De Aenea quidem meo," etc. In MACROBIUS, *Sat.*, i. 24, 11.

[12] For the composition of the Aeneid and the chronology of its various parts, *vide* SABBADINI, *Studi storici sull' Eneide.* Lonigo, 1889, p. 70 seqq.

[13] "Hoc loco per transitum tangit historiam quam per legem artis poeti-cae aperte non potest ponere. . . . Lucanus namque ideo in numero poetarum esse non meruit quia videtur historiam composuisse non poema." SERV. *ad Aen.*, i. 382. Cp. MARTIAL, xiv. 194; FRONTO, p. 125; QUINTIL., x. 1, 90.

[14] Cp. SCHWEGLER, *Röm. Gesch.*, i. p 279 seqq; PRELLER, *Röm. Mytholog.*, p. 666 seqq.; HILD, *La légende d'Énée avant Virgile.* Paris, 1883.

[15] NIEBUHR is greatly mistaken when he maintains (*Röm. Gesch.*, i. 206

entirely of the Homeric kind, this subject would have proved
sufficiently unsuitable by reason of the heterogeneous nature of
the incidents and characters which it introduced; but the
purpose of the Vergilian epic was so entirely different that
these defects in its subject, even if noticeable, are far less
pronounced than would otherwise have been the case.   Homer
moves constantly in an atmosphere of idealism; he can take
no account of history, for history did not begin till centuries
after him; the limits and the proportions of actual humanity
are so far from his thoughts, that it is but rarely, and then
merely as a term of comparison, that he takes note of the
weakness of man as he is (οἷοι νῦν βροτοί εἰσιν); the child of
an age without history, he is the interpreter of a national
idealism which is of itself already eminently poetical.   The
Latin poet, on the other hand, living at a period when his
nation had reached its highest historical development, was
compelled, while keeping just so much idealism as the nature
of an epic required, to fix his eyes on history, for history was
the basis of that universal national feeling which had just then
reached its highest pitch of intensity, and was more than ever

seqq.) that Vergil condemned his Aeneid to the flames because he did not
consider it national enough.   Such an idea would never have entered his
head, and the absurdity of it is shown by the immense success that the
Aeneid immediately gained, owing to its being so in sympathy with contemporary feeling.   The history of Livy, which is so thoroughly national,
begins with the story of Aeneas, and Livy has explained his reasons for so
doing in unmistakably plain language in his preface: "Et si cui populo
licere oportet consecrare origines suas et ad deos referre auctores, ea belli
gloria est populo Romano, etc."   How perfectly the legend of Aeneas was
in harmony with the rest of Roman tradition may be seen from the words
which Horace (*Od.*, iv. 4. 53) puts into the mouth of Hannibal:—

> " Gens quae cremato fortis ab Ilio,
>   iactata Tuscis aequoribus, sacra
>   natosque maturosque patres
>   pertulit Ausonias ad urbes,
>   duris ut ilex," etc.

When this was written the Aeneid had only just appeared (the 4th Book of
the Odes is generally supposed to have come out in 18 B.C.).   The Emper-
or's partiality for Troy as the sacred city of Rome and the Gens Iulia is
clearly shown by the well-known passage in *Od.*, iii. 3, which is certainly
earlier than the Aeneid.   To describe these and similar passages as merely
so much rhetoric and flattery, and to ignore the existence of a real and
intense national feeling on the subject is wilfully to sacrifice fact to theory.

in need of adequate expression.[16] Conscious, therefore, of his
office, and aided in fulfilling it by a power of sympathy all
his own,[17] he brought his poem, both in subject and treatment,
into such close connection with Roman history that it might
almost be described as an introduction to it, while at the same
time it is a poetical summing-up of the impression that that
history made on the minds of all those who contemplated it.[18]
And so, as is always the case when the long-sought formula
which expresses some universal feeling is at length found, the
Aeneid was received with a burst of enthusiasm throughout
the Roman world.

It is wonderful to watch the interest with which the cultured classes of the time kept themselves informed as to the
progress of this great work, and how powerful and marked
was its influence on Latin literature from the very first. While
it was being composed, Augustus, Maecenas, and the whole
crowd of friends, courtiers, dilettanti, poets and orators who
surrounded them, were all more or less well posted in the
development of the work, various passages from which were
every now and then recited by the poet in this private circle.
At the time of Vergil's death, this was all the publicity which
the poem had had, nor was any part of it, in the opinion of its

[16] The original title of the poem was, according to some, not the *Aeneis*,
but the *Gesta populi Romani* : " unde etiam in antiquis invenimus opus hoc
appellatum esse non Aeneidem sed Gesta populi Romani ; quod ideo mutatum est, quod nomen non a parte sed a toto debet dari." SERV., *ad Aen.*,
vi. 752.

[17] Nothing can be stranger than the theory advanced by some modern
critics (*e.g.* TEUFFEL, *Gesch. d. röm. Lit.*, p. 891) that the " soft and gentle "
disposition of Vergil rendered him unfit for epic poetry. Which of all the
various epic poets has had the proper disposition for epic poetry ? Was it
the platonic Tasso, or the pious Milton, or the mystical Klopstock ? And
how is it that the " gentle " Vergil has succeeded better than them all,
while the Titanic Goethe could produce nothing in this category but the
Achilleis?

[18] " Qui bene considerat inveniet omnem Romanum historiam ab Aeneae
adventu usque ad sua tempora summatim celebrasse Vergilium, quod ideo
latet quia confusus est ordo ; nam inversio Ilii et Aeneas errores adventus
bellumque manifesta sunt ; Albanos autem reges, Romanos etiam consules,
Brutos, Catonem, Caesarem Augustum et multa ad historiam Romanam
pertinentia hic indicat locus, caetera quae hic intermissa sunt in ἀσπιδοποιίᾳ
commemorat " SERV. *ad Aen.*, vi. 752. Cp. too PROBUS, *ad Georg.*, iii. 46,
p. 58 seq., ed. KEIL.

author, thoroughly complete; yet a vast public was aware of its existence, and the effect produced by such passages of it as had been privately recited raised expectation to the highest pitch. Its actual publication was undertaken by Vergil's two friends and literary executors, Varius and Tucca, who had been appointed by Augustus to see to this delicate business. How long they took in accomplishing it we do not know, but very long it cannot have been.[19] The impression produced was profound and universal. In this work, which from that time onward became its author's chief claim to distinction, all recognised the greatest achievement of Latin poetry,[20] and by virtue of it Vergil became to the Romans the "prince of song."[21] Traces of the study of Vergil and his phraseology can be recognised in his great contemporary, Livy, in whose work evident reminiscences of the Aeneid are to be found.[22] Especially rich again in such reminiscences is Ovid,[23] who was twenty-four years old when Vergil died, and had only known him by sight.[24] And it is worthy of note that in the cases of Livy and Ovid this cannot have come about, as it did with so many other Latin writers, through the use of Vergil in the schools. From the memoirs, too, of Seneca the Elder [25] we see

---

[19] According to Boissier (*La publication de l'Énéide* in the *Revue de Philologie*, 1884, pp. 1–4), it was already published when Horace wrote his *Carmen Saeculare*, in 737 (17), *i.e.* within two years of the poet's death.

[20] The first passage in which this is definitely stated is in Ovid :

"et profugum Aeneam, altaeque primordia Romae,
quo nullum Latio clarior exstat opus."

Ars Amat., iii. 387.

"tantum se nobis elegi debere fatentur,
quantum Vergilio nobile debet epos."

Rem. Am., 395.

The *Ars Amatoria* appeared in 2–1 B.C. ; the *Remedia Amoris* in 1–2 A.D.

[21] "Inter quae (ingenia) maxime nostri aevi eminent princeps carminum Vergilius, Rabirius," etc. Vell. Paterc., ii. 37.

[22] Cp. Wölfflin in the *Philologus*, xxvi. p. 130.

[23] *Vide* the numerous instances in Zingerle's *Ovidius und sein Verhältniss zu den Vorgängern und gleichzeitigen römischen Dichtern*. (Innsbrück, 1869–71), ii. pp. 48–113. For Tibullus, Propertius, Horace and Livy, *vide* Sabbadini, *Studi critici sull' Eneide*. Lonigo, 1889, pp. 134–173.

[24] "Vergilium vidi tantum," *Trist.*, iv. 10, 15.

[25] These memoirs, which go back to the orators of the reign of Augustus, give the earliest known instances of quotations from Vergil. The following are the chief passages :—"Sed ut sciatis sensum bene dictum dici tamen

clearly that the Aeneid was well known and that lines from it
were commonly quoted during the first decade after the poet's
death.   The pathetic story of Dido,[26] which in later times
moved even St. Augustine to tears,[27] had particular attractions
for a certain class of readers, and was throughout the following centuries one of the parts of the poem most greatly
admired.

A prejudiced and paradoxical school of criticism may say
what it pleases of this great poet, as of so many other great
Latin writers.   If it is mistaken, the loss is all its own.
Science will find it hard to pardon the excesses of an intellectual reaction, however powerful such a reaction may be for
progress.   The work of Vergil considered, as it should be, in
its proper historical place, is, and will always remain, a work
without equal, and the fascination which it has exercised for
so many centuries on all cultured minds, from the least to the
greatest, is entirely legitimate.   Vergil appears as imitator
merely in his accessories, and even there he is great; he is an
imitator because he was compelled to be so, because no genius,
however powerful, could at that period have been otherwise.
A complete revolt from the rules of art, as laid down in the
still living literature of Greece, was a thing that no one de-

posse melius, notate prae caeteris quanto decentius Virgilius dixerit hoc,
quod valde erat celebre, " belli mora concidit Hector "; " Quidquid apud
durae," etc. (*Aen.*, xi. 288).   Messala (ob. 8 B.C.) aiebat hic Vergilium
debuisse desinere, quod sequitur " et in decimum," etc., explementum esse.
Maecenas hoc etiam priori comparabat," *Suasor*, 2.   "Summis clamoribus
dixit (Arellius Fuscus) illum Vergili versum " Scilicet is superis," etc. (*Aen.*,
iv. 379).   Auditor Fusci quidam, cuius pudori parco, cum hanc suasoriam
de Alexandro ante Fuscum diceret, putavit aeque belle poni eundem versum ; dixit, Scilicet is superis," etc.   Fuscus illi ait : si hoc dixisses audi-
ente Alexandro, scires apud Vergilium et illum versum esse " . . . capulo
tenus abdidit ensem " (*Aen.*, ii. 553), *Suasor*, 4.   " Montanus Iulius qui
comis fuit quique egregius poeta, aiebat illum (Cestium) imitari voluisse
Vergili descriptionem " Nox erat et terras," etc. (*Aen.*, vii. 26), *Controv.*, 16
(Cestius came to Rome shortly after Vergil's death, cp, MEYER, *Orat. rom.
fragmenta*, p. 537).   *Vide*, too, *Suasor.*, 1.

[26] " et tamen ille tuae felix Aeneidos auctor
contulit in Tyrios arma virumque toros,
nec legitur pars ulla magis de corpore toto,
quam non legitimo foedere iunctus amor."
OVID, *Trist.*, ii. 533.

[27] *Confessiones*, lib. i.; op. i. 66.

sired, and it would have been received with indignation as a
monstrous and unintelligible enormity. There are conditions
of the human intellect in which genius cannot be entirely free.
But none the less is this genius real and apparent to all who
are not wilfully blind; nor must it be discounted by treating
it, as has been done in the case of Vergil, as if it were mere
technical skill. The work of Vergil belongs to an entirely
different sphere from that of Homer and the Greek epic-
writers generally,[28] and must, consequently, be regarded as to
all intents and purposes an original creation. A tincture of
Hellenism there was in the mind of the poet, as there was
in all Roman thought, and he would not have been true to
himself had he failed to give utterance to it; but the first
and most profound characteristic of Vergil is that he was, as
Petronius with true critical insight calls him, a Roman.[29]

[28] Even TEUFFEL allows that " Ton und Geist der Aeneis steht freilich zu
Homer in diametralem Gegensatze." *Gesch. d. röm Lit.*, p. 400. The
point is treated more fully by PLÜSS in his *Vergil und die epische Kunst*,
(Leipz., 1884), p. 339 seqq.

[29] " Homerus testis et lyrici, Romanusque Vergilius et Horati curiosa
felicitas." PETRON., *Sat.*, 118.

CHAPTER II

BUT such results could not be obtained by simple natural genius ; genius alone was not sufficient in the conditions then prevailing ; it is never sufficient to produce great works of art in times of great culture. Both by reason of its own nature and origin, and also owing to the influence of contemporary Greek writers, the poetry of the Augustan age, like most Roman poetry, was essentially of a learned character. Much erudite philological study was necessary before a poet could produce work in harmony with the surrounding conditions of culture. The direction of contemporary Greek poetry, dominated by the Alexandrians, was so essentially learned, that neither was the language of poetry an actual living language, nor was the poetry itself intended for any but a learned audience. If there is any one fact which brings into special relief the peculiar genius of Roman poetry as compared with Greek, it is the use which the former made of its ancient models. The decay of Greek poetry after the time of Alexander is such that students of its history are compelled, if they wish to fill up the great gaps that occur in it, to have recourse to the Romans, for it is in these latter alone that a continuation of its aims and activity is to be found.

But for all their pedantic study, not merely of Greek works, but also of the works of the earlier native writers, the best of the Roman poets were able to infuse into their poetry a national character which is entirely wanting in the Alexandrians. Unlike these, they did not write for a narrow circle of learned critics, but for a vast public, whose education was such that it required of its poet that he should be at the same time rhetorician, grammarian, and antiquary. And in these latter qualities, essential in a Roman poet, no one could equal Vergil, who, in addition to many other artistic studies, had bestowed particular attention to the Latin language, both as it then existed and also in its earlier forms, with a view to bringing it to the greatest possible perfection, and making it an adequate vehicle of expression for his artistic conceptions, and had also, both in his library and on his journeys, made a special study of all local myths, usages, and the like, which were in any way connected with his work.[1] He knew moreover the secret of concealing this great learning of his, never ostentatiously displaying it in such a way as to make the poetry subordinate to it—a virtue which his ancient critics already thoroughly appreciated;[2] and he was thus able to satisfy two entirely different classes, the learned few and the general public. The wonderful genius of Vergil in his use and creation of poetical diction and in his treatment of metre, and the minuteness of his antiquarian researches, made with a view to giving his work the most correct local colouring, are such self-evident facts that even the most severe and prejudiced of modern critics have been

---

[1] To Augustus, who, while engaged in his war with the Cantabri, had asked how the Aeneid was getting on, he answered : " De Aenea quidem meo, si me hercle iam dignum auribus haberem tuis, libenter mitterem ; sed tanta inchoata res est, ut paene vitio mentis tantum opus ingressus mihi videar, cum praesertim, ut scis, alia quoque studia ad id opus multoque potiora impertiar." MACROB., *Sat.*, i. 24, 11.

In a task of such difficulty and delicacy it is not surprising that, as his biography states (p. 59), " traditur cotidie meditatos mane plurimos versus dictare solitus, ac per totum diem retractando ad paucissimos redigere, non absurde carmen se informe more ursae parere dicens et lambendo demum effingere. Aeneida prosa primum oratione formatam digestamque in xii. libros particulatim componere instituit, prout liberet quidquid, et nihil in ordinem arripiens, ut ne quid impetum moraretur, quaedam imperfecta transmisit, alia levissimis verbis veluti fulsit, quae per locum pro tibicinibus interponi aiebat, ad sustinendum opus, donec solidae columnae advenirent."

The Aeneid as we have it took eleven years to compose, and Vergil had intended to devote three more to polishing it. It was with this object that he undertook the journey to Greece which proved fatal to him. DONAT., p. 62.

[2] " Vergilium multae antiquitatis hominem sine ostentationis odio peritum." GELL., v. 12, 13. QUINTILIAN too notices this when comparing Vergil with Homer: " et hercle ut illi naturae caelesti atque immortali cesserimus ; ita curae et diligentiae vel ideo in hoc plus est, quod fuit ei magis laborandum et quantum eminentibus vincimur fortasse aequalitate pensamus." *Inst.*, x. 1, 86.

compelled, in these points, to join in the eulogies of the ancients.[3]

The needs and the nature of Roman thought were such, that the impression produced by those characteristics of the poem which were the most extrinsic and mechanical was the most profound. Throughout the vicissitudes which the conception of the poet underwent, this impression survived and remained, however much it may have been distorted and debased, most vivid in all the literary tradition of the Latin middle ages. Perfection of language was to the Romans such an essential in a work of art, that it may be said to have been the chief point to which they looked in forming a judgment; in their opinion perfection of language would atone for the absence of many other merits. And, in fact, the Latin writers were in this respect in an entirely different position to the Greeks. Among the latter, the forms of art, having their birth in natural and spontaneous movements of national thought, were seconded by a simultaneous and equally spontaneous development of the language, which enabled the poets to apply it to their needs without any special grammatical or philological study. The development of Roman literature, on the other hand, was a far less natural one. To reduce a rough and barbarous language into a form in which it could be the vehicle of a literature, not national in its origin, but imported, as it were, suddenly from abroad, was a matter of the greatest difficulty; it was with this that the earliest Latin writers had to contend, and it was on this that their attention was mainly concentrated.[4] From this point of view one may describe the

---

[3] Cp. BERNHARDY, p. 437 ; TEUFFEL, p. 397 ; BAEHR, p. 371; HERTZBERG (*Uebers. d. Aeneis*), p. xi. seqq. ; HERMANN, *Elem. doctr. metr.*, 357 ; MÜLLER, *De re metr.*, p. 140 seq., 183, 190 seq. ; NIEBUHR, *Röm. Gesch.*, i. p. 112 (3rd ed.). For the legend of Aeneas and the use made of it by Vergil *vide* KLAUSEN, *Aeneas und die Penaten*, ii. p. 1249 seq.; RUBINO, *Beiträge zur Vorgeschichte Italiens*, p. 68 seqq., 156 seqq., 178, and particularly pp. 121-8, where the learning and accuracy of the poet are deservedly praised. WEIDNER in the preface to his *Commentar zu Vergil's Aeneis, Buch I., II.* (Leipz., 1869) has summed up Vergil's merits in a manner which, if somewhat superficial, is yet not without discernment. Stronger arguments against the prevailing German views are to be found in PLÜSS, *Vergil und die epische Kunst*, Leipzig, 1884.

[4] Cp. LERSCH, *Die Sprachphilosophie der Alten*, i. p. 103.

C

whole of Latin literature, from Livius Andronicus to Cicero
and Vergil, as nothing but a series of experiments in which
efforts were continually being made to mould the language
according to those æsthetic requirements which Greek influence
had imposed upon taste.[5] For this reason therefore, in addition
to the particular influence of Alexandrian culture, special grammatical studies were made by almost every Roman writer, as
long as the literature had not reached its full development and
as long as national thought was still seeking for the means of
adequate expression. But these objects were attained by Cicero
and Vergil, the former in prose, the latter in poetry ; and both
of them succeeded so entirely in satisfying the ideal of a perfect
language, that all subsequent attempts in this direction were
foredoomed to failure. This achievement of theirs, which was
certainly a great one, was regarded by the ancients as actually
their chief merit, and it was, without doubt, owing to the intensity and universality of the desire which it satisfied, the
chief cause of their fame in ancient times. The influence of
both orator and poet was so dependent on merits of this kind
that the latter came actually to serve as the standards by which
the poet as poet and the orator as orator were judged.

That a merely external quality should be so highly regarded
in the popular estimation as to practically usurp the place of
all others, or lead to their being unduly exaggerated on its
account, is certainly not what is to be desired for the formation
of a true opinion of the artistic value of a writer. Without
subscribing to the harsh opinion of Mommsen as to the merits

---

[5] LUCRETIUS, who died when Vergil was fifteen, not only shows evident
traces of this effort throughout his work, but also openly alludes to it (lib.
i. 137) :—
> " Nec me animi fallit Graiorum obscura reperta
> difficile illustrare Latinis versibus esse,
> multa novis verbis praesertim cum sit agendum,
> propter egestatem linguæ et rerum novitatem."

Cp. i. 831, iii. 259; HEFFTER, *Gesch. d. lat. Sprache währ. ihr. Lebens-
dauer*, p. 124 ; and HERZOG, *Untersuchungen über die Bildungsgeschichte der
griechischen und lateinischen Sprache* (Leipz., 1871), p. 196 seqq. The latter
however judges the Augustan poets with haste and levity (p. 213), and entirely
ignores the influence of Vergil in the matter of language on the schools, on
grammar, and on literature !

of Cicero as an orator, it cannot be doubted that a great part
of his oratorical fame was due to the excellence of his style as
a writer.[6] The same canons of criticism led Terence, notwithstanding his marked inferiority as a comedian, to be preferred
to Plautus down to the end of the middle ages.[7] But however
much the judgment of the ancients may have been led astray
in their estimate of Cicero by their predilection for his graces of
style, however different may be the place they assigned him in
the history of eloquence from that which he really deserves to
occupy, there can be no doubt that in forming a judgment of
Cicero they were moving in a sphere in which they were far
more competent to form an opinion than was the case in their
judgment of Vergil; for the practical use of oratory in the
days of the republic had taught the Romans to be far better
judges of orators than of poets, and the former were far more
characteristic of national life and feeling than the latter. And
it is further noteworthy that while in the judgments passed on
Cicero his quality as orator is often separately examined and
compared with that of his rivals, both Latin and Greek, no
such separate estimate of Vergil in his character as poet is anywhere to be found; and yet more was written about him than
about any other Roman author. The very enthusiasm which
his work evoked, not only when it finally appeared, but also
while it was still in course of preparation and only certain
passages from it were known, gave rise to rancorous criticisms
upon it.[8] But while a few, rather enemies than critics, attacked

---

[6] Cp. BLASS, *Die griesch. Beredsamkeit in dem Zeitraum von Alexander bis
auf Augustus*, p. 125 seqq.

[7] " Sciendum tamen est Terentium propter solam proprietatem omnibus
comicis esse praepositum, quibus est, quantum ad cetera spectat, inferior."
SERV. *ad Aen.*, i. 410. Much earlier, CICERO (*ad Att.* vii. 3, 10) had said :
" secutusque sum, non dico Caecilium . . . malus enim auctor latinitatis est, sed Terentium cuius fabellae propter elegantiam sermonis putaban-
tur a C. Laelio scribi." VULCATIUS SEDIGITUS assigned the first place among
comedians to Caecilius, the second to Plautus, and only the sixth to Terence.
(GELL. xv. 24.)

[8] DONATUS (*Vit. Verg.*, p. 65) mentions some ribald anonymous parodies of
passages in the Bucolics and Georgics, the Aeneomastix of Carvilius Pictor,
a work by Herennius on the faults, and one by Perellius Faustus on the
"thefts" of Vergil, and eight books entitled Homoeon Elenchon, by Q.
Octavius Avitus, in which was recorded " quos et unde versus transtulerit."

or derided it, the great mass of those who heard it gave expression to their admiration in terms of enthusiasm which, without doubt, faithfully represent the general spirit with which it was received. But enthusiasm and abuse are not criticism. How far the works on Vergil of the many grammarians contemporary with the poet or shortly subsequent to him were of an æsthetic character, and concerned themselves with what would at the present day be called real criticism, the scanty notices of them that remain render it difficult to judge; but there can be little doubt that if the genius of Vergil had received in them any satisfactory general definition, grammatical tradition, which is full of the poet's name, would not have failed to preserve it. Instead of this, the best that has been preserved is a single remark of Domitius Afer, which, though just, is yet insufficient, and merely superficial in the manner in which it assigns Vergil a place in that hierarchy of poets over which Homer presides;[9] for, as we have seen, the ancients were not in a position to judge otherwise than superficially of the connection between Vergil and Homer.

Of contemporary opinions only one has come down to us,[10] but this, though maliciously expressed, yet contains a good deal of truth in it; it regards Vergil's work, however, merely from the rhetorical point of view, and might equally well be a criticism on an orator.[11] Moreover, it is clear that those who

Asconius Pedianus, who lived in the time of Claudius, wrote a work defending Vergil against these and similar critics.

[9] "Utar enim verbis eisdem quae ex Afro Domitio iuvenis excepi, qui mihi interroganti quem Homero crederet maxime accedere: secundus, inquit, est Vergilius, propior tamen primo quam tertio." QUINTIL., x. i. 86. Domitius Afer was praetor under Tiberius in 26 A.D.; he died in 59. This saying is versified by ALCIMUS AVITUS (5th–6th centuries) in the *Anthologia Latina*, No. 259 (ed. MEYER).

[10] "M. Vipsanius a Maecenate eum suppositum appellabat novae cacozelae repertorem, non tumidae nec exilis sed ex communibus verbis, atque ideo latentis." DONAT., *Vit. Verg.*, p. 65.

[11] Equally true is the criticism of HORACE (*Sat.*, i. 10, 44):—

> "molle atque facetum
> Vergilio annuerunt gaudentes rure Camenae."

It is to be noticed however that these words, as they themselves expressly state (*rure*), refer only to the Bucolics and Georgics. When Horace wrote the first book of the Satires (41–35 B.C.) Vergil had not so much as

attacked Vergil for the frequent use he had made of Homer,
did so chiefly in a spirit of hostility, wilfully ignoring the
similar use made of him by other illustrious poets,[12] Greek as
well as Latin, and also (as Vergil himself used to retort) the
great difficulty of doing so successfully.[13] The free use which
Vergil made of writers, both Latin and Greek, who had gone
before him, had its justification, or rather its *raison d'être*, in a
way of looking at such things peculiar to the ancients, and any
hostile criticism of him on that account was more clearly prejudiced then than would be the case now, when opinions on
this subject have so greatly changed.[14]

For the most part the criticism of these grammarians confines itself to details; it discusses words, forms, and metrical
licenses, examines certain parts of the narrative, noticing inconsequences and contradictions, or deals with purely antiquarian questions. Observations on style are few, and always
limited to isolated passages; for the most part they consist of
comparisons; here is a metaphor which Vergil has used better
or less well than Homer, there is a description in which he has
been surpassed by Pindar. For the rest, an examination of
these criticisms, as far as they have been preserved,[15] will show
a considerable freedom and independence of judgment; though
looked upon as the highest authority in the fields of grammar,

thought of the Aeneid; he was at that time busy with the Georgics. Were
the dates not so very uncertain, one might almost venture to say that
this criticism of Horace refers to the Bucolics alone. Certainly, if Horace
had known the Aeneid, he would not simply have described his friend's
poetry in these words. Vergil was dead, and his work had already appeared
when Horace wrote the *Ars Poetica* (10-9 B.C.); but the single mention of
Vergil in this (v. 53) is merely concerned with a contrast between the old
and new schools in the general matter of language.
  [12] Cp. WALTHER, *De scriptorum Romanorum usque ad Vergilium studiis
Homericis.* Vratisl., 1867.
  [13] "Hoc ipsum crimen sic defendere assuetum ait (Asconius Pedianus):
cur non illi quoque eadem furta temptarent? verum intellecturos esse faci-
lius esse Herculi clavem quam Homero versum surripere." DONAT, p. 66.
  [14] See the just and acute observations of HERTZBERG on this point in the
Introduction to his translation of the Aeneid, p. vi. To find in these "furta"
of Vergil's a proof of his want of originality, as TEUFFEL does (*Gesch. d. röm.
Lit.*, p. 392), is a grave error.
  [15] A review of the criticisms passed on Vergil in classical times appears
in the *Prolegomena* of RIBBECK, c. viii. These criticisms refer almost entirely to the Aeneid, very rarely to the Bucolics or Georgics.

rhetoric, and erudition, Vergil is not, during this first period, an
object of blind admiration; various faults are recognised and
pointed out, and Asconius Pedianus himself is willing, to a
certain extent, to admit these in the book he wrote against the
detractors of the poet. But these detractors, who were animated
in their criticisms by a spirit of hostility, are only to be found
among Vergil's contemporaries; the unfavourable opinions of
Hyginus and Probus, and the more bitter and less just attacks
of Annæus Cornutus,[16] had no influence on the poet's reputation.
These faults were looked upon for the most part as merely such
as are inevitable in everything human—even Homer was not
exempt from them—and there was a very general opinion that
many of them would have been removed but for the poet's
premature death. Some even went so far as to assert that he
had purposely put certain difficulties and obscurities into his
poem to try the skill and acumen of the grammarians.[17]

During this first period therefore the influence of Vergil was
felt rather than defined. As the most faithful expression of national feeling ever given, and as a work of art in entire harmony
with the taste of the time, the Æneid had gained an immense
and well-deserved prestige, in comparison with which the fame
of the great Roman orator sank into insignificance. But when
contemporary criticism wished to analyse the processes by
which this success had been attained, it failed to penetrate
beyond such parts of the work as were entirely external, partly
because of the tendency of the age to interest itself chiefly with
such matters, partly because its knowledge of literature was

[16] This grammarian, who was the master of Lucan and Persius, did not
hesitate to criticise Vergil in strong terms (*abiecte, sordide, indecore*, etc.).
But all his criticisms which have been preserved are either mere cavils, or
else point out obvious errors. He too was an admirer of the poet, as we
learn from his own words: "iamque exemplo tuo etiam principes civitatum,
o poeta, incipient similia fingere." CHARIS., p. 100 (ed. KEIL).

[17] "Asconius Pedianus dicit se Vergilium dicentem audisse, in hoc loco
se grammaticis crucem fixisse, volens experiri quis eorum studiosior invenir-
etur." SERV. *ad Ecl.*, iii. 105. Cp. PHILARGYR., and SCHOL. BERN., *ibid.*
Probably Asconius was citing the authority of some one else, for he can
hardly have been born when Vergil died. Cp. RIBBECK, *Prolegg.*, p. 97 seq.
We find this idea again in the middle ages, where it is spoken of as a regular
habit of ancient authors, not confined to Vergil, *e.g.*, in the Prologue of Maria
de France, who states it on the authority of Riscian.

not sufficient to give it an insight into the true nature of the
epic. We have already noticed how this habit of mind, which
occupied itself merely with externals, tended not a little to
prevent a just estimate of the eloquence of Cicero, notwithstanding the fact that oratory was a subject on which Romans
were especially qualified to decide, and the further fact that a
parallel between Cicero and Demosthenes was a far truer one
than any between Vergil and Homer could be. In the case of
Vergil, this same method of criticism resulted in confining his
merits as poet to a field far too narrow for the nature and
universality of the enthusiasm he had evoked. Hence his
poetical and national qualities, which, while generally felt,
could not be truly judged within the restricted limits of contemporary appreciation, acted like leaven on those qualities
of scholar and grammarian which could be understood and
defined, and served to expand them to undue proportions. The
idea of Vergil's universal knowledge does not, it is true, as yet
appear; but there does already appear an idea of his universal
authority, whether in poetry or prose, grammar or rhetoric—
that is to say, in all the first elements of the culture of the
time. Every one who speaks of him is prone to exaggerate
more or less the nature and the variety of his powers, and
Martial is certainly not giving utterance to an idea exclusively
his own when he says that, had Vergil chosen to devote himself to lyric poetry or the drama, he could easily have surpassed
the highest masters in either of those branches of literature.[18]
From the very beginning therefore of the history of Vergil's
fame there are traces to be found of those aberrations of judgment which attained subsequently to such striking proportions.

[18] " Sic Maro nec Calabri tentavit carmina Flacci,
        Pindaricos nosset cum superare modos ;
     et Vario cessit Romani laude cothurni,
        cum posset tragico fortius ore loqui."
                                        MART., viii. 18.

It is worthy of note that, though Virgil exercised a great influence on Latin
prose, he had no great reputation himself as a prose writer. " Vergilium
illa felicitas ingeni in oratione soluta reliquit." SENECA, Controv., iii. p. 361
(ed. BURSIAN); cp. DONAT., Vit. Verg., p. 58.

CHAPTER III

VERGIL belongs to that small class of poets who have been altogether fortunate. Admired not only for his rare genius, but also for his rare character, which made him one of the most sympathetic men of his age,[1] he was spoken of with enthusiasm by all his fellow-poets, the best of whom were ready, as we may learn from their works, freely to acknowledge his superiority. He had enemies—genius always has—but he could well afford to forget them in the esteem with which he was regarded by great men of every kind and by the whole Roman people, which, on hearing his verses recited in the theatre, rose as one man and saluted the poet, who happened to be present, with the acclamations usually reserved for Augustus.[2] He certainly, from what he saw in his lifetime, had every reason to anticipate the immortality of his fame in future ages.

Signs of the poet's popularity are apparent in every sphere. In the upper classes, among whom it was the fashion to take an interest in literature, the learned lady described by Juvenal,

[1] " Cetera sane vitae et ore et animo tam probum constat ut Neapoli Parthenias vulgo appellatus sit." DONAT., *Vit. Verg.*, p. 57. " Anima candida." HOR., *Sat.*, i. 5, 41. An ancient commentator thought that Vergil was meant in Horace's well-known lines, " Iracundior est paulo," etc. *Sat.*, i. 3, 29 seqq.

[2] " Malo securum et secretum Vergili recessum, in quo tamen neque apud divum Augustum gratia caruit, neque apud populum Romanum notitia. Testes Augusti epistulae, testis ipse populus, qui, auditis in theatro Vergili versibus, surrexit universus, et forte praesentem spectantemque Vergilium veneratus est sic quasi Augustum." *Dial. de Oratt.*, 13. How great was this " notitia apud populum Romanum " is clear too from his biography, " ut . . . si quando Romae, quo rarissime commeabat, viseretur in publico, sectantes demonstrantesque se suffugeret in proximum tectum." DONAT., *Vit. Verg.*, p. 57.

(according to the scholiast Statilia Messalina, the wife of Nero,) who appears surrounded by grammarians and rhetoricians, dealing earnestly and voluminously with the literary questions of the day, discusses the character of Dido, and considers the relative merits of Vergil and Homer.[3] Polybius, the freedman of Claudius, a courtier of much influence and a dilettante in literature, probably very much of the same calibre as his imperial master, undertook a Latin paraphrase of Homer and a Greek one of Vergil, and on these Seneca, in his work addressed to him, pours forth eulogies,[4] which are probably as sincere as those he at the same time bestowed on the future hero of the Apocolocyntosis. In the theatre too Vergil's popularity was no less striking; not only were his poems recited there[5] for many centuries after his death, but special dramatic representations of them were given. Thus Nero, towards the end of his life, when threatened from every side, made a vow that if he escaped he would himself perform a pantomime entitled Turnus, taken from the Æneid.[6] It was further the fashion at sumptuous entertainments to have, among other forms of diversion, recitations from Homer and Vergil. Thus at the table of the parvenu Trimalchio, the Homeristae duly appear, and a passage from the fifth book of the Æneid is cruelly

³ " Illa tamen gravior, quae cum discumbere coepit
    laudat Vergilium, periturae ignoscit Elissae,
    committit vates, et comparat; inde Maronem,
    atque alia parte in trutina suspendit Homerum."
                           Sat., vi. 434 seqq.

⁴ " Homerus et Vergilius tam bene de humano genere meriti quam tu et de omnibus et de illis meruisti, quos pluribus notos esse voluisti quam scripserant, multum tecum morentur." *Dial.*, xi. (*Ad Polyb. de Consol.*) 8. 2. " Agedum illa quae multo ingeni tuo labore celebrata sunt, in manus sume, utriuslibet auctoris carmina, quae tu ita resolvisti ut quamvis structura illorum recesserit, permaneat tamen gratia. Sic enim illa ex alia lingua in aliam transtulisti, ut, quod difficillimum erat, omnes virtutes in alienam te orationem secutae sunt." *Ibid.*, 11. 5.

⁵ " Auditis in theatro Vergili versibus," *Dial. de Oratt.*, l. c.; " bucolica eo successu edidit ut in scena quoque per cantores crebro recitarentur." DONAT., *Vit. Verg.*, p. 60.

⁶ " Sub exitu quidem vitae palam voverat, si sibi incolumis status permansisset, proditurum se partae victoriae ludis etiam hydraulam et choraulam et utricularium, ac novissimo die histrionem, saltaturumque Vergili Turnum." SUETON., vi. 54. Cp. JAHN, in *Hermes*, ii. p. 421; FRIEDLÄNDER, *Sittengeschichte*, etc., ii. 274.

murdered.[7]   Among the presents too, (Xenia,) which it was
customary to give on certain occasions, books which happened
to be in fashion would often figure.   Such a book would
contain some short poem of Homer or Virgil, or sometimes
even their complete works, written elegantly on a small scroll,
and occasionally further ornamented with the author's portrait.[8]

Nor did the fame of Vergil and his contemporaries of the
"new school" remain confined to Rome; it spread rapidly
throughout the provinces.   Among the various graffiti still
visible on the walls of Pompeii occur several verses of Vergil.[9]
One of these is the twentieth line of the eighth Eclogue:—

CARMINIBVS CIRCE SOCIOS MVTAVIT VLIXIS;

another,—

RVSTICVS EST CORYDON; [10]

[7] " Ecce alius ludus. Servus qui ad pedes Habinnae sedebat, iussus, credo,
a domino suo, proclamavit subito canora voce:—

' Interea medium Aeneas iam classe tenebat.'

Nullus sonus unquam acidior percussit aures meas; nam praeter recitantis
barbarie aut adiectum aut deminutum clamorem, miscebat Atellanicos versus, ut tunc primum me Vergilius offenderit."   PETRON., *Sat.*, 68.

[8] " Accipe facundi Culicem, studiose, Maronis,
    ne nugis positis Arma virumque canas."

MART., xvi. 185.

" Quam brevis immensum cepit membrana Maronem,
    ipsius vultus prima tabella gerit."

ID., xiv. 186.

Besides Homer and Vergil, there occur also in Martial's Xenia Menander,
Cicero, Propertius, Livy, Sallust, Ovid, Tibullus, Lucan, and Catullus.

[9] Cp. BÜCHELER, *Die pompejanische Wandinschriften*, in the *Rhein. Museum*,
N.F., xii. p. 250 seqq. GARRUCCI, *Graffiti*, tab. vi. 5 (*Aen.*, ii. 148). As the
excavations are extended the number of Vergilian lines discovered increases
daily. In the collection of ZANGEMEISTER, *Inscriptiones parietariae Pom-
peinae, Herculanenses, Stabianae* (vol. iv. of the *Corpus Inscrr. Lat.*), Berlin,
1871, the following numbers are lines or parts of lines of Vergil: 1237 (*Aen.*,
v. 110), 1282 (*Aen.*, i. 1), 1524 (*Ecl.*, ii. 56), 1527 (*Id.*), 1672 (*Aen.*, i. 1), 1841
(*Aen.*, ii. 148), 2218 (*Aen.*, ii. 1), 2361 (*Aen.*, i. 1), 3151 (*Aen.*, ii. 1), 3198 (*Aen.*,
i. 1). To these may be added two others published recently in the *Giornale
degli Scavi di Pompei*, ser. ii. vol. i. p. 281 (*Aen.*, i. 234), vol. ii. p. 35 (*Aen.*,
i. 1). A Roman wall-inscription has the words, " colo calathisque Minervae"
(*Aen.*, vii. 805); *vide* FEA, *Varietà di notizie*, p. xxvii.; JORDAN in *Bursian's
Jahresbericht*, i. 784.

[10] The common reading is, " *Rusticus es Corydon*," but the *Codex Romanus*
has " *est*," like the Pompeian inscription.

another, which sounds sadly in the deserted city,—

CONTICVERE OM[NES].

These inscriptions are probably the work of schoolboys, like the alphabets, or parts of alphabets, which occur in various parts of Pompeii.[11] The date of the Pompeian catastrophe was 79 A.D., when Vergil had already been dead ninety-eight years; but though doubtless the great mass of the Pompeian graffiti were written between that date and the eruption of sixteen years previously, yet many are clearly much earlier. One belongs certainly to the year 79 B.C., and one of the alphabets also seems to belong to the time of the Republic.[12] The fame of Vergil in Campania, where he spent most of his time, was very great even during his life, and his grave at Naples moreover gave him a particular connection with that neighbourhood. Hence there is no real reason why these Vergilian verses should not have been written on the walls of Pompeii at a period much nearer the poet's lifetime, or even during his lifetime itself. The two passages, ' Rusticus est Corydon,' and ' Conticuere omnes,' are at the present day still two of the most familiar passages in Vergil. Nor are these graffiti the only proof of his popularity at Pompeii; verses of his occur also, in epigraphs properly so-called, on a singular variety of objects, on a silver spoon, on a tile, on a bas-relief representing a woman selling game, and on tombstones.[13]

---

[11] Cp. GARRUCCI, *Graffiti*, tab. i. Elementary schoolmasters, as is well known, used to hold their classes in the open air, in the streets or the squares. Cp. USSING, *Darstellung der Erziehungs- und Unterrichtswesen bei den Griechen und Römern* (transl. by FRIEDRICHSEN, Altona, 1870), p. 100 seqq. For the Pompeian wall-paintings that have reference to the schools, see JAHN, *Ueber Darstellungen des Handwerks und Handelsverkehrs auf antiken Wandegemälden* (Leip., 1868), p. 288 seqq. There is among the Pompeian graffiti one very curious one of a grammatical character. Cp. GARRUCCI, tab. xvii.; JAHN, *op. cit.*, p. 288.

[12] BÜCHELER, *op. cit.*, p. 246.

[13] On a silver spoon is the seventeenth line of Ecl. i.; on a bas-relief of the Villa Albani are the lines 607 seqq. of Aen., i.; *vide* JAHN in the *Berichte d. sächs. Gesellsch. d. Wiss.*, 1861, p. 365. On a tile of the 1st century appear the first two lines of the Aeneid; *vide Archäolog. Anz.*, 1864, No. 184, p. 199. Vergilian lines are cited from epitaphs by MARINI, *Frat. arv.*, p. 826 seq., *Papiri diplom.*, p. 332 seq.

But the greatest triumph gained by Vergil and the other
Augustan poets was in the domain of education.   And, in fact,
they had with their works so entirely satisfied what had been
a long-standing want, that it would have been mere folly on
the part of the schools to keep up the old tradition, and not to
profit by this new and quickening nourishment which was
offered them. It was without doubt the perfection to which
the Latin language had been brought by Vergil and Cicero
which tended far more than any reform of Augustus to
encourage the study of grammar as a special profession. No
sooner had the new poetry appeared than there were grammarians who made use of it for purposes of education,—the
earliest of them perhaps Q. Caecilius Epirota, a freedman of
Atticus, of whom Suetonius says that he was the first to use
as reading-books in his elementary courses the works of Vergil
and the other poets of the new school.[14]   It is difficult for anyone who has not made a special study of the conditions of
culture at this epoch to form any idea of the power and influence of the grammarians in promoting literary fame.   In
this fever of literary activity, induced not only by the tastes of
an Emperor, but also by the dictates of a fashion so universal
that even a Trimalchio had to put on the airs of an author,
every possible method of obtaining publicity and favour was
eagerly adopted; while some hired a claque to applaud their
recitations,[15] others would shrink from no expedient, however
base, to obtain admission into the schools of the grammarians,
and thus shelter the poor products of their Muse under the
shadow of education. The contempt with which Horace speaks
of these devices [16] shows how common they were.   But there
can be no doubt that the honour of being read in the schools
was one for which it was well worth striving, and was a

---

[14] " Primus dicitur Latine ex tempore disputasse, primusque Vergilium
et alios poetas novos praelegere coepisse."   SUET., De Gramm. et Rhett. 16.
[15] Cp. HELWIG, De recitatione poetarum apud Romanos, p. 20 seqq.

[16] " Non ego ventosae plebis suffragia venor
impensis cenarum et tritae munere vestis ;
non ego nobilium scriptorum auditor et ultor
grammaticos ambire tribus et pulpita dignor."
HOR., Epist., i. 19, 37 seqq.

matter of consequence, even for us at the present day; for it
was the grammarians who selected the canon of poets that,
through the medium of the schools and by no other way, has
come down to us. Many works which have been lost would
not have been so had they had the fortune to be used as text-
books, just as many works have for this reason alone been
preserved. While a certain amount of good taste still prevailed, the first place in the schools was occupied by Vergil;
after him came Terence and Horace, while other writers of the
good period, such as Ovid and Catullus, were not without their
advocates. In later times, when rhetoric had invaded the domain of poetry, the works of Lucan, Juvenal, Statius, and others
who compare even more unfavourably with their predecessors,
were thought worthy of taking a place as text-books. But
in addition to these the earlier writers continued to be read
and studied, and it was always with Vergil, and, as long as
a knowledge of Greek prevailed, with Homer, that the course
began.[17]

During the whole first century of the Empire and part of
the second, the study of grammar was highly developed and
dominated the field of literature, giving rise to learned and
important works by specialists, the contents of which were
largely drawn upon by grammarians of a later date. The system of these early writers was, up to a certain extent, modelled
on the grammatical studies of the Greeks. But though their
methods of elucidation were very similar, the use they made of
Vergil as an authority on grammar was naturally different from
that made by the Greeks of Homer; for in this respect the

---

[17] "Ideoque optime institutum est ut ab Homero atque Vergilio lectio in-
ciperet." QUINTIL., i. 85.

> "Cui tradas, Lupe, filium magistro
> quaeris sollicitus diu rogasque.
> omnes grammaticosque rhetorasque
> devites moneo; nihil sit illi
> cum libris Ciceronis aut Maronis."
>> MART., v. 56.

> "Dummodo non pereat, totidem olfecisse lucernas
> quot stabant pueri, cum totus discolor esset
> Flaccus, et haereret nigro fuligo Maroni."
>> IUV., vii. 225 seqq

importance of the Latin writer differed fundamentally from
that of the Greek. Homer had been largely studied and
illustrated by the Alexandrians, but his language and his
forms had merely a historical interest, and though they might
be and actually were adopted in some kinds of poetical com--
positions, such adoption was entirely academic and artificial,
and they could not in any way form the basis of a universal
theory of grammar destined to govern the universal usages of
ordinary writers. Vergil, on the other hand, embodying as he
did the highest development of which the Latin language was
capable, was, and was bound to be, the supreme authority on
all grammatical questions.[18] He is, as it were, the pole-star of
the grammarian, and every one destined for the profession of
grammar must steep himself in him.[19] No other Latin writer
was made a subject of study by so many grammarians or called
forth so many grammatical works.

His literary eminence, and his authority on questions of
language, required a corresponding security as to the true reading of his text; many critics therefore busied themselves with
this, emending not merely by conjecture, but also by the use of
MSS. of authority belonging to his family, or even of his
actual autographs, which were still known in the times of
Pliny, Quintilian, and Gellius.[20] In addition to textual criticism, explanations of difficult passages, of words, or of mythological and geographical allusions, and observations on the

---

[18] Speaking of *cortex* being used of both genders, QUINTILIAN says :
"quorum neutrum reprehendo, cum sit utriusque Vergilius auctor " (i. 5.
35) Later grammarians kept up the same tradition : " stiria dicuntur ab
stillis, quae Vergilius genere feminino, Varro neutro dixit : sed vicit Vergili
auctoritas." *Lib. de dubiis nominibus*, ap. KEIL, v. 590 ; "mella tantum
triptoton est ; vicit propter auctoritatem Vergilianam." *Fr. bob. de nomine*,
ap. KEIL, v. p. 558.
[19] " Grammaticus futurus Vergilium scrutatur." SENECA, *Epist.*, 108.
[20] "Iamvero Ciceronis ac divi Augusti Vergilique (monimenta manus)
saepenumero videmus." PLIN., *Nat. hist.*, xiii. 83. " Quomodo et ipsum
(Ciceronem) et Vergilium scripsisse manus eorum docent." QUINTIL., i. 7.
11. " Quod ipse (Hyginus) invenerit in libro qui fuerit ex domo atque
familia Vergili." GELL. N. A., i. 11, 1. " In primo Georgicon, quem ego,
inquit (Probus), manu ipsius correctum legi." ID., xiii. 2. 4. " Qui scripserunt idiographum librum Vergili se inspexisse." ID., ix. 14. 7. " Osten-
disse mihi librum Aeneidos secundum mirandae vetustatis, emptum in
sigillariis viginti aureis, quem ipsius Vergili fuisse credebatur." ID., ii. 3. 5.

style of various passages, considered either separately or as
compared with similar passages in Greek writers, formed the
subject of learned treatises by Hyginus, the friend of Ovid and
the new school of poets generally,[21] by Probus, who deserves
to be called the Roman Aristarchus, by Annaeus Cornutus, and
many others, whom it would be long to mention. Others again,
like Asper, wrote expository commentaries, which accompanied
the text of the poems.[22]

In addition to these works treating directly of Vergil,
numerous grammatical works appeared in which the instances
were drawn more largely from Vergil than from any other
writer. Hence that close connection, still noticeable in such
parts of this literature as are preserved, between commentaries
on Vergil and treatises on grammar, by nature of which remarks which form part of a commentary appear again in a
grammatical treatise, and *vice versâ*;[23] and though these works
are not known to us at first hand, yet the later grammarians,
who made use of them in their compilations, can give us an
idea of the extent to which Vergil was employed in them.
The chief merit of Vergil which they recognised was the apt-
ness of his diction.[24] A good example of the esteem in which
he was held on this account is furnished us by the work of
Nonius, composed towards the end of the 3rd century, to which
the author contributed little or no original matter, making it
entirely a compilation from earlier works,—a fact which con-
stitutes its chief value at the present day. In this work, which
is of no great bulk, and which sums up in itself, as it were, the
various authorities employed by preceding grammarians,[25] the
number of examples from Vergil is well-nigh 1,500. No other
of the numerous authors cited, either from republican or im-

---

[21] "Vatum studiose novorum," as Ovid says of him (*Trist.*, iii. 14. 7).
[22] For these early critics of Vergil, *vide* THOMAS, *Essai sur Servius et son
commentaire sur Virgile.* Paris, 1880; GEORGII, *Die antike Aeneis-kritik.*
Stuttgart, 1891.
[23] Cp. KEIL, *Gramm. Lat.*, v. 7 (*Praef. ad Cledonium*).
[24] "Quis ad sophisticas Isocratis conclusiones, quis ad enthymemata
Demosthenis, aut opulentiam Tullianam, aut proprietatem nostri Maronis
accedat?" AUSON, *Epist.*, xvii. 8.
[25] SCHMIDT, *De Nonii Marcelli auctoribus grammaticis*, p. 4 seq., 96 seqq.

perial times, (the latest is Martial,) comes anywhere near this
figure ; neither Cicero, who after Vergil is the chief authority,
nor Varro, who of the rest is one of the most quoted.   And
throughout the field of grammatical studies Vergil's predominance is the same, as one can easily satisfy oneself by merely
casting an eye over the index of authorities in Keil's edition.
To be brief, the use which the grammarians made of Vergil is
so extensive that, if all the MSS. of him had been lost, it would
be possible from the notices given us by the ancients of the
Vergilian poems, and the passages quoted from them by the
grammarians alone, to reconstruct practically the whole of the
Bucolics, the Georgics, and the Aeneid.[26]   The great mass of
these grammatical examples might doubtless have been taken
from other authors ; but the authority of Vergil was supreme,
and his poetry was, so to speak, the Bible of the ancients ; it
was the first of all scholastic books, and was always in every-
body's hands.

The centre of the activity of all these grammarians was the
school with its oral instruction ; but such parts of their works
as are known to us certainly do not belong to the elementary
department of education.   Valerius Probus, the most famous
of all the Vergilian commentators, did not keep a school strictly
speaking, but used to discuss learned questions with a small
and select circle.   Others, however, of well-nigh equal learning
and eminence, such as Asper, wrote expressly with a view to
education, and, in general, many of the remarks and explanations contained in learned and critical treatises were adopted
by the authors of commentaries intended for the use of schools.
Thus, from such remains of the learned literature of the period
as still exist, it is possible to form a very fair idea of the
methods of the more elementary instruction.   Vergil was the
first book given to children as soon as they could read and
write, and from thenceforth formed the staple means of
elementary no less than of advanced education.   From him
the master first taught his scholars to read with expression,
and to modulate the voice according to the sense ;[27] and this

[26] *Vide* the foot-notes in RIBBECK'S edition.
[27] QUINTIL., i. 8. 1.

choice, like that of Homer for a similar purpose, is approved by Quintilian, not only on account of the beauty of these two poets, but also on account of the noble and elevated sentiments they express. ' To appreciate them,' he adds, ' a maturer judgment is no doubt necessary ; but for this there is time enough, for they will not be read once only.'[28] Then the master would make use of these same reading-lessons to practise his pupils in turning the poetry into prose, noting the quantities and commenting on all irregularities and licenses, ' not, of course, with a view of blaming the poets, to whom much must be excused on the plea of metrical necessity.'[29] And from this the student advances to the interpretation of the actual text. But all this was more or less dependent on the knowledge of the individual grammarians, which was in most cases not very profound. Many of them were quite without any higher culture, to say nothing of the absolute charlatans who abounded. For the more ignorant among them Quintilian recommends an adherence to what was to be found in the ordinary manuals of elementary education.[30]

[28] " Quanquam ad intelligendas eorum virtutes firmiore iudicio opus est ; sed huic rei superest tempus, neque enim semel legentur. Interim et sublimitate heroici carminis animus assurgat, et ex magnitudine rerum spiritum ducat, et optimis imbuatur." QUINTIL., i. 8. 5.

[29] QUINTIL., i. 8. 13 seqq.

[30] " Et grammaticos offici sui commonemus. Ex quibus si quis erit plane impolitus et vestibulum modo artis huius ingressus, intra haec quae profitentium commentariolis vulgata sunt consistet ; doctiores multa adicient." QUINTIL., i. 5. 8.

CHAPTER IV

A SIMILAR position to that which Vergil held in grammatical
instruction was held by him also in the kindred study of
rhetoric ; for so closely were these two connected, and so immediately did the one follow the other, that many of the
rhetorical figures were taught already by the grammarian,[1] and
many teachers, especially in earlier times, devoted themselves
equally to both branches of learning.[2] But while the study
of grammar made a distinct advance during the first century,
the art of rhetoric was marked by a no less notable decline.
Having lost its true habitat through the downfall of civil
liberty, it had come to be a mere parasite, intruding upon every
branch of literature, paralyzing it and contaminating all its
products.   In the frenzy for declamation then prevailing,
which demanded that all the aims and methods of education
should be based on rhetoric, the use made of Vergil was very
varied.   In matters of theory, numerous instances illustrative
of principles would naturally be drawn from his works, already made familiar through the preliminary courses of education and the habit of the grammarians of setting their pupils
to examine the force of the various figures and metaphors.   In
the practical part of the subject too, which would receive the

---

[1] " Enimvero iam maiore cura doceat (grammaticus) tropos omnes, quibus
praecipue, non poema modo, sed etiam oratio ornatur, schemata utraque,
id est figuras, etc." QUINTIL., i. 8. 16.

[2] " Veteres grammatici et rhetoricam docebant ac multorum de utraque
arte commentarii feruntur ; secundum quam consuetudinem posteriores
quoque existimo, quanquam iam discretis professionibus, nihilominus vel
retinuisse vel instituisse et ipsos quaedam genera institutionum ad elo-
quentiam praeparandam ut problemata, paraphrases, allocutiones, ethologias
atque alia hoc genus ; ne scilicet sicci omnino atque aridi pueri rhetoribus
traderentur." SUET., De Gramm. et Rhett., 4.

most attention in the ordinary schools, not only were themes for declamation taken from his works, but his images and ideas and rhetorical expedients were drawn upon, his descriptions were imitated, his felicities of expression copied; and such a use of the poet was common from the earliest times among the most celebrated orators of the Augustan age, among whom Arellius Fuscus, one of the numerous friends of the elder Seneca, was notorious for his frequent adaptations of Vergil, made chiefly with a view of gaining favour with Maecenas.[3] A similar use had been made, and was still made, of Homer, whom the ancients looked upon as furnishing the earliest monuments of the oratorical art; the speeches of his heroes were looked upon as masterpieces of rhetoric, even Quintilian, usually so sparse in his praises, breaking into enthusiasm on the subject of Homeric eloquence.[4] And rhetorical qualities were the easier to find in Vergil, seeing that he, like all the poets of the Augustan era,[5] had gone through the regular course of studies in grammar and rhetoric. It may be chance, but perhaps it is less chance than it seems, that the earliest quotations from Vergil with which we are acquainted are made by orators contemporary with the poet, who either employ him in their compositions or speak of him from the rhetorical point of view.[6]

But if the Augustan poets understood how to keep rhetoric within due bounds and to save poetry from becoming identified with it, this was not the case with their successors, who became so subject to the influence of this dominant factor in Latin literature that many of them, such as Lucan, Silius

[3] "Solebat autem ex Vergilio Fuscus multa trahere ut Maecenati imputaret." SENEC., *Suasor.*, 3.

[4] "Hic enim, quemadmodum ex Oceano dicit ipse amnium fontiumque cursus initium capere, omnibus eloquentiae partibus exemplum et ortum dedit . . . Nam, ut de laudibus, exhortationibus, consolationibus taceam, nonne vel nonus liber quo missa ad Achillem legatio continetur, vel in primo inter duces contentio, vel dictae in secundo sententiae omnes litium ac consiliorum explicant artes? Iam similitudines, amplificationes, exempla, digressus, signa rerum et argumenta ceteraque probandi ac refutandi sunt ita multa ut etiam qui de artibus scripserunt plurimi harum rerum testimonium ab hoc poeta petant." QUINTIL., x. 1. 16 seqq.

[5] The best instance of the care devoted by these poets to the study of rhetoric is furnished by the Heroides of Ovid.

[6] *Vide* the passages of Seneca the Elder quoted on p. 12.

Italicus, Valerius Flaccus and Statius, are merely orators in
verse. And this *rapprochement* between poetry and rhetoric
naturally led to an interchange of materials between the two.
Poetry, guided by the bad taste which dominated poets and
orators alike, proceeded to avail itself of all the machinery of
rhetoric; while eloquence, confined to themes bare of any subjective interest and abandoning logic in favour of the mere
graces of style, placed the orator in the same position as
the poet, perversely giving to an art which is essentially
practical that character of idealism which belongs properly
to poetry alone. Those who had to declaim, often extempor-
aneously, on puerile and fictitious subjects were compelled
to conceal the lack of interest they felt in their material by a
recourse to poetical imagery; and this abuse became greater
and greater, the more that the public grew to admire what was
bombastic and affected.[7] The form of poetry best adapted for
such a class of writers was naturally the epic, both as being
the least subjective and also as affording the greatest variety
of rhetorical situations. For rhetorical no less than poetical
qualities, Vergil was looked upon as second only to Homer
among poets, a view which Quintilian also approves, though he
is not in favour of an immoderate use of the poets on the part
of an orator, and describes Lucan's want of poetical feeling
by saying he is fitter for orators to imitate than for poets.[8]
Evidently Vergil was largely studied by the rhetoricians of that
period, as we may learn from the fact that the rhetorician-poet
Annius Florus at the beginning of the second century, like
Macrobius subsequently, devoted a special treatise to a discus-

---

[7] We have a specimen of the sort of compositions which were admired at
the Capitoline contest instituted by Domitian in the inscription on the
recently discovered tombstone of Q. Sulpicius Maximus, a boy of twelve
years of age, who distinguished himself by improvising the Greek verses
which appear there. They are pure rhetoric both in subject and tone;
there is nothing poetical about them except that they are written in verse.
Vide VISCONTI, *Il Sepolcro di Q. Sulpicio Massimo*, Roma, 1871.

[8] "Ut dicam quod sentio, magis oratoribus quam poetis imitandus."
x. 1, 90. Orators are recommended to study him, as well as Vergil and
Horace, also in the *De Oratoribus*, 20: "exigitur enim iam ab oratore etiam
poeticus decor, non Acci aut Pacuvi veterno inquinatus, sed ex Horati et
Vergili et Lucani sacrario prolatus."

sion of the question whether Vergil were really orator or poet.[9] The authority of Cicero was naturally great in the rhetorical schools, but that of Vergil was so pre-eminent that, as the author of the dialogue *De Oratoribus* says, it would have been easier to find a detractor of Cicero than one of Vergil.[10]

It was the fortune of Vergil to be always on the crest of the wave, whether the current that carried him along the ages were clear or turbid. Seneca, who strove to wed the worst extravagances of rhetoric with philosophy, and yet, in spite of all his failings, startles us with his genius, quotes no author so often as Vergil, for whom he has the deepest veneration,[11] and whom his father had known personally. Vergil satisfied the rhetoricians, and he satisfied also those who were opposed to the rhetorical tendencies of the times; he satisfied Quintilian,[12] who tried in vain to bring back good taste in matters of style, he satisfied the author of the *De Oratoribus*, and, if he be not the same, he satisfied Tacitus also, a man who was great in his contempt for the schools and the popular taste, but yet shows in his works frequent traces of having studied the Mantuan poet.[13] But the universality of this admiration becomes even more striking, when we encounter, as we shortly do, a reaction unfavourable to the Augustan poets and observe how none the less the fame of Vergil and of certain of his contemporaries suffers no harm thereby.

Among the various artifices to which rhetoricians had recourse in their desire to satisfy the universal craving for novelty, was that of endeavouring to give their compositions

---

[9] *Vergilius orator an poeta.* Of this work only a fragment of the beginning has been preserved; this was first published by RITSCHL and then reproduced by JAHN in his FLORUS. (Leip., 1852.)

[10] " Plures hodie reperies qui Ciceronis gloriam quam qui Vergili detractent." *De Oratt.*, 12.

[11] He expresses this veneration with enthusiasm : " Clamat ecce maximus vates et velut divino ore instinctus salutare carmen canit; *optima quaeque dies*, etc." *Dial.*, x. (*de brev. vit.*) 9, 2. Elsewhere he says : " Homerus et Vergilius tam bene de humano genere meriti." *Dial.*, xi. (*ad Polyb. de consolat.*) 8, 2 ; " Vir disertissimus." *Dial.*, viii. 1.

[12] " Auctor eminentissimus," i. 10, 10 ; " acerrimi iudicii," viii. 3, 24; " poesis ab Homero et Vergilio tantum fastigium accepit," xii. 11. 26.

[13] Cp., besides the remarks of ERNESTI on the subject, the parallels adduced by DRÄGER, *Syntax und Styl des Tacitus*, Leip., 1868.

a grand and severe character by making them tortuous and obscure. To write simply and clearly would have seemed to many then, as it would seem to some too at the present day, an act of high treason against the laws of eloquence. A rhetorician kept saying to his pupil, who brought him an exercise, "Darker, darker!" The pupil made it darker, till at length his master exclaimed, "Bravo, now it will do; even I cannot understand a word of it." [14] This species of affectation, which strove to make an impression by an appearance of profound erudition, led naturally to the use of unusual and obsolete words, with a consequent reaction in favour of the pre-Augustan writers. The Latin language had been formed by a series of experiments; hence even after a final style had been discovered both for prose and poetry, those earlier writers, who had contributed towards this discovery without actually attaining to it, were clearly entitled to a certain amount of respect. But in addition to their intrinsic worth, which gave these early poets and prose authors a certain claim to admiration, there was a theoretical tradition which kept their authority alive; for the whole of that science of grammar and philology which was so essential to a writer, even in later times, was almost entirely based on these ancient authors; and hence the grammarians, to whom every writer would be indebted for his education, had perpetual occasion to refer to the ancient literature. The new literary tendency, due to the influence of Cicero and Vergil, offered, it is true, in the models it provided, a large wealth of choice phrases, but it was a wealth which was hard for those to employ judiciously who did not combine with the purely mechanical rules of grammar and rhetoric a natural refinement of taste. In an epoch when philological erudition was admired and even required by the public, an epoch too in which a large part of the literary treasure of the nation consisted of early authors who were admittedly imperfect, it was easy for the taste of a writer to be at fault in the choice of his models. An old-fashioned style has often a force of its own,[15]

---

[14] QUINTIL., viii. 2. 12 seqq.

[15] " Propriis (verbis) dignitatem dat antiquitas. Namque et sanctiorem

and may well be useful for rhetorical purposes ; but to employ
it without falling into grave errors requires a refinement of
artistic feeling which is accorded to very few.[16]   There were,
it is true, even in the best period of Latin literature, certain
grammarians and writers who affected an antiquated style.
Caesar [17] already blames this propensity, as did Horace and
Vergil,[18] no less than Seneca, Quintilian and others in later
times.   But the excellency of both prose and poetry in the
Augustan age and the general good taste prevailing at the time
prevented this movement in favour of antiquity from gaining
any considerable proportions.   In the age of the Antonines
however, when literature was less concerned with matter than
with manner, the tendency becomes more evident.   The Greek
propensities of several of the emperors, the affection shown,
especially by Hadrian, for certain products of the Alexandrian
school, the admiration for everything that was pompous, mysterious, and foreign which prevailed in this age, so favourable
for charlatans of every kind, and the need of supplying by
artificial means the lack of creative power, induced many to
have recourse to archaisms and unusual expressions with the
object of giving apparent force and weight to empty and ver-
bose phrases.

The best known representative of this tendency is the Cicero
of the period, M. Cornelius Fronto, the tutor of M. Aurelius
and L. Verus, a past-master in every kind of pedantry, who
taught that one should go hunting up 'insperata atque inopi-
nata verba' and try to give one's diction a certain tinge of antiquity (colorem vetusculum appingere).   He, as far as one can
judge from his remains, made very little use of the Augustan
poets in his studies of style and language.   Here and there
in his writings appears an occasional reminiscence of Vergil or

---

et magis admirabilem faciunt orationem ; quibus non quilibet fuerit usurus."
QUINTIL., viii. 3. 24.

[16] "Odiosa cura; nam et cuilibet facilis, et hoc pessima quod rei stud-
iosus non verba rebus aptabit, sed res extrinsecus arcesset quibus haec
verba conveniant."   QUINTIL., viii. 3, 30.

[17] "Tanquam scopulum sic fugias inauditum atque insolens verbum."
Ap. GELL., i. 10. 4.

[18] *Catalect.*, 2.

Horace, but these are clearly due to the influence of his early education.[19]   Vergil is scarcely quoted by him at all,[20] and of Horace he merely speaks as "poeta memorabilis."[21]   Fronto was the head of a school of considerable importance and left behind him a certain rhetorical tradition which was of particular weight in Gaul.[22]   But his influence was practically confined to the narrow field of purely rhetorical prose, and there are not many distinct traces of it in those writers who have come down to us.   Moreover, it seems possible to infer from certain indications that several of Fronto's disciples did not follow their master rigorously in his estimate of the Augustan poets.   Thus, in the very circle itself of Fronto's friends and admirers, there were several who not only made use of Vergil in their grammatical studies, but even devoted special treatises to him, as for instance Sulpicius Apollinaris, the tutor of Pertinax, who prefixed to an edition of the Aeneid the three famous distichs on the subject of Vergil's dying request that his work should be burnt, and composed too the arguments in verse to the various books, which have also been preserved.[23]

[19] Cp. Herz, *Renaissance und Rococo*, not. 76.   The work entitled *Quadriga, seu exempla elocutionum ex Vergilio, Sallustio, Terentio, Cicerone*, was formerly attributed to Fronto, but it has now been established that it is by Arusianus Messius.   Cp. Teuffel, § 427, 4.

[20] In Gellius, ii. 26. 1.

[21] "Plane multum mihi facetiarum contulit istic Horatius Flaccus, memorabilis poeta, mihique propter Maecenatem et Maecenatianos hortos meos non alienus." *Ad Caes.*, ii. 1.   The poets whose works his imperial pupil read were Plautus, Accius, Lucretius and Ennius.   "Aut te Plauto expolires, aut Accio expleres, aut Lucretio delenires, aut Ennio incenderes." *De feriis Alsiensibus*, 3, p. 224 (ed. Du Rieu).   The opposite school, to which Quintilian and the author of the *De Oratoribus* belonged, read Vergil, Horace and Lucan.   Cp. *Dial. de Oratt.*, 20.

[22] Most of the writers who admire Fronto come from Gaul; such are Ausonius, Claudius Mamertus, Eumenius, and Sidonius.   The grammarian Consentius, who cites Fronto (Keil, v. 333), also comes from Gaul.   Leo, the counsellor of Eurich, King of the Goths, boasted of his descent from Fronto.   To him wrote his friend Sidonius, "Suspende perorandi illud quoque celeberrimum flumen quod non solum gentilitium sed domesticum tibi, quodque in tuum pectus per succiduas aetates ab atavo Frontone transfunditur." (Sidon., *Ep.*, viii. 8).   Fronto was also admired by his fellow-countrymen in Africa, as we learn from Minucius Felix and Marcianus Capella, but his chief eulogist, after his contemporary Gellius, is Sidonius, who admires principally his "gravitas."

[23] Donat., *Vit. Verg.*, p. 63.   The last of the three distichs is noteworthy for its emphasis :—

Anyhow, it is quite clear that the movement originated by
Fronto had only a limited influence, and that in purely literary
circles, and did not in any way affect the common schools,
which were under the Empire the main educational institutions.
In these the authority of Vergil remained unimpaired and ran
no risk of being supplanted by that of Ennius, Lucilius or
Lucretius, however much the influence of Fronto might be
exercised on their behalf.

As a matter of fact, this reaction in favour of the ancients
was not confined to Fronto and his school, and Fronto's excesses
in this direction appeared rather in his method of teaching and
his choice of examples than in his literary style, for others,
who were less well-known, carried this affectation to much
greater lengths. But in his methods Fronto went far beyond
even those who on the whole shared his tastes; for before him
the most ardent admirers of the ancient literature had not
dreamt of daring to dethrone Vergil.

A work which throws much light on the literary ideas of
this period and on the tendencies of contemporary studies is the
work of Aulus Gellius. Gellius was not a disciple of Fronto;
as a grammarian he can hardly be said to have belonged to one
school more than to another.[24] He seems to have been just an
erudite dilettante, who made a collection, both from books and
from various learned circles that he frequented, of views on all
manner of subjects; his chief researches, however, are concerned with the history of the language, and everything which
had to do with the meaning and usage of words seems to have
had a special interest for him.[25] He is a sort of philological
antiquarian, and hence his extreme veneration for the old

> " Infelix gemino cecidit prope Pergamon igni,
>   et paene est alio Troia cremata rogo."

The Periochae attributed, in all probability rightly, to Sulpicius are in the
Anth. Lat., No. 653 (ed. RIESE). Sulpicius also discussed Vergil in his
letters (cp. GELL., ii. 16. 8 seqq.). For his relations with Fronto, *vide* GELL.,
xix. 13. 1.

[24] I cannot bring myself to accept the contrary view maintained by HERTZ
and accepted by KRETSCHMER in his *De auctoribus Aul. Gellii grammaticis*,
p. 3 seq.

[25] " Ei libro (Aeli Melissi) titulus est ingentis cuiusdam illecebrae ad
legendum ; scriptus quippe est, *De loquendi proprietate*." xviii. 6. 8.

writers of the republic, and his contempt for the grammarians of the Empire,[26] not excepting the famous Verrius Flaccus.[27] He does not so much as mention Tacitus or Quintilian, and, like Fronto, he savagely attacks Seneca,[28] not merely for his mistakes in style and language, but also because he speaks mockingly of those searchers after archaisms who made a study of the early poets. Hence Gellius moves in the same atmosphere as Fronto, of whom he speaks with enthusiasm, and has much in common with him; but yet, though his style and language show evident traces of his antiquarian tendencies, he is much too independent of Fronto to be called an actual follower of his.[29] While on this subject, it is worth noticing a chapter in which Gellius refers without disapproval to certain sayings of Favorinus in which the latter deprecates the use of archaisms.[30] But the most important point for us in this work, which is such a precious document for the literary life of the epoch, is the regular use which is made of Vergil.

In the work of Gellius, Vergil appears as an authority of great weight in all questions of language, of usage and of elegance;[31] and in these matters, which are Gellius' proper sphere, Vergil is not only cited as an authority, but is also defended against the attacks of certain grammarians of the previous century,[32] such as Hyginus and Annaeus Cornutus, who are censured in no measured terms.[33] Only rarely is it

[26] "Isti novicii semidocti," xvi. 7. 13 ; "turba grammaticorum novicia," xi. 1. 5. Cp. too xvii. 2. 15.

[27] "Cum pace cumque venia istorum, si qui sunt, qui Verri Flacci auctoritate capiuntur," xvii. 6, 5.

[28] He even calls him "ineptus atque insubidus homo," xii. 2. 11.

[29] I cannot agree here with BERNHARDY (p. 872). Fronto is an orator and his school is strictly an oratorical one, and one cannot expect to find Frontoniani except among orators. One need not think of Fronto to explain certain peculiarities in the style of Gellius.

[30] "Vive moribus praeteritis, loquere verbis praesentibus," i. 250 seq.

[31] "Poeta verborum diligentissimus," ii. 26. 11 ; "elegantissimus poeta," xx. 1. 54 ; "multae antiquitatis hominem sine ostentationis odio peritum," v. 12, 13.

[32] "Grammatici aetatis superioris haud sane indocti neque ignobiles," ii. 6. 1.

[33] "Insulsa et odiosa scrutatio," (he is speaking of a quibbling criticism of Annaeus Cornutus) ix. 10. 5 ; "sed Hyginus nimis hercle ineptus fuit cum, etc.," vii. 6, 5.

admitted that a word has been improperly or infelicitously used by Vergil.[34] Certain criticisms dealing with questions of fact, or with contradictions and inconsequences in the story, are repeated, and various explanations quoted for what they are worth; but all this is confined to minutiæ, and even when such a subject as Vergil's art is discussed, the question is never regarded from a broad point of view. The discussion is restricted to certain parallels between Vergil and various Greek poets, and even so only in the matter of individual passages. In some cases Vergil's imitation is regarded as felicitous, in others as the reverse; passages are quoted in which he is inferior to Homer; Favorinus compares Vergil's description of Etna with that of Pindar (Pyth. I.), and finds it much less perfect,[35] in which he is doubtless right. But the reasons he adduces are of little weight; he merely compares expression with expression without going at all below the surface or considering the different requirements of two such different branches of poetry as the epic and the lyric. The criticism of the age was not capable of this; and if at times it shows itself sufficiently independent to find fault with a writer of authority, its strictures are confined to externals and to that formal part of literature which was all that the literary mind of the period was able to appreciate.

It was the fashion at this time for grammarians to give séances at which they displayed their learning, and there was always a public eager to listen to them. When Gellius was at Brundisium, one of these grammarians was giving a specimen of his accomplishments by reading the Seventh Book of the Aeneid and offering to answer any questions on it. His reading was barbarous and he gave a ridiculous answer to a question which Gellius put.[36] Such charlatans are often mentioned in the *Noctes Atticae*. One thing however is clear from this,

---

[34] Once the charge is introduced by " existimatur " (x. 29. 4) ; in another place however it is distinctly admitted (i. 22. 12).

[35] " Ut Pindaro quoque, qui nimis opima pinguique esse facundia existimatus est, insolentior hoc quidem in loco tumidiorque sit . . . Audite nunc Vergili versus, quos inchoasse eum verius dixerim quam fecisse, etc." xvii. 10. 8 seqq.

[36] " Oves bidentes dictae quod duos tantum dentes habeant," xvi. 6. 9.

and that is the frequent use made of Vergil by grammarians, from the highest to the lowest. There were some, it is true, who preferred Lucilius to Horace, and Ennius or Lucretius to Vergil, but they were exceptions.[37] One of the chief of these latter was the Emperor Hadrian;[38] but his admiration for Ennius did not prevent his consulting the Sortes Vergilianae, and frequently quoting lines from Vergil.[39] The way in which Gellius speaks of a would-be Ennianistes, who read Ennius in the amphitheatre at Puteoli, shows clearly that the practice was an unusual one. Martial too, who belonged to no special literary clique and may be taken as a representative of common contemporary feeling on questions of literature, was sure of the approbation of the majority when he blamed the Romans for continuing to read Ennius after they had Vergil, or when, in a pungent epigram, he satirised one of those pedants who neglected Vergil for the unintelligible Helvius Cinna.[40] In fact, the grammarians as a whole deplore the small amount of study bestowed on the ancient writers.[41]

Vergil moreover, of all the Augustan poets, was the one

[37] "Illi qui Lucilium pro Horatio et Lucretium pro Vergilio legunt . . quos more prisco apud iudicem fabulantes non auditores sequuntur, n n populus audit, vix denique litigator perpetitur." *Dial. de Oratt.*, 23.

[38] "Ciceroni Catonem, Vergilio Ennium, Sallustio Coelium praetulit, eademque iactatione de Homero ac Platone iudicavit." SPARTIAN., *Hadrian.*, 16.

[39] SPARTIAN., *Hadrian.*, 2: "quos versus (*Aen.*, vi. 869 seqq.) cum aliquando in horto spatians cantitaret." SPARTIAN., *L. Ver.*, 4. L. Verus, who used to admire Ovid and Apicius to the extent of taking them to bed with him, could find no better way of expressing his appreciation of Martial than that of calling him his Vergil. SPARTIAN., *L. Ver.*, 5.

[40] "Ennius est lectus, salvo tibi, Roma, Marone."

MART., v. 10. 7.

"Scribere te, quae vix intelligat ipse Modestus
et vix Claranus, quid, rogo, Sexte, iuvat?
non lectore tuis opus est, sed Apolline, libris;
iudice te, maior Cinna Marone fuit.
sic tua laudentur; sane mea carmina, Sexte,
grammaticis placeant et sine grammaticis."

ID., x. 21.

[41] "Legerat (Probus) in provincia quosdam veteres libellos apud grammatistam durante adhuc ibi antiquorum memoria, necdum omnino abolita sicut Romae; . . . quamvis omnes contemni magisque opprobrio legentibus quam gloriae et fructui esse animadverteret." SUET., *De Gramm. et Rhett.*, 24.

whom the lovers of antiquity found most to their taste. In the
Noctes Atticae the authors most frequently cited are Ennius,
Laberius, Plautus, Caesar, Cicero, Lucilius, Nigidius Figulus,
Cato, Sallust, Varro, and Vergil.[42] Thus the authority of
Vergil in matters of grammar and philology is put on a level
with that of the writers of the republic. Of the other Augustan
poets, Horace alone is quoted more than once. A similar
tendency is apparent in the already-mentioned work of Nonius;
here the chief authority is Vergil, then, after a long interval,
comes Cicero, then Plautus, then Varro, and then in succession
Lucilius, Terence, Accius, Afranius, Ennius and Lucretius,
Sallust, Pacuvius, Pomponius, Caecilius, Naevius, Novius, Tur-
pilius, Titinius, Laberius, Livius Andronicus, etc. Quotations
from any Augustan poet, or indeed from any writer of the
Empire, except Vergil, are very rare in Nonius. In addition
however to the other causes which led Vergil to be regarded
as a supreme authority in matters of grammar, there was a
special reason for this association of him with the writers of an
epoch from which his art was in reality quite distinct. Vergil
was the only one of the Augustan poets who understood how to
use antiquated words without seeming affected; without any
contingent loss, his poetry gave evident signs of a careful study
of the early Latin writers. Hence he was able to satisfy two
opposite tastes, not only that of men of the modern school, like
Seneca, who were the very opposites of Fronto and Gellius, but
also that of the philological antiquaries, who were ready to give
him, on account of his archaisms, a high place among those
" hircosi " from whom his art was really so very far separated.
Quintilian, when commenting on the difficulty of using antiquated words with effect, makes special mention of Vergil's
success in this respect, and says that he was the only man who
ever knew how to do it.[43] Seneca believed that he introduced

---

[42] In a discussion with a second-rate grammarian, the authorities cited
are Plautus, Sallust, Ennius and Vergil (vi. 17). In another place a quack-
grammarian says to Gellius, " Si quid ex Vergilio, Plauto, Ennio quaerere
habes, quaeras licet." (xx. 10. 2.)

[43] "Eoque ornamento acerrimi iudicii P. Vergilius *unice* est usus," viii. B.
24 ; " Vetustatis, cuius amator *unice* Vergilius fuit," ix. 3. 14 ; " Vergilius
amantissimus vetustatis," i. 7. 16.

this archaic element into his poetry to please the 'populus Ennianus'; [44] but such a judgment could hardly be true of a writer of Vergil's exquisite taste, and was probably generated by Seneca's admiration for the Augustan writer coupled with his contempt for the early literature. For Vergil himself still belonged to this 'populus Ennianus,' only he was artist enough to know to what extent he ought to make use of Ennius and the other ancient writers; and he knew it better than Horace, who was more capable in this respect of formulating the rules which a writer should follow [45] than of following them himself.

In fact, Vergil's reputation did not suffer in the least from that reaction which took place in a certain department of literature, however little he might enjoy the sympathy of Fronto. The vitality of his fame was too great to be injured by any temporary indiscretion, however important. In the century which admired Apuleius, a man of great talent, no doubt, but one who makes himself ridiculous and impossible as a writer by the affectation and barbarity of his diction, in the century which set up a statue to him and listened with admiration to this new Latin produced by a set of Africans, it might well have been expected that the language of Vergil would appear weak, enervated, and insipid. Yet so great was his reputation and so great the authority which, thanks to the famous scholars of the preceding generation, he had acquired, that, in the midst of this triumph of degraded taste, his irresistible prestige and his inseparable connection with general education preserved his fame undiminished. In the schools of the grammarians and rhetoricians, and among all classes, whatever their various degrees of culture, he continued to be an object of veneration, and we see him growing constantly greater and greater throughout that decay of Latin literature which became more and more rapid from the reign of Marcus Aurelius onwards.

---

[44] " Vergilius quoque noster non ex alia causa duros quosdam versus et enormes et aliquid supra mensuram trahentes interposuit, quam ut Ennianus populus agnosceret in novo carmine aliquid antiquitatis." In GELLIUS, xii. 2.

[45] *Epist.*, ii. 1. 64 seqq.

But though his fame did not diminish, and though he kept his original place among the great names of antiquity, it was inevitable that, in the altered conditions of the intellectual environment through which he passed, the nature of his reputation should undergo a certain degree of change. True poetical creations were as entirely wanting in this epoch of Latin literature as they were in the epochs which followed. Rhetoric had taken the place of poetry, and this was kept alive merely by virtue of its imitation of the older models, among whom Vergil occupied the highest place. And here may be noticed an essential difference in the respective influences of Vergil and Homer. Homer exercised an influence over the living development of Greek poetry and art, of which he was merely the first representative, with whom all successive productions were naturally connected by the most intimate organic ties ; the influence, on the other hand, of Vergil on the moribund Latin poetry of the ages subsequent to him was a purely formal and external one, for that poetry was a poetry of form rather than of substance. But however careful might be the study of the poet, and however close the imitation of his language and style, it could not serve to bridge over the immense gulf that existed between the Augustan writers and their successors in their appreciation of poetry ; and yet the public of their time listened to these later poets with enthusiasm. So far was this the case that it seems hard to believe that the audiences that applauded Statius [46] can have had any true understanding of Vergil, and did not rather read into the works of the Augustan writer that false and degraded taste which led them to admire his pompous and bombastic imitator.

Without doubt the fame of Vergil was far beyond the comprehension of this later age, and his traditional greatness was so far misunderstood as to lead to his being regarded with a wellnigh superstitious veneration. Already under the Antonines we

[46] " Curritur ad vocem iucundam et carmen amicae
    Thebaidos, laetam cum fecit Statius urbem,
    promisitque diem ; tanta dulcedine captos
    afficit ille animos tantaque libidine vulgi
    auditur."
                    IUVENAL, vii. 82 seqq.

find the custom, practised even by the emperor, of enquiring the future by opening at random a volume of Vergil; these so-called 'sortes Vergilianae' were consulted by Hadrian no less than by many of his successors, and continued popular throughout the middle ages. This practice shows not only the immense popularity of Vergil, but also the veneration with which he was regarded; for such powers of prophecy were only ascribed to books which were venerated because of their sacred character or on account of the extraordinary wisdom they were supposed to contain, such as Homer, the Sibylline books, and, at a later period, the Bible.[47] If at one time the madman Caligula, to show his contempt for everyone, proposed to remove from the libraries the works and the busts of Vergil,[48] two centuries later Alexander Severus called Vergil the Plato of poets, and put his bust in a special 'lararium' with those of Achilles and certain other heroes and writers.[49] But long before this the enthusiasm of certain poets had well-nigh deified Vergil. Silius Italicus used to celebrate his birthday every year, visiting his tomb as if it were a temple;[50] as a temple the Neapolitan Statius too used to regard it.[51] Martial

---

[47] Cp. *Hist. lit. de la France*, iii. p. 11 seqq., and the curious passage in RABELAIS, iii. 10 seqq.

[48] " Sed et Vergili ac Titi Livi scripta et imagines paulum abfuit quin ex omnibus bibliothecis amoveret, quorum alterum ut nullius ingeni minimaeque doctrinae, alterum ut verbosum in historia negligentemque carpebat." SUET., iv. 34.

[49] " Vergilium autem Platonem poetarum vocabat, eiusque imaginem cum Ciceronis simulacro in secundo larario habuit, ubi et Achillis et magnorum virorum." LAMPRID., *Alex. Sev.*, 30.

[50] " Quas (imagines) non habebat modo, verum etiam venerabatur, Vergili ante omnes, cuius natalem religiosius quam suum celebrabat, Neapoli maxime, ubi monimentum eius adire ut templum solebat." PLIN., *Epist.*, iii. 7. 8. This veneration for Vergil, which seems to have been almost a monomania with Silius Italicus, is confirmed too by several epigrams of Martial (vii. 63; xi. 48, 49). Cornutus dedicated a work of his on Vergil to Silius : " *Annaeus Cornutus ad Italicum de Vergilio.*" CHARIS., p. 100, cp. p. 102 (ed. KEIL).

[51] " Maroneique sedens in margine templi
sumo animum et magni tumulis accanto magistri."
STAT., *Silv.*, iv. 4. 54.

"nec tu divinam Aeneida tenta
sed longe sequere et vestigia semper adora."
ID., *Theb.*, xii. 816.

speaks of the Ides of October as sacred to Vergil, just as those of August were sacred to Hecate or those of May to Mercury.[52] Vergil was then already the saint of poets; and, of all the apotheoses of the Roman empire, this deification of Vergil, though ill-defined in its origin and exaggerated in its effects was, without doubt, the only one inspired by a really generous sentiment.

[52] " Maiae Mercurium creastis Idus,
    Augustis redit Idibus Diana,
    Octobres Maro consecravit Idus.
    Idus saepe colas et has et illas
    qui magni celebras Maronis Idus."
                                MART., xii. 67.

Martial is full of enthusiasm for Vergil, whom he calls magnum (iv. 14), summum (xii. 4), immensum (xiv. 186), aeternum (xi. 52). The idea as to the Ides of October occurs again in Ausonius (Idyll. v. 23).

    " Sextiles Hecate Latonia vindicat Idus,
    Mercurius Maias superorum adiunctus honori,
    Octobres olim genitus Maro dedicat Idus."

CHAPTER V

THE vicissitudes which Latin literature underwent during the
3rd and 4th centuries are known to all. With a court and
public entirely dominated by the military element, where any
slave or barbarian who had influence with the ignorant soldiery
could ascend the throne of the Caesars, literature could hardly
be in a flourishing condition. Under such circumstances too
it was inevitable that literature should grow less and less in
touch with the general public, and become confined to a class
of persons whose sole inspiration, as well as their sole audience,
was in the schools. One result of this divorce between literature and general contemporary thought was that the difference
between the written and spoken language became steadily more
sensible, and thus the Latin of the common people came more
and more to the front; hence the position of the grammarian
grew to be a far less exalted one, and it soon sufficed if he
could teach his pupils to write simply correctly. Nor was
the productive power of the grammarians of these centuries
of decadence out of proportion to the quality of their pupils'
requirements; for, while rich enough in quantity, it was ex-
tremely poor in originality. In the field of grammatical
studies, as in every other, there is apparent a quite extraordinary poverty of ideas; no one dares to move a step without
supporting himself on some earlier authority. Just as every
work of art during this period is a mere unintelligent imitation, so every learned or scientific work is a mere unintelligent
compilation or compendium. Culture, being forced to live an
artificial and restricted life, was already beginning to abandon
everything that seemed superfluous, and was looking out for
short cuts and showing a great desire for reducing everything

to the smallest possible compass. In such compendia and compilations, intended to spare the reader the trouble of studying
a number of authors, this age of the decadence is remarkably
rich, and by far the greater part of the grammatical works
which have been preserved belong to this class. As was only
to be expected, under this process of compilation many of the
earlier works were lost for ever. The emperors still sometimes
patronised grammarians, as they did philosophers and rhetoricians, but it was merely as a luxury or from caprice, or
sometimes even from cowardice, out of fear of what they might
write, as was said to be the case with Alexander Severus.[1]
The imperial taste moreover, when it was literary, was generally more in sympathy with Greek, and was not of a kind
to exercise a beneficent influence; on the contrary, it tended
rather to encourage what was futile and vain. Thus Geta,
who wished to appear a patron of the alphabet by ordering
dinners all the dishes of which began with a certain letter,
used also to amuse himself now and then by inviting grammarians to submit to him lists of words expressive of the
cries of various animals.[2]

After the time of Alexander Severus, who, in spite of his
Greek proclivities, yet venerated Vergil (though perhaps rather
as philosopher than poet) in the way we have seen, the study
of letters became almost entirely foreign to the palace of the
Caesars. The old imperial tradition was completely destroyed,
and among the various usurpers who held or fought for the
chief power, such a man as Gordian the Elder[3] was quite an
exception. From this time onward we find the soldier, as such,
directly contrasted with the man of letters, which had never
been the case formerly ; and this fact could not fail to make
literary studies unpopular, even with those who had received
a certain amount of education. The writers of the ' Historia
Augusta,' who describe the events of their time just as they

---

[1] " Amavit litteratos homines, vehementer eos etiam reformidans ne quid
de se asperum scriberent." LAMPRID., *Alex. Sev.*, 8.

[2] SPARTIAN., *Antonin. Geta*, 5.

[3] " Hic enim vita venerabilis, cum Platone semper, cum Aristotele, cum
Tullio, cum Vergilio ceterisque veteribus agens, etc." CAPITOLIN, *Gordian*, 7.

actually were, without any attempt at embellishment, give us
a good idea of the general intellectual level of the time,
especially in political and military circles. Thus Vopiscus
wonders that his grandfather, in describing the assassination
of Aper, should have attributed to the murderer Diocletian
the words, 'gloriare Aper Aeneae magni dextra cadis'; 'for
this,' he says, 'in a soldier, seems to me marvellous, though I
know that many people are accustomed to cite passages from
the comedians and the other poets, both Greek and Latin.'[4]
At the end of the second century Clodius Albinus, though by
no means fond of learning, had studied Vergil at school as a
boy, though his study of the poet had only given him an opportunity of displaying his military instincts.[5]   But in spite of
everything Vergilian reminiscences are common, even among
these classes; for a large number of Vergilian lines had come
to be regarded almost as proverbs, and, thanks to the school
and the theatre, well-nigh every one had some knowledge of the
Aeneid.   Thus quotations from Vergil, made à propos of political
events, are not only met with in the case of Gordian the Elder,
who was a man of culture,[6] but they occur in a letter of Diadumenus to his father Macrinus,[7] and in one of Tetricus the
Elder to Aurelian.[8]   Under Alexander Severus, Iulius Crispus,
tribune of the Praetorians, expressed his displeasure in a Vergilian quotation which proved fatal to him.[9]   A pun in praise
of Diadumenus and at the expense of Macrinus, which went
the round of the circus, consisted of two half-lines of Vergil;[10]

---

[4] VOPISC., *Numerian.*, 13.

[5] "Omnem pueritiam in Africa transegit, eruditus litteris Graecis et
Latinis mediocriter, quod esset animi iam inde militaris et superbi.   Fertur
in scholis saepissime cantasse inter puerulos, 'Arma amens capio nec sat
rationis in armis.'"   (*Aen.*, ii. 314.)   CAPITOLIN., *Clod. Alb.*, 5.

[6] "Cantabat praeterea versus senex, cum Gordianum filium vidisset, hos
saepissime, 'Ostendent terris hunc tantum fata, etc.'"   (*Aen.*, vi. 870.)
CAPITOLIN., *Gord. iun.*, 20.

[7] "Si te nulla movent, etc." (*Aen.*, iv. 272).   LAMPRID., *Ant. Diadum.*, 8.

[8] "Versus denique illius fertur, quem statim ad Aurelianum scripserat:
'Eripe me his, invicte, malis'" (*Aen.*, vi. 865).   TREB. POLL., *Trig. tyrann.*, 24.

[9] "δύο ἄνδρας τῶν ἐπιφανῶν ἀπέκτεινεν, Ἰούλιον Κρίσπον χιλιαρχοῦντα τῶν
δορυφορῶν, ὅτι ἀχθεσθεὶς τῇ τοῦ πολέμου κακώσει ἔπος τι τοῦ Μάρωνος τοῦ
ποιητοῦ παρεφθέγξατο, ἐν ᾧ κ.τ.λ." (*Aen.*, xi. 371).   DION CASS., 75. 10.

[10] "Egregius forma iuvenis, dignus cui pater haud Maxentius esset"
(*Aen.*, vi. 862; vii. 653).   CAPITOLIN., *Opil. Macrin.*, 12.

and similarly, a Vergilian hemistich was included in the acclamations with which the Senate proclaimed the already elderly
Tacitus emperor.[11]

But if among the orgies and crimes of the imperial palace
an echo, as it were, of Vergilian verse might still sometimes
be heard, that was no proof of the existence of any real
poetical feeling; it only showed that the fame of the poet was
so universal that it was able to survive even under the most
unfavourable circumstances. His chief office now was to teach
children in the schools and so give them the means of emphasising their childishness when they grew up. In fact, he was
so thoroughly studied at school that to know his works by
heart from one end to the other was no uncommon feat. This
great familiarity with his writings, coupled with the general
poverty of ideas of the period, led to the production of the
' Centos,' [12] in which, by the adroit combination of isolated
lines and hemistichs, Vergil was made to say the most unexpected things. The idea of such ' Centos ' could only have
arisen among people who had learnt Vergil mechanically and
did not know of any better use to which to put all these verses
with which they had loaded their brains. And moreover, the
use which had already been made of Vergil by so many poets
was related closely enough to the work of the cento-makers,
and led naturally up to it.[13] Nor is this a case of the caprice

[11] " Et tu legisti, ' incanaque menta regis Romani ' (Aen., vi. 810), dixerunt decies." VOPISC., Tacit., 5.

[12] The earliest collection of Vergilian centos is in the famous Codex
Salmasianus, which forms the nucleus of the Anthologia Latina and goes
back to the 8th century at least. This MS. contains twelve by various
authors and of various periods, including the Medea of HOSIDIUS GETA.
Only one of these is Christian ; this last was not published by either BURMANN
or MEYER in their Anthologia Latina ; it was first published by SURINGAR
(De ecclesia, anonymi cento Vergilianus ineditus. Traiect. ad Rh., 1867), and
it is in the Anthologia Latina of RIESE (Leip., 1869, i. p. 44).

On the subject of centos in general, and those of Vergil in particular, see
HASELBERG, Commentat. de centonibus, Puttbus, 1846 ; BORGEN, De centonibus
Homericis et Vergilianis, Havniae, 1826 ; Revue analytique des ouvrages
écrits en centons depuis les temps anciens jusqu'au XIX. siècle (DELEPIERRE,
London, Trübner, 1868) ; Tableau de la littérature du centon chez les anciens
et les modernes (ID., Lond., 1875) ; MÜLLER, De re metr., p. 465 seq. ; MIL-
BERG, Memorabilia Vergiliana, pp. 5–12.

[13] Noteworthy in this connection is the Ciris, attributed to Vergil, which
is so full of Vergilian phrases and turns of expression as to be well-nigh a
cento.

of one or two individuals; it is a regular form of literary
composition, which began early and lasted long. Already in
the time of Tertullian, a certain Hosidius Geta had composed
out of Vergilian lines a tragedy entitled ' Medea,' which is
still in existence; another writer had put together in a similar
manner a translation of the *Tabula* of Cebes. Then there
were Christians too, who wished Vergil to bear witness to
their faith, such as Proba Faltonia,[14] who told the story of
the Old Testament in Vergilian verses; Pomponius, who produced a work of the kind in honour of Christ, entitled
' Tityrus';[15] Marcus Victorinus (4th century), who composed
in this way a Hymn on the Passion; Sedulius (5th century),
author of a poem on the Incarnation, etc.[16] The Emperor
Valentinian, as if jealous of Vergil's fame as a pure writer,
even composed an obscene poem out of verses of his, and compelled Ausonius to compete with him in this field; this is
the origin of the famous *Cento Nuptialis*, which is without
doubt the best of the various centos that have been preserved. Now-a-days such work would be looked upon as
childish, but then it was regarded as showing respect for the
poet, and the memory and skill of these writers were very
generally admired.[17] Vergil must be treated in every way like
Homer, and, as there had been Homeric centos, so there must
be Vergilian ones also. In the case of either poet there were
certain men who achieved a special reputation for this class
of performance, and who used to style themselves Homeric or
Vergilian poets.[18] But the highest degree of absurdity was

[14] Cp. ASCHBACH, *Die Anicier und die römische Dichterin Proba* (Vienna,
1870), p. 57 seqq.

[15] Published by BURSIAN in the *Sitzungsber. d. Münch. Akad.*, 1878, 2. 29.

[16] So much were these Christian centos the fashion that Pope Gelasius,
in his note on the canon, thought it necessary to declare them apocryphal :
" Centimetrum de Christo, Vergilianis compaginatum versibus, apocry-
phum." *Decret. Gelas. Pap.* (ann. 494), ap. LABBÉ, iv. 1264.

[17] Ausonius excuses himself in the dedicatory letter to his friend Paulus :
" Piget Vergiliani carminis dignitatem tam ioculari dehonestasse materia,
sed quid facerem ? iussum erat; quodque est potentissimum imperandi
genus, rogabat qui iubere poterat, S. imperator Valentinianus, vir meo
iudicio eruditus."

[18] An ancient Roman inscription runs : " Silvano coelesti Q. Glitius Felix

reached by one Mavortius, author of a cento on the
Judgment of Paris, who got at last to *improvising* Vergilian
centos; and one of these improvisations, in which he
modestly declines the title of the 'modern Vergil,' is still
extant.[19]

The manner in which Vergil was regarded could not fail to
be greatly influenced by the various commentaries with which
he was illustrated in the schools; for here, as we have seen,
his works continued to serve as the basis of education. A
critical history of the various commentators on Vergil, though
attempted by Suringar,[20] remains still to be written, and this
cannot be satisfactorily done until numerous special researches
have been made in this most intricate subject. The commentaries on Vergil, which kept being produced down to the end
of the middle ages, were, owing to the use made of them
for educational purposes, subject to perpetual alterations. No
master ever scrupled to condense or modify or gloss them in
any way he might think best. One would compile from a
number of earlier authorities and then give the compilation his
own name, another would insert glosses from various quarters
and remain anonymous, another would embellish or interpolate
the regular commentaries according to his taste and pass off
the result as the work of the original author. The mass of
commentaries which has come down to us is like a swollen
torrent, fed by tributaries of every sort and origin. All have
been condensed or rearranged or interpolated from various

Vergilianus poeta d. d." OBELLI-HENZEN, No. 1179. In a Greek inscription from Egypt appears an Homeric cento by an author who calls himself
an "Homeric poet." *Vide* LETRONNE, *Inscr. de l'Egypt*, ii. p. 397.

[19] It too is found in the Codex Salm., and was first published by QUI-
CHERAT in the *Bibl. de l'école des chartes*, ii. p. 182. SURINGAR republished
it, without knowing of the first edition, after the *De ecclesia* (p. 15), but did
not discover either the name of its author or its subject. In this respect
RIESE, who has been the first to include it in the *Anthologia Latina* (i. p. 48),
was more successful.

[20] *Historia critica scholiastarum Latinorum* (Lugd. Bat., 1834), vol. ii.
Special treatises on several of the Vergilian commentators have been written
by WAGNER, TEUBER, RIESE, and others. There are valuable critical materials
in the *Prolegomena* of RIBBECK (pp. 114–198), to which must be added the
important work of HAGEN, *Scholia Bernensia ad Vergili Bucolica et Georgica*,
Lips., 1867, p. 696 seqq.

sources; none has remained in its original form. Those which bear the names of Probus and Asper may serve to show to what an extent the later grammarians corrupted the work of their more capable predecessors. The principal compilations of Vergilian epexegesis, like the principal grammatical compilations, belong to this period of decadence, and here two names stand out conspicuously, Donatus and Servius.

For a judgment of the commentary of Donatus,[21] now lost, but mentioned by his pupil Jerome among those that were in regular use in the schools,[22] a consideration of the parts of it preserved by Servius will be sufficient.[23] Donatus wished to pose as a critic, and consequently judges very freely of the poet, finding fault with many passages; but not only are his strictures unjust, but they often show a surprising ignorance, even of the elementary rules of prosody. This critical attitude did not prevent him from admiring Vergil, but his admiration was of such a kind as to lead him to present the poet to his pupils in an altogether false light, attributing to him, as certain philosophical schools had already done to Homer, an extraordinary degree of wisdom, and searching in his lines for hidden philosophical meanings which had certainly never so much as entered his head. He explained the order of the Vergilian poems as follows:—' One must know,' he said, ' that Vergil, in composing his works, followed an order corresponding to the life of man. The first condition of man was pastoral, and so Vergil wrote first of all the Bucolics; afterwards it was agricultural, and so he wrote next the Georgics. Then, as the number of the race increased, there grew up therewith the love of war; hence his final work is the Æneid, which is full of

[21] RIBBECK states (*Prolegg.*, p. 179) that nothing is known of a commentary by Aelius Donatus on the Bucolics. But he is mistaken. The Biography of Vergil, which bears the name of Donatus, was originally prefixed to a commentary on the Bucolics, and concludes with general remarks on these which have been preserved. Cp. HAGEN, *Schol. Bern.*, p. 740 seqq.

[22] " Puto quod puer legeris Aspri in Vergilium et Sallustium commentarios, Vulcati in orationes Ciceronis, Victorini in dialogos eius et in Terenti comoedias praeceptoris mei Donati, aeque in Vergilium." HIERONYM., *Apol. adv. Rufin.*, i. p. 367.

[23] *Vide* the passages in Servius referring to Donatus collected by SURINGAR, *op. cit.*, p. 37 seqq. ; and RIBBECK, *Prolegg.*, p. 178 seqq.

wars.'[24] We shall see further on to what an extent this allegorical method of interpreting Vergil was developed.

But the most popular of all the commentaries on Vergil,
and the only one which has come down to us complete, if not
intact, is that of Servius, a work which was in regular use
in the schools of the middle ages, and is of the greatest importance still, not so much for its elucidation of Vergil as for
the numerous valuable notices of every kind that it has preserved. To estimate fairly the work of Servius by what we
possess now, is a difficult matter;[25] for while on the one hand
it is clear that he compiled it from earlier commentators and
grammarians, on the other it is equally clear that, owing to
the constant use made of it, it has undergone various alterations, and has been steadily interpolated throughout the course
of the middle ages, sometimes with such stupidity as to make
Servius cite himself as an authority.[26] It is clear however
that Servius was, for the time in which he lived, an eminent
grammarian, and superior to Donatus, whose errors he often
corrects with much taste and sense. But this was not enough
to enable him to overcome the defects of the scholarship of his
age. There was something stereotyped about the whole grammatical tradition of the period, which lasted throughout the
middle ages, and did not fail to make itself apparent in that
practical part of instruction which was concerned with the
exposition of authors. Thus not a few of the views which
appear crystallised in Servius are due to a certain mistaken
tendency noticeable already at an earlier date. Those un-
answerable questions which the Alexandrians were so fond
of asking about Homer,[27] and which interested Tiberius so
greatly,[28] were also put forward about Vergil, and may often

[24] Serv., *Prooem. Eclog.*, p. 97. Cp. too a Latin MS. published by
Quicherat in the *Bibl. de l'école des chartes*, ii., p. 128.
[25] Very valuable in this connection is the critical edition of Servius and
other Vergilian commentators, undertaken by Thilo and Hagen (Leipz.,
1878 seqq.). Cp. Georgii, *Die alte Aeneiskritik* (Stuttg., 1891), p. 9 seqq.
[26] " Ut Servius dicit."   *Ad Ecl.*, i. 12 ; iii. 20 ; ix. 1.
[27] Cp. Lauer, *Gesch. der homer. Poesie*, p. 6 seq. ; Gräfenhan, *Gesch. d.
class. Philologie im Alterth.*, ii. p. 11 seq. For the ἐνστατικοί and the λυκτικοί
vide also Lehrs, *De Aristarchi studiis homericis*, pp. 199–224.
[28] Suet., *Tiber.*, 70. Cp. Gell., xiv. 6 ; Lauer, *op. cit.*, p. 11.

be recognised by their regular formula in Servius.[29] Con-
scientious criticism and sound scholarship were by no means
indispensable to satisfy the demands of fashion in this branch
of learning, where the grammarian was too often little more
than a charlatan,[30] and where it was required of his answers
that they should be subtle, brilliant, and specious rather than
that they should be useful, just, or true. A curious instance of
this is afforded by the twelve or thirteen passages of Vergil
which were supposed to present insuperable difficulties.[31] This
insuperable difficulty had come to be well-nigh an article of
faith, and the commentator simply left these passages alone,
saying, 'This is one of the Twelve.' And yet several of the
lines which Servius includes in his list do not in reality present
any special difficulty.

However much one may claim that the work of Servius has
been tampered with, yet it cannot be denied that certain allegorical interpretations—as, for instance, that of the golden
branch with which Aeneas descends into Hades [32]—are too much

---

[29] "Cur" or "quomodo dixit . . .? Solvitur sic . . ." *Ad Aen.*,
iii. 203, 276, 341, 379 ; iv. 399, 545, etc.

[30]   ". . . ut forte rogatus,
     dum petit aut thermas aut Phoebi balnea, dicat
     nutricem Anchisae, nomen patriamque novercae
     Anchemoli, dicat quot Acestes vixerit annos,
     quot Siculi Phrygibus vini donaverit urnas."
                                        Iuvenal, vii. 232.

[31] " Sciendum est locum hunc esse unum de xii. (al. xiii.) Vergili sive
per naturam obscuris, sive insolubilibus, sive emendandis, sive sic relictis
ut a nobis per historiae antiquae ignorantiam liquide non intellegantur."
Serv., *ad Aen.*, ix. 363. " Sciendum tamen et locum hunc esse unum de
his, quos insolubiles diximus supra." Id., *ad* ix. 412. Cp. too *ad* v. 622 ;
xii. 74 ; Lehrs, *De Aristarchi stud. hom.*, p. 219 seq. ; Ribbeck, *Prolegg.*,
p. 109 seqq. To this category belong also the *antapodoses* (quibus locis
commemorantur quae non sunt ante praedicta), of which one is noticed by
Servius, *ad Aen.*, ix. 453, as the tenth. Cp. Ribbeck, *Prolegg.*, p. 108 seq.

[32] " Ergo per ramum virtutes dicit esse sectandas, qui est Y litterae imi-
tatio, quem ideo in silvis dicit latere, quia re vera in huius vitae confusione
et maiore parte vitiorum virtutis integritas latet." Serv., *ad Aen.*, vi. 186.
For this reason, in the earlier editions of Vergil, there often appear attributed
to him the lines of Maximinus on the symbolical meaning of the letter Y
(*Anthol. Lat.*, No. 632, ed. Riese) :

     " littera Pythagorae, discrimine secta bicorni,
      humanae vitae specimen praeferre videtur, etc."

in accord with the ideas of Servius' own time to be due to any
one but him. But if here and there Servius gives to certain
lines or certain parts of the narrative a philosophical meaning,
there is no sign of any general and systematic theory of allegorical interpretation which would make all the incidents of
the work tend in this one direction. Of such an interpretation
we shall have occasion to speak shortly, and we shall then have
an opportunity of regarding this question at closer quarters.

Vergil had in fact made use of allegory, as every one knows,
in the Bucolics, but here it was when dealing with facts
rather than with ideas. An ancient tradition, going back to
Asconius Pedianus and even to the times of the poet himself, as to the authenticity of which there can be no reasonable
doubt, stated that Vergil had in the Bucolics alluded to the
incidents of his own life and to the events of the day. But
this vague and general statement left it indefinite as to what
were the actual passages in which Vergil had made use of
allegory, and thus from the very earliest times we find the
commentators divided in opinion as to the meaning of various
lines, which some understood literally, or, as Servius has it,
'simpliciter,' while others interpreted them 'per allegoriam,'
and spent their time in hunting up events to which they
might refer. Servius, in judging between the two schools,
shows a very reasonable tendency to limit the range of allegory,[33] and often pronounces for the literal interpretation on
the ground that the allegorical is 'non necessaria.' But he is
not always consistent in this, and at times he accepts or passes
as possible allegorical interpretations which are quite without
foundation,[34]—for to ascribe all such errors of judgment to
interpolators would be to exaggerate his merits and to fail to
recognise the nature of the period in which he lived. To what
lengths the mania for allegorical interpretations could go is
shown at once at the beginning of the first Eclogue. Directly
after saying that Tityrus stands for Vergil, 'not indeed every-

[33] "Refutandae enim sunt allegoriae in bucolico carmine, nisi cum ex
aliqua agrorum perditorum necessitate descendunt." *Ad Ecl.*, iii. 20.
[34] Cp. SCHAPER, *Ueber die Entstehungszeit der Virgilischen Eclogen*, in the
Jahrbb. f. Philolog. u. Paedagog., vol. 90 (1864), p. 640 seqq.

where, but only where the passage reasonably admits it,' he proceeds to explain 'sub tegmine fagi' as a most beautiful allegory, because 'fagus' comes from the Greek φαγεῖν, to eat, and hence the poet alludes with this word to those estates which were necessary to support him and which had been restored to him by the kindness of Augustus. A little lower down again, in the words—

> · ipsae te, Tityre, pinus,
> ipsi te fontes, ipsa haec arbusta vocabant '—

he explains Tityrus as being Vergil, the pines Rome, the fountains the poets or the senators, and the shrubs the grammarians. Perhaps this last interpretation is not due to Servius,[35] but for our purpose it is sufficient to observe that interpretations of this kind were current, not only in Servius time, but even earlier.

To Servius himself is also doubtless due that exaggeratèd idea of the exceptional and extraordinary wisdom of Vergil which prevails in various parts of his commentary. Thus he quotes with evident satisfaction the view of Metrodorus, who held that it was an error to accuse Vergil, as some had done, of being ignorant of astrology ; [36] while at the beginning of the Sixth Book of the Aeneid, which was supposed to contain the most recondite learning of all, he puts the following note : 'All Vergil is full of wisdom, but especially this book, the chief part of which is taken from Homer. Some things in it are stated simply, others are taken from history, many from the exalted sciences of Egyptian philosophy and theology, so that several passages of this book have had entire treatises devoted to them.'

The commentary of Servius is essentially the work of a grammarian, intended to be used in the schools of grammar ; there are, it is true, certain rhetorical notices, for the studies of rhetoric and grammar were closely akin, but an exposition of Vergilian poetry from the rhetorical point of view is not

---

[35] SURINGAR, *Hist. crit. scholl. Lat.*, ii. p. 79. LION, instead of " *Arbusta*, fruteta, id est scholastici," edits " *Arbusta*, fructeta scholastici vocabant."

[36] *Ad Georg.*, i. 230. Nor are there wanting expressions of admiration, such as, " Unde apparet divinum poetam aliud agentem verum semper attingere." *Ad Aen.*, iii. 349.

the main object of the work. The commentary of Tiberius Claudius Donatus, who lived a little later than the Donatus already mentioned, is, on the other hand, professedly rhetorical. The author had written it, without sparing his words,[37] to supply a deficiency which he noticed in the commentaries in use at the time. He believed that Vergil's first quality was rhetorical, and that his works ought to be elucidated by orators quite as much as by grammarians;[38] hence his notes are not in any way grammatical or philological, but are confined to explaining the meaning and the rhetorical fitness of every passage in the Aeneid. From its nature, therefore, this commentary is not one which can give us much help for an understanding of the poet or a knowledge of antiquity, and this will account for the general neglect into which it has fallen among scholars; in fact, it has not been reprinted since the 16th century.[39] Contrary to the custom of his contemporaries, Donatus has been at no pains to give his work a learned air, having purposely eliminated from it every note of an erudite nature, and not even made use of those technical terms of rhetoric which one would naturally have expected. But this vague and colourless manner in which he treats his subject has made him to a certain extent better able than others to discern the real purpose of the Aeneid, in which he sees nothing but an account of the deeds of Aeneas and a glorification of Rome and Augustus, rigorously excluding the idea that it is in any way a scientific or philosophical work.[40] In this

---

[37] " . . . melius existimans loquacitate quadam te facere doctiorem quam tenebrosae brevitatis vitio in erroribus linquere." *Praef.*

[38] " Si Maronis carmina competenter attenderis et eorum mentem commode comprehenderis, invenies in poeta rhetorem summum; atque inde intelliges Vergilium non grammaticos sed oratores praecipuos tradere debuisse." *Praef.*

[39] I quote from a Venetian (Juntine) edition of 1544. Another appeared at Naples in 1535, another at Bale (*cura* G. Fabricii) in 1561. Crinitus, in 1496, made some extracts from a Florentine MS. of this commentary, but without much admiring them, apparently : " Videtur opera ludi ; non enim omnino doctus hic . . . Donatus," he says. Cp. MOMMSEN, in the *Rhein. Museum*, N. F. xvi. p. 139 seq. ; VALMAGGI, in the *Riv. di filol. cl.* xiv. (1886), p. 31 seqq. ; BURCKAS, *De Tib. Cl. Donati in Aen. Comment.* (Jena, 1888).

[40] " . . . inveniemus Vergilium id esse professum ut gesta Aeneae per-

way he answers the critics who found certain inconsequences
or contradictions in Vergil's philosophical views; but he is
none the less convinced of the vastness and variety of Vergil's
learning, which is such, according to him, that the student of
any branch of human knowledge may find valuable information
in Vergil's works.[41] This is, of course, quite in accordance with
the idea of the perfect orator, who, as Cicero had already said,
must be a man of universal knowledge.[42]

As a matter of fact, Donatus had no reason to complain that
Vergil was not sufficiently studied by the rhetoricians. The
first elucidation and exposition of the poet belonged naturally
to the grammarians, but the use which the rhetoricians made
of him in their schools and their works at this period left
nothing to be desired. Most of the writers on rhetoric drew
their illustrations from him, chiefly when treating of the figures,
as is clear from several commentaries and also from short
treatises on the figures attached to various MSS. of Vergil.[43]
In Iulius Rufinianus' treatise on the figures, the instances are
almost exclusively taken from Vergil.[44] Arusianus, towards
the end of the 4th century, drew his *Exempla locutionum*,
for the use of the schools of rhetoric, from Terence, Cicero,
Sallust, and Vergil.[45] In the same century the rhetoricians
Titianus and Calvus brought together in a special work the
themes taken from Vergil and adapted as exercises in the
rhetorical schools.[46] Declamations of this period, both in prose

curreret, non ut aliquam scientiae interioris vel philosophiae partem quasi
assertor assumeret." *Praef.* (Cp. too the beginning of the preface, which
deals with the aims of the Aeneid).

[41] " Interea hoc quoque mirandum debet adverti, sic Aeneae laudem esse
dispositam ut in ipsa exquisita arte omnia materiarum genera convenirent,
quo fit ut Vergiliani carminis lector rhetoricis praeceptis instrui possit, et
omnia vivendi agendique officia reperire." *Praef.*

[42] Cp. QUINTIL., ii. 21.

[43] Cp. HAGEN, *Scholia Bernensia*, pp. 733, 984.

[44] *Rhetores Latini minores*, ed. HALM, p. 38 seqq.

[45] Cp. HAUPT, in *Hermes*, iii. p. 223.

[46] " Et Titianus et Calvus, qui themata omnia de Vergilio elicuerunt et
afformarunt ad dicendi usum, in exemplo controversiarum has duas posue-
runt allocutiones, Venerem agere statu absolutivo cum dicit Iunoni, ' Causa
fuisti periculorum his quibus Italiam fata concesserunt,' Iunonem vero niti
statu causativo et relativo, per quem ostendit non sua causa Troianos
laborare, sed Veneris." SERV., *ad Aen.*, x. 18. This custom of taking

and verse, on subjects taken from Vergil are still preserved.[47]
Avienus undertook a task half antiquarian half rhetorical when,
in his work which is now lost, he treated in verse at length
those legends or facts which had been merely briefly alluded to
by Vergil.[48] Throughout this period, during which rhetoric
exercised an absolute sway over the minds of men,[49] Vergil's
fame continued bright, merely altering its colour according to
the taste of the time, and losing more and more its rational
nature.

Those therefore who studied in the grammatical and rhetorical schools were taught to look upon Vergil as the supreme
type of the grammarian and of the rhetorician, and as the final
authority on all those questions of learning and culture which
were regarded at the time as important. The result of such
a training on a grown-up man and a professed scholar may
be learned from the *Saturnalia* of Macrobius, in which Vergil
appears as an encyclopædic authority on every conceivable
subject.

Macrobius (4th–5th century) is the author of the only ancient work we now possess, apart from the commentaries,
which deals professedly with Vergil. It was his wish to form
a collection, for the use of his son, of the criticisms and the
comments of every kind which he had found in the course of
wide and varied reading. To bring all these various materials
together, he has not only adopted, like so many others, a sym-
posium as his framework, but has confined the greater part of
the dialogue to an argument on the merits of Vergil, in which
he makes use of the poet's name to introduce discussions on

themes from Vergil was equally common in the African schools of rhetoric,
as we learn from Augustine, *Conf.*, i. 17.

[47] " Qui in Vergilium scripsit declamationes de hoc loco hoc ait, etc."
Serv., *ad Aen.*, x. 532. We possess the prose declamation of Ennodius,
" *Verba Didonis cum abeuntem videret Aeneam*," on the theme of *Aen.*, iv.
365 seqq. (*Dictio*, xxviii.). Of the declamations in verse we shall speak
further on.

[48] Cp. Ribbeck, *Prolegg.*, p. 186 seq.

[49] " Post apicem divinitatis ego illa sum quae vel commendo si sint
facta vel facio . . .: nos regna regimus et imperantes salubria iubemus.
. . . Ante scipiones et trabeas est pomposa recitatio. . . . Poetica,
iuris peritia, dialectica, arithmetica cum me utantur quasi genitrice, me tamen
asserente sunt pretio." Thus speaks Rhetoric in Ennodius, *Opusc.* vi.

the most varied topics, thus showing how important a position
Vergil occupied in the learning of the time. But though Macrobius has wished to give his work the appearance of a discussion
as to the merits of Vergil's poetry, it is, in fact, nothing but a
eulogy of it; for such the tone of enthusiastic admiration which
pervades every page, and the programme in the first book of
the part to be devoted to Vergil, prove it to be. In this dialogue Macrobius—himself a distinguished and learned man for
his time—introduces as speaking all the most eminent scholars
of the period, and rises with these, in his contemplation of the
poet, to a far higher level than the common. He has before
his eyes the school-conception of Vergil,[50] and rightly enough
finds it mean and inadequate; he feels that there is far more
in the poet than the grammarians of the time were capable
of perceiving. He wishes therefore to penetrate more deeply
into the poem and to bring to light those hidden beauties
which few or none besides were able to appreciate. And yet
throughout his work, which claims to be a protest against the
false and dwarfed notions of the age, the ideas of that age do
not fail to make themselves apparent and at times strangely to
warp the author's judgment without his perceiving it.

In the eyes of Macrobius, Vergil is not merely an authority
in every branch of learning,[51] but he is distinctly infallible.

[50] To the use of Vergil in the schools at this period and later, there
allude, besides MACROBIUS, OROSIUS (i. c. 18): "Aeneas qualia per trien-
nium bella excitaverit, quantos populos implicuerit, odio excidioque afflixerit,
ludi litterari disciplina nostrae quoque memoriae inustum est," and from a
point of view more in accordance with that of Macrobius, FULGENTIUS, who,
speaking of Vergil, says, "Sed illa tantum quaerimus levia quae mensualibus stipendiis grammatici distrahunt puerilibus auscultationibus," *De Verg.
cont.*, p. 742; "Si me scholarum praeteritarum non fallit memoria," *Ib.*,
p. 748; "Unde et infantibus, quibus haec nostra (Vergili) materia traditur,
isti sunt ordines consequendi," *Ib.*, p. 747. In the 4th century, as we learn
from AUSONIUS, Vergil and Homer were read in the schools just as in the
time of Quintilian, and after them Menander, Terence, Horace, and Sallust
(*Idyl.*, 4, 46). A grammarian is described by Ausonius (*Epig.*, 187) as "arma
virumque docens atque arma virumque peritus." SIDONIUS APOLLINARIS
(5th cent.), in his panegyric on Anthemius, puts Vergil first in the list of
authors studied by him, then Cicero, Livy, Sallust, Varro, Plautus, Quintilian, and Tacitus (*Carm.*, ii. 184 seqq.).

[51] "Nullius disciplinae expers," *Somn. Scip.*, i. 6. 44; "disciplinarum
omnium peritissimus," *Ib.*, i. 15. 12; "omnium disciplinarum peritus,"
Sat. i., 16. 12.

Macrobius does not admit, as so many of his predecessors had done, that there are defects or errors in Vergil's poetry; he considers that the power of solving any difficulty which may be found depends entirely on the capacity of the student.[52] His whole work is occupied in bringing to light the immense store of Vergil's learning, which was to a great extent hidden from the ordinary reader of the time,—'the many things which the commentators lightly pass over, as if it were not given to a grammarian to concern himself with anything beyond mere words.' 'We, who feel conscious of a finer taste, will not suffer the entrance to the sacred poem to remain hidden any longer, but will examine the road that leads into its most secret recesses and throw open its inmost shrine for the veneration of scholars.'[53] In the dialogue, a certain Evangelus is made to take up a position opposed to the poet, but there is nothing really earnest about this character; he cannot be taken as a representative of the unprejudiced critics of an earlier period, still less of those of the time of Macrobius, among whom such a personage certainly never existed. He is merely introduced to afford an opportunity of eulogising Vergil, and, as if the author were afraid that his criticisms might be taken too seriously, care is taken when describing his arrival on the scene to paint his personal character in the' blackest colours. As soon as he is announced every one gives signs of disapprobation;[54] each time that he opens his mouth to attack Vergil every one shudders.[55] Some of his criticisms had already been made by earlier scholars; but, as a rule, he sets himself to attack just those points in which Vergil is strongest, and even goes so far as to deny that a man born, like the poet, in

[52] "Quem nullius unquam disciplinae error involvit," *S. Scip.*, ii. 8. 1; "manifestum est omnibus quid Maro dixerit, quem constat erroris ignarum; erit enim ingeni singulorum invenire, quid possit amplius pro absolvenda hac quaestione conferri." *S. Scip.*, ii. 8. 8.

[53] *Sat.*, i. 25. 12 seqq.

[54] "Corrugato indicavere vultu plerique de considentibus Evangeli interventum otio suo inamoenum, minusque placido conventui congruentem. Erat enim amarulenta dicacitate et lingua proterve mordaci procax, ac securus offensarum, quas sine delectu cari vel non amici in se passim verbis odio serentibus provocabet." *Sat.*, i. 7. 2.

[55] "Cumque adhuc dicentem omnes exhorruissent." *Sat.*, i. 24. 8.

F

a Venetian village can have known anything about Greek
or Greek writers.[56]   This foolish remark, which could not so
much as have occcurred to Vergil's bitterest detractor in the
Augustan age, serves however to introduce, by way of reply,
a lengthy exposition of the profundity of the poet's knowledge
of Greek, a theme which occupies almost the whole of the Fifth
Book.   Similarly, it is a remark of Evangelus that opens the
whole discussion on Vergil, which forms the most important
part of the work.   Evangelus refuses to recognise in Vergil
anything more than a mere poet, whose work moreover contains many faults and was rightly judged by its author worthy
to be burnt.[57]   Symmachus, on the other hand, maintains that
Vergil is not only suitable for teaching children, but can serve
far higher purposes.   'You seem to me,' he says to Evangelus,
'to regard Vergil from the same point of view as we did when
we learnt him by heart at school; but the fame of Vergil is
such that no praise can increase it nor any blame detract from
it.'   At this point the other speakers join in and combine to
attack Evangelus, each taking upon himself to expound a part
of Vergil's wisdom, and so fill up the programme of the remain-
ing books, which have only been preserved in a fragmentary
condition.   Thus Eustathius is to deal with Vergil's knowledge
of astrology and philosophy, Flavianus and Vettius to point
out how intimate was his acquaintance with the augural and
pontifical ceremonies, Symmachus to dilate on his knowledge
of rhetoric, Eusebius on his power as an orator, Eustathius to
show what use he made of Greek writers, Furius Albinus and
Caecina Albinus to explain how he borrowed from earlier Latin
writers in the matter of lines and words respectively, while
Servius, as the chief Vergilian commentator, is to expound the
meaning of certain difficult passages.—All that part of the

---

[56] "Unde enim Veneto rusticis parentibus, inter silvas et frutices educato,
vel levis Graecarum notitia litterarum?"   Sat., v. 2; x. 4.

[57] "Qui enim moriens poema suum legavit igni, quid nisi famae suae,
posteritati subtrahendo, curavit?   Nec immerito; erubuit quippe de se
futura iudicia, si legeretur petitio deae precantis filio arma a marito cui sola
nupserat, nec ex eo prolem suscepisse se noverat. vel si mille alia multum
pudenda, seu in verbis modo Graecis modo barbaris, seu in ipsa dispositione
operis deprehenderentur."   Sat., i. 25, 6, 7.

work which deals with astrology and philosophy has been lost,
but there can be little question as to how a neo-platonist would
treat such a subject; and we have moreover a sample in the
'Dream of Scipio,' where Macrobius recognises in Vergil's
'terque quaterque beati' the Pythagorean doctrine of numbers.[58] More worthy of acceptance, notwithstanding its frequent exaggerations, is that part of the work which deals with
Vergil's knowledge of augury and with his erudition generally;
this and, for a quite different reason, the parallels adduced from
the Greek and Latin writers [59] are the most valuable portions
of the book. In these parallels we are surprised not only by
the knowledge displayed by Macrobius of a number of authors
who were at that time no longer read, but also by a certain
fineness of critical discernment hardly to have been expected
in a writer of his date. But the fact is that Macrobius was
often simply compiling, not merely from Servius,[60] who himself compiled from others, but also from various earlier authorities, whom he often quotes verbatim without acknowledgment; [61] as, for instance, where he copies out of Gellius the
whole passage comparing Vergil's description of Etna with that
of Pindar. In collecting these parallels from the earlier works
on Vergil, Macrobius keeps clearly before him throughout his
intention of eulogising the poet. The passages in which Vergil is judged superior to Homer are mentioned first, then those
in which he is equal; those in which he is inferior are spoken

[58] *S. Scip.*, i. 6. 44. The character of this part of the work is clear from
the words in the First Book, " De astrologia totaque philosophia, quam
parcus et sobrius operi suo nusquam reprehendendus aspersit." *Sat.*, i.
24. 18.

[59] Vergil's learning in Greek matters is summed up by Eustathius in the
following hyperbole: " Cave, Evangele, Graecorum quemquam vel de summis auctoribus tantam Graecae doctrinae hausisse copiam credas quantam
sollertia Maronis vel assecuta est, vel in suo opere digessit." *Sat.*, v. 2. 2.

[60] According to others, Macrobius did not make use of Servius, but the
text of Servius has been interpolated from Macrobius. *Vide* WISSOWA, *De
Macrobii fontibus* (Bresl., 1880), p. 55.

[61] He admits as much in the preface (4): "Nec mihi vitio vertas si res
quas ex lectione varia mutuabor ipsis saepe verbis quibus ab ipsis auctoribus enarratae sunt explicabo . . . et boni consulas oportet si notitiam
vetustatis modo nostris non obscure modo ipsis antiquorum fideliter verbis
recognoscas."

of last, and then often in modified terms.[62] Similarly, when
about to discuss the use made by Vergil of the ancient Latin
poets, Macrobius thinks it necessary to point out that this is
no failing on Vergil's part, but that he rather deserves the
gratitude of the original authors for having in this manner
immortalized them, adding that these passages sound far better
in Vergil than in their original context.[63] The two treatises
dealing with Vergil as orator and as rhetorician have only
survived in a fragmentary condition. In what remains of the
first we find put the question which, after all that we have
seen, will no longer surprise us, namely, whether a good orator
could learn more from Cicero or from Vergil. In spite of all
the speaker's respect for Cicero and his unwillingness to decide
between two such great names, the answer is finally in favour
of Vergil. Cicero, according to Eusebius, has only one style
(copiosum); Vergil has four (copiosum, breve, siccum, pin-
gue); he is like nature, with its varied aspects; one might
say of him that he combines the qualities of all the ten Attic
orators, and yet not say enough.[64] This enthusiasm of Macrobius for the eloquence of Vergil reminds one of that of Quintilian for the perfection and universality of the eloquence of
Homer. But the most foolish part of the work is that which
deals with Vergil as rhetorician. What remains of it treats
principally of the emotions, and amounts to nothing more than
a proof that Vergil observed the laws of rhetoric relative to

[62] " Et quia non est erubescendum Vergilio si minorem se Homero vel
ipse fateatur, dicam in quibus mihi visus est gracilior auctore." v. 13. 1.

[63] " Cui etiam gratia hoc nomine est habenda, quod nonnulla ab illius
in opus suum quod aeterno mansurum est transferendo, fecit ne omnino
memoria veterum deleretur; quos, sicut praesens sensus ostendit, non
solum neglectui, verum etiam risui habere iam coepimus. Denique et
iudicio transferendi et modo imitandi consecutus est ut quod apud illum
legerimus alienum aut illius esse malimus aut melius hic quam ubi natum
est sonare miremur." Sat., vi. 1. 5. 6.

[64] " Nam qualiter eloquentia Maronis ad omnium mores integra est, nunc
brevis, nunc copiosa, nunc sicca, nunc florida, nunc simul omnia, interdum
levis aut torrens; sic terra ipsa hic laeta segetibus et pratis, ibi silvis et
rupibus hispida, hic sicca harenis, hic irrigua fontibus, pars vasta operitur
mari. Ignoscite, nec nimium me vocetis, qui naturae rerum Vergilium com-
paravi. Intra ipsum enim mihi visum est si dicerem decem oratorum, qui
apud Athenas Atticas floruerunt, stilos inter se diversos hunc unum per-
miscuisse." v. i. 19. 20.

pathos ; to establish this point, the laws in question are passed in review and the Vergilian passages cited which are in accordance with them. Thus, while the rhetoricians in forming their laws had quoted Vergil as their chief authority, Macrobius now praises Vergil for having observed the laws of rhetoric ! Hence the impression which this part of the book conveys is that of a chapter of rhetoric inverted, and such, in all probability, it actually is.

Macrobius had found the soil ready for his work, not only in the way of materials from which to compile it, but also by reason of the intellectual environment in which it was produced. That decadence of taste which, notwithstanding all the author's efforts to rise above the level of his contemporaries, is so apparent in it had already been going on for some time ; we have already noticed the origin and gradual expansion of those false ideas relative to Vergil in respect of which it marks the close of one period and the beginning of thé next. Written at a moment when the old pagan world was just coming to an end, by an eminent man who belonged entirely to that world, it serves to define clearly the nature of the views held relative to the poet at the very close of paganism, before the influence of the new atmosphere of the Christian middle ages, which was so strangely to transform him, had begun to make itself felt.

To this period of decadence belong still two other authors, both adherents of the old pagan tradition,[65] who were not without influence in propagating Vergil's fame during the centuries of barbarism which followed ; these are the two famous grammarians, Donatus and Priscian. These two compilers, separated from one another by well-nigh two hundred years, dominated the schools of the middle ages to such an extent that their influence, direct or indirect, is still felt at the present day.[66] Donatus' Vergil-commentary, already mentioned, was eclipsed by that of Servius ; but so great was the fame that he acquired

[65] Priscian, though a Christian, entirely follows the pagan tradition in choosing his examples, differing greatly in this from Isidorus, who is only a little later.

[66] Cp. KEIL, *Gram. Lat.*, ii. p. ix. seq. ; xxix. seqq. ; iv. p. xxxv. seqq.

by his grammar, which was adopted in all the schools and familiar to all who frequented them, that grammar and Donatus became well-nigh synonymous terms. Priscian too with his compilations, still more extensive and learned than those of Donatus, achieved so high a reputation that the writers of the middle ages cannot speak of him except in terms of greatest enthusiasm and veneration.[67] Keeping to the traditions of their predecessors, these two grammarians drew most of their instances from Vergil; and so constant was the use they made of him that, even had he been little known at the time, the force of their authority would have got him readers.[68] Priscian, in a special treatise which was very popular, gives us a curious instance of the way in which Vergil was used for the practical teaching of grammar. He takes the first line of each book of the Aeneid and asks the pupil to explain every word and to analyze it grammatically and metrically; and so, passing from one question to another, he finds occasion to propound, in reference to these twelve lines, all the chief rules of grammar and prosody.[69] It is noticeable that Lucan, who was fashionable in the middle ages, is quoted by Priscian almost as often as Horace; but the two chief authorities remain Terence and Vergil.

But even outside the domain of education the poet did not cease to be popular, as he had always been. Theatrical representations founded on his works continued to be given, one of

[67] Thus his pupil Eutychis, a grammarian much read in the middle ages, writes, "De quibus omnibus terminationibus et traductionibus quia Romanae lumen facundiae, meus, immo communis omnium hominum praeceptor in quarto de nomine libro summa cum subtilitate disseruisse cognoscitur, etc." EUTYCHIS, *Ars de verbo*, ap. KEIL, *Gram. Lat.*, v. 456. Cp. THUROT, in *Notices et Extraits*, t. xxii. p. 63.

[68] The instances in the *Ars Maior* of DONATUS are about a hundred in number, and some eighty of them are from Vergil. Priscian offers in his various works, which are far more extensive and learned than those of Donatus, a very great number of quotations. The author most used is Vergil, who is cited more than 1,200 times; Terence, who comes second in the list, does not reach half this number; then come Cicero and Plautus, then Horace and Lucan, then Juvenal, and after him Sallust, Statius and Ovid, then Lucretius, Persius, etc.

[69] *Partitiones xii. versum Aeneidos principalium*, ap. KEIL, *Gram. Lat.*, iii. pp. 459–515.

the favourite themes being the tragic adventure of Dido, which used to move the audiences to tears, and was a most fashionable subject for tapestries, pictures, and other works of art.[70] Nor was there any want of public recitations, and in the 6th century still people crowded into the Forum of Trajan to hear the Aeneid.[71] It must not be forgotten however that this was an age which admired the poems of Arator on the Acts of the Apostles, and called on him to recite them in public no less than seven times.[72] The name too of Vergil had come to be applied to men of so little mark that Ennodius grows indignant over it.[73] The hand of a consul transcribed and emended the text of Vergil in the precious codex which we have;[74] but this was a distinction which other writers, even contemporary ones, enjoyed at this period.

Rome and the Romans were sadly changed from what they once had been. The pompous and empty rhetoric of Sym-

---

[70] " Quod ita elegantius auctore (Apollonio Rhodio) digessit ut fabula lascivientis Didonis, quam falsam novit universitas, per tot tamen saecula speciem veritatis obtineat et ita pro vero per ora omnium volitet, ut pictores fictoresque et qui figmentis liciorum contextus imitantur effigies hac materia vel maxime in efficiendis simulacris tanquam unico argumento decoris utantur, nec minus histrionum perpetuis et gestibus et cantibus celebretur." MACROB., *Sat.*, v. 17. 5.

" Quod Maro Phoenissae cantatur et Naso Corinnae."
VICTORIN., *Epist. ad Salm.*, 73.

Cp. AUSON., *Epig.*, 118. The *Cupido cruci affixus* of AUSONIUS was suggested by a picture of the " Lugentes Campi " in a house at Treviri.

[71] "Aut Maro Traiano lectus in urbe foro."
VENANT. FORT., vi. 8. 26.

" Vix modo tam nitido pomposa poemata cultu
audit Traiano Roma verenda foro."
ID., iii. 20. **7.**

[72] Cp. LABBÉ, *Biblioth. nova mss.*, i. p. 688.

[73] " In tantum prisci defluxit fama Maronis,
ut te Vergilium saecula nostra darent.
si fatuo dabitur tam sanctum nomen homullo
gloria maiorum curret in opprobrium, etc."
ENNOD., *Carm.*, ii. **118.**

It is wrong to suppose that Vergil the Grammarian, of whom we shall speak in due course, is meant here ; many people took the name of Vergil during the decadence and the middle ages. Cp. OZANAM, *La civilisat. chrét. chez les Francs*, p. 426.

[74] For this codex see RIBBECK, *Prolegg.*, p. 209 seqq.

machus and the other panegyrists, who united in applying to
the reign of Gratian the happy prophecies of the Fourth
Eclogue,[75] serves only to render more gloomy the spectacle of
general ruin.   More sincere and just was the feeling of Jerome,
who, on hearing in his hermit-cell how Rome had been taken
by Alaric, gave vent in verses of the Aeneid to the deep sorrow
which the momentous news inspired, and exclaimed with the
Psalmist, ' Deus, venerunt gentes in haereditatem tuam!' [76]
With the memories of a glorious past were contrasted the sad
facts of decay, the humiliating intercourse with insolent barbarians, who had been slaves and now were masters, and the
mournful presentiment of a terrible end.   But though Rome
and her empire might fall, that union of nations which it had
been her great work and her true mission to bring about
remained.   Rome was still in all men's eyes the mother of
civilization, the symbol of miraculous power, the supreme ideal
of human greatness ; that Roman sentiment to which the epic
of Vergil had so perfectly responded was, even after the fall
of the Empire, too closely connected with the essential spirit
of Latin culture to disappear from men's minds as long as
that culture continued.   The deep traces left by the Roman
dominion and the benefits that mankind had derived therefrom give to the innumerable expressions of the Roman sentiment, which long survived the actual empire, a reality and a
sincerity which precludes the possibility of regarding them as
so many frigid and automatic imitations of antiquity.   And
yet, without doubt, the conditions of thought were greatly
changed, and in many departments of ancient culture this
sentiment could not be more than merely passive, unable in
its present activity to harmonise at all intimately with that
culture.   Taste had been entirely spoilt, and any true æsthetic
or artistic idealism was an impossibility.

Those intellectual powers from which art results were at
this time either paralyzed or entangled in a new environment

[75] " Si mihi nunc altius evagari poetico liceret eloquio, totum de novo
saeculo Maronis excursum, vati similis, in tuum nomen exscriberem.
Dicerem de caelo rediisse iustitiam, etc." SYMM., *Laud. in Gratian. Aug.*, 8,
ed. MAI, p. 27.
[76] Cp. AM. THIERRY, *Saint Jérome*, ii. p. 191 seqq.

to which art was in reality quite foreign. In this period of great struggles and great upheavals, both social and moral, there was no doubt an immense fund of poetical energy, but it was one which found expression not in individual artistic productions, but in the great general fact of the universal renewal. Christ wrote no verses, it is true, but there was poetry enough in His personality and in that of His followers. But art, in this shock of heterogeneous elements, in this decay and regeneration of imperfect thoughts and feelings, missed those conditions which are indispensable to its existence ; the minds of men were disturbed, vaguely agitated, and, as it were, hardened against all æsthetic impressions. They still followed blindly the models of ancient culture, and kept before them the products of ancient art; but their level had sunk so low, their aims and ideals were so changed, that it is hard to believe that the works of antiquity, however much they may have studied and admired them, can have had any more real influence upon them than that of a wonderful dream.—As we have seen from Macrobius, from the grammarians and from other writers, the central place in this body of traditional authority was occupied by Vergil, who seemed like the sun round which the other stars revolved. Those real qualities of learning which distinguished him, and which, even at an early period of his fame, had been gauged with considerable inaccuracy, had become by this time his only claim to distinction and were, owing to the great prestige of his name, amplified and exaggerated according to the spirit of the age, which, under the influence of neo-platonism and still more of Christianity, tended irresistibly towards symbolism, mysticism and allegory. The poets of the period could achieve but little which rose as high as mediocrity, and even such verses as they produced found their sole inspiration in the schools of grammar and rhetoric. The art of the greatest of Roman poets seemed to these people a mystery, the clue to which could only be found in vast and recondite learning. Hence it was considered a sure proof of refined taste and superior erudition to be able to discover hidden in his verses scientific dicta and profound philosophical doctrines of every kind.

As supreme centre of the literary inheritance left by the Romans, as representative of classical learning, as interpreter of that Roman sentiment which survived the downfall of the Empire, the name of Vergil acquired in Europe a significance well-nigh equivalent to that of civilization itself.[77] Such was his charge to the nations of the future, committed to him by paganism as it died. Some centuries before Dante spoke of Vergil as 'virtù somma,' Justinian had said almost as much when, in the most perfect monument of the practical wisdom of the Romans which has survived, he put Vergil by the side of the divine Greek epic poet, who was to him 'the father of every virtue.'[78]

[77] In the panegyric in honour of Avitus, SIDONIUS APOLLINARIS makes the king of the Goths say (v. 495 seqq.) :—

> " mihi Romula dudum
> per te iura placent ; parvumque ediscere iussit
> ad tua verba pater, docili quo prisca Maronis
> carmine molliret Scythicos mihi pagina mores."

[78] " Sicuti cum poetam dicimus nec addimus nomen subauditur apud Graecos egregius Homerus, apud nos Vergilius." IUSTIN., *Inst.*, § 2 : ". . . et apud Homerum, patrem omnis virtutis." ID., *in fin. prooem Digest.*

CHAPTER VI

WE have now to follow Vergil's fortunes during the course of the middle ages. The barbarians and the Christians had entirely changed the face of the ancient world. On the one hand literature ran a risk of perishing at the hands of religious fanaticism or of being swamped in the sea of theological productions; on the other it was clear enough that the invaders had not been led to occupy the civilised countries out of any affection for civilisation or with any wish to pursue classical studies. Oppressed and oppressors, laity and clergy alike, were too much concerned with the safety of their bodies or their souls to have any time to bestow on classical ideals. But there was one thing which saved Latin literature. Latin remained the language of the Church and its writers, and in order to be able to write Latin that would pass muster it was still necessary to study it to a certain extent. While Latin was sinking to the condition of a dead language, the local European languages, though in process of formation, were not as yet sufficiently advanced to have attained to the position of vehicles for literature. Hence the schools, and especially those of the grammarians, had to continue to exist, and round the study of grammar were grouped those various other educational subjects which were thought necessary for the equipment of a writer. Even without the evidence collected by various scholars as to the continued existence of the schools during this whole period, their existence would be sufficiently proved by the fact that the Latin language continued in use long after it had become purely literary and different from the spoken vernacular. But we must be careful not to rate these schools at more than their true worth. Nothing was taught in them beyond what was

absolutely necessary, or rather, what was considered necessary;
for the study of profane subjects had ceased to be an end in
itself and was looked upon merely as a means for the attainment of higher things.   Hence the Seven Arts, into which even
before the time of Augustus educational subjects had been
divided,[1] became more and more attenuated, and in the middle
ages were reduced within the narrowest possible limits.   Formerly such compendia as those of Varro or Cato had taken but
an unimportant place in literature, because the various branches
of learning of which they united the elements were all in a
state of activity and development.   But now that this development had come to an end and the activity of every department
of learning had become straitly and rigorously circumscribed,
such general handbooks became common owing to the same
cause as had led to the publication of compendia of the separate branches of study; and as they supplied what was at the
time a felt want, it was only natural that they should attain
to an importance which would at an earlier period have been
impossible.   This serves to explain the origin of such works
as the encyclopædias of the Seven Arts made by Cassiodorus,
Capella, Isidorus, Bede and others, in which the whole of profane learning was contained in a small volume, and to account
for the favour with which they were received and the popularity which they enjoyed throughout the middle ages.   A
feature of these encyclopædias is that, among the serious subjects of which they treat, the one which seems most after the
author's heart is nearly always grammar; in fact, the author's
system and treatment is generally such that he cannot be called
anything but a grammarian.   And indeed grammar always
appears as the first and most important of the liberal arts, and
it is amusing to hear the barbarian Atalaric eulogising it in his
decree to the Senate concerning the payment of professors of
these subjects.   'The school of the grammarians,' he says, 'is
the most excellent foundation of culture, the glorious mother of
eloquence, which knows how to think and to speak correctly.

---

[1] Cp. RITSCHL, *Quaestiones Varronianae*, Bonn, 1845; MERCKLIN in the
Philologus, xiii. p. 736 seqq.; JAHN, *Ueber die röm. Encyklopedien*, in the
Berichte d. Sächs. Gesell. d. Wiss., 1850, p. 263 seqq.

. . . Grammar is the mistress of speech; she adorns the
human race, which by making use of the most excellent literature can avail itself of the wisdom of the ancients. . . . The
barbarians do not know it . . . for arms belong to every
nation, but eloquence accompanies the Romans alone.' [2]

And where there was grammar there was also Vergil as its
inseparable companion and its supreme authority. Vergil and
grammar became synonyms, one may almost say, in the middle
ages. Thus when Gregory of Tours (6th cent.) says of Andar-
chius that he had been instructed in his youth 'in the works
of Vergil, in the Codex Theodosianus and in arithmetic,' [3] by
'the works of Vergil' he means nothing more than that he had
been taught grammar; as it is said in the Life of S. Bonitus,
that he was instructed 'in the elements of grammar and the
laws of Theodosius.' [4] Hence a good grammarian at once compared himself with Vergil.[5] A curious instance of this is the
case of the grammarian of Toulouse, dating apparently from
the 6th century, who in bringing forward a most extraordinary
Latin, of which we shall have occasion to speak further on,
could not think of a better name to call himself than P. Vergilius Maro, and this, in fact, is the only name by which he is
now known.

This state of affairs lasted well-nigh throughout the middle
ages, up to the commencement of modern literature, when the
laity resumed their intellectual activity and the study of secular
things. The reasons which induced the medieval clergy to
devote themselves to the study of the Seven Arts were not of
such a kind as is necessary to give literature and science that
motive power which renders them capable of development. The
ancient traditions which had already become stagnant towards
the end of paganism became during the following centuries,

[2] CASSIODOR., *Variarum*, lib. ix. c. 21.
[3] "De operibus Vergili, legis Theodosianae libris, arteque calculi adprime
eruditus est." GREGOR. TURON., iv. 47.
[4] "Grammaticorum imbutus initiis, nec non Theodosi edoctus decretis."
ap. MABILLON, *Act. S.*, iii. pars. 1. pag. 90.
[5] "Et si aliquis de Aquitanis parum didicerit grammaticam, mox putat se
esse Vergilium." ADEMAR., *Epist.* (12th cent.) ap. MABILLON, *Annales ord.
S. Bened.*, iv. 725; GIESEBRECHT, *De literar. stud.*, etc., p. 18.

in which Christianity exclusively dominated the feelings and thoughts of mankind, like a substance in suspension in a medium incapable of absorbing it, and sank in a mass to the bottom. In itself it remained quite unchanged throughout the whole period; it was so much dead matter passed from hand to hand and was only modified by the rough and unskilful treatment it experienced during the process. If here and there the study of it decayed to such an extent as to well-nigh disappear, the practical inconveniences resulting therefrom soon induced some authority to restore it; but once restored, it was the same as it had been before. If any attempt at innovation was made, it consisted merely in endeavouring to bring the already greatly reduced mass within yet narrower limits. To discover some method of further abridgment was the only object after which any one strove.[6] Charlemagne might resume the classical studies; he could not renew them. Grammar, which of all the Seven Arts was the one most benefited by that monarch, remained unchanged, except for the childish ignorances of the compilers and adapters, from the times of paganism to the 12th century, when its theories at length began to come under the influence of scholasticism.[7] Modern literature and modern speculation had then already commenced, but grammar still held in the popular estimation that pride of place which in the 6th century the Ostrogoth king had assigned to it.[8] And what is

---

[6] This mania for abridgment led at length to the making of travelling-grammars. Such the work of PHOCAS (5th cent.) professes to be, as we learn from its preface:

> "Te longinqua petens comitem sibi ferre viator
> ne dubitet parvo pondere multa vehens."

Ars Phocae Grammatici de nomine et verbo, ap. KEIL, *Gramm. Lat.,* v. p. 410.

[7] Vide THUROT, *Notices et extraits de divers manuscrits pour servir à l'histoire des doctrines grammaticales au moyen-âge,* Paris, 1868. (It is the 22nd volume of the *Notices et extraits des manuscrits de la bibl. imp.*)

[8] In the legend of Charlemagne it is said, "Premièrement fist Karlemaine paindre dans son palais gramaire qui est mère de tous les ars." In the *Image du monde* this supremacy of grammar is explained by the mystical reason that it is the science of words, and God created the world with a word:

> "Par parole fist Dex le monde
> Et tous les biens qui ens habunde."

Vide JUBINAL, *Oeuvres complètes de Ruteboeuf,* ii. p. 417.

true of grammar is true also of Vergil, who with it continued to dominate secular study throughout medieval times. The middle ages had taken over ready-made from the period of decadence not merely its materials for secular education, but also its opinions as to the ancient authors. The echo of Vergil's renown and of the conception formed of him then lasted on throughout the middle ages and was heard in those naïve utterances which were the natural expression of an epoch of such debased culture and with ideas so little in harmony with the ancient world.

The works of classical antiquity were only able to survive during the middle ages through the medium of the schools, and those authors who were known at all during this period owed such fame as they enjoyed to the schoolmasters. Of these the first was of course Vergil, and then, like accompanying planets, Ovid and Lucan, Horace, Juvenal and Statius, and then others according to individual taste. The names of the chief writers of antiquity, like those of the chief grammarians, were so impressed upon children at school, that when they grew up, if they interested themselves at all in literature, they could not lose these early reminiscences of that Latin language in which they wrote. Hence the enormous number of quotations from Vergil and other pagan writers to be found in the works of many Christian authors both before and after the total extinction of paganism and right on through the middle ages. But the spirit of ascetic Christianity could not fail to feel a great repugnance towards these expressions of pagan sentiment, and hence it will be necessary for us to examine the position of Vergil and the other classical authors in the midst of the fierce attacks made upon paganism by the Christians, and still more after the complete victory of the new religion.

The ecclesiastical writers [9] might feel a strong aversion towards pagan authors, and attack them, as did Arnobius, Ter-

[9] As this work deals only with the Western countries, it will be unnecessary to examine the state of the classical studies in the Greek world. On the whole, however, it may be said that what is true of the West is true of the East also, except that the Eastern Church showed itself in this, as in some other respects, more liberal than the Western. The homily of Basil on the reading of pagan literature is well known.

tullian and others, with a violence which even persecution and
enthusiasm will hardly excuse, but they had none the less to
read and study them, partly to refute them, partly for the
no less important reason that they formed the foundations of
general culture and that from them alone could one learn to
write the language of the world which was to be converted.
Hence the rage provoked among the Christians by the decree
of the Emperor Julian debarring them from the study of grammar and rhetoric, although in this he was merely adopting the
logical results of their own ideas. He maintained that it was
not right that people who made such objections to the pagan
writers on grounds of morality and religion should use these
same writers as the basis of their education,[10] a view which
many of the more intolerant Christians had already themselves
expressed. But all the more enlightened Christians at once
perceived the hidden malice of the decree; for to separate
Christianity entirely from the ancient civilisation and to bind
it by a rigorous logic within the limits of its unworldly nature
was the best way to oppose it and hinder its development in a
society of Graeco-Roman culture. Nothing however was strong
enough to resist the flood of the movement, and Julian's decree,
like the rest of his endeavours, came to nothing. Subsequently,
when paganism had disappeared and there was no longer any
object in refuting the pagans, the tradition of the Christian
schools was already formed, and no longer capable of alteration.
Some might wish to substitute Christian for pagan writers;
but what grammarian could admit that the substitution was a
satisfactory one ? In the new grammatical compilations quotations from the Vulgate and other Christian works were
sometimes added to those from the classical authors,[11] but the

---

[10] "ἄτοπον μὲν οἶμαι τοὺς ἐξηγουμένους τὰ τούτων ἀτιμάζειν τοὺς ὑπ' αὐτῶν
τιμηθέντας θεούς." JULIAN, Epist., 42, p. 422. The decree forbade the Christians to teach grammar or rhetoric (AMMIAN. MARCELL., xxii. 10. 7; JOH.
CHRYSOST., ii. p. 579, etc.); hence they could not send their sons to the
schools, for they could not entrust them to pagan schoolmasters. Cp.
LASAULX, Der Untergang des Hellenismus, p. 65; KELLNER, Hellenismus und
Christenthum (Köln, 1866), p. 226 seq.

[11] Among the most noteworthy instances of this is the work of ISIDORUS.
SMARAGDUS too (9th cent.) states expressly that he draws his instances from
the Vulgate (cp. THUROT, op. cit., p. 63): ". . . quem libellum non Ma-

latter always remained, as they were bound to do, the chief authorities.

The necessity of a radical change was not felt, for paganism was dead for good, and any one with any sense could see that it would not be resuscitated in the schools. Hence we do not find any official decrees of the ecclesiastical authorities forbidding the use of the pagan writers;[12] and we are met by the apparent contradiction that, while on the one hand the ancients are steadily hated and maligned as pagans, on the other their works are assiduously read and studied, and they are looked up to by the most enlightened Christians as men of learning and genius. The middle ages found a traditional usage already formed and to this they scrupulously adhered. The Fathers

ronis aut Ciceronis vel etiam aliorum paganorum auctoritate fulcivi, sed divinarum scripturarum sententiis adornavi, ut lectorem meum iucundo pariter artium et iucundo scripturarum poculo propinarem, ut grammaticae artis ingenium et scripturarum pariter valeat comprehendere sensum." SMARAGD., Prolog. tractat. in part. Donat. ap. KEIL, De quibusdam grammaticis Latinis infimae aetatis (Erlangen, 1868), p. 20. A similar proceeding was adopted in rhetoric. Thus BEDE, in his De schematibus et tropis, says, " Sed ut cognoscas, dilectissime fili, cognoscant omnes qui haec legere voluerint, quia sancta scriptura ceteris scripturis omnibus non solum auctoritate quia divina est, vel utilitate quia ad vitam ducit aeternam, sed et antiquitate et ipsa praeeminet positione dicendi, placuit mihi collectis de ipsa exemplis ostendere, quia nihil huiusmodi schematum sive troporum valent praetendere saecularis eloquentiae magistri, quod non in illa praecesserit." Ap. HALM, Rhett. Lat. min., p. 607.

[12] One cannot regard as a canonical authority the apocryphal Constitutiones Apostolorum, notwithstanding their considerable antiquity. In these rules, full of the simplicity of primitive Christianity, the reading of pagan literature is discouraged, the Bible being regarded as a sort of encyclopaedia in which all information of value is to be found. (Constit. Apost., i., c. 4.)

At the Fourth Council of Carthage (5th cent.) it was decided (cap. xvi.), " ut episcopi libros gentilium non legant, haereticorum autem pro necessitate et tempore," and ISIDORUS in his Liber Sententiarum (iii. cap. 13) says, " Prohibetur Christianis figmenta legere poetarum," stating the reasons in full. It is clear, however, that all this must not be taken literally and must be regarded rather as advice against excess than as an actual prohibition to read pagan authors. The whole thing was a matter of conscience, and the various works of Isidor himself show how he meant his words to be understood. The passage of Isidor and the canon of the Council of Carthage are repeated in GRATIAN'S collection of canons (dist. 37). Vide the note of BERARDI, i. 193 seqq. Various passages from both Greek and Latin Fathers, expressing various views on the subject of the pagan writers are collected in the note on the Constit. Apost. in the Patr. temp. apostolic., ed. COTELERIUS, i., p. 204. Cp. too LOAISE and AREVALO ad Isid. lib. sent., iii. c. 13 ; GAZAEUS, ad Cassian. Coll., xiv. c. 12.

had said and written much against these authors, but they had
none the less made use of them; their successors did the same.
Pagan writers were studied at school, they were quoted when
necessary in literary works even of a theological and religious
character, and at the same time they were spoken of as "idola-
trous dogs." Some of the most authoritative of the Fathers
had said that it was not good to read them; but did they not
contradict this by their very words and actions? Jerome,
whose love for Cicero led to the blows in his famous dream
and to the angel's well-known reproof, 'Ciceronianus es, non
Christianus,' had said of Vergil that he was 'not the second,
but the first Homer of the Romans.'[13]   And yet, in a letter to
Damasus on the Prodigal Son, he blames severely those priests
who 'lay aside the Gospels and the Prophets and read comedies,
who repeat the amorous words of the Bucolics, who have Vergil
always in their heads and make a sensual sin of that study
which for children is a necessity.'   But this did not at all
agree with Augustine, who observes without disapproval that
'children read Vergil so often, that they do not easily forget
him.'[14]   These reminiscences of profane studies which had to
be undergone troubled many scrupulous minds so much that
we find the Hermit Cassianus actually working out a remedy
for them.[15]   But how difficult it was to forget them is clear

---

[13] *Comm. in Michaeam.*, Op. vi. 518.

[14] " Vergilium pueri legunt ut poeta magnus omniumque praeclarissimus
atque optimus, teneris imbibitus annis, non facile oblivione possit aboleri."
De Civ. Dei, lib. i. cap. 8. This passage is often misquoted with *legant*, but
the true reading is *legunt*, and indeed an exhortation would be out of place
in the context.

[15] *Germanus.* "Speciale impedimentum salutis accedit pro illa quam
tenuiter videor attigisse notitia litterarum, in qua me ita vel instantia pae-
dagogi vel continuae lectionis maceravit intentio, ut nunc mens, poeticis
velut infecta carminibus, illas fabularum nugas historiasque bellorum quibus
a parvulo primis studiorum imbuta est rudimentis, orationis etiam tempŏre
meditetur, psallentique vel pro peccatorum indulgentia supplicanti, aut im-
pudens poematum memoria suggeratur, aut quasi bellantium heroum ante
oculos imago versetur, taliumque me phantasmatum imaginatio semper
eludens ita mentem meam ad supernos intuitus aspirare non patitur ut
quotidianis fletibus non possit expelli."

Nosteros. "De hac ipsa re unde tibi purgationis nascitur desperatio
citum satis atque efficax remedium poterit oboriri, si eandem diligentiam
atque instantiam quam te in illis saecularibus studiis habuisse dixisti ad

from Jerome, with his frequent involuntary reminiscences of
the classics. Thus, when speaking[16] of the catacombs at Rome
which contained the graves of the Apostles and Martyrs, and
of the darkness reigning in their subterranean passages, he
says, ' Here one can only move step by step, and in the darkness one is reminded of Vergil's " Horror ubique animos simul
ipsa silentia terrent." ' One of the pillars of the Church, bor-
rowing the words of a pagan to express the feelings with which
the most venerable recesses of this Christian sanctuary inspired
him! How can this be the same Jerome who elsewhere in the
height of his religious fervour exclaims, ' What has Horace to
do with the Psalter, or Vergil with the Gospel, or Cicero with
the Apostle?'[17] And many similar passages might be found
in his writings. Nor did his adversaries spare him for his
studies of classical literature. When he established at Beth-
lehem a school of grammar in which he expounded Vergil and
other profane Latin and Greek writers to children, Rufinus
attacked him for it in a way that affected him deeply.[18]

If any one were to collect from the ecclesiastical writers all
the passages in which they inveigh against the reading of pagan
authors and the pursuit of profane studies generally, the collection would be a considerable one; but far greater would be a
collection of the passages which prove that none the less these
same writers occupied themselves with studies of this very
kind. There were Christian poets and prose writers, but every
one of them with the least claim to literary merit owes that
merit entirely to the ancients, of whom he is the disciple and
often the servile imitator. And not only was the study of the
ancient writers not discouraged; it was even recommended.
Thus a letter of Sidonius Apollinaris (5th cent.) introduces
us to a villa in Gaul, the owner of which had collected together

spiritalium scripturarum volueris lectionem meditationemque transferre.''
CASSIAN., *Coll.*, xiv. cap. 12, 13.
    [16] *Comm. in Ezechiel*, c. 40.
    [17] *Epist. ad Eustochium*, Op. i. 112.
    [18] " Maronem suum comicosque ac lyricos et historicos auctores traditis
sibi ad discendum Dei timorem puerulis exponebat; scilicet ut praeceptor
fieret auctorem gentilium." RUFIN., *Apol.*, ii. ap. HIERON., p. 420. Cp. AM.
THIERRY, *Saint Jérome*, i. p. 314.

everything calculated to delight the body and the mind. Here
among the books we find Christian and pagan authors mixed
together in a manner which shows clearly enough how little
relation to real life had the declarations of the fanatics.[19]   Or
again, when Cassiodorus is impressing on his monks the necessity of the study of the Seven Arts,[20] he confronts them with
the example not only of Moses, who was learned in all the
wisdom of the Egyptians, but also that of 'the Holy Fathers,
who did not consider that the study of profane literature should
be rejected, but were themselves examples to the contrary,
showing themselves most skilled in such studies, as one may
see in the cases of Cyprian, Lactantius, Ambrose, Jerome,
Augustine, and many others. And who could hesitate in the
face of such illustrious examples?'   And this is the commonplace with which ecclesiastics always defend themselves when
they write on profane matters and think an excuse necessary.[21]

---

[19] "Qui inter matronarum cathedras codices erant, stylus his religiosus
inveniebatur; qui vero per subsellia patrumfamilias, hi cothurno latialis
eloqui nobilitabantur.   Licet quaepiam volumina quorundam auctorum
servarent in causis disparibus dicendi parilitatem.   Nam similis scientiae
viri, hinc Augustinus, hinc Varro, hinc Horatius, hinc Prudentius, lectita-
bantur." SIDON., *Epist.*, i. 9.   Between this, however, and the idea of CHAIX
(*Sidoine Apollinaire*, Paris, 1867) and other modern Catholics, that the
Church was always the great protector of the ancient culture, there is a
considerable difference.   Cp. KAUFMANN in the *Gött. Gel. Anz.*, 1868, p.
1009 seqq.

VERGIL GRAMMATICUS (ap. MAI, *Class. auctt.*, v. p. 5) states that it was the
established custom of the Church to keep works by Christian and pagan
authors in separate libraries.   "Hocce subtilissime statuerunt ut duobus
librariis compositis, una fidelium philosophorum libros, altera gentilium
scripta contineret."   But there seems no occasion to take this extraordinary
writer's assertion as seriously as is done by OZANAM (*La civilisat. chrét. chez
les Francs*, p. 434 seq.).   There were doubtless some who divided their books
in this way; we have an instance of it in the passage of Sidonius just cited;
but there is no proof that they were ordered to do so by the Church, and in
the numerous catalogues of medieval libraries which we possess Christian
and pagan writers are nearly always enumerated indiscriminately.

[20] *Divin. lectt.*, cap. 28.

[21] In an unpublished compendium of Quintilian made by STEPHEN OF
ROUEN (12th cent.), of which there is a MS. in the Bibl. Nat. at Paris, the
author excuses his undertaking as follows: "Hoc pariter notandum quod
ecclesiae doctores gentilium libros non incognitos habebant. . . . Probat
hoc et beatus Augustinus qui in disciplinis liberalibus libros singulos edidit.
. . . Beatus etiam Ambrosius cuiusdam philosophi epistulam in quadam
sua epistula integram ponit.   Origenes vero philosophorum libros adoles-
centibus summopere ediscendos praecipiebat, dicens eorum ingenia in divinis

In those monasteries in which silence was the rule, use was made of conventional signs to denote objects which might be required; here, when one wanted a book by a pagan writer, after the sign for ' book' he made a gesture in imitation of a dog scratching its ear, ' because a pagan is rightly compared to that animal.'[22] One despised the pagans, but one read them. The rule of some of the more modern monastic orders, such as those of Isidor, Francis, and Dominic, forbade the reading of pagan authors, or only allowed it after special permission;[23] but the rules of the older orders not only did not forbid it, but even admitted it in their schools and caused manuscripts to be copied without distinction of author.[24] Had there been any wish faithfully to follow the precepts of Christianity, even if all pagan writers had not been forbidden, at least those works ought to have been destroyed which would be regarded as im-

scripturis capaciora et tenaciora fore cum horum subtilitates et ingeniorum acumina animo perceperint. Quod Iulianus Augustus, magnus equidem philosophus, sed errore maior, considerans, postquam a fide discessit, edicto publicato prohibuit ne Christianorum filii artem oratoriam addiscerent, quod quanto in eloquentiae studiis edocti forent tanto in Christiana fide ac religione, ut in revincendis gentilium, quos sequebatur, erroribus acutiores ac disertiores exsisterent; simul dicens hostes adversariorum armis non armandos. Karoli etiam magni magister Alcuinus de hac arte dialogum sub proprio Karoli nomine conscripsit," etc.

[22] " Pro signo libri scholaris quem aliquis paganus composuit, praemisso signo generali libri, adde ut aurem digito tangas, sicut canis cum pede pruriens solet; quia non immerito infidelis tali animanti comparatur." BERNARD, *Ordo Cluniacens.* in the *Vetus disciplina monast.*, p. 172 (ZAPPERT, *Virgil's Fortleben im Mittelalter*, p. 81).

[23] "Gentilium autem libros vel haereticorum volumina monachus legere caveat." HOLST., *Cod. reg. monast.*, p. 124. Cp. HEEREN, *Gesch. d. class. Lit. im Mittelalter*, i. p. 70; LE CLERC, *Hist. lit. de la France*, xxiv. p. 282; SPECHT, *Gesch. d. Unterrichtswesens in Deutschland* (Stuttg., 1885), p. 40 seqq. (*Das Mönchthum u. d. prof. Studien.*)

[24] The modern discoveries of classical manuscripts in palimpsest have led some to think that the monks used systematically to obliterate the works of the ancient pagan writers and substitute works of a sacred character, out of their hatred for pagan literature. This is a great mistake. The cancelled texts are often themselves Christian works; sometimes even secular works take the place of sacred, as for instance in a palimpsest which has the Iliad written over the Epistles of St. Paul. Too often (I know it from experience) the palimpsests play one false in this way, and disappoint one when one thinks to have made some great discovery of classical literature. For further information on this subject *vide* MONE, *De libris Palimpsestis* (Carlsr., 1855), and WATTENBACH, *Das Schriftwesen im Mittelalter* (Leip., 1871), p. 174 seq.

moral by any religion. And yet the *Ars Amatoria* of Ovid and
the obscene epigrams of Martial figure in the monastic libraries
by the side of the Bible and the Fathers, and the numerous
manuscripts of these works which we possess are in great part
the work of monks. Some of these indeed had not the courage
to transcribe certain passages in full, which accordingly we
find sometimes omitted, sometimes arbitrarily altered on moral
grounds,[25] while others copied their author faithfully and in
full, but avenged themselves by calling him opprobrious names
in the margin ;[26] most of them, however, had easier consciences
than is generally supposed. Thus Horace, certain of whose
poems the pagan Quintilian already had considered unfit for
schools,[27] was not only read, copied, and glossed by the monks,
but some of his most amorous odes were sung by them to
hymn-tunes, the music of which is found added in more than
one manuscript.[28]

There were a few fanatics, but the mass of mankind was
tolerant. Anselm not only allowed the reading of Vergil, but
even recommended it ;[29] Lupus of Ferrières not only advised

[25] In a MS. of Ovid in the library at Zurich, in the verse "Hoc est quod
pueri tangar amore minus" (*Ars Am.*, ii. 684), *minus* is changed into *nihil*,
and a note in the margin states, "ex hoc nota quod Ovidius non fuerit
sodomita." Cp. L. MÜLLER in the *Jahrbb. f. Philol. u. Paedagog.* (1866),
p. 395. In the famous Paris MS. of *Excerpta* (Notre Dame, 188) many of
the verses are thus treated: thus the line of TIBULLUS (I. i. 25) "Iam modo
non possum contentus vivere parvo," becomes "Quippe ego iam possum
contentus vivere parvo," while in another line of the same author (i. 1. 89),
"lusisset amores" is altered into "dampnasset amores"   For further
instances *vide* WÖLFFLIN in the *Philologus*, xxvii. (1867), p. 154.

[26] Among Greek writers the one most often treated in this way is LUCIAN,
of whom the Byzantine copyists regularly remark in the margin, ὦ κάκιστε
ἀνθρώπων, ὦ μιαρώτατε, and the like. Cp. L. MÜLLER in the *Jahrb. f. Philol.
u. Paedagog.*, 1866, p. 395.

[27] ". . . nam et Graeci multa licenter, et Horatium nolim in quibusdam interpretari." QUINTIL. i. 8. 6.

[28] In a Montpelier MS. of Horace the Ode to Phyllis, "Est mihi nonum
superantis annum" (iv. 11), is accompanied by musical notes which have
been recognised as the tune of the famous hymn "Ut queant laxis resonare
fibris." Cp. LIBRI, *Catal. génér. des MSS: des bibl. publ. des départ.*, i. p.
454 seq.; BAITER, *Horat.*, ii. p. 915 seqq.; JAHN in *Hermes*, ii. p. 419;
NISARD, *Archives des miss. scient. et litt.*, 1851, p. 98 seqq.

[29] "Et volo quatenus ut fiat quantum potes satagas, et praecipue de
Vergilio et aliis auctoribus quos a me non legisti; exceptis his in quibus
turpitudo sonat." ANSELM, Op. 351. Thus too many others. In an early
poem entitled *Ad pueros* we read:

Regimbert to study Vergil, as appears from his letters,[30] but
was a diligent searcher after classical manuscripts, and even
wished to borrow of Pope Benedict III. a Cicero, a Quintilian,
and a Commentary on Terence.[31] Often the invectives which
we find directed against the study of pagan literature are merely
so much rhetoric with no real meaning. Where literature has
become rhetorical it is always difficult to know how far to take
the author seriously. When Gregory of Tours lifts up his
voice against the fables and the pernicious doctrines of the
'philosophers,' that is to say, the ancient writers, and then
proceeds to narrate the chief incidents of the Æneid and the
other poetical legends, condemning them one by one, he does
not seem to observe that he is merely making a display of
his own learning and showing that he is himself well acquainted with those very authors of whom he disapproves.[32]
He strikes one as being very much more in earnest when he
deplores, like so many others, the misery brought about in his
times by the general decay of literary studies.[33]

The greatest enemies of profane studies were the authors of

" Pervigil oro legas cecinit quod musa Maronis,
        quaeque Sophia docet, optime, carpe, puer."

Vide AMADOR DE LOS RIOS, *Hist. crit. de la lit. Españ*. ii. pp. 238, 339.

[30] ". . . satius est ut apprime sis, et in Vergiliana lectione, ut optime
potes, proficias." LUP. FERRAR., *Epist.* 7.

[31] *Epist.* 103. *Vide* also *Epistt.* 1, 5, 8, 16, 37, 62, 104, in which he asks
for or sends copies of Cicero, Gellius, Servius, Macrobius, Boethius, Caesar,
Quintilian, and Sallust. His correspondence justifies what he says of
himself to Einhard (*Ep.* i.): "Amor litterarum ab ipso fere initio pueritiae
mihi est innatus, nec earum, ut nunc a plerisque vocantur, *snperstitiosa
otia* fastidio sunt. Et nisi intercessisset inopia praeceptorum, et longo situ
collapsa priorum studia paene interissent, largiente Domino, meae aviditati
satisfacere forsitan potuissem."

[32] "Non enim oportet fallaces commemorare fabulas, neque philosophorum
inimicam Deo sapientiam sequi, ne in iudicium aeternae mortis Domino
discernente cadamus. . . . Non ego Saturni fugam, non Iunonis iram,
non Iovis stupra, non Neptuni iniuriam, non Aeoli sceptra, non Aeneadum
bella, naufragia vel regna commemoro; taceo Cupidinis emissionem; non
exitia saeva Didonis, non Plutonis triste vestibulum, non Proserpinae stup-
rosum raptum, non Cerberi triforme caput; non revolvam Anchisae colloquia,
non Ithaci ingenia, non Sinonis fallacias; non ego Laocoontis consilia, non
Amphitrionidis robora, non Iani conflictus, fugas, vel obitum exitialem
proferam," etc. GREGOR. TURON. (6th cent.), *Lib. Miracul.*, 714.

[33] "Vae diebus nostris quia periit studium litterarum a nobis." *Praef.
Hist. Eccl. Franc.*

the Lives of Saints, who held, not unnaturally, that it was better to read the Life of a Saint than to read the doings of Æneas.[34] A few of these authors were men of some learning, but the great mass of them were uncultivated and ignorant. Coming from the lowest ranks of the monastic orders, they despised everything worldly, even in the region of intellect, and boasted cynically of their own ignorance.[35] 'The reader must not,' says one of them, 'be troubled by the heap of bar-

[34] "En meliora meo narrantur carmine gesta;
    non gladios nec tela refert pharetramque Camillae."
Milo, *Vit. S. Amandi, Act. S. Febr.*, i. 881 seq. Cp. Petrus, *Vit. S. Theobaldi, Act. S.* ix. 165; Anon. *Vit. S. Remacli, Act. S.*, ii. 469. etc. Vide Zappert, *op. cit.*, not. 62; *Prolog. Vitae Wirtonis*, ap. Pez, *Thes.*, i. 3. 339. Cp. Watten-bach, *Deutsch. Geschichtsq.* (6th ed.), ii. p. 250. It is a commonplace with the Christian poets to contrast the pagan glories of Homer and Vergil with the lowly but Christian nature of their own subject. Such is the purport of the Preface to Juvencus' versification of the Gospels, while Bede writes:

    "Bella Maro resonet, nos pacis dona canamus,
        munera nos Christi, bella Maro resonet."
                                            Hist. Angl., p. 295.

Cp. too Wipone (*Prolog. Vit. Chuonradi imp.*): "Satis inconsultum est Superbum Tarquinium, Tullum et Ancum, patrem Aeneam, ferocem Rutulum, et huiusmodi quoslibet et scribere et legere: nostros autem Carolos atque tres Ottones, imperatorem Heinricum secundum, Chuonradum imperatorem patrem gloriosissimi regis Heinrici tertii, et eundem Heinricum regem *in Christo triumphantem* omnino negligere."
[35] "Curiosum ceterum lectorem admoneo ut barbarismorum foedam congeriem in hoc opusculo floccipendat, et veritati in vulgari eloquio fidei aurem apponat, et quod hic inveniet simpliciter perlegat et acsi in sterquilinio margaritam exquirat." Wolfhardus (9th cent.), *Vit. S. Walpurgis, Act. Sanct.*, iv. 268. "Sed et si quis movetur rusticitate sermonis soloecismorumque inconcinnitatibus, quas minime vitare studui, audiat quia regnum Dei non est in sermone sed in virtute, neque apud homines bonos interesse utrum vina vase aureo an ligneo propinentur." *Miracul. S. Agili, Act. Sanct.* ii. 812. Cp. Anon., *Vit. S. Geraldi, Act Sanct.*, ix. 851. Many writers, feeling that their grammar is not above reproach, revolt strangely against the "tyranny of Donatus." Instances abound; it must suffice to quote the following curious passage from the *Indiculus luminosus* (No. xx.) of Alvarus Cordubensis (9th cent.): "Agant eructuosas quaestiones philosophi et Donatistae genis impuri, latratu canum, grunnitu porcorum, fauce rasa et dentibus stridentes, saliva spumosi grammatici ructent. Nos vero evangelici servi Christi discipuli rusticanorum sequipedi," etc. These words agree remarkably with a horrible biography of Donatus, inspired perhaps by this same repugnance for his grammar, which is found in a Paris MS. and has been several times published (most recently by Hagen, *Anecdota Helvetica*, p. 259). Yet Alvarus shows himself by his works to have been a diligent student of Vergil. Cp. Amador de los Rios, *Hist. crit. de la lit. Españ.*, ii. p. 102 seqq.

barisms he will find in this book, but must rather lend the ear
of faith to hear the truth in simple language; let him read with
simplicity what he finds here, and as it were search for a pearl
in a dungheap.' Others not only confess to solecisms and bar-
barisms, but actually glory in them. Even persons in high
places [36] had recourse at times to this low form of rhetoric, and,
when accused of their own ignorance or of that of the clergy,
answered disdainfully with such commonplaces as 'the kingdom
of God does not consist in words but in virtue,' or 'the gospel
was entrusted to ignorant fishermen, and not to skilled orators.' [37] Thus, when the bishops of Gaul in convocation at

---

[36] One of these is GREGORY THE GREAT. " Non metacismi collisionem
fugio, non barbarismi confusionem devito, situs motusque praepositionum,
casusque servare contemno ; quia indignum vehementer existimo ut verba
caelestis oraculi restringam sub regulis Donati." *Praef. Iobi,* t. i. p. 6.
With this affected knowledge of grammatical terms the great man endeavours to show that his want of will is not the result of want of power. That
he was thus indifferent to the laws of grammar is not however manifested
in his works. In fact, the supposed animosity of Gregory the Great towards
secular studies has been much exaggerated by various writers, who have
been unable to appreciate the true meaning and value of certain expressions
of his, and have not perceived that Gregory's attitude was merely that of a
hundred other famous medieval Churchmen. A misunderstanding of a
passage of JOHN OF SALISBURY (*Polycrat.*, ii., c. 26) has led to the belief that
Gregory burnt the Palatine library, while, as a matter of fact, all that is
referred to in that passage is the works on astrology and the like, which
had already been equally rudely treated by the Emperor Valens and others.
Nor is it easy to believe that there should have been any library at Rome
left for Gregory to burn, after the Goths and Vandals. These errors have
already been pointed out by more than one critic, and the whole question is
dispassionately discussed by GREGOROVIUS, *Gesch. d. St. R. im Mittelalt.*, ii.
p. 90 seqq., hence there was no need for TEUFFEL (*Gesch. d. röm. Lit.*,
p. 1026) to introduce them again. The thesis of LEBLANC, *Utrum Gregorius
Magnus litteras humaniores et ingenuas artes odio persecutus sit,* Paris, 1852,
is an apology inspired merely by Catholic sentiment.
[37] These commonplaces are summed up by the anonymous and really
modest author of the *Miracula S. Bavonis* (10th cent.) : " Suscipiant alii
copiosum variae excusationis suppellectilem, videlicet quod veritas, nativa
vivacitate contenta, non quaerat altrinsecam colorum adhibitionem; et quod
Christianae fidei rudimenta non ab oratoribus sed a piscatoribus et idiotis
sint promulgata ; et quod regnum Dei magis virtutis quam sermonis constet
efficacia, aliaque perplura in id orationis cadentia ; mihi facilis apologiae
patet occasio, scilicet cui nullius eruditionis favet exercitatio." *Act. S.*, ii.
389. Cp. SULP. SEV., Op. i. 2 ; FELIX, *Vit. S. Guthlaci, Act. S.*, iii. 59 ;
ANON., *Vit. S. Convoionis, Act. S.*, vi. 212 ; ANON., *Vit. S. Martini, Act. S.*,
i. 557 ; WARMANNUS, *Vit. S. Priminii, Act S.*, iv. 128 ; OTHLO, *Vit. S. Boni-
fatii,* ap. PERTZ, *Mon. Germ.*, ii. 358, etc. ; ZAPPERT, *op. cit.*, not. 62.

Rheims inveighed against the ignorance of the Roman clergy
the apostolic legate, Leo, abbot of S. Boniface, replied, in his
letter to the kings Hugo and Robert, that 'the vicars and disciples of Peter do not wish to have as their masters Plato,
Vergil, Terence, and the rest of the herd of philosophers, who
fly proudly in the air like birds, or dive like fishes into the
abysses of the sea, or wander like sheep over the earth; and
since the foundation of the world the elect of God have not
been orators or philosophers, but rude and illiterate men.' [38]
That all this was not meant seriously is clear enough, for both
accusers and accused show, if nothing else, a pride and a
haughtiness anything but apostolic. The fact which the
bishops at Rheims deplored could not be denied, and so the
ecclesiastical rhetoric had to find some way of justifying it.

It is further worth noticing that such declamations against
profane studies betray not unfrequently an evident jealousy of
those, probably among the writer's co-religionists, who were
honoured on account of their proficiency in these studies. But
at the same time it must not be forgotten that even the most
enlightened of ecclesiastical writers were under the influence of
a powerful and profound religious sentiment, which might at
any moment develop into enthusiasm and fanaticism. Continually preoccupied with thoughts of the highest good and the
future life, they were subject, like all minds concentrated on
religious matters, to the attacks of sudden scruples, which led
them to contradict themselves. Thus Augustine, who used at
one time to find an innocent pleasure in the daily perusal of
half a book of the Æneid, when forty-three years old deplores those days 'in which he let himself be moved by the
death of Dido, forgetting that all the time he was himself
dying to God.' [39] But these fervent words, uttered in a moment of enthusiasm, did not prevent him from rating Vergil
highly and from making considerable use of him in his *De*

---

[38] LEONIS *Epist.* ap PERTZ, *Mon. Germ.*, v. 687.   Cp. GREGOROVIUS, *Die
Stadt Rom im Mittelalter*, iii. 527.

[39] " Et plorare Didonem mortuam quia se occidit ob amorem, cum interea
me ipsum in his a te morientem, Deus vita mea, siccis oculis ferrem
miserrimus." AUGUSTIN., *Conf.*, lib. i., op. 1. 53.

Civitate Dei, which he finished in his seventy-second year. And
then again, at seventy-four, we find him repenting of having
used the word 'fortuna' so often, and of having called upon
the Muses as goddesses. Alcuin, who had in his youth, as
his anonymous biographer puts it, read 'the books of the
philosophers and the lies of Vergil,' and at the age of eleven
preferred Vergil to the Psalms,[40] when he became old, refused
to have anything more to do with such things, and forbade
his disciples to read the Æneid, saying, 'The divine poets are
enough, nor is there any need that you should be contaminated
by the sensuous eloquence of Vergil.'[41] But he did not succeed in imposing his views upon others, and had severely to
reprimand Sigulph for persisting, in spite of the prohibition, in
expounding Vergil in secret. Some[42] have refused to believe
the account of the anonymous biographer, owing to the frequent
Vergilian reminiscences occurring in Alcuin's letters; but from
what has been already said, it is clear that the one fact need not
necessarily exclude the other.[43] The same thing happened in
the case of Theodulph, who excuses himself in his verses for
having read Vergil, Ovid, Pompeius, and Donatus,[44] and in that
of many others. Nor was Alcuin the only one who found it

---

[40] *Vit. Beati Alcuini, Act. S.*, iv. 147; *Monumenta Alcuiniana*, ed. HAT-
TENBACH et DUEMMLER. Cp. MONNIER, *Alcuin et Charlemagne*, p. 9 seq.

[41] In the verses prefixed to his commentary on the Song of Solomon
Alcuin says:

" Haec rogo menti tuae iuvenis mandare memento,
carmina sunt nimium falsi haec meliora Maronis,
haec tibi vera canunt vitae praecepta perennis,
auribus ille tuis male frivola falsa sonabit."
Monumenta Alcuiniana, p. 714.

[42] *Vide* WRIGHT, *Biographia Britannica litteraria; Anglo-Saxon period*,
p. 42. For Alcuin's hatred of the classics, *vide* LORENZ, *Alcuin's Leben*
(Halle, 1829), pp. 267 and 277.

[43] There is in the library at Berne a MS. of Vergil supposed to have been
written by Alcuin, or at any rate copied from one so written. Cp. MÜLLER,
Analecta Bernensia, iii. pp. 23–25.

[44] " Et modo Pompeium, modo te, Donate, legebam,
et modo Vergilium, te modo, Naso loquax ;
in quorum dictis quanquam sint frivola multa,
plurima sub falso tegmine vera latent."
THEODULPH., *Carm.*, iv. 1.

necessary to check the ardour with which these profane studies were carried on.[45]

Scruples of this kind even broke the sleep of some. Herbert, bishop of Norwich, relates how one night Christ appeared to him in a dream, and said, 'I know that from your youth till now you have served in the sacerdotal office; but why do you keep with you the lies of Ovid and the inventions of Vergil? It is not fitting that the same mouth should preach Christ and recite Ovid.' Then the bishop remembered the blows of St. Jerome, and answered, 'I have sinned, I confess it, and that not only in reading the Gentile writers, but also in imitating them.'[46] The author of the Life of St. Odo relates how this saint, having conceived a wish to read Vergil, saw one night in a dream a vessel which was beautiful without but within was full of serpents, which at once twined themselves about him; and when he awoke, he perceived that the vessel was Vergil and the serpents were the pernicious doctrines hidden within him.[47] An anonymous writer of the 11th century relates further of a certain scholar, who in a moment of delirium cried out that

---

[45] Curious in this connection is the ironical admonition contained in some lines entitled *Versus S. Damasi Papae ad quendam fratrem corripiendum*, first published by AMADUZZI, *Anecd. Litt.*, ii. p. 387, and afterwards by RIESE in his *Antholog. Lat.*, No. 765:

> "Tityre, tu fido recubans sub tegmine Christi,
> divinos apices sacro modularis in ore,
> non falsas fabulas studio meditaris inani.
> illis nam capitur felicis gloria vitae,
> istis succedunt poenae sine fine perennes.
> unde cave frater vanis te subdere curis," etc.

[46] HERBERT. DE LOSINGA, *Epist.*, pp. 53–56; cp. pp. 63, 98.

[47] JOHANNES, *Vit. S. Odonis*, *Act. S. saec. V*, p. 154. Cp. BRUCKER, *Hist. Philos.*, iii. p. 651; DU MÉRIL, *Mélanges arch.*, p. 462. A similar story is told of St. Hugo, Abbot of Cluny, by VINCENT DE BEAUVAIS (*Spec. hist.*, 26, 4): "Alio tempore cum dormiret idem pater, vidit per somnium sub capite suo cubare serpentum multitudinem et ferarum, subitoque capitale excutiens et exquirens supposita, invenit librum Maronis forte ibi collocatum; mox, abiecto codice singulari, in pace requievit, cognovitque modum materiae libri visioni congruere, quem obscoenitatibus et gentilium ritibus plenum indignum erat cubiculo sancti substerni." Cp. LIEBRECHT (*Germania* of PFEIFFER, x. p. 418), who is however wrong in supposing that there is an allusion here to a work of Vergil's on necromancy, of which we shall have occasion to speak further on. A similar legend occurs in JACQUES DE VITRY (cp. LÉCOY DE LA MARCHE, *La chaire française au moyen-âge*, p. 439) and in PASSAVANTI, *Specchio di vera penitenza*, dist. 1, cap. 2.

he saw a troop of devils who assumed the forms of Æneas, Turnus and other characters in the Æneid.[48]

But while some were troubled with such scruples, others carried their admiration for Vergil to the point of fanaticism. Ruthbert used to express his opinion in the Chapter in lines of Vergil. The monk Probus showed such enthusiasm for Vergil and Cicero that his fellows used to accuse him in jest with wishing to put them among the saints.[49] Rigbod, bishop of Trèves, was said to know the Æneid better than the Gospels.[50] This enthusiasm, which was carried to the extremest degrees, appears also in legend. Thus a writer of the 11th century relates that 'Wilgard pursued the study of grammar at Ravenna with an excessive assiduity, surpassing even the Italians in his diligence. He had begun to pride himself like a fool on his learning, when one night there appeared to him three devils in the forms of Vergil, Horace, and Juvenal, who began with deceitful words to thank him for the study he had bestowed upon them and to promise him a share in their fame. Thus depraved by the evil arts of the devil, he began to teach many things contrary to the Holy Faith and to maintain that the words of the poets must in all things be believed. He was at length convicted of heresy and condemned by the Archbishop Peter. But in Italy,' adds the writer, 'many souls were found to be infected with these same views.'[51] Another legend[52] tells of two scholars who visited the tomb of Ovid, to endeavour to learn something from him. One of them asked which was the best line in his poems, and a voice from the grave answered:

'Virtus est licitis abstinuisse bonis.'

The other wished to know which was the worst, and was told:

---

[48] *Vit. S. Popponis, Act. S.*, viii. 594.
[49] Cp. LUPUS FERRAR., *Epist.*, 20.
[50] Vide OZANAM, *La civil. chrét. chez les Francs*, p. 485, 501, 546.
[51] GLABER, *Histor.*, ap. BOUQUET, *Réc. des hist.*, etc., x. p. 23. Cp. OZANAM, *Documents inédits*, p. 10; GIESEBRECHT, *De litterarum studiis apud Italos primis medii aevi saeculis*, p. 12 seq.
[52] In WRIGHT, *A selection of Latin stories from MSS. of the 13th and 14th centuries*, p. 43 seq. For further examples *vide* WATTENBACH, *Deutsch. Geschichtsq.* (6th edit.), i. 324 seqq.

'Omne iuvans statuit Iuppiter esse bonum.'

Wishing to do something for this great lost soul, the two scholars
began to pray for him, using the Pater Noster and the Ave;
but the voice, ignorant of the virtue of these prayers, cried
impatiently:

'Nolo Pater Noster: carpe, viator, iter.'

These scruples lasted long, though at the Renaissance Boccaccio[53] did not think it necessary to combat them; and, as every
one knows, they have made themselves very prominent again
of late years. But fortunately, in the middle ages as well as
now, victory has always been on the side of the ancient tradition.[54] In the 12th century, a party headed by an eccentric
individual, who, independently of religion, declared the historians and poets to be injurious and despised the masters of
rhetoric, grammar, and dialectic, found its most vigorous opponent in the learned and enlightened John of Salisbury.[55]
Jacques de Vitry and Arnaud de Humblières also discussed the
question, and had no hesitation in affirming the value of classical studies, if pursued with proper safeguards.[56] One of the
most noteworthy signs of the complete triumph of classicism
at the time of the Renaissance is the catalogue of the private
library of Pope Nicholas V., which contained absolutely nothing
but secular classical authors.[57]

The fulminations, therefore, and the intolerances of certain
individuals had but little weight as against that practical necessity which would not permit of sacred studies without a
certain amount of previous secular education. And so this last
continued to exist, though its existence was a sufficiently miserable one. The schools of grammar went on, even though they
might at certain moments, through want of teachers or similar

[53] *Comm. a Dante*, Inf. i. 72.

[54] Recently it has found defenders even among the Jesuits, and that too
in a department which touches Christianity far more nearly than that of
poetry. *Vide* the notable work of Father KLEUTGEN, *Die Philosophie der
Vorzeit vertheidigt*, Münster, 1860–1863.

[55] *Metalogicus*, i. cap. 3 seqq. Cp. *Hist. lit. de la France*, xiv. 13;
SCHAARSCHMIDT, *Johannes Saresberiensis*, p. 212 seqq.

[56] Cp. LÉCOY DE LA MARCHE, *La chaire française au moyen-âge*, p. 438 seq.

[57] Published by AMATI in the *Archivio storico*, iii., t. iii. 1 (1866), p. 207
seqq.

reasons, come to a standstill in certain localities; the monks continued to copy manuscripts. In the catalogues of the medieval monastic libraries, as far as they have been preserved, sacred and profane writers figure indiscriminately,[58] the latter sometimes under the title of 'libri scholares'; among these the commonest are Vergil, the two Donati, Priscian, and a multitude of other grammatical works.[59] The extraordinary number of Vergil MSS. which we possess is a further proof of the use made of him in the schools; for many of these MSS. are just scribbled down anyhow, evidently for school use, and are utterly valueless for purposes of text-criticism. Some Vergil MSS. bear a dedication to some saint, such as St. Martin, St. Stephen, or the patron saint of the church or monastery to which the manuscript was given.[60] Such manuscripts were sometimes very valuable owing to their miniatures and their binding, or as specimens of calligraphy, and hence they figure, strangely enough, among the Bibles, the Missals, the Breviaries, the candlesticks, the chalices, and the ostensories, in the catalogues of the treasures of convent, abbey, and church.

[58] In a catalogue made in the 11th century of the MSS. at the famous monastery of Pomposa, the writer foresees that some will object to the presence in the library of pagan authors, and answers their objections thus. After the usual commonplaces, "Sed . . . non ignoramus," he adds, "futurum fore quosdam superstitiosos et malevolos, qui ingerant procaci cura indagare cur idem venerabilis abbas Hieronymus voluit gentilium codices fabulasquae erroris exactosque tyrannos divinae inserere veritati paginaeque librorum sanctorum. Quibus respondemus," etc. Cp. BLUME, *Iter Italicum*, ii. p. 117.

[59] *Vide* the instances collected by ZAPPERT, *op. cit.*, not. 42, to which many more might be added.

[60] In a Vatican MS. of Vergil (No. 1570) of the 10th or 11th century, there is a statement by the monk who copied it, which, after saying that he did so to avoid idleness and to serve the common good, adds, "Quem (codicem) ego devoveo Domino et Sancto Petro perpetualiter permansurum per multa curricula temporum, propter exercitium degentium puerorum laudemque Domini et Apostolorum principis Petri." Another MS. bears a dedication to St. Stephen; *vide* PEZ, *Thesaur.*, i. *Dissert. isagog.*, xxv. In a MS. in the Berne library one reads, "Hunc Vergili codicem obtulit Berno, gregis B. Martini levita, devota mente Domino et eidem Beato Martino perpetuiter habendum; ea quidem ratione ut perlegat ipsum Albertus consobrinus ipsius et diebus vitae suae sub praetextu B. Martini habeat, et post suum obitum iterum reddat S. Martino." DE SINNER, *Catal. codd. MSS. bibl. Bern.*, i. 627.

CHAPTER VII

THE subject of the preceding chapter was a sufficiently wide one, and it may perhaps at first sight seem as if the limits of the special theme of this work had been exceeded. But it is easy to perceive how closely that subject and our theme have been connected by the name of Vergil, so constantly mentioned during the course of our enquiry. In fact, so constant has been the mention of this name when medieval writers were expressing either their hate or their love for the ancients, that it is clear that Vergil was to them the chief representative of the classical tradition. But while we have thus been able to obtain a general idea of the fame of Vergil during this long period and of the conditions under which it survived, it will now be necessary to study that fame and those conditions somewhat more closely and in greater detail.

When the ecclesiastical and civil authorities wished at any time during this period to promote the study of the Seven Arts, the principal reason which they adduced was, in addition to the example of the great lights of the Church, the necessity of these Arts for purposes of sacred study. We see this in the case of Cassiodorus, Bede, Alcuin and others, while a memorable instance of it is the circular sent by Charlemagne to the bishops and abbots in 787. The king here states that he has noticed in the official documents forwarded to him from various monasteries a rudeness of style which can only proceed from a neglect of the study of letters. 'Wherefore,' he adds, 'we have begun to fear lest, if the knowledge of how to write should be lost, the knowledge of how to interpret the Scriptures should be lost also. And while errors of speech are harmful, we all know that errors of thought are more harmful still. Therefore we exhort you not merely not to neglect the study of letters, but to pursue it with diligence, that you may be able to penetrate with ease and security into the mysteries of the Holy Scriptures. For, inasmuch as there are in the sacred books figures of speech, metaphors and other ornaments of style, it is clear that every reader will the more readily grasp the spiritual sense in proportion as he is the more in-structed in the art of letters."[1] This was unquestionably what saved classical literature from utter ruin. For while Charle-magne maintained that the Scriptures should form the basis of instruction,[2] at the same time he sought in every direction for teachers of grammar, and thus resuscitated, as is generally known, the secular part too of general education.[3] But the ecclesiastical writers did not look upon the ancient pagan authors merely as great masters of tropes and figures; when-ever they found in their works any passage calculated to con-firm the principles of the Faith, they promptly availed them-selves of it, even to the extent of straining the sense, or even of resorting to forgery. The supreme authority enjoyed by Vergil as a writer of extraordinary wisdom, as the first of the ancient poets, and at the same time the best in moral respects, made a great impression on many Christian theologians, who felt more at home with him than with the other pagan poets, and did not disdain to quote his words in support of the great principles of Christianity, or with a view of showing that of all the pagans he was the one who had approached nearest to that faith. The numerous Vergilian centos on Christian subjects show not only that Vergil occupied in literature the same position among the Christians as he had done among the pagans, but also that there was a keen desire among the

---

[1] *Encycl. de litteris colendis* ap. SIRMOND, *Conc. Gall.*, ii. p. 127.

[2] BALUZ., i. 237 (*Capitolar. of* 789).

[3] Cp. I. LAUNOII, *De scholis celebrioribus seu a Carolo Magno seu post eundem Carolum per occidentem instauratis liber*, publ. with the *Iter Ger-manicum* of MABILLON, Hamburg, 1717; and BAEHR, *De literarum studiis a Carolo Magno revocatis ac schola Palatina instaurata*, Heidelb., 1856. It is known that Vergil was held in high honour at this Palatine school, and the pseudonyms of several of the academicians were derived from him. Thus we hear of a Vergilius, a Damoetas, a Menalcas, etc.

H

former to assimilate the words of the poet they admired to the
ideas imposed upon them by the new faith, and to purify him
from what was in their eyes his only fault, the pagan spirit.[4]
He was the first of those Gentiles to whom could be applied
the words of the Gospel, 'They heard that Jesus passed by.'[5]
It seemed pitiable to think that this great man should have
been born in 'the time of the false and lying gods,' when his
works and the story of his life showed him to have possessed a
pure and noble soul and one eminently fitted to accept the
words of Christ. Hence he is the first of those whom Dante,
that faithful interpreter of the religious sentiment of the
middle ages, would not put among the damned, but placed
among those whose one involuntary fault was that they were
not baptized. This spirit of compassion is well expressed in
those lines, so often cited, which used to be sung at Mantua
(in the 15th century still) in the Mass of St. Paul, relating how
the apostle visited the poet's grave at Naples and burst into
tears, exclaiming, 'What would I not have made thee had I
found thee still alive, O greatest of the poets!'[6] But besides
this, it had become traditional from the time of the first apologists
to demonstrate in the pagan writers themselves a certain anti-
pagan spirit and a certain tendency, within limits, towards Christianity, which was the more pronounced the greater the writer
was. Hence it would even appear that at the time of Arnobius
a petition was made to the Senate by the pagans themselves for

---

[4] " Vergilium cecinisse loquar pia munera Christi." PROBA, *Praef. ad Cen-*
tonem. "Dignare Maronem mutatum in melius divino agnoscere versu,"
says a grammarian to the Emperor Honorius in dedicating to him a Christian cento. Vide *Anth. Lat.* No. 735 (ed. RIESE).

[5] MATTH. xx. 30.

[6] " Ad Maronis mausoleum
    Ductus fudit super eum
      Piae rorem lacrimae;
    Quem te, inquit, reddidissem,
      Si te vivum invenissem,
        Poetarum maxime."

BETTINELLI, *Risorg. d' Ital.*, ii. p. 18; DANIEL, *Thes. Hymnolog.*, v. 266. It
is not true, as some have asserted, that these lines are still sung in the Mass
of St. Paul at Mantua. A graceful anecdote of the life of St. Cadoc (5th
century) expresses this same feeling of compassion for the pagan Vergil.
Vide *Vita St. Cadoci* ap. KEES, *Lives of Cambro-British Saints* (Lond., 1855),
p. 8. Cp. LA VILLEMARQUÉ, *La Légende Celtique* (Paris, 1864), p. 202 seqq.

the destruction of certain books, such as Cicero's *De Natura Deorum*, which, by laying bare the weak side of paganism, rendered it liable to attack on the part of the Christians.[7] Out of this association of the great pagans with the ideas of the Christian faith grew those legends of the conversion of Seneca, Pliny and others, which were taken seriously by enlightened men and lasted a long time. I myself remember hearing as a boy at a school in Rome that the dying words of Cicero were, ' Causa causarum, miserere mei ! '

Augustine, Jerome, Lactantius, Minucius Felix and others among the Fathers and ecclesiastical writers are in the habit of quoting lines of Vergil in which they recognise principles of philosophy or theology which bear a certain resemblance to Christian doctrines, such as the unity, the spirituality, or the omnipotence of God.[8] But on this point we need not dwell, for such quotations are by no means confined to Vergil alone, but are common in the case of various other ancient writers.[9] More noteworthy is the fame achieved by the poet among the Christians owing to his Fourth Eclogue, by virtue of which he was elevated to the rank of those prophets who had foretold the coming of Christ.[10] The expectation of an immediate regeneration of the world in an era of happiness, justice, love and peace which inspires the whole of this Eclogue, the connection of this expectation with the birth of a child, and the ancient authority of the Sibyl on which the whole prophecy is based, could not fail to induce a Christian when reading it to think of

[7] ARNOB., *Adv. Gentes*, iii. 7. Cp. BERNHARDY, *Grundr. d. röm. Litt.*, p. 92.

[8] *Vide* the passages collected by PIPER in his *Virgilius als Theolog und Prophet des Heidenthums in der Kirche*, pub. in the *Evangelischer Kalender* for 1862, pp. 17-55.

[9] There exist ancient collections of passages both of Greek and Latin pagan writers having reference to Christianity. Thus a MS. in the Vienna library contains, " Veterum quorundam scriptorum Graecorum ethnicorum praedictiones et testimonia de Christo et Christiana religione, nempe Aristotelis, Sibyllae, Platonis, Thucydidis et Sophoclis." Cp. OEHLER, in the *Philologus*, xiii. 752; xv. 328.

[10] Cp. VERWORST, *Essai sur la 4e Eclogue de Virgile* (Paris, 1844); FREYMÜLLER, *Die Messianische Weissagung in Virgils vierter Ecloge.* Metten., 1852; (I have been unable to obtain either of these two works.) PIPER, *op. cit.*, pp. 50-80; CREUZENACH, *Die Aeneis, die vierte Ecloge und die Pharsalia im Mittelalter.* Frkf. a. Main, 1864, pp. 10-14

the birth of Christ and the regeneration of the world which his pure and gentle teaching promised. It would be out of place here to describe the causes and the vicissitudes of the Messianic prophecies among the Jews and in the Graeco-Roman world, and the curious lucubrations of the Sibyllists, whether Jewish or Christian. It will suffice to point out that to the complicated history of this subject belongs also the Christian interpretation of the Fourth Eclogue, which was already well in vogue among Christian writers of the 4th century. The most circumstantial interpretation of the kind appears in the address delivered by Constantine to an ecclesiastical assembly.[11] According to Eusebius, this discourse was given by the Emperor in Latin and then translated by the interpreters into Greek.[12] At any rate the translation of the Eclogue into Greek verse,[13] which accompanies the address as at present existing, shows evident traces of the work of the Sibyllists; in many places indeed it alters the sense in an arbitrary manner with a view to bringing it into accordance with the Christian interpretation.[14] The emperor examines the various parts of the poem, and finds in them a detailed prophecy of the coming of Christ, pointing out that the Virgin who returns is Mary, the child sent from the sky is Jesus, the serpent which shall cease to be is the Tempter, the balsam which will grow everywhere is the race of Christians, pure from sin (amomum = $\check{\alpha}\mu\omega\mu\omega\nu$), and so on. He maintains that the poet wrote with the full knowledge that he was foretelling Christ, but expressed himself darkly and introduced the mention of heathen deities to avoid affronting the pagans and provoking the anger of the authorities. But not all of the ecclesiastical writers who adduced this argument in favour of the Faith believed that Vergil understood the true significance of the Sibylline prophecy; the general view was that he did

[11] CONSTANTINI M. *Oratio ad Sanct. coet.*, c. 19-21. This address of Constantine's forms the subject of a very lengthy work by ROSSIGNOL (*Virgile et Constantin le grand*, Paris, 1845), which is not yet complete. At the end of the part which has appeared the author expresses his intention of proving that the address is not by Constantine, but by Eusebius.

[12] EUSEB., *Vit. Constantini*, iv. 32.

[13] This translation has often been published separately, most recently by HEYNE, *Excurs. I. ad Bucol.*, and ROSSIGNOL, *op. cit.*, p. 96 seqq.

[14] Cp. ROSSIGNOL, *op. cit.*, p. 181 seqq.

not know what it really meant, but wished to apply it to the birth of the son of Pollio or some other illustrious patron. In the same century as Constantine, Lactantius also interpreted this Eclogue in a Christian sense, but, being a follower of the doctrine of the millennium, he referred it, not to the coming of Christ, but to His promised return.[15] Augustine too admits the existence among the Gentiles of prophets who foretold the coming of Christ, and quotes the Fourth Eclogue, with special reference to the lines 13, 14, which he interprets of the remission of sins through the merits of the Saviour.[16] Jerome, on the other hand, throws ridicule on those who maintained that Vergil was a Christian without Christ, and treats the whole subject as childish and worthy to rank with the centos and similar puerilities.[17] It is worth remembering however that a certain theological doctrine, supported by various passages of Scripture, induced men to look for prophets of Christ among the Gentiles, and that, though there were Sibylline oracles, such as the famous acrostic, which clearly foretold His coming, unbelievers used to maintain that these latter were apocryphal, and the accusation was hard to rebut, for it was true; hence this Fourth Eclogue, based on a Sibylline prophecy the authenticity of which could not be disputed, was looked upon as evidence of the greatest possible value, and as such it was regarded by Augustine no less than Constantine. Hence too even those who did not believe that Vergil understood the true meaning of his words yet looked upon him as an unconscious witness to the Faith. And so, as the story

---

[15] LACTANT., *Div. Instit.*, i., vii. c. 24.

[16] " Nam omnino non est cui alteri praeter dominum Christum dicat genus humanum :

> Te duce, si qua manent sceleris vestigia nostri,
> irrita perpetua solvent formidine terras.

Quod ex Cumaeo, id est ex Sibyllino carmine se fassus est transtulisse Vergilius; quoniam fortassis etiam illa vates aliquid de unico Salvatore in spiritu audierat quod necesse habuit confiteri." AUGUSTIN., *Epist.* 137 *ad Volusian.*, c. 12, Opp. ed Bened., t. ii. p. 809 seq. Cp. *Epist.* 258, c. 5, Opp. t. ii. p. 670 ; *De Civ. Dei*, x. 28.

[17] " Quasi non legerimus Homerocentonas et Vergiliocentonas; ac non sic etiam Maronem sine Christo possimus dicere Christianum qui scripserit : Iam redit et Virgo etc. Puerilia sunt haec et circulatorum ludo similia, docere quod ignores." HIERONYM., *Epist.* 53 *ad Paulin.*, c. 7, Opp. t. i. p. 273.

spread among the people,[18] Vergil became the companion of
the Sibyl and figured in sacred pictures and mysteries right
down to the Renaissance in company with David, Isaiah and
the other prophets; and this idea, assuming legendary forms
and becoming connected with the popular conception of Vergil
as magician, was developed in various remarkable ways, of
which we shall have occasion to speak further on.   The supposed irresistible nature of this argument was the origin of the
ecclesiastical legends of the conversions brought about by this
Fourth Eclogue, such as that of Statius,[19] rendered famous by
Dante, or that of the three pagans Secundian, Marcellian, and
Verian, who, being suddenly enlightened by the lines ' Ultima
Cumaei,' etc., became, instead of persecutors, martyrs for
Christ.[20]   Another legend tells how Donatus, bishop of Fiesole
(9th century), just before his death appeared at a meeting of
his friars and made a confession of his faith before them, using
the words of the poet 'Iam nova progenies,' etc., after which
he immediately died.[21]   Pope Innocent III. quoted these lines
as a confirmation of the Faith in a Christmas sermon,[22] and
they were understood in a Christian sense by numerous men of
the highest importance in the middle ages, such as Dante,[23]
Abelard,[24] and Marsilius Ficinus,[25] not to mention others.
And Vergil, as prophet of Christ, is a common enough object in
ecclesiastical art.   In the stalls of the cathedral of Zamora
in Spain (12th century) among numerous figures from the
Old Testament appears also that of the poet, with the word

---

[18] Cp. FULGENT., *De contin. Verg.*, p. 761; *Scholl. Bern.* (ed. HAGEN), p. 775
seqq.   CHRISTIAN DRUTHMAR (9th century), remarks on Matth. xx. 30, "Audierunt quia Iesus transiret : Iudaei audierunt per prophetas, gentes quoque non per omnia ignoraverunt, sed sophistae eorum similiter denuntia-
verunt; unde illud Maronis, Iam nova progenies," etc.   *Bibl. Patr. max.*
(Ludg.) xv. 147.   *Vide* also AGNELLUS, *Lib. Pontific.*; *Vit. Grat.*, c. 2, in
MURATOR., *Script. rer. It.*, t. ii. pars i. p. 180 ; COSM. PRAG., *Chronic.* in
PERTZ, *Mon. Germ.*, t. ix. p. 36.
[19] Cp. RUTH in the *Heidelburger Jahrbb.*, 1849, p. 905 seqq.
[20] VINCENT. BELLOVAC., *Spec. hist.*, xi. c. 50 ; *Act. Sanct. Aug.*, t. ii. p. 407.
[21] OZANAM, *Documents inédits*, p. 55.
[22] *Serm. II. in fest. Nativit. Dom.*, Opp. p. 80.
[23] *Purgator.*, xxii. 67 seqq.
[24] *Introd. ad Theolog.*, lib. i. c. 21; *Epist.* 7 *ad Helois.*, p. 112.
[25] *De Christ. relig.*, c. 24.

' progenies' taken from the famous line; [26] similarly Vergil figures in the pictures of Vasari in a church at Rimini, while in the frescoes of Raphael in S. Maria della Pace at Rome the words 'Iam nova progenies' serve to mark the Cumaean Sibyl. After the Renaissance scholars argued both for and against the Christian interpretation of the Eclogue; [27] and even at the present day there are still some to be found who take this ancient farce seriously.[28]

[26] *Vide* STREET, *Some Account of Gothic architecture in Spain.* (Lond., 1869), p. 95.

[27] *Vide* the notices collected by PIPER, *op. cit.*, p. 75 seqq.

[28] As for instance VERWORST in the dissertation mentioned above. *Vide* also SCHMITT, *Rédemption du genre humain annoncée par les traditions de tous les peuples* (French transl. by Henrion). Paris, 1827, p. 122 seqq.

CHAPTER VIII

BUT apart from those merits which recommended the classical
writers, and especially Vergil, to the Christians, there were
also other means of diminishing that repugnance which the
adherents of the new faith could not fail to feel for the immo-
ralities and the absurdities of the ancient mythology. Such
repugnance was of course natural enough, for even before the
times of Christianity it had been felt by the pagan philosophers. Some of these, such as Xenophanes and Heraclitus,
had ruthlessly condemned this mythology and the poets who
had served to spread it; but both mythology and poets were
too closely bound up with the life of the people to allow such
general condemnations to seem more than individual eccentricities. Others however, more tolerant and better able to appreciate the greatness of these products of the national genius,
sought for some means whereby to reconcile the legends and
the poets with the results of philosophical speculation, and
found it in allegory, a method of interpretation which in such
cases suggests itself spontaneously.[1] But while many availed
themselves of this, it was the Stoics who reduced it to the
form of an exact science, owing to the importance in their
system of the religious idea and its close connection there
with practical morality, which compelled them to take into
consideration the existing popular beliefs and to define their
actual significance.[2] The use however made of allegory was
naturally far more extensive when the ancient religion, instead
of being subjected to the dispassionate criticism of a body of

[1] Cp. GRÄFENHAN, *Gesch. d. class. Phil. im Alterth.*, i. p. 211 seqq.
[2] Cp. ZELLER, *Die Philosophie der Griechen*, iii. 1, p. 290 seq., 300 seqq.

calm thinkers, was brought face to face with a new religion in
sympathy with the spirit of the age and supported by the
fanaticism of adherents who were determined that it should
triumph throughout the world. In this long and obstinate
struggle, allegory was employed as a weapon of defence by
either side indifferently, being equally familiar to both. The
pagans took refuge in allegory because it was only natural that
their religion, already vanquished by the development of speculation, should seek by this means to ally itself to the latter.
The religious idea sank into mysticism and opened the door to
the religions of the East, which were positive and dogmatic and
more full of abstractions than the old naturalistic mythology,
thus in reality preparing the way for the triumph of Christianity. A philosophy which, if not exactly critical, was at
any rate charitable, threw its mantle over the too striking
nudity of the ancient gods and heroes, who were still kept
continually before the eyes of all by means of the general
system of education. The mantle of this philosophy could not
long defend the religion which was doomed to fall, but it did
not a little service in protecting the ancient literature in the
midst of Christian society, both while the latter was still strug-
gling for supremacy and when it was enjoying the fruits of
victory. And it was the more efficacious in that allegory and
symbolism were traditional with Christianity, in itself a mystical religion and long accustomed to seek in the enigmas of the
prophets and the parables of the Jews and of Christ Himself
a deep significance hidden beneath the obvious meaning of the
words. Nay more, the Bible itself, different as it might be in
origin and nature from the works of the classical poets, needed
no less in many points to be reconciled with the results of experience and reflection. The Alexandrian Jews had already made
a free use of allegory, to reconcile, as they said (they meant the
converse), philosophy with the Bible, while the use made of
allegory in Christian exegesis at every period is well known.[3]
Nor must one think any the worse, as one is easily tempted to

---

[3] CELSUS already, who in his polemic made use of allegory to explain the
pagan mythology, accuses the Jews and Christians of their abuse of this
method of argument, iv. 50, 51.

do, of either religion for its recourse to this expedient, as if it were the result of cold calculation or a deliberate 'pious fraud.' It is the instinctive and honest resource of men whose minds are dominated at one and the same time by two contradictory influences of equal power, from neither of which are they able to free themselves. Allegory is a species of dialectical hallucination, which owes its origin to those earnest convictions which are natural to a vigorous and impulsive temperament.

Allegory was applied by the ancients to mythology generally and to the language of the poets particularly, as these latter formed, in the absence of a religious code, the only written authority for the common faith. The only ancient poets however who have been submitted to a complete allegorical interpretation are Homer and Vergil, though the reasons for such treatment are very different in the two cases. For those who were anxious to find documentary authority for the common beliefs, no other writer could have the weight of Homer, whether on account of his prehistoric antiquity or the marvellous power of his genius or the character and national importance of his poems. Hesiod could only occupy a second place. In a religion which was the child of nature, and hence the sister of poetry, the first and the greatest of the poets was inevitably also the highest concrete authority to whom religious beliefs could be referred, and therefore Herodotus is right enough in the one sense, though mistaken in another, when he thinks of Homer as the father of Greek religion and morals. Hence the numerous allegorical interpretations of Homer which, though they began in the philosophical schools, were by no means confined to them.[4] But Vergil, being an essentially modern poet as compared with Homer, was far from having any such authority, for which age was above all things indispensable; and while this modernity continued, no one could pretend to regard as an allegory a poem which was universally known to be nothing of the kind. An authority so generally known and respected as Vergil was naturally looked upon by different persons from different points of view; the gram-

----

[4] Cp. BERNHARDY, *Grundr. d. Griesch. Lit.*, ii. 1, p. 201 seq.

marian, Seneca tells us, regarded him as a grammarian, the philosopher as a philosopher;[5] but these latter did not, we may be sure, search for allegories in him, or Seneca, the enemy of all allegorical exposition, would not have failed to notice it; they confined themselves to commenting on such ideas of the poet as were of a genuinely philosophical nature. But when the character of the intellectual atmosphere became changed, and the fame of Vergil grew in consequence to cloudy and irrational proportions, he too was compelled to submit to allegorical interpretation. But this only took place because, for reasons we have already noticed, allegory was the fashion, and the spirit of the times, eager for fantastic speculations, could not bring itself to believe that a man of such exceptional wisdom as it considered Vergil to have been should not have hidden beneath the simple legend of Aeneas something more profound and important. Vergil was not interpreted allegorically in defence of paganism or as a weapon to be used against the Christians,— such an idea would never have occurred to a pagan,—but solely from a philosophical point of view and by reason of the exaggerated conception of him as a philosopher which was prevalent at the time, this method of interpretation being then in vogue not merely among philosophers but also among grammarians. Hence it was here applied with equal conviction and without polemic by pagans and Christians alike, and the hidden meanings which both discovered in Vergil were of a purely ethical and philosophical character, dealing generally with the vicissitudes of human life in its aspirations towards perfection.

The traces that remain in pagan literature of this method of interpretation are very few, and we have already noticed them in speaking of Donatus, Servius, and Macrobius. The most important specimen of it that we possess is the work of a Christian writer, Fabius Planciades Fulgentius, of uncertain date,[6]

---

[5] *Epist.* 108, 24–29.

[6] The only certain datum is that Fulgentius was later than Marcianus Capella, whom he quotes ; Capella, according to the researches of his most recent editor, EYSSENHARDT (Lips., 1866), completed by L. MÜLLER (*Neue Jahrbb. f. Phil. u. Paedag.*, 1867, p. 791 seq.), must have written before 439. No other date has as yet been fixed. ZINK (*Der Mytholog Fulgenz*, Wurz-

but unquestionably not later than the 6th century. His *De Continentia Vergiliana*, in which he describes *what is contained*, or rather, *what is hidden* in the work of Vergil, is one of the most curious productions of the Latin middle ages, while at the same time it is the most characteristic monument we possess of Vergil's celebrity during the times of Christian barbarism.[7] In his preface the author hastens to state that he will confine himself to the contents of the Aeneid, because the Bucolics and Georgics contain truths of such profundity that it is impossible fully to fathom them. He abandons this part of the work therefore [8] as requiring more learning than he possesses, for the First Georgic deals entirely with astrology, the Second with physiognomy and medicine, the Third with augury, and the Fourth with music, the end of it, futher, being apotelesmatic, while the contents of the Bucolics are equally remarkable. The good man is by rights a philosopher, but with the words 'leaving the somewhat rancid bitterness of the hellebore of Chrysippus, I will dally awhile with the Muses', he launches out into five hexameters, in which he calls on the Muses to assist him in the great work he is about to undertake—'not

burg, 1867) has put the composition of the *Mythologicon* in the years 480–484. REIFFERSCHEID, making use of the work *De aetatibus mundi et hominis* (pub. by himself in the *Rhein Mus.*, xxiii., 1868, p. 133 seq.), which is very possibly by this same Fulgentius, recurs to an old view which refers the *Mythologicon* to the time of King Huneric (528). While L. MÜLLER (*N. Jahrbb. f. Phil. u. Paedag.*, 1867, p. 796) fixes his date as 456, JUNGMANN (*Quaestiones Fulgentianae*, in the *Acta Societatis philologae Lipsiensis*, ed. PRID. RITSCHELIUS, Lipsiae, 1871, t. i. p. 49 seqq.) believes him to have been born in 480, and to have written the *Mythologicon* in 523 or 524. For the earlier opinions, *vide* LERSCH in his edition of the *De abstrusis sermonibus* (Bonn, 1844), p. 1 seqq.

[7] The *De Continentia* has been published in the *Mythographi Latini* of VAN STAVEREN (Ludg. Bat. 1742). A more modern edition does not exist. For this work of Fulgentius *vide* GASQUY, *De Fabio Planciade Fulgentio Vergilii interprete* in *Berl. Stud. f. cl. Philol.*, vi. (1887).

[8] " Bucolicam Georgicamque omisimus in quibus tam mysticae sunt interstinctae rationes," etc., p. 738. " . . . Ergo doctrinam mediocritatem temporis excedentem omisimus, ne dum quis laudem quaerit nominis fragmen reperiat capitis," p. 39. In the Padua library is a MS. bearing the title, " *Fulgentius super Bucolica et Georgica Vergili* " (cp. LERSCH. p. 96). I have examined this MS., and at once came to the conclusion that it has no right to the name of Fulgentius. *Vide* my article in the *Revue critique*, Aug., 1869, p. 136.

one Muse, that will not be enough, but all the Muses.' [9]
Thanks to the Muses, he is brought face to face with the
spectre of Vergil himself. The appearance of this venerable
shade is imposing and severe, as that of a poet deep in meditation. With a humility which contrasts strangely with the
presumption which pervades this book no less than the rest of
his works Fulgentius calls on the poet to descend from his
pinnacle and to reveal to him the mysteries of his poetry,—
not indeed the more profound, but such as would be compre-
hensible to a poor barbarian; [10] this Vergil consents to do,
though he speaks to his disciple with a sternness which is
positively terrifying,[11] and addresses him throughout as ' ho-
muncule.' He declares that he intended in the twelve books
of the Aeneid to display an image of human life. On proceeding to explain this in detail, he dwells for a long time on the
first line, in which the subject of the poem is revealed, and
arrives only after several lengthy digressions at the hidden
meaning of the three words ' arma, virum, primus,' which
that line contains. ' There are three stages,' he says, ' in the
life of man; the first is *getting*, the second, *keeping what one
has got*, the third, *adorning what one keeps*. These three stages
you will find in my line. *Arma, i.e.* valour, refers to what is
physical; *Virum, i.e.* wisdom, to what is intellectual; *Primus,
i.e.* prince, to what is ornamental and artistic. Thus you have
the three in their proper order of *getting, keeping* and *adorning*.
And thus I have symbolised by a story the normal conditions
of human life; firstly nature, then wisdom, then happiness.'
Having thus concluded his preamble (antilogium), the poet
poceeds to expound the contents of the individual books. He

[9] " Maius opus moveo, nec enim mihi sufficit una,
  currite Pierides," etc.
    p. 740.

[10] " Serva istaec, quaeso, tuis Romanis quibus haec nosse laudabile com-
petit et impune succedit. Nobis vero erit maximum si vel extremas tuas
contigerit per stringere fimbrias." p. 742.

[11] " Quatenus, inquit, tibi discendis non adipata crassedo ingenii, quam
temporis formido periculo reluctat, de nostro torrentis ingenii impetu urnu-
lam praelibabo quae tibi crapulae plenitudine nauseam movere non possit.
Ergo vacuas fac sedes tuarum aurium, quo mea commigrare possint elo-
quia." p. 742.

shows scant respect for his listener here, and tells him openly
that before he begins he wishes to assure himself that he is not
speaking to 'Arcadian ears,' and, as if doubting whether Fulgentius had ever even read the Aeneid, he asks him to give a
short summary of the contents of the first book,[12] which, without taking offence in the least, Fulgentius proceeds to do.
Thus re-assured, Vergil commences his exposition of the first
and following books. We need not do more than touch upon
the most important points here, as to follow the interpretation
in detail would be as wearisome for the reader as for me.

Vergil declares that the shipwreck denotes the birth of man,
who enters with pain and sorrow upon the storms of life; Juno,
who brings about the storm, is the Goddess of Birth, and Aeolus, who does her bidding, is Perdition;[13] Achates signifies the
troubles of infancy;[14] the song of Iopas is the song of the
nurses. The facts of the Second and Third Books all refer to
childhood, with its love of the marvellous, to which refers also
the Cyclops at the end of Book III., who with his one eye
symbolises ignorance and quarrelsomeness, conquered by Ulysses, who is good sense. The period of childhood ends with the
death and burial of Anchises, which denotes the termination of
parental authority. Being thereupon free, the man (Book IV.)
devotes himself to the pleasures of the chase and love; over-
whelmed by his passions (the storm) he enters upon an illicit
liaison (Dido), till, admonished by the intellect (Mercury), he
returns to his senses; the flame of abandoned love sinks into
ashes (the death of Dido). Recovering himself (Book V.) he
remembers his father's example and devotes himself to noble
exercises (the funeral games of Anchises), and the triumphant
intellect destroys the means of wandering (burning of the
ships). Thus strengthened (Book VI.) he returns to wisdom
(the temple of Apollo), not without first being freed from hal-

[12] " Sed ut sciam me non Arcadicis expromptare fabulam auribus, primi
nostri continentiam libri narra." p. 747.
[13] " Aeolus enim Graece quasi Aionolus, id est saeculi interitus dicitur."
p. 748.
[14] " Achates enim Graece quasi ἀχῶν ἔθος, id est tristitiae consuetudo."
p. 750.

lucinations (Palinurus) [15] and having laid aside vain-glory
(Misenus).[16] Fortified with the golden branch, which is the
wisdom which opens the way to hidden truths, he undertakes
philosophical investigations (the descent into Hades). First
of all there appear to him the sorrows of human life; then
after passing, guided by Time (Charon),[17] the troubled waters
of youth (Acheron),[18] he hears the quarrels and strifes that
divide men (the barking Cerberus), which are stilled by the
honey of wisdom. Thus he proceeds to a knowledge of the
future life and a discernment of good and evil, and reflects on
the passions (Dido) and the affections (Anchises) of his youth.
Thus made wise (Book VII.), he frees himself from tutelage
(the burial of the nurse Caieta) and reaches his sought-for
Ausonia, that is, increase [19] of good, chooses as his mate labour
(Lavinia) [20] and allies himself (Book VIII.) with the good
man (Euander); from him he learns of the triumph of virtue
over crime (Hercules and Cacus). Making himself a breast-
plate of his fiery spirit (the arms of Vulcan), he dashes into
the struggle (Books IX., X., XI., XII.) against anger (Turnus),[21] who, led first by drunkenness (Metiscus) and then by
obstinacy (Iuturna = Diuturna), is assisted by impiety (Me-
zentius) and folly (Messapus).[22] Finally Wisdom triumphs
over all.

This brief summary of the work has doubtless seemed sufficiently strange; but no summary can give a really full appreciation of the strangeness of the original. It is naturally vain
to seek for a basis of fact in any allegorical speculation; yet
such speculations are capable, as is clear from various examples
both ancient and modern, of considerable refinement and of attaining a degree of speciousness which renders them attractive

[15] " Palinurus enim quasi Planonorus, id est errabunda visio." p. 753.
[16] " Misio enim Graece obruo dicitur; αἶνος vero laus vocatur." p. 753.
[17] " Caron vero quasi Cronon, id est tempus." p. 756.
[18] " Acheron enim Graece sine tempore dicitur." p. 756.
[19] " Ausonia enim ἀπὸ τοῦ αὐξάνειν dicitur, id est cremento." p. 763.
[20] " et uxorem petit Laviniam, id est laborum viam." p. 763.
[21] " Turnus enim Graece dicitur quasi θοῦρος νοῦς, furibundus sensus." p.
764.
[22] " Messapus, quasi μισῶν ἔπος." p. 765.

and even plausible to a certain class of minds. But the process of Fulgentius is so violent and incoherent, it disregards
every law of common sense in such a patent and well-nigh
brutal manner, that it is hard to conceive how any sane man
can seriously have undertaken such a work, and harder still to
believe that other sane men should have accepted it as an
object for serious consideration. So far, indeed, is the author
from being bound by any rule, that he does not even respect
the machinery of his own imagination, and makes Vergil speak
at times as if he were Fulgentius.[23]   And to his carelessness is
added ignorance in proportion, as when he makes Vergil quote
from Petronius and even from Tiberianus! The book has not
even any proper conclusion, for the author quite forgets that, as
Vergil has been speaking hitherto, he himself ought to appear
and say farewell to the reader.[24]   The proportions of the work
are no less remarkable, for while several pages are spent over
the first line, in other places whole books are passed over in a
few sentences. The only part treated with care is the Sixth
Book, which, as we have already seen when speaking of Servius,
was generally considered as the one most replete with hidden
meanings. Of the language it is needless to speak; it is the
abortive offspring of a barbarism as deficient in taste as in
knowledge, which strives none the less to make a show of
learning by torturing its constructions out of all shape and
dragging in strange words hunted up from every quarter and
then often used in a wrong sense; [25] while of the etymologies
it may safely be said that they are without parallel in any other
author.

Worthy of notice however is Fulgentius' type of Vergil.
The poet appears as a proud and gloomy mystic, the direct

[23] Thus Vergil says in one place, " Tricerberi autem fabulam iam superius
exposuimus " (p. 756). This means that Fulgentius has discussed the question in his *Mythologicon*, i. 5.

[24] ZINK (*op. cit.*, p. 27) believes that the end of the work is lost, or that
its author left it unfinished. JUNGMANN (*op. cit.*, p. 73) points out rightly
that neither of these suppositions is necessary. And indeed it is clear from
the eighth book onwards that the writer is growing tired of his work and so
hastens to finish it in this abrupt manner.

[25] An accurate examination of the Latin of Fulgentius has been undertaken for the first time by ZINK, *op. cit.*, pp. 37–62.

opposite of that frank, genial and modest spirit which we recognise in all his poetry, which all his biographers have described and which Dante has so faithfully reproduced. But such to these barbarians was the natural type of the wise man; he too, like wisdom itself, was surrounded with darkness; for all learning was going back, as it were, to its original state, and hiding itself beneath a veil of poetical mysticism. Among these people, as we see not only in Fulgentius but already in Macrobius (especially in the Dream of Scipio), in Marcianus Capella, in Boethius and others, learning, having lost its rational basis and abandoned those logical exigencies which compel a certain calmness of consideration, appears always accompanied and regulated by a kind of poetical enthusiasm more or less pronounced; it appears as it were from without, and, attaching itself to minds ill-prepared to receive it, drives them in their astonishment to commit various extravagances. Hence that curious mixture of prose and verse which is so noticeable in Capella, Boethius, and also Fulgentius. Such enthusiasm, which to a cultured mind accustomed to scientific criticism can seem little else than a disease, has clearly no kinship with that poetic spark which a happy inspiration of the truth may engender. To it the man of learning must always appear as a mystic being, superhuman and divinely inspired; and such in fact is the Vergil of Fulgentius. And on careful consideration it becomes clear that this type is really nothing but an ulterior development of that which we have already found in Macrobius and other pagan writers of the decadence. Fulgentius has followed this same direction, merely adding of his own whatever the rudeness and barbarity of his age could suggest; nor is he in any way an unfair representative of that age, for though it may have produced men who were greatly his superiors, yet in the matter of secular learning at any rate he would appear to furnish an average specimen both of its taste and of the extent of its knowledge. Anyhow, the fundamental principle of his interpretation is not his own, for, as we have seen, the idea that Vergil contained an allegory of the vicissitudes of human life is of much earlier origin. Still less can his other and larger work, his *Mythologicon*, be regarded as at all original in conception. How much of it is his own, how much actually taken from other sources, is not easy to ascertain, nor is this the place for such an enquiry. But what is necessary for us to observe is the fact that, though Fulgentius was clearly a fervent Christian, yet neither is the *Mythologicon* nor the *De Continentia* written, as one might naturally think, with any apologetic object or with any view of reconciling the classical tradition with Christianity. There is not a word which alludes to the struggle between Christianity and that tradition; the fundamental principle of the work is purely philosophical, and its object is to reconcile the ancient mythology with the truths, not of Christianity, but of philosophy. It is evident that the *De Continentia* is directly connected with the *Mythologicon*, to which it is subsequent in date, and to which it forms as it were an appendix.[26] It was only natural, if one takes into consideration the position of Vergil in contemporary culture, that a man who had employed allegory to interpret philosophically the general body of the ancient mythology should have been led by the same motives to undertake a similar interpretation of the famous story of Aeneas, which seemed to form a small cycle of legends distinct from the rest, which were mostly of Greek origin. And as the basis of the first work was the general idea of the profundity of ancient thought, so that of the second was the particular conception of the extraordinary wisdom of Vergil; and hence, while in the *Mythologicon* Urania and Philosophy are introduced as speaking, in the *De Continentia* it is Vergil himself. Fulgentius therefore appears as a pupil of the Stoics and the philosophers and grammarians of the decadence, and his quality of Christian, though appearing incidentally, contributes nothing to the nature of the work. And yet it is easy to recognise throughout the *De Continentia* the privileges which Vergil, among pagan writers, enjoyed at the hands of the Christians The idea is dominant that the miraculous power of his genius has enabled him to approach very close to the doctrines of

---

[26] The close connection between the *De Continentia* and the *Mythologicon*, as well as the priority of the latter, is clear from the words already quoted: "'Tricerberi autem fabulam iam superius exposuimus." p. 756.

Christianity, chiefly in ethical and philosophical matters, and
hence, when he makes a statement which that religion could
not possibly admit, Fulgentius cannot refrain from expressing
his astonishment that he should have fallen into such an error
when he was able to write, ' Iam redit et Virgo,' etc.[27]   Vergil answers, ' If among all these Stoic truths I had not admitted any Epicurean errors, I should not have been a pagan.
For the knowledge of the whole truth is given to none but to
you, for whom there shone the Sun of Truth.   But we have
not come here to speak of this.'   We find the same impatient
assent in two other passages where Fulgentius quotes words of
Scripture or Christian doctrine which agree with what the
poet has said; in two others Vergil does not answer at all.[28]
And in fact these interruptions are foreign to the aim of the
work, and as such the author himself regards them; yet they
were naturally suggested by the ideal type of Vergil current
among contemporary Christians.   Thus, without any violent
transitions, by a perfectly natural and continuous process, the
Vergil of Fulgentius, that is, the Vergil of Christian barbarism,
arrived at awakening sympathies which bridged over in a remarkable manner the gulf that separated the pagan writer
from the adherents of Christianity.   In fact this type, dominated already by the medieval idea that human reason, in spite
of all causes of error, had succeeded in attaining before the
birth of Christ to principles which were, as far as was possible
without miracle or revelation, homogeneous with Christianity,
is nothing else than a rough prototype of the ideal of Dante.

Fulgentius is anything but a scholar or a thinker, but he
makes great efforts to appear both, not hesitating even to in-
vent the names of authors and works that never existed,[29] to
give a more striking character to his learning—an old trick
already employed with success in more enlightened times,[30]

---

[27] " O vatum Latiaris autenta! itane tuum ingenium clarissimum tam
stultae defensionis fuscare debuisti caligine? qui dudum in Bucolicis mys-
tice persecutus dixeras: Iam redit et Virgo, etc." p. 761.
[28] pp. 743, 746, 753, 755.
[29] Cp. LERSCH, op. cit., p. 19 seqq.; ZINK, op. cit., p. 75 seqq.
[30] " . . . unde improbissimo cuique pleraque fingendi licentia est,

and sufficiently common during the decadence and the middle
ages.[31] He may be looked upon as the caricature of all who
went before or followed after him in the field of allegorical interpretation, among whom were some men of unquestionable
ability. And yet he was too much a child of his time not to be
welcomed by his contemporaries. The middle ages, with that
naiveté which distinguished them, thought to have found in
him a man of much learning and profound intellect, and set
much store on his works. The frequent use made of these is
clear from the numerous MSS. of them which have been preserved. Siegbert of Gembloux (11th century) is well-nigh
terrified by such acumen,[32] and is full of admiration for the
man who has been able ' to seek out gold in the mud of Vergil.' [33] The scholiast of Germanicus is interpolated from the
Mythologicon, and there are some similar interpolations in the
Fables of Hyginus, while the second and third Vatican Mythographer, and to some extent also the first, have all made use of
Fulgentius—facts of no small importance when it is remembered that Hyginus and some of the Vatican mythographers
(principally the first) were certainly used as school-books.[34]

This system of allegorical interpretation flourished well
enough under the reign of scholasticism. Bernard of Chartres
wrote a commentary to the first six books of the Aeneid, in
which he maintained that Vergil in these books 'described as
a philosopher the nature of human life . . . and all that
the human soul does or suffers during its temporary abode in
the body.' [35] The same view was held by one of the most

adeo ut de libris totis et auctoribus, ut succurrit, mentiantur tuto, quia in-
veniri qui nunquam fuere non possunt." QUINTIL., i. 8. 21.
    [31] The Ravenna cosmographer is famous for this. Cp. for other instances
HERSCHER, *Ueber die Glaubwürdigkeit der neuen Geschichte des Ptolemäus
Chennus,* in the *N. Jahrb. f. Phil. u. Paedag.,* 1853, Supplem. i. p. 269 seqq. ;
ZELLER, *Vorträge und Abhandlungen geschichtlichen Inhalts,* p. 297 seqq.
    [32] "Hic certe omnis lector expavescere potest acumen ingenii eius qui
totam fabularum seriem secundum philosophiam expositarum transtulerit
vel ad rerum ordinem vel ad humanae vitae moralitatem." *De script eccle-
siast.,* c. 28.
    [33] "Qui totum opus Vergili ad physicam rationem referens, in lutea quo-
dammodo massa auri metallum quaesivit." ID. *ibid.*
    [34] Cp. ZINK, *op. cit.,* p. 13 seqq.; BERNHARDY, *Grundr. d. röm. Litt.,* p.
868.
    [35] "Scribit enim (Vergilius) in quantum est philosophus humanae vitae

important men of the 12th century, John of Salisbury. He observes that Vergil had 'under the guise of legend expressed the truths of all philosophy,' [36] and traces the successive steps in the development of the human soul through the first six books of the Aeneid. Aeneas, according to him, is nothing else than the human soul, *i.e.* the inhabitant of the body, 'for *Ennaios* signifies inhabitant.' Following out this idea, he finds expressed in the First Book, under the image of the shipwreck, the troubles of childhood; in the Second, the development and frank curiosity of boyhood, which learns much both true and false; in the Third, the errors of youth; in the Fourth, illicit love; in the Fifth, developed manhood verging towards old age; in the Sixth, old age itself with its failing powers and imminent decrepitude.[37] And just as formerly Donatus had thought to recognise in the order in which Vergil's three works were composed a connection with the three great phases in the history of human development, so in the middle ages there were not wanting those who saw in it those three modes of life which were generally distinguished in the philosophy of that time, the contemplative life in the Bucolics, the sensual in the Georgics, and the active in the Aeneid.[38] There was at that time neither book, fact nor story which was not considered capable of a moral or philosophical interpretation, and it was a common doctrine that every work might be understood in four ways, the literal, the allegorical, the moral and the anagogic. One class of ideas dominated the minds of men, and therefore

naturam. Modus vero agendi talis est; sub integumento describit quid agat vel quid patiatur humanus spiritus in humano corpore temporaliter positus, etc." *Vide* Cousin, *Ouvr. inéd. d'Abélard*, p. 283 seqq. Cp. De-mimuid, *De Bernardo Carnotensi grammatico professore et Vergili interprete.* Paris, 1873.

[36] " Procedat poeta Mantuanus, qui sub imagine fabularum totius philo-sophiae exprimit veritatem." *Polycrat.*, vi. c. 22: " Vergilium in libro (Aeneidos) in quo totius philosophiae rimatur arcana." *Ib.*, ii. c. 15.

[37] *Polycrat.*, viii. c. 24. Cp. Schaarschmidt, *Joh. Saresberiensis*, p. 97 seq.

[38] " Et sciendum est quod Vergilius considerans trinam vitam, scilicet, contemplativam, voluptuosam et activam, opera tria conscripsit, scilicet, Bucolicam per quam vitam contemplativam demonstrat, et Georgicam per quam vita voluptuosa intelligitur, . . . et Aeneidos per quam datur in-telligi vita activa." *Comm. in Verg. Aen.*, Cod. Bibl. S. Marc. Venet. cl. xiii. (Lat.) n. 61, col. 3. The same words are cited from a Vienna 14th century MS. by Zappert, *op. cit.*, p. 16.

they sought in everything for hidden traces of that which interested them most. And so allegory, after having served
firstly as a means of reconciliation between the philosophy and
the half poetical, half religious mythology of antiquity, and
secondly as the defensive weapon of the two conflicting faiths,
remained as an integral part of the theological armour, adapting itself as well to the exigencies of Christian dialectic as it
had ever done to those of Greek philosophy. And hence it
took no small part in the formation of that fragile but not un-
serviceable bridge built by scholasticism between the monastic
theology and lay speculation, and at a time when these two
tendencies had so profound an influence it attained to a sovereignty over thought which, though it would not now any
longer be tolerable, was then accepted without demur, so that
not only was it admitted in exegesis and given weight in ratio-
cination, but it even became the natural vehicle of expression,
as we see in such a work as the *Divina Commedia*, the most
important product of this epoch.   Dante indeed makes explicit
reference to this doctrine in the *Convito*, where he actually
applies it to Vergil, speaking of 'the allegory of the ages of
man contained in the Aeneid,' and giving at the same time an
allegorical interpretation of the poem differing little from that
of John of Salisbury.[39]   Nor did the Renaissance entirely
abandon this method of Vergilian exegesis, which even found
supporters in such celebrated scholars as L. B. Alberti and
Christopher Landin.[40]

[39] *Convito*, iv. 24, 26.
[40] CHRIST. LANDINI *Disput. Camaldul.*, lib. iii., iv. (*in P. Verg. Maronis al-
legorias*).

CHAPTER IX

THOUGH there may be in the books intended for school use a few instances of legends interpreted after the allegorical methods of the *Mythologicon* of Fulgentius, there is no reason to suppose that any allegorical interpretation of the Aeneid such as we find in the *De Continentia* was in vogue in those elementary schools of grammar to which the use of Vergil as a text-book properly belonged. This search for hidden meanings in the work of the great poet, this scrutiny of the depths of that marvellous wisdom which was attributed to him, was the business, as we have already seen in Macrobius and as is equally apparent from Fulgentius, of those who considered themselves far above the level of the class-room.[1] The master who wished to expound such an allegory would have had to give a special course of lectures on Vergil, commenting on the whole Æneid continuously, and any such proceeding would have been very far removed from that practical instruction in Latin grammar which was the chief object of Vergilian exposition in the mediæval schools. It would be very interesting to know something of these schools, their masters, and their methods of teaching, and to study the use that they made of Vergil and the idea that their scholars had of him. But throughout the middle ages a thick cloud covers this important branch of intellectual activity, which was then more than ever modest and retiring. And yet we may form some idea of the

---

[1] No one would take seriously the words addressed by Fulgentius to Vergil, "tantum illa quaerimus levia quae mensualibus stipendiis grammatici distrahunt puerilibus auscultationibus" (p. 742). This is evidently nothing but an hyperbole to express the unfathomable depths of the wisdom of Vergil and the author's modesty in his presence.

nature and amount of the instruction there given by examining
the numerous books intended for the use of schools that have
survived, consisting mainly of grammars and commentaries on
Vergil and other authors.

The number of grammatical works written after the fall of
the empire during the middle ages is very considerable. Some
are the work of men who had gained their reputations in some
other sphere of activity, at that time regarded as more important; others are written by professed grammarians who limited
their productions to this branch of secular study. The value of
both the one class and the other is absolutely nil; the latter
are naturally the more humble, though several of them too
enjoyed wide popularity. This sort of composition had so little
pretension to originality, its production had become so entirely
a matter of mere routine and business, and the place which it
occupied in the intellectual life of the time was so low, that it
seems quite to have lost its personal character. As is the case
with most of those articles which supply the ordinary needs of
every-day life, the name of the producer was a matter of indifference. Hence the grammarians of whom we know most
are men who gained distinction in the sphere of ecclesiastical
matters and only afterwards felt called upon to descend to the
more humble field of grammar. Of the others in many cases
the very name is unknown, and very seldom indeed does our
knowledge extend beyond this; not unfrequently the absence
alike of external evidence and any special internal characteristics renders it impossible even to give them a date. Many
grammatical works, which were evidently not published anonymously, have reached us without their authors' names, having
lost them in the process of being copied for use in the schools.
These works were generally looked upon as common property;
they were added to, modified or abridged to suit individual
taste, and without the least regard for the author's intentions;
and this system of usage lasted on to the very end of the middle
ages. Alexandre de Villedieu (13th century) begs the reader,
in the versified prologue to his glossary, to make additions
or alterations with moderation, and only in the margin, and
deplores the extreme liberty with which this practice was

indulged.[2] As for any philological object, properly speaking, in these works, there was none; their sole purpose was practical. This was so with Cassiodorus, Isidorus and the English and Irish scholars, distinguished for that period, such as Bede, Aldhelm and Clement; it was so with the authors of the numerous grammatical works called forth by Charlemagne's revival of these studies; Smaragdus, Alcuin, and Rabanus Maurus wrote on grammar with no further object than that of supplying the needs of the schools that their prince had called into being. Nor is the character of the grammatical works of the 12th to the 15th centuries, after the theoretical part of grammar had come under the influence of scholasticism, a philological one. Such had been the universal decay of secular learning that the mere ability to do anything in any of its branches was sufficient to win a name; as to how it was done, no one troubled to ask; criticism did not concern itself with such things. When one considers the poverty of ideas and the absence of knowledge apparent in the most distinguished grammars of the time, it is simply appalling to think of the depths of ignorance and barbarism which must have been reached by the mass of those schoolmasters who could only boast of average attainments.

The general intellectual level indeed was so low that the masters found no less difficulty in propounding what they wished to teach than the pupils had in comprehending it. It was this general embarrassment and preoccupation which necessitated that perpetual curtailment and abridgment of the original materials of education—'*pro fratrum mediocritate*,' as is modestly stated in the title of a compendium of Donatus wrongly attributed to Augustine.[3] The following characteristic words which occur prefaced to an adaptation of Donatus which bears the name of Bede[4] may serve as a further instance among

---

[2] " Si quaecunque velit lector addat seriei
non poterit libri certus sic textus haberi."

Vide THUROT, *op. cit.*, p. 32.

[3] *Ars S. Augustini pro fratrum mediocritate breviata*, ap. KEIL, *Grammat. Lat.*, vol. v. p. 494.

[4] *Cunabula grammaticae artis a Beda restituta*, in BEDAE Opp. i. p. 2. This treatise does not occur in the list of Bede's works; cp. WRIGHT, *Biogr. Brit. lit.*; *Anglo-Saxon period*, p. 271 seqq. The introduction from which

many others. 'The work of Donatus has been so spoilt and interpolated by some, every one freely adding what pleased him
or what he had found in other authors, to the extent of insert-
ing new declensions, conjugations, and the like, that only in
the most ancient manuscripts is the text of the author to be
found as he left it. But in order that no one may believe that
we have done the same, we wish here to explain our intentions
in publishing the present volume. All those who are better
acquainted with grammar than we, know that the above-
mentioned grammarian compiled his *Ars prior* for the use of
children, arranging it in question and answer, to suit what he
considered to be the requirements of his own time. But inasmuch as we and others like us are so blunted and dull of intellect that we do not for the most part know either how to
question or how to answer, we have compiled this little book
in conformity with the smallness of our understanding; and
though it may not be necessary for minds better exercised and
more acute, it will yet, we think, be useful for the more simple
and less ready-witted.'

When Charlemagne revived the ancient classical studies by
means of the Latin, which was still the universal literary
language, there were already beginning to appear signs of the
vulgar new Latin, as had happened before in the case of the
vernacular of the non-Latin or non-Latinised Celtic and
Teutonic races, while at the same time the decay of learning and
the great national wars had served to bring about a feeling of
nationality among peoples hitherto united under the common
name of Romans. All this rendered the task of the grammarians still more difficult, for they had to reclaim a class of minds
which had already become too far estranged from Latin; and as
most of them were themselves of non-Latin origin and thoroughly
conscious of their own proper nationality, they felt and often
confessed their own barbarism in handling the ancient Latin
materials,[5] and the difficulties they encountered in consequence.

---

we quote is also published without the author's name in KEIL, *Gramm. Lat.*,
vol. v. p. 325.

    [5] " . . . et irrisione dignum arbitrabar . . . Romanae urbanitatis
facundia disertissimis rhetoribus, me paene de extremis Germaniae gentibus

Hence in the wilderness of their various works there prevails
an ignorance and a confusion of ideas calculated to startle even
those best prepared for it. Their knowledge of Latin is always
vague and rude, and greatly disturbed by the influence of the
' *Usus*,' [6] *i.e.* that barbarous form of low Latin which was commonly employed by ecclesiastical writers [7]—a fact which, in
the case of men who were unable to form any judgment from
a purely secular point of view, naturally led to its gaining a
certain degree of grammatical authority. In the absence of any
solid or coherent criterion, everything was unstable, and though
everything rested on authority of some kind, any appreciation
of the comparative values of various authorities was out of the
question.[8] It is all one walk in the dark, without light, direction or guide, clutching eagerly at the words of any book that
might be found, without regard for contradictions, incoherences,
or incompatibilities.

ignobili stirpe procreatum . . . inter talium dissona decreta virorum
ex persona iudicis disputando iudicare." ANON., *Gram.* (cod. saec. xi.) ap.
KEIL, *De quibusdam grammaticis,* etc., p. 26 ; EKKEHART IV., in his *De lege
dictamen ornandi* writes :—

> " Teutonicos mores caveas, nova nullaque ponas ;
>   Donati puras semper memorare figuras."

Vide HAUPT, *Zeitschrift f. deutsch. Alterth.,* N.F., ii. p. 33 : " proprietas
autem eiusdem verbi Latinis magis patet quam barbaris." *ibid.,* p. 52.
Noteworthy is the delicacy displayed by GOZBERT (*De Mirac. S. Galli,* in
PERTZ, *Mon. Germ.,* ii. p. 22) ; " Siquidem nomina eorum qui scribendorum
testes sunt vel fuerunt, propter sui barbariem, ne Latini sermonis inficiant
honorem, praetermittimus." ELMOLDUS NIGELLUS however has no such
scruples and writes cheerfully (*Carm.,* i. 373 seqq.) :

> " Parte sua princeps Wilhelm tentoria figit
>   Heripreth, Lihutard, Bigoque, sive Bero,
>   Santio, Libulfus, Hilthibreth, atque Hisimbard
>   sive alii plures quos recitare mora est."

[6] " Duplex est grammatica ; nam est quaedam quae dicitur analogica et
alia quae dicitur magis usualis." *Vide* THUROT, *op. cit.,* p. 211.

[7] The grammatical peculiarities of the Christians had been commented on
by their pagan adversaries from the earliest times. ARNOBIUS defends them
in his accustomed style. *Adv. gent.,* i. 59.

[8] NOTKER BALBULUS (9th century), one of the many monks of this name
at the famous medieval monastery of S. Gallen, speaking of Alcuin's *Dia-
logus de grammatica,* says, " Alcuinus talem grammaticam condidit ut
Donatus, Nicomachus, Dositheus et noster Priscianus in eius compara-
tione nihil esse videantur." Cp. MAITRE, *Les écoles épiscopales et monas-
tiques de l'occident,* etc. (Paris, 1866), p. 220.

To attempt to follow the processes of these minds would be
at once a wasted endeavour and an outrage on common sense.
But any one who has penetrated sufficiently into this Babel to
form an idea of the nature and degree of the confusion there
reigning, will feel no astonishment at seeing arise from its
midst that enigmatical monstrosity, at once comic and tragic,
the Vergil of Toulouse,[9] who, considered in respect of his surroundings and origin, gives the impression of little else than
a grim joke. He is perhaps the only medieval grammarian
who deserves to be called original, but his originality takes
a strange turn. Ideas, facts, names of authors, words and rules
are all alike invented by his fertile brain, which ends by distinguishing twelve different kinds of Latin, and putting Vergil
in the time of the Flood. This strange writer, with his claims
to great grammatical authority and his adoption of the name
of Vergilius Maro to enforce those claims, reminds one irresistibly in the squalor of his time (6th–7th century) of those
hideous and putrid fungi which are generated in the rotting
leaves of autumn. Before the phantasies of his fatuous imagination one stands perplexed and bewildered, unable to understand what it all means ; no one has ever yet succeeded in explaining what this Vergil really was. To call him a charlatan
is not enough, when one considers the extent of his work and
its complete isolation from all the ordinary ideas and traditions;
the nature and tone of his writings will not allow one to regard
them as a satire ; it is easy to say he was a madman, but we do
not find in all the middle ages a single voice raised against
him ; his works, preserved in numerous MSS., are quoted
seriously by Bede, Clement of Ireland, and other distinguished
grammarians, and the strange and mysterious Latin of the

---

[9] Some of this author's works were published for the first time by MAI,
Class. auctores, v. p. 1 seqq., another by HAGEN, *Anecdota Helvetica*, p. 189
seqq. A complete edition of his remains was made by I. HUEMER, *Virgilii
Mar. Gramm. opera*, Lips. (Teubner), 1886, which may be amplified and corrected by reference to TH. STANGL, *Virgiliana*, Munich, 1871 (and *Wochenschr.
f. class. Philol.*, 1890, No. 29–31), and M. HERTZ, *De Verg. Mar. gramm.
epitomar. cod. Ambiensi*, Vratisl. (Ind. schol.) 1888. On the subject of this
Vergil, *vide*, besides MAI and HAGEN (cp. *Jahrbb. f. Philol.*, 1869, p. 732
seq.), OSANN, *Beitr. z. gr. u. röm. Literaturgesch*, ii. p. 131 seqq. ; QUICHERAT,

anonymous *Hisperica famina*,[10] the *Polyptychum* of Atto of Vercelli,[11] and various other medieval productions,[12] so suggestive of this Vergil, seems to prove beyond doubt that he was looked up to as the authoritative head of a school. Facts such as these give us an idea of the state of the classical studies in the middle ages. Nowhere is there a sign of reason or intelligence applied to them; they are as it were in a trance; while learning, having lost those logical fibres and that theoretical framework which keeps it alive, lies dead and rotting in men's minds, intermixed and permeated with hallucinations and phantasies of every kind.

The chief authorities on grammar remain Donatus and Priscian, and next to them Charisius, Diomedes, and the other compilers of the decadence ; but about these are accumulated a number of new authorities, who are in reality, however, merely derived from them, with nothing added but what is wrong ; the number of the editors and abridgers of Donatus especially is something astonishing. The confusion in many of these grammatical compilations arrives at last to such a pitch that the hallucinations of Vergil Grammaticus are cited as of equal weight with the views of Donatus and Priscian.[13] No less complete is the chaos which reigns in the choice of grammatical examples and in the exegesis of the authors used in the schools. Vergil still keeps his place as the chief authority in grammatical works and as the author most commonly used at school; his ancient fame as a master of style remains ;[14] but to the other ancient authors who used to be read after him have been added

---

Fragm. inéd. de littérat. lat. in the *Bibl. de l'école des chartes*, ii. p. 130 seqq.; WUTTKE, *Ueber die Aechtheit des Aethicus*, p. 49 ; OZANAM, *La civil. chrét. chez les Francs*, p. 420 seqq. ; HAASE, *De medii aevi studiis philologicis*, p. 8 ; KEIL, *De quibusd. gramm. inf. aet.*, p. 5 ; ERNAULT, *De Verg. Mar. gramm. Tolos.*, Paris, 1886.

[10] Publ. by MAI, *Class. auctores*, vol. v. p. 479 seqq., and recently by STOWASSER, Vienna, 1886.

[11] Publ. by MAI, *Scriptt. vett. nova collectio*, vol. vi. p. 43 seqq.

[12] *Vide* STOWASSER, *Stolones Latini*, Vienna, 1889.

[13] For a good instance *vide* the anonymous grammar publ. from a 10th century MS. by HAGEN, *Anecdota Helvetica*, p. 62 seqq.

[14] "Latinae quoque scientiae valde potatus rivulis, etiam proprietate partium aliquis eo melius nequaquam usus est post Vergilium," FARIC., *Vit. Aldhelmi*, fol. 140.

a motley crew of writers of the vilest sort, who none the less are
regarded as good models and as great authorities on matters of
language.   Prudentius, Juvencus, Sedulius, Avitus, Prosperus,
Paulinus and Lactantius figure side by side with Vergil, Lucan,
Statius and Juvenal.   And this custom began in early times, as
is clear from Isidor's famous work *De dubiis Nominibus* of
which the oldest MSS. go back to the 9th century,[15] where the
author most often quoted next to Vergil is Prudentius, then
Juvencus, and then Varro; then Paulinus, Lactantius, Sidonius,
etc.   Sometimes one MS. contains glosses on two authors of the
most diverse nature, as for instance Vergil and Sedulius.[16]
Among the Christian poets, the most fashionable and the most
read in the schools was Prudentius, 'prudentissimus Prudentius,' as Notker Balbulus calls him; [17] and in reality this writer,
himself an imitator of Vergil, is the most noteworthy of his
class.   His popularity is attested by the numerous MSS. of
him which remain, one of these even going back to the 6th
century.   Nor was it only the Christian poets and fathers who
were quoted in the grammars and read in the schools by the
side of classical authors; even the text of the Vulgate was
looked up to by these pious barbarians as an authority on
language, for it was 'inspired by the Holy Ghost, which knows
more than Donatus.' [18]

The ignorance that prevails is wonderful.   Smaragdus is not
alone in taking the '*Eunuchus Comoedia*' and the '*Orestes
tragoedia*' cited by Donatus as the names of two authors.   Of
Greek they do not even know enough to explain the commonest
terms, and their etymologies are occasionally amazing.   '*Poema*,'

[15] *Gramm. Lat.*, ed. KEIL, vol. v. p. 567 seqq.
[16] *Gloss. in Vergilium et Sedulium*, 9th century MS. in the library at
Laon.   Vide *Catal. génér. des MSS. des bibl. pub. des départ.*, vol. i. p. 250.
[17] " Si vero etiam metra requisieris, non sunt tibi necessariae gentilium
fabulae, sed habes in Christianitate prudentissimum Prudentium de Mundi
Exordio, de Martyribus, de Laudibus Dei, de Patribus novi et veteris Testa-
menti dulcissime modulantem." NOTKER BALBULUS, *De interpretibus div.*
scriptt., c. 7, ap. PEZ, *Thes. anecd.*, i. p. 9.
[18] " In his omnibus Donatum non sequimur, quia fortiorem in Divinis:
Scripturis auctoritatem tenemus." SMARAGD. ap. THUROT, *op. cit.*, p. 81 ;:
" de scala et scopa et quadriga Donatum et eos qui semper illa dixerunt:
pluralia non sequimur, quia singularia ea ab Spiritu Sancto cognovimus:
dictata." ID., *ibid.*

according to Remigius of Auxerre (9th century), means '*positio*';
'*emblema*' means '*habundantia.*'[19] Of the futile questions and
the imaginary difficulties raised it is needless to speak, any more
than of the grotesque and arbitrary solutions suggested. In
the quotations, which are generally at second-hand, the name
of one author is constantly substituted for that of another.[20]
How far their minds could wander is shown by the instances,
not unfrequent, in which they endeavoured to give the rules of
grammar a mystical interpretation, as when an anonymous
writer of the 9th century sees in the three persons of the verb
a reference to the three persons of the Trinity,[21] or when
Smaragdus recognises in the eight parts of speech a Biblical
number.[22] Nor was the study of orthography any more to the
point, in spite of the numerous treatises upon it, as is clear
from the many MSS. which show in their spelling evident
traces of the influence of the barbarous pronunciation of the
districts in which they were copied.[23]

The manner in which the various authors were interpreted
may be gathered from such commentaries of the period

[19] *Vide* THUROT (*op. cit.*, p. 65 seqq.). This whole work is valuable for
the study of the medieval grammarians.

[20] There are some instances in KEIL, *De quibusd. gramm. Lat. inf. aet.*,
p. 16.

[21] "Personae autem verbis accidunt tres. Quod credo divinitus esse
inspiratum, ut quod in Trinitatis fide credimus in eloquio inesse videatur."
ANON. MS. saec. ix. ap. THUROT, *op. cit.*, p. 65.

[22] "Multi plures, multi vero pauciores partes esse dixerunt. Modo autem
octo universalis tenet ecclesia; quod divinitus inspiratum esse non dubito.
Quia enim per notitiam Latinitatis maxime ad cognitionem electi veniunt
Trinitatis, et ea duce regia gradientes itinera festinant ad superam tendunt-
que beatitudinis patriam, necesse fuit ut tali oraculo Latinitatis compleretur
oratio. Octavus etenim numerus frequenter in divinis Scripturis sacratus
invenitur." SMARAGD. ap. THUROT, *op. cit.*, p. 65.

[23] Cp. SCHUCHARDT, *Der Vokalismus des Vulgärlateins*, i. p. 17 seqq. et
passim. Noteworthy for their preservation of the barbarous local pronunciation are several MSS., earlier than Charlemagne, in the library of the
Seminary at Autun, which may be compared in this respect with the inscriptions at the same place; cp. *Catal. génér. des MSS. des bibl. pub. des
départ.*, i. 20, 21, 23, 24, 27, 107.
Even in matters of orthography the religious idea comes to the front.
Thus HILDEMAR (9th century), in his commentary on the *Regula S. Bene-
dicti*, observes, "Sunt multi qui distinguunt voluntatem per n attinere ad
Deum, et voluntatem per m ad hominem, voluptatem vero per p ad
diabolum." *Vide* SCHUCHARDT, *op. cit.*, p. 4 seq.

as have survived. In these, even more than in the grammatical works, the chaotic, the ignorant and the arbitrary
nature of their writers stands confessed, while the mania
for interpolation and abridgment is at least equally pronounced. Among commentators Servius held the same place
as Donatus among grammarians and Vergil among poets;
but the mass of notes which has come down to us from the
middle ages under Servius' name, though doubtless mainly due
to him, is yet in great part the product of the medieval copyists, who down to the very end of the 15th century did not
cease to corrupt and interpolate his text. In addition however to the works of Servius, of Donatus, of Asper, and other
ancient commentators, which have all reached us from the
middle ages in an equally mutilated condition, there are in
the libraries, for the most part still unpublished, innumerable
commentaries of medieval origin (generally anonymous) on
Vergil and other writers. The patience of modern scholars
has not hitherto proved equal to the wearisome task of searching in this enormous mass of glosses for those which may be
of ancient origin. And yet the recent publication by Hagen
of the Berne Scholia of the 9th century [24] has shown that not
a little of interest may still be found in this quarter. But in
all that part of these works which is of actual medieval origin,
what is most noticeable is the ignorance, which at times
reaches such proportions that one feels constrained to pause
and ask oneself whether the writer is not really an escaped
lunatic. What is one to think of a commentator who explains
'*efficiam*' by '*effigiem, imaginem*,' [25] or who, in the passage '*Quo
te, Moeri, pedes,*' would read '*Quot Emori pedes,*' recognising in
this an allusion to the four feet of a swift kind of Arab horse
called *Emoris* ? [26] Or of one who begins his commentary on the

---

[24] *Scholia Bernensia ad Vergili Georgica atque Bucolica*, ed. HERM. HAGEN.
Lips., Teubner, 1867. *Vide* p. 696 seqq.

[25] *Ad Ecl.*, iii. 51 : "*Efficiam*, pro effigiem, imaginem." *Scholl. Bern.*,
p. 769.

[26] *Ad Ecl.*, ix. 1 : " alii dicunt : *Emoris*, equus velocissimus Saracenorum,
quem interdum accipi potest. Quot Emori pedes : id est, utinam quattuor ut
me in urbem cito veherent ad accusandum Cladium (*sic*)." *Scholl. Bern.*,
p. 827.

Bucolics with these words, in strangely barbarous Latin: 'At this time, when Julius Cæsar was at the head of the Empire, Brutus Cassius was ruler of the twelve parishes of Tuscany, and there arose war between Cæsar and Brutus Cassius, with whom Vergil was living, and Brutus was conquered by Julius; and after this Julius was killed by a blow with a stool'?[27] In another MS. commentary at Venice the three kinds of style, of which Servius also speaks at the beginning of his work, are thus distinguished: 'The sublime style is that which treats of exalted personages, such as kings, princes or barons; this is the style of the Aeneid. The middle style treats of middle-class people; this is the style of the Georgics. The low style is that which treats of the lower classes, and hence this is the style of the Bucolics.'[28] There is a commentator on Juvenal who simply swarms with absurdities, set down with a frank-ness and confidence well-nigh incredible.[29] 'Elenchus,' accord-ing to him, means 'the title of a book,' and comes from the Greek 'elcos' (sic) which means 'sun,' 'for as the sun illu-minates the world, so does the title throw light on the whole book.' 'Provincia' is an adverb, and means 'swiftly,' and has besides the senses of 'foresight, district, and country.' 'Circenses' is derived from 'circum enses,' 'because on one side ran the river, on the other they set up swords, and between the two was the race-course.'[30] One would never come to an end if one wished to record all the follies of this commentator and

[27] Vide *Catal. génér. des MSS. des bibl. pub. des départ.*, vol. i. p. 428, and cp. HAASE, *De medii aevi studiis philologicis*, p. 7. The passage has been published by BOUCHERIE, *Fragment d'un commentaire sur Virgile*, Mont-pellier (Soc. pour l'étude des langues romanes), 1875.

[28] "Stilus in hoc opere est sublimis . . . nam est monendum quod triplex est stilus, scilicet sublimis, mediocris et infimus. Sublimis stilus est qui tractat de sublimibus sive maximis personis, ut regibus, principibus et baronis, et hic stilus in Aeneide servatur. Mediocris stilus est qui de medio-cribus personis tractat, et servatur in libro Georgicorum. Infimus stilus vel humilis . . . est qui tractat de infimis personis, et quia pastores sunt inferiores personae hic stilus in libro Bucolicorum servatur." *Comment. in Verg. Aen.*, cod. saec. xv., bibl. S. Marci, Lat., class. xiii. n. 61, col. 6.

[29] *Vide* C. F. HERMANN, *De scholiorum ad Iuvenalem genere deteriore*, Götting., 1849, p. 4 seqq.

[30] This etymology of "circenses" occurs already in ISIDOR., *Orig.*, xviii. 27, and in CASSIODORUS, *Variar.*, iv. 51.

K

numberless others like him.[31]   But it is worth observing that
many of these errors seem due to the fact that in many
countries Latin had fallen into disuse and been replaced by the
vernacular. At any rate, in a country where Latin or any
kindred language was spoken, it would have been impossible
for any one to explain, as the doubtless German [32] scholiast
of Juvenal has done, ' umbella ' as ' a sort of green stone,' or
' asparagus ' as ' a fish, or a kind of mushroom.'

The difficulty felt by the non-Latin nations in understanding Latin is further proved by the fact that, from the 7th
century onwards, the vernacular German or Celtic is substituted for Latin in the glosses. The custom of explaining in
Latin notes the meaning of the author read was no longer
found convenient, and hence those numerous Celtic, Anglo-
Saxon, and Old High German glosses, so highly prized for
philological reasons, which accompany the MSS. of the Bible,
many ecclesiastical writers, and poets both Pagan and Christian.[33] Among the Christian poets Prudentius was always the
most popular ; Raumer enumerates no fewer than twenty-one
MSS. of his works glossed in Old High German.[34] Among the
classical poets, the one most frequently glossed is naturally
Vergil, and there exist old Latin-German vocabularies derived
entirely from these Vergilian glosses.[35]—This movement was
bound eventually to end in translations made into these
languages. The earliest Gothic translation, that of the Bible,
need not be considered here, as it was the outcome of special
causes and circumstances ; but in the 9th century Alfred the

---

[31] Cp. WAGNER, De Iunio Philargyrio, P. ii. pp. 11, 13, 17, 19 seqq.

[32] Vide HERMANN, op. cit., p. 4.

[33] The work most frequently glossed in Anglo-Saxon is the treatise of
ALDHELM, De laude virginitatis, which is full of Graecisms and written for
women ; next to this the Gospels, the Psalms, and the poems of Prudentius,
Prosperus and Sedulius. Vide WRIGHT, Biogr. Brit. lit.; Anglo-Saxon
period, p. 51.

[34] Die Einwirkung des Christenthums auf die althochdeutsche Sprache,
p. 104 seqq. ; cp. p. 222.

[35] For the German glosses on Vergil vide WACKERNAGEL in HAUPT's Zeitschrift f. deutsch. Alterth., v. p. 327 ; STEINMEYER, De glossis quibusdam
Vergilianis, Berlin, 1869 ; and Die deutschen Virgilglossen of the same
author in HAUPT's Zeitschrift, etc. (N.F.), vol. iii., 1870, p. 1 seqq. Some
Celtic glosses have been published by HAGEN, Scholl. Bern., p. 691,

Great, the Augustus of the Anglo-Saxons, translated into Anglo-Saxon Boethius and the *De cura Pastorali* of Pope Gregory. He was compelled for the purposes even of these translations to employ others to reduce the Latin text to a simpler and clearer form,[36] and did not therefore venture to attempt Vergil, though he, like all the rest, regarded him as the father of Latin poets and the pupil of Homer; [37] but in the 10th century the German Notker translated the Bucolics, Marcianus Capella, Boethius, and others.[38] The class of writers with whom Vergil divides the honour of being thus translated is full of significance as showing the taste of the age and the sort of conception which men must have had of the author of the Aeneid.

As for the rhetoric of the middle ages, as far as it is a continuation of the rhetoric of classical times, there is even less to be said of it than of medieval grammar. Rhetoric is held in honour as the second of the Seven Arts, but it is very far from retaining that proud position which Ennodius, Capella, and other rhetoricians of the decadence were wont to assign to it. Commentaries, abridgments and editions of ancient works on rhetoric are no doubt to be found, but they do not reach anything like the number of the works devoted to grammar. All that remained of classical rhetoric, properly speaking, was the configuration, the terminology, certain definitions, and especially that part relating to tropes and figures which had already in ancient times formed the connecting link between rhetoric and grammar, the former thereby becoming as it were a sort of appendix of the latter.[39] Christian rhetoric and the

[36] "Libros Boethii . . . planioribus verbis elucidavit (episc. Asser) . . . illis diebus labore necessario, hodie ridiculo. Sed enim iussu regis factum est ut levius ab eodem in Anglicum transferrentur sermonem." WILH. MALMESB., p. 248.

[37] "Theah Omerus se goda sceop, the mid Crecum selest was; se waes Firgilies lareow, se Firgilius waes mid Laedenwarum selest." (Homer, the good poet, who was the best among the Greeks; he was Vergil's master; Vergil was the best among the Latins.) ALFRED'S *Boethius*, ed. CARDALE, p. 327; WRIGHT, *Biogr. Brit. lit.*; *Anglo-Saxon period*, p. 56.

[38] For the ancient translations in Old High German, *vide* RAUMER, *Die Einwirkung des Christenthums*, etc., Chap. ii., passim.

[39] It forms part of the "scientia sermocinalis," which includes the three sciences of logic, rhetoric and grammar. For the connection between the

Christian style generally had resources peculiar to itself, and any one who has considered these in their essence will not be surprised when the treatise of Alcuin on rhetoric,[40] after beginning with the usual divisions and definitions of the parts and kinds of the oration, glides insensibly into a series of definitions belonging to dialectic and finishes with a series of definitions referring to virtue.

Given the character of the Christian style and the ideas and the aims of the Christian writers, it was obviously far more justifiable to make use of the Scriptures by way of illustration when expounding rhetoric than when treating of grammar; and yet, as a matter of fact, though the same chaotic mixture of authorities is here too noticeable,[41] the proportion of Scriptural examples in the works on rhetoric is not so great as one might naturally have expected or as some zealots would have wished it to be. The great difficulty was the intimate connection between rhetoric and grammar and the solid manner in which the latter was based on the classical tradition,—a fact which tended to preserve the authority of secular studies in the case of the former also. And, in addition to this, the whole ancient apparatus of terms, definitions, divisions, etc., served to keep in vogue the ancient system, for while the indifference felt for these studies was not sufficient to cause them to be entirely forgotten, on the other hand there was an utter absence of that energy which would have been necessary for thoroughly reorganising them.[42]

---

two latter during the middle ages and especially in the times of scholasticism, *vide* THUROT, *op. cit.*, p. 470 seqq. Cp. SPECHT, *Geschichte des Unterrichtswesens in Deutschland*, p. 86 seqq.

[40] *Disputatio de rhetorica et de virtutibus sapientissimi regis Karoli et Alcuini Magistri*, reprinted by HALM in his *Rhett. Lat. minores*, p. 523 seqq.

[41] "Cognoscite ergo, magistri saecularium litterarum, hinc (ex Scriptura scilicet) schemata, hinc diversi generis argumenta, hinc definitiones, hinc disciplinarum omnium profluxisse doctrinas, quando in his litteris posita cognoscitis quae ante scholas vestras longe prius dicta fuisse sentitis." *De schem. et tropis ap. Cassiodor.* (Introd.) in CASSIOD., op. (MIGNE) ii. p. 1270. Cp. the passage of BEDE already cited on p. 81.

[42] In a treatise on rhetoric coming from the school of S. Gallen and contained in a MS. of the 11th century occur the following words, which give a noteworthy picture of the miserable state of this study in the middle ages: "Olim disparuit, cuius facies depingenda est, et quae nostram excedit memoriam; eam qualis erat formare difficile est, quia multi dies sunt ex quo

As an authority in matters of rhetoric, Vergil continued to
occupy that position which his universal popularity and the
treatises of the ancient rhetoricians had assigned to him; and
although the importance of Cicero as an orator rendered allusions to the poet less necessary here than was the case in
matters of grammar, yet the intimate connection which existed
between rhetoric and grammar, and the fact that the two were
generally taught by the same master, naturally tended to bring
Vergil into prominence in this branch of study also, as had
already been the case in early times. Gerbert, like the rhetoricians of the decadence, considered the study of poetry indispensable for the formation of an orator's style, and used to
lecture on Vergil, Statius, Terence, Juvenal, Persius, Horace
and Lucan by way of introduction to the study of rhetoric.[43]
That part of the work of Macrobius which dealt with Vergil's
rhetorical qualities occurs in several MSS. united with the
biography of the poet attributed to Donatus,[44] and evidently
these chapters, which form as it were a compendium of rhetoric,

---

desinit esse. Oporteret eam immortalem esse, cuius amore languent ita
homines, ut abstractam tam diu et mundo mortuam resurgere velint. Ubi
Cato, ubi Cicero, domestici eius? nam si illi redirent ab inferis; haec illis
ad usum sermonis famularetur; sine qua nihil eis certum constabat, quod
ventilandum esset pro rostris. Quid autem est quod in suam non redigatur
originem? Naturalis eloquentia viguit, quousque ei per doctrinam filia
successit artificialis, quae deinde rhetorica dicta est. Haec postquam
antiquitate temporis extincta est, illa iterum revixit; unde hodieque plurimos cernimus qui in causis solo naturali instinctu ita sermone callent, ut
quae velint quibuslibet facile suadeant, nec tamen regulam doctrinae ullam
requirant." Publ. by Docen in the *Beiträge zur Geschichte und Literatur* of
Aretin, vii. p. 283 seqq. Cp. the text publ. by Wackernagel in the *Zeitschr.
f. deutsch. Altherth.*, iv. p. 463–478. Remarkable for its grotesque originality, and important for the light it throws upon the state of rhetoric in
Italy in the 11th century, is the *Rhetorimachia* of Anselm, publ. by
Duemmler (*Anselm der Peripatetiker*, Halle, 1872); cp. Gaspary, *Gesch. d.
ital. Lat.*, i. p. 24 seqq.

[43] " Cum ad rhetoricam suos provehere vellet, id sibi suspectum erat,
quod sine locutionum modis, qui in poetis discendi sunt, ad oratoriam artem
perveniri non queat. Poetas igitur adhibuit, quibus assuescendos arbitra-
batur. Legit itaque ac docuit Maronem et Statium Terentiumque poetas,
Iuvenalem quoque ac Persium Horatiumque satiricos, Lucanum etiam
historiographum. Quibus assuefactos locutionumque modis compositos, ad
rhetoricam transduxit." Richer., *Hist.*, lib. iii. 47.

[44] *E.g.* in a MS. in the National Library at Florence, copied by Pier
Cennini.

were much read in the middle ages; to them may be referred
some curious remarks in the *Fiore di Rettorica* of Fra Guidotto
which speak of Vergil as comprising within a small compass all
that is to be said on the subject of this art.[45]

In the medieval prose-writers Vergilian reminiscences are
very common, and occur equally in Orosius in the 5th century[46]
and Liutprand in the 10th.[47] But rhetoric had particular influence on poetry, and occasioned, chiefly at the beginning of
the middle ages, the production of a number of works intimately associated with Vergil. To prepare for the discussion
of these, however, we shall be compelled, in the first place, to
retrace our steps a little.

---

[45] " . . . e come conteremo per lo innanzi del versificato che fece il
grande poeta Virgilio nel tempo che fu Attaviano imperadore Augusto,
figliuolo adottivo di Giulio Cesare ; nell' imperio della sua dignitade nacque
Cristo glorioso salvatore del mondo ; il quale Virgilio si trasse tutto il
costrutto dello intendimento della rettorica, e più fece chiara dimonstranza,
sicchè per lui possiamo dire che l' abbiamo, e conoscere la via della ragione
e la etimologia dell' arte di rettorica ; imperocchè trasse il grande fascio in
piccolo volume e recollo in abbreviamento." FRATE GUIDOTTO, *Fiore di
rettorica*, ap. NANNUCCI, *Manuale*, etc., ii. p. 118.

[46] Cp. MÖRNER, *De Oros. vit.*, p. 117 seq.

[47] Cp. KÖPKE, *Vit. Liudprand*, p. 138.

CHAPTER X

THOSE notices which we possess of the life of Vergil have come down to us through the medium of the schools of grammar and rhetoric, and we owe them especially to the custom, dating from early times, of prefixing notices of the authors' lives to the school-commentaries on their works; in fact, all the biographies of Vergil, more or less detailed as the case may be, either are, or originally were, an integral part of commentaries of this kind. Such portions of these biographies as are derived from ancient sources belonging to the early days of the empire are of no particular importance for our present purpose; the only part of them which need concern us is that which is distinctly due to the period of decadence or the middle ages. This is why we have postponed to the present moment the examination of the traditions relative to the poet's life; for it will now be possible for us to study the whole of these various traditions in the light of the middle ages, a fact which will enable us to arrive at truer conclusions than would have been the case had we been compelled to regard them from a purely classical point of view.

The important position occupied by Vergil in the fields alike of literature and of education led naturally to more being written about his life than was the case with the other Latin poets. We have consequently a number of authentic notices of him, which enable us to appreciate his actual personality in a very marked degree; and this is rendered the more striking by the fact that such notices were not in any way gathered, as, for instance, is the case with Ovid, from his own writings, but were derived from reminiscences and biographical documents,

which spread together with his fame. Vergil had seldom
occasion, owing to the nature of his works, to speak of himself,
as Ovid, Horace, and others had done; and even where he did
so, as in the Bucolics, the allusion was of such a nature that it
could only be understood by means of external evidence preserved by tradition in the commentaries. It was only natural
that a man who aroused such exceptional interest should have
had much written about him by his contemporaries.[1] His
friends, Varius and Melissus,[2] and others who were on terms of
particular intimacy with him, left special treatises dealing with
his life and character. Others, again, who had not known him
themselves, but who lived near enough to his times to have
heard his contemporaries speak of him, wrote works about
him; such a one was Asconius Pedianus, who had not known
the poet personally, but wrote his book against the latter's
detractors at a time when the subject was fresh in every one's
memory, and first-hand evidence as to Vergil's life and habits
could easily be obtained. At the end of the reign of Tiberius
still, Seneca the Elder, by this time a nonagenarian, who had
known all the chief men of the Augustan age, recorded many
reminiscences of Vergil;[3] and finally, as is always the case
with celebrities, numerous anecdotes, both true and false, were
disseminated by means of oral tradition. Of such oral tradition in the case of Vergil traces are already to be found at the
beginning of the 2nd century.[4] It was at this very period that
Suetonius was compiling his learned *De Viris Illustribus*, and,
making use of the materials above-mentioned, gave, in the
section relating to poets, an abstract of the life of Vergil.
The work of Suetonius was largely used by grammarians, who
derived from it the biographical notices which they prefixed to
their school-commentaries on the various authors. From this

---

[1] "Amici familiaresque P. Vergili in iis quae de ingenio moribusque eius
memoriae tradiderunt." GELL., xvii. 10.

[2] Cp. QUINTILIAN, x. 3. 8; DONAT., *Vit. Verg.*, p. 585; RIBBECK, *Prolegg.*,
p. 89.

[3] "Et Seneca tradidit Iulium Montanum poetam solitum dicere invola-
turum se Vergilio quaedam," etc. DONAT., *Vit. Verg.*, p. 61. This passage
does not occur in any work of Seneca the Elder which has survived.

[4] "Nisus grammaticus audisse se a senioribus aiebat," etc. DONAT., *Vit.
Verg.*, p. 64.

work therefore, which is now lost, though considerable frag-
ments of it remain, come also the chief biographical notices
which we possess concerning Vergil ; they are contained in the
most important biography which has survived, viz., that which
bears the name of Aelius Donatus,[5] owing to the fact that
this grammarian prefixed it in the 4th century to his commentary on Vergil.[6]

[5] There is much confusion among scholars as to the works which bear
the name of Donatus. It is worth while therefore to observe that the
larger biography which we possess was part of the lost commentary of
AELIUS CLAUDIUS DONATUS, and does not belong to that of TIBERIUS CLAU-
DIUS DONATUS, as has been erroneously asserted by FABRICIUS, GRÄFENHAN
(Gesch. d. class. Phil. im Alterth., iv. p. 317) and others. REIFFERSCHEID
(op. cit., p. 400 seq.) has proved conclusively the falsity of this view. VAL-
MAGGI, however (La biografia di Virgilio attribuita al grammatico Elio
Donato in the Riv. di filol. class., 1886, p. 1 seqq.), has reopened the ques-
tion, maintaining that the biography is not by Donatus, and that it is not
derived from Suetonius, but is part of an anonymous commentary on the
Bucolics, based probably on the commentary of Servius.

[6] Of the various editions of this biography I have, as said above, adopted
that of REIFFERSCHEID, who has restored the genuine parts of Suetonius to
him (Suetoni praeter Caesarum libros reliquiae, Lips., 1860, p. 54 seqq.).
For the criticism and history of this ancient biography it is indispensable
to consult the important work of HAGEN, who has published a new critical
edition of it (Scholl. Bern., p. 734 seqq.), including that part of the commentary of Donatus which immediately followed it and treats of Bucolic
poetry. Vide also NETTLESHIP, Ancient lives of Vergil, Oxford, 1879 ; BECK,
ad Verg. Vit. Suetonian. in the Jahrbb. f. Philol., 1886, p. 502 seqq.
WÖLFFLIN published in the Philologus of 1866 (p. 154) the preface of Donatus, which is found prefixed to the biography in a Paris MS., with the title,
"Fl. (leg. Ael.) Donatus L. Munatio suo salutem." The editor, BAEHR
(p. 367), and others have erroneously supposed that this was a preface to
the biography. In that case, as Baehr points out, the words " de multis
pauca decerpsi " would prove that the biography is not taken straight from
Suetonius. But it is only necessary to read this preface with a little
attention to become convinced that it is a preface to the whole commentary
and not to the biography alone. Donatus is clearly speaking of the interpretations in the commentary when he says that he has added his own
views to those of others (admixto sensu nostro), while the words with which
he concludes, " si enim haec grammatico, ut aiebas, rudi ac nuper exorto
viam monstrant ac manum porrigunt satisfecimus iussis," are in an equal
degree only applicable to the commentary as a whole. From this preface it
appears that the work of Donatus was in the main a compilation, though
he did make additions of his own, as we learn too from Servius. Like
Macrobius, he quotes (without acknowledgment) the actual words of his
predecessors: " Agnosces igitur in hoc munere collatitio sinceram vocem
priscae auctoritatis. Cum enim liceret usquequaque nostra interponere,
maluimus optima fide quorum res fuerat eorum etiam verba servare." This
too is the system on which· he borrows from Suetonius in the biography.

The foundation therefore of the notices we possess is not any special work on Vergil's life but a compendious article in a biographical dictionary. Donatus has merely copied Suetonius, often word for word; in fact, in that part of the biography which may be regarded as genuine, and which is alone found in the better MSS., the dry and cold style of Suetonius is clearly recognisable, as well as his habit of stringing together a series of anecdotes without any comments or observations of his own. Although it is evident throughout that the writer is dealing with a poet of unusual distinction, and one regarded as superior to any other Latin poet, yet the tone of the biography is everywhere natural and realistic, and there is a complete absence of that fervour of enthusiasm which usually marked everything that was written on the subject of Vergil. This tone is very characteristic of Suetonius, as we learn from his biographies of the Twelve Caesars. From Suetonius too comes that dose of the marvellous which belongs to the clearly ancient part of the work, and consists of presages indicative of the poet's future greatness; such as the dream of his mother, the fact that he did not cry when born, and the great height attained by the poplar-tree planted, according to custom, at his birth.[7] These anecdotes Suetonius doubtless derived from oral tradition, or from earlier written records of such tradition, and similar stories occur in all his biographies of the Caesars. Such stories are too common in antiquity to be in any way specially characteristic of Vergil, though they serve to put him on a level with the most distinguished characters of history and to raise him above the rest of Roman poets, and they must not therefore be confounded with the medieval Vergilian legends, which had a very different origin. Perhaps Donatus did not copy all that Suetonius had written; but be that as it may, this part of his commentary was more fortunate than the rest, and survived as

For the MSS. and the text of this biography, vide HAGEN, op. cit., p. 676 seqq., 683 seqq.

[7] Noteworthy, and not incredible is the statement which follows : " quae arbor Vergili ex eo dicta atque etiam consecrata est summa gravidarum ac fetarum religione et suscipientium ibi et solventium vota." DONAT., Vit. Verg., p. 55.

a separate work; it was read throughout the middle ages, and
served as the basis for many other short biographies affixed to
Vergilian commentaries or MSS. Through it was preserved
in the literary tradition that historical personality of the poet
which has come down to the present day.[8]

For the most part the prose biographies which remain are
not marked by that enthusiasm with which we are accustomed
to hear Vergil spoken of even in classical times, and still more
during the decadence and the middle ages. They regard the
poet as a subject of unusual interest, but they are all too simple
and too wanting in any subjective or rhetorical colouring to
convey any due impression of such interest. The reason of this

[8] The Latin Anthology contains several epigrams which stood beneath
portraits of him (No. 158, ed. RIESE). It is strange, considering the unin-
terrupted course of Vergil's fame, that no really trustworthy likeness of him
has come down to us. Busts of Vergil were the commonest things imagin-
able in ancient times, especially in public (cp. SUET., iv. 34) and private
libraries, down to the very end of the decadence. We shall quote presently
an inscription which stood under a portrait of Vergil in the 5th century.
Equally ancient was the custom of ornamenting MSS. with a portrait of
their authors (MART., xiv. 186), and it lasted down to the Renaissance. The
most ancient portrait of Vergil of this kind which we possess is the well-
known one in the famous Codex Romanus, referred by some to the 4th or
5th century. But the makers of these miniatures soon became indifferent
as to whether they were true portraits or not, and, in fact, this Vatican
miniature presents a sufficiently vague and insignificant type, though, as it
occurs three times in the MS., it may perhaps be a rough copy of a traditional portrait which had already served to ornament earlier MSS. In the
later middle ages and during the Renaissance fidelity was quite disregarded,
and the numerous portraits of the poet on MSS. of this date present a
wonderful collection of fanciful types. Sometimes he has a long beard,
sometimes none at all; sometimes he has long flowing locks, sometimes he
is bald; sometimes he wears a Phrygian cap, and so on. I have been quite
unable to discover any fixed type in the numerous MSS. I have examined.
The many MSS. too which contain portraits of Dante are equally arbitrary
in their representations of this poet, of whom there can have been no
difficulty in procuring a correct likeness, so that it is clear that accuracy
was at a discount in this class of ornamentation.
Two miniatures of Vergil, one by Simon Memmi, are published in MAI's
Vergilii Maronis interpret. vet., Mediol., 1818. The one from the Codex
Romanus has often been reproduced. On these miniatures and the bust at
Mantua, vide VISCONTI, Icon. Rom., p. 385 seqq. : LABUS, Museo di Mantova,
i. p. 5 seqq.; CARLI, Dissert. sopra un antico ritratto di Virgilio, Mantua,
1797 ; MAINARDI, Dissert. sopra il busto di Virgilio della R. Accad. di Man-
tova, Mantua, 1833 ; RAOUL ROCHETTE in the Journal des Savants, 1834,
p. 68 seqq. ; Beschreibung von Rom., ii. 2, p. 345 seq. ; MÜLLER, Handb. d.
Archäol. d. Kunst., p. 734 ; DE NOLHAC, Les peintures des manuscrits in the
Mél. d'arch. et d'hist. de l'École fr. de Rome, iv. (1884), p. 327, tab. xi.

is that none of these biographies was undertaken for its own
sake, but they were all, as we have already noticed, intended
to serve the practical purposes of education and to act as
introductions to commentaries, the cold and matter-of-fact
style of which they accordingly adopt.   The objects of Donatus' work were certainly not of a kind to inspire him to supply
any want of warmth which might be characteristic of Suetonius ; and this was still more the case with those who compiled
from him.   The same may be said of the brief and confused biographical notices prefixed to the commentaries of Probus [9] and
Servius.[10]   But if the exaggerated enthusiasm for Vergil prevailing throughout the literary world found no expression in
the style of these styleless compilations, it yet acted as a leaven
which was bound to result in the admixture with the historical
notices of a number of facts invented, perverted, or misunderstood, some of which even found their way into the text of his
principal biography.   The middle ages left their mark on this
no less than on other things, and herein lies the particular
interest that this subject presents to us just now.[11]

[9] For this short biography, also included in REIFFERSCHEID'S *Suet. Reliq.*,
p. 52, *vide* STEUP (*De Probis grammaticis*, Jena, 1871, p. 120 seqq.), who
maintains that it formed part of a commentary by a Valerius Probus
Iunior.

[10] REIFFERSCHEID maintains (*Suet. relic.*, p. 398 seq.) that the biography
which bears the name of Servius is not really the work of this grammarian,
and that the biography which he actually wrote, and which he quotes in
the Introduction to the Bucolics, is lost.   HAGEN (*Scholl. Bern.*, p. 682)
argues forcibly against this idea, which has been accepted by BAEHR (R. L.,
p. 366) and TEUFFEL (R. L., p. 389), and points out that this biography of
Servius is found already in a Berne MS. of the 8th–9th century.

[11] The biography which bears the name of Donatus is found in certain
MSS. augmented by a number of absurd or irrelevant interpolations ; but
the earliest of these MSS. is not, as far as is yet known, earlier than the
14th century (cp. HAGEN, *Scholl. Bern.*, p. 680 ; ROTH in the *Germania*, iv.
p. 285), while the uninterpolated biography occurs already in MSS. of the
10th or 11th century.   Quite independently of the notices which they contain, the language and style of these interpolations show clearly that they
are not additions made by Donatus to the text of Suetonius.   None the less,
however, the idea of ROTH (*op. cit.*, p. 286 seq.) that they are the work of a
Neapolitan scholar of the beginning of the 12th century is, without doubt,
erroneous.   Though the interpolated MSS. do not differ from one another
in the number or nature of the interpolations, it is clear that these interpolations are not the work of one man or of one time ; the contents of some
of them is found already in Servius, Cassiodorus or Aldhelm, and the
Neapolitan scholar would have had to have been a man of erudition truly

Before everything it is necessary to emphasize the fact that this invasion of the Vergilian biography by new and apocryphal elements was not brought about, as many who have treated the subject have supposed, by the legends which speak of Vergil as magician. The common error which ascribes the interpolations in Donatus and various other facts found in other medieval biographies to this legend has had its rise in a confusion of two things entirely distinct alike in their nature, their age, and their origin, viz. the literary and the popular Vergilian legends. These two classes of fabulous productions have, it is true, one connecting link, for both of them originated in an exaggerated conception of the wisdom of Vergil; but they differ entirely from one another, both as to the nature of the conception, which is of course much cruder among the people, and also as to the field of activity in which they consider the extraordinary wisdom to have been exercised. The Vergil of the popular legends entirely loses his character as poet; in the literary legends he always retains it, his poetry serving as the vehicle of expression for his vast and varied learning. For the origin of this latter class of legends we have seen sufficient cause in the historical and psychological phenomena which we have already examined; but these would not be

surprising for his time. Roth, moreover, has not considered that though these interpolations are pretty poor stuff, they are yet on the whole much less barbarous than one would have reason to expect from a native of Southern Italy living at this period.

Unauthentic Vergilian anecdotes of various kinds begin to be current at a very early period, and in several of these interpolations it is impossible not to recognise anecdotes which went the round of the schools in the times of the decadence; indeed it would be unreasonable to suppose that the various biographies of the poet should, in passing through so many hands, have remained quite free from additions of this kind. I have no hesitation in believing that Aldhelm and Cassiodorus read in some biography those anecdotes which they quote as well known, and which reappear subsequently as interpolations in the biography of Donatus or Suetonius. It may be that some grammarian, in copying or abridging the work of Suetonius, which Donatus left untouched, added to it the stories which he found current in the schools. However this may be, it seems clear that in these interpolations, though they occur only in MSS. of recent date, there is a nucleus of considerable antiquity, which was contained already in some biography anterior to the 6th century, and has gone on being augmented down to the 12th century, to which latter period one of the anecdotes, differing from the rest, clearly belongs.

enough of themselves to explain the rise of the former, to
which, as we shall see presently, an entirely special cause must
be assigned. The two met eventually, as they were bound to
do, but the popular legend did not leave the home of its birth
or acquire any celebrity by means of literature earlier than the
12th century. Its influence does not make itself felt in the
biographies of the poet till very late, and even then only to a
limited extent. Into the biography of Donatus there has only
been introduced one single anecdote, of which we shall speak
elsewhere, in which any influence due to the popular legends
can be traced; and this not because it forms in any way part
of them, but because it is the only one in the whole biography,
whether genuine or interpolated, which describes the wonderful learning of the poet as being displayed in any other than
a literary field. A biography published by Hagen,[12] from a
Berne MS. of the 9th century, contains many original statements, but nothing suggestive of Vergil as magician, as we
find him in those biographies that are later than the 13th century. We shall encounter the popular legend, strangely mixed
with biographical notices derived from Donatus, in the 15th
century poem by Bonamente Aliprandi, of which we shall speak
in the second part of this work.

The literary legend (understanding by this general expression every unauthentic statement concerning Vergil as poet,
scholar, or man of letters current in the literary tradition)
cannot be said to offer anything specially characteristic of its
subject; it is rather characteristic of the medium in which his
fame was preserved throughout the middle ages. It consisted
of a number of particulars or anecdotes which occur either
separately or in combination with the historical notices, and
which, though evidently incredible for historical reasons, yet
contain nothing in itself impossible or supernatural. They
were the direct product of the grammarians and the students
of Vergil, and were rarely simple efforts of imagination, being
generally based on some anecdote which was exaggerated, or
on some allusion or verse which was misunderstood. Already
in the earliest times one finds more than one 'dicitur' adduced

[12] *Scholia Bern.*, p. 996 seqq.

by Asconius Pedianus, or by the grammarians and commentators. At a later period the accumulation of poetical exercises bearing Vergil's name, the confusion and loss of the links of the ancient tradition and the general increase of ignorance afforded ample opportunity for the multiplication of erroneous and legendary ideas.

Thus there is the familiar story of the distich :

> ' Nocte pluit tota, redeunt spectacula mane ;
> divisum imperium cum Iove Caesar habet,'

the honour for which some plagiarist claimed, causing Vergil to lament in the lines, also anonymously published :

> ' Hos ego versiculos feci ; tulit alter honorem.
> sic vos non vobis—— '

This story and these verses, which are certainly not by Vergil, enjoyed great celebrity in the schools of the middle ages, and their fame has lasted on to the present day.[13] The verses occur in numerous Vergilian MSS. of various dates, and they are mentioned by more than one medieval writer. The Codex Salmasianus, which contains them,[14] and Cassiodorus [15] and Aldhelm,[16] who quote them, show clearly that they were as well known in the 6th and 7th centuries already as they were

---

[13] To this incident, too, may be referred the line, " Iuppiter in caelis, Caesar regit omnia terris," which bears the title " Vergilius de Caesare," *Anth. Lat.*, no. 782 (RIESE). Although this line is not found in any MS. earlier than the 14th or 15th century, yet I believe it to be of considerable antiquity. RIESE (*Jahrbb. f. Philol.*, 1869, p. 282) fancies, with little reason, that there is a reminiscence of it in the *Nux Elegia*, v. 143 : " Sed neque tolluntur, nec dum regit omnia Caesar, incolumis," etc.

[14] *Anth. Lat.*, 256, 267 (RIESE).

[15] " Ut est illud : Divisum imperium cum Iove Caesar habet." CASSIOD., *De Orthogr.*, c, 8. (This chapter of Cassiodorus is taken from the work of an unknown grammarian, CURTIUS VALERIANUS.)

[16] ALDHELM cites as from Vergil " in tetrastichis theatralibus " the line, " Sic vos non vobis mellificatis apes." (ALDH., *Opp.* ed. GILLES, p. 309.) *Vide* MANITIUS, *Aldhelm u. Beda*, Vienna, 1886, p. 27. From the expression " in tetrastichis theatralibus " it is clear that these verses consisted then of only two couplets. It is thus that they appear in the Cod. Salmas., the line quoted being the last of the four. It is evident moreover on other grounds that the three other ways of finishing the line " Sic vos non vobis " are a later addition, though they are found already in MSS. of the 10th century. The last two are wanting in several MSS. of DONIZO (11th cent.), who also tells the story. (*Vit. Math.* ap. MURATORI, *Scriptt. rer. It.*, v. p. 860.)

at a subsequent period. In the biography of Donatus however they and the story relative to them occur only in the interpolated MSS.[17] How exactly they came to be attributed to Vergil is difficult to divine; perhaps they were introduced in the first instance into his epigrams and passed thence into those collections of his minor poems of which the Codex Salmasianus affords a specimen.[18] This at least is the only way of explaining how, in this same codex, a distich from the Tristia of Ovid appears as an epigram of Vergil.[19]

Another story current among the commentators was one having reference to the hemistich of the Aeneid which describes Ascanius as 'magnae spes altera Romae.' In this case the admiration for the poet is expressed by setting him side by side with the greatest master of Latin prose. Cicero, having heard the Sixth Eclogue recited in the theatre of Cytheris, being struck by the extraordinary genius it displayed, asked for the name of its author, and, having learnt it, exclaimed, 'Magnae spes altera Romae!'—he himself was, of course, the first. Vergil then afterwards introduced these words into the Aeneid, referring them to Ascanius. The good people who started the story did not of course consider that at the date of

----

[17] HAGEN (*Jahrbb. f. Philol.*, 1869, p. 784) maintains that the narrative accompanying these verses in the interpolated biography cannot be earlier than the 12th century. But it is evident that the verses presuppose the narrative, which is therefore at least as old as they. To determine the exact date of the narrative is difficult, but there is certainly nothing in it to prevent its being earlier than the 12th century. But however this may be, I have no doubt that the two distichs had already been introduced into the biography when the Codex Salmasianus was written. These two epigrams, and the two (261, 264) which stand so close to them in this MS., are evidently taken from the biography itself. Especially noteworthy in this connection is No. 264, which is nothing but the Propertian couplet, " Cedite Romani scriptores," etc., quoted in the biography. Moreover, the work " Cnutonis regis gesta," in which the "Nocte pluit tota " is quoted as Vergilian, is certainly earlier than the 12th century.

[18] HAGEN (*loc. cit.*) suggests a similar explanation, except that he introduces quite gratuitously the idea of Vergil as magician. When he asserts that from verses such as these to the conception of a magician is but a step, he shows that he has not examined the question with his usual care.

[19] " Si quotiens homines peccant, sua fulmina mittat
          Iuppiter, exiguo tempore inermis erit."
                                        Ov., *Trist.*, ii. 33.

the publication of the Eclogues Cicero was already dead.[20]
This anecdote, which is found also in Servius,[21] passed from
the commentaries into the biography, as a proof of the great
success achieved by the Bucolics when recited in the theatre;
it evidently arose from some saying which brought Vergil and
Cicero together as the chiefs of Roman literature and applied
to Vergil the words of his own hemistich.[22]   The interpolated
biography concludes with a series of seven or eight sayings
attributed to Vergil, some of them founded on passages from
his poems.   These sayings do not offer any very striking
features, and are for the most part little more than commonplaces, yet they portray Vergil as a man of a mild and genial
temperament, with a good supply of tact and commonsense.
They describe him too as in high favour at court, and several
of them take the form of answers to questions addressed to
him by Augustus or Maecenas.   The admiration in which he
was held comes out too in several cases in the very words put
into his mouth.[23]   The date of this part of the legendary

---

[20] Cicero died in B.C. 43, while the Eclogues were certainly not earlier
than B.C. 41. Cp. RIBBECK, prolegg. p. 8 seq. Such anachronisms are not
uncommon, and we find a similar one in the MSS. which attribute to Vergil
the two well-known elegies on the death of Maecenas (cp. RIBBECK, Appendix Verg., p. 61, 192 seqq.).   When Maecenas died, Vergil had already
been dead eleven years. And such errors occurred before the middle ages.
Thus MARTIAL says calmly (iv. 14) : "Sic forsan tener ausus est Catullus
Magno mittere Passerem Maroni," forgetting that when Catullus died,
Vergil was only sixteen.

[21] "Dicitur autem (ecloga vi.) ingenti favore a Vergilio esse recitatam,
adeo ut, cum eam postea Cytheris meretrix cantasset in theatro, quam in
fine Lycoridem vocat, stupefactus Cicero cuius esset requireret, et cum eum
tandem aliquando agnovisset, dixisse dicatur et ad suam et illius laudem :
Magnae spes altera Romae ; quod iste postea ad Ascanium transtulit, sicut
commentatores loquuntur." SERV., ad Ecl., vi. 11.

[22] To praise the poet with his own words was no such uncommon thing ;
RUSTICUS in his letter to Pope Eucherius (5th cent.) quotes the following
epigram, which he had read under a portrait of Vergil, in which three lines
of the Aeneid (i. 607 seqq.) are applied to him :—

"Vergilium vatem melius sua carmina laudant ;
in freta dum fluvii current, dum montibus umbrae
lustrabunt convexa, polus dum sidera pascet,
semper honos nomenque tuum laudesque manebunt."

Vide SIRMOND., ad Sidon., p. 34.

[23] " . . . ea tuba cum volo loquor quae ubique et diutissime audie-
tur." DONAT., Vit., Verg., p. 68.

L

biography is very uncertain; though there is much in it indicative of the middle ages, yet it would seem beyond doubt that some of it belongs to an earlier period, in substance if not in form. One of these sayings of Vergil, that on Ennius, is already found quoted in the 6th century by Cassiodorus.[24] The liking of the ancients for collections of apophthegms by great men is well known, and probably some such collection of the sayings of Vergil was preserved in the works on his life. Suetonius, or Donatus in his abridgment of Suetonius, left them on one side, but they spread none the less from their original sources and attached themselves, not without a due admixture of invention, to the minor grammatical literature, now for the most part lost, and to the oral tradition of the schools. A work in which one might naturally have expected to find them is that of Valerius Maximus; but this tasteless compiler, who wrote so near to the age of the poet that he might have proved a most valuable fountain of knowledge for us, has chosen servilely to imitate authorities which, owing either to their date or their nature, contain no mention of Vergil; in fact, Vergil is not no much as once named in the whole work of Valerius.

In those biographies, derived for the most part from Donatus, which accompany Vergilian commentaries on MSS. of the 9th, 10th and 11th centuries, there do not occur any anecdotes deserving of special attention, nor is there any trace of supernatural powers attributed to the poet. There soon appears, however, an exaggerated idea of his learning, especially in philosophical matters, a feature which is foreign to the larger biography, although such an idea was already current in the time of Donatus. Noteworthy in this connection are several strange etymologies of the name of Vergil. In a biography found in a 9th century MS. this name is said to be ' equivalent to *vere glisceus*, Vergil being a famous philosopher and manifold

---

[24] " Cui et illud aptari potest quod Vergilius, dum Ennium legeret, a quodam quid faceret inquisitus, respondit: aurum in stercore quaero." Cassiod., *De instit. div. lit.*, cap. i. " Cum is (Maro) aliquando Ennium in manu haberet rogareturque quidnam faceret, respondit se aurum colligere de stercore Ennii." Donat., *Vit. Verg.*, p. 67.

in his fecundity, like the spring.' [25] In the Vergilian Codex
Gudianus (9th cent.), in which his biography occurs three or
four times, we find that ' he was called *Maro* from *mare*, for
as the sea abounds in water so did he abound in wisdom more
than any other man.' [26] After the 12th century this idea
becomes still more accentuated in some biographies; in these,
however, there is already apparent the influence of the popular
legends gaining a foothold in literature. In a Marcian Codex
of the 15th century, which contains a Vergil commentary,
there is a biography in which the author gives free rein to his
enthusiasm for the poet : ' Of Vergil it may be said, " omne
tenet punctum " ' ; to him may be applied the words of the
Psalmist, ' omne quod voluit facit ' ; and hence it was written
of him,—

> ' Hic est musarum lumen per saecula clarum,
> stella poetarum non venerenda parum.' [27]

The motto prefixed to the whole commentary is,—

> ' Omnia divino monstravit carmine vates.'

But among the other Vergilian attributes we here find magic
expressly mentioned,[28] which is not the case in any biography
earlier than the 12th century.

In addition to what occurs in the biographies, there are to
be found in medieval writers not a few erroneous or legendary
ideas concerning Vergil. We have already noticed how the
commentators on the Bucolics used to imagine facts to which
the poet was supposed to make allegorical allusions. Thus,

---

[25] " Alii volunt ut a vere Vergilius, quasi *vere gliscens*, id est crescens, sit
nominatus. Erat enim magnae philosophiae praeclarissimus praeceptor et
multiplex sicuti vernalia incrementa." HAGEN, *Scholl. Bern.*, p. 997.

[26] *Vide* HEYNE, *ad Donat. Vit. Verg.*, § 22.

[27] "De eo potest dici illud oratoris : omne tenet punctum ; de quo ait
Macrobius : Vergilius nullius disciplinae expers fuit ; unde dictum est de eo :
Hic est Musarum," etc. ; . . . "potest dici id psalmistae ; omnia quae-
cunque voluit fecit." *Cod. Marcian. Lat.*, cl. xiii., No. lvi., col. 2. "Ideo
Vergilius proprio nomine Vates vel Poeta antonomastice nuncupatur, sicut
beatus Paulus Apostolus, et Aristoteles Philosophus." *Ibid.*, col. 3.

[28] Et fuit magnus magicus, multum enim se dedit arti magicae ut patet
ex illa ecloga "Pastorum Musam Damonis et Alphesiboei." *Ibid.*, col. 8.
" Ex faucibus sanguinem spuebat sed per medicinam se sanabat, erat
enim magnus medicus et astrologus." *Ibid.*, col. 13.

according to a note in a 9th century MS., Vergil is described as
keeping a public school of poetry at Rome, to which he alludes
in his 'Formosam resonare doces Amaryllide silvam.'[29]
Striking is the colossal anachronism of the Anglo-Saxon writer
who, taking literally certain metaphorical expressions, considers
Vergil as the contemporary and pupil of Homer.[30]   By a
strange confusion of the various ideas of which we have
already spoken, we find Paschasius Rathbert asserting that
the Sibyl recited in person Vergil's Ten Eclogues before the
Senate.[31]   Neckam refers to the incident which forms the
subject of the *Culex* as having happened to Vergil himself,
though at a later period, after reading the poem, he retracts
this view.[32]   There was further a tradition, not in itself improbable, which spoke of Vergil as receiving large sums from
Augustus as a reward for his work;[33] and this tradition was
particularly connected with the lines on Marcellus that made
such an impression on Octavia, for which Servius says that he
received a sum of money in cash on the spot.[34]   This sum is
fixed in the interpolated biography at 100,000 sesterces per

---

[29] "Formosam, etc.: . . . Tropice ad Maronem hoc dicitur docen-
tem in Roma artem poeticam. Amaryllis Romam allegorice significat."
HAGEN, *Scholl. Bern.*, p. 1000.

[30] "Omerus waes east mid Crecum, on thaem leod-scipe leotha craeftgast,
Firgilies freond and lareow, thaem maeran sceope magistra betst." (Homer
lived in the East among the Greeks; in that nation he was the greatest
poet; he was the friend and master of Vergil, that great bard, the best of
all the masters."

Metres of Boeth., ed. Fox, p. 137. This metrical version of Boethius has
been attributed to King Alfred, but wrongly, as is shown by WRIGHT, *Biogr.
Brit. lit.; Anglo-Saxon period*, p. 56 seq., 400 seqq.

[31] "Legimus vero, quod Sibylla decem eclogas Vergilii in senatu salta-
vit." PASCH. RATHB., *in Matth. Ev.*, c. 35; in the *Bibl. max. vett. patr.*,
xiv., p. 130.

[32] "Vergilius igitur repatrians, dulcibus Athenis relictis, etc. Sed quid?
Rara fides ideo est quia multi multa loquuntur. Hoc adicio quia postquam librum Vergili *De culice* inspexi, alium esse tenorem relationis adverti.
Ut enim refert Vergilius, pastor quidam," etc. ALEX. NECKAM, *De naturis
rerum* (ed. WRIGHT, Lond., 1863), cap. 109, p. 190 seq.

[33] "Ab Augusto usque ad sestertium centies honestatus est." PROB., *Vit.
Verg.* (ap. REIFFERSCHEID, *Suet. reliq.*, p. 53).

[34] "Et constat hunc librum tanta pronuntiatione Augusto et Octaviae
esse recitatum, ut fletu nimio imperarent silentium, nisi Vergilius finem
esse dixisset, qui pro hoc aere gravi donatus est." SERV. *ad Aen.*, vi. 862.
Cp. MOMMSEN, *Gesch. d. röm. Munzwesen*, p. 303.

line.[35]   The same story, with curious additions, occurs later in
connection with the lines, ' Nocte pluit tota,' etc.   Benzone di
Alba (11th cent.) states that Vergil was rewarded for these
verses by Augustus with a large sum of money and *his freedom*.[36] The same statement appears in Donizo.[37] Not content
with this, Alexander of Telese (12th cent.) asserts that Vergil
obtained for them from Augustus the fief of the city of Naples
and the province of Calabria.[38] Now here we see an encounter
between the literary and the popular legend, which latter was
Neapolitan in its origin, and in which Vergil always figures as
lord or patron of the city of Naples.   These elements, which
tended to prepare the way for the admission of the popular
legend into literature, are worthy of note for their importance
in connection with the second part of this work.

But if, for reasons on which we have already dwelt, the
tone of enthusiasm generally used when speaking of Vergil
does not appear in his prose biographies, it is given a loose
enough rein in those poetical compositions which treat of him.
The poetry of the middle ages, which was based on classical
models, kept Vergil continually before its eyes.   It looked
upon him as a sort of poetical and rhetorical emporium, and
took from him the themes on which it declaimed (for poetry

---

[35] "   .   .   . defecisse fertur (Octavia) atque aegre focillata dena sester-
tia pro singulo versu Vergilio dari iussit."   DONAT., *Vit. Verg.*, p. 62.

[36] "Liber cum rebus, Maro, cunctis esto diebus
       et de thesauro Iulii sis dives in auro.

Certe pro duobus carminibus a Iulio Caesare est honoratus duplici honore
Vergilius."   *Ad Henricum*, iv., *imp.*; Lib., i. 30 (Ap. PERTZ., xiii. p. 610).

[37] *Vit. Mathild.* ap. MURATORI, *Scriptt. rer. Ital.*, v. p. 360.

[38] "Nam si Vergilius, maximus poetarum, apud Octavianum imperatorem
tantum promeruit ut pro duobus quos ad laudem sui ediderat versibus
Neapolis civitatis, simulque Calabriae dominatus caducam ab eo receperit
retributionem, multo melius," etc.   *Alloq. ad reg. Roger.*, ap. MURATORI,
Scriptt. rer. Ital., v. p. 644.   To this munificence displayed by Augustus to
Vergil alludes also WILLIAM OF APULIA at the close of his poem :—

> " Nostra, Rogere, tibi cognoscis carmina scribi
>   mente tibi laeta studuit parere poeta ;
> semper et auctores hilares meruere datores.
> Tu, duce Romano dux dignior Octaviano,
>   sis mihi, quaeso, boni spes, ut fuit ille **Maroni**."

Ap. MURATORI, *Scriptt. rer. Ital.*, v. p. 278.

had been, for a long time past, nothing but so much declamation), and these not only from his works but also from his qualities and the chief events of his life. This was the origin of the bombastic Vergilian biography in verse, written in the 6th century by the grammarian Phocas; only part of it has been preserved, but its tone is sufficiently marked by the Sapphic ode which precedes it.[39] But many of the incidents in the poet's life were commonly known either from the biographies in the school-commentaries, or from these commentaries themselves (particularly those on the Bucolics), and the most striking of these incidents were made the subjects of special poetical exercises. Thus the story of the lost estate recovered through the favour of Augustus and the intercession of Maecenas and other friends was familiar to every reader of the Bucolics, and more than one Latin poet found inspiration in this anecdote, honourable alike to the poet and his protector.[40] In a 10th century MS. occurs a medieval poetical exercise, purporting to be an epistle in verse written by Vergil to Maecenas when Mantua had been occupied by the veterans.[41] An epigram in the Anthology refers to the poet's brother Flaccus, immortalised, according to the commentators and the larger biography, as the Daphnis of Eclogue V.[42] Of anecdotes derived direct from the biography, none was so famous

[39] It is founded on the biography of Suetonius as read in Donatus; the differences are of little moment. Cp. REIFFERSCHEID (*Suet. reliq.*, p. 403 seq.), who has included this text in his work (p. 68 seqq.). It has also been printed in various collections, most recently by RIESE, *Anth. Lat.*, No. 671.

[40] *E.g.* MART., viii. 56; SIDON., *Carm.*, iii., iv.; *Auct. panegyr. Pison.*, v. 217 seqq. Cp. HAUPT in *Hermes*, iii. p. 212.

[41] Published by USENER in the *Rhein Mus.*, xxii. p. 628, from a S. Gallen MS. of the 10th century, where it has the title *Maro Maecenati salutem*. It is found in other MSS. also, but without this title. RIESE has included it in his *Anth. Lat.*, No. 686 (cp. vol. i. pars. 2, p. 23), but neither he nor Usener have understood the real purport of the poem, and have supposed that it was descriptive of the deplorable state of Italy when overrun by the barbarians. DONIZO, in the dispute between Mantua and Canossa, discourses at length on this incident in Vergil's life, mentioning various details not found in the biography. *Vit. Mathild.* ap. MURATORI, *Scriptt. rer. Ital.*, v. p. 360.

[42] " Tristia fata tui dum fles in Daphnide Flacci,
      docte Maro, fratrem dis immortalibus aequas."
                                        Anth. Lat., No. 778 (RIESE).

as that of Vergil's dying command that the Aeneid should be burnt; it was a subject which lent itself to declamation, and the opportunity was not allowed to pass. Thus, already in the time of Gellius and Suetonius, Sulpicius Apollinaris composed on this subject the three distichs quoted in the biography.[43] To a later period belong the lines in the Codex Salmasianus, in which the Romans pray Augustus to prevent the carrying-out of the poet's command.[44] But the declamation on this subject takes up an even more elevated tone when it makes Augustus himself speak, as in the famous ' Ergone supremis,' etc., which perhaps formed part of the biography of Phocas already mentioned.[45]

Vergil's actual works, moreover, served to supply poets and verse-makers with subjects. This was the case, too, with several of the short poems quoted in the biography. Thus the epigram which, according to the biographer, Vergil composed as a boy on the robber-chief Balista, achieved great notoriety, and occurs in many Vergilian MSS., into which it has evidently been introduced from the biography.[46] It was imitated by

---

[43] "Iusserat haec rapidis," etc. DONAT., *Vit. Verg.*, p. 63. They occur in the various editions of the Latin Anthology. Three other couplets of the same significance are prefixed to the arguments in verse of the books of the Aeneid which bear the name of this same Sulpicius. L. MÜLLER (*Rhein. Mus.*, xix. p. 120) maintains successfully that the original distichs are those in the biography.

[44] "Temporibus laetis," etc. *Anth. Lat.*, No. 242 (RIESE). The earliest editions of Vergil and some MSS. attribute these lines to CORNELIUS GALLUS. In a Vatican MS. (No. 1586) of the 15th century we find "Egerat Vergilius cum Varrone (*i.e.* Vario) antequam de Italia recessisset, ut si quid sibi acciderat, Aeneidam combureret, quod adimplere volens et Cornelius Gallus hoc sentiens, Caesari pro parte Romanorum et totius orbis supplicavit ne combureretur, in hunc modum videlicet: Temporibus laetis," etc.

[45] *Anth. Lat.*, No. 672 (RIESE). This declamation in verse was very famous, and some even among modern scholars have treated it as if it were a real work of Augustus. Of an ancient imitation of it only the end has survived ("Nescio quid, fugiente anima," etc.), *Anth. Lat.*, No. 655. We may quote as a specimen of it the last lines, in which Augustus says of Vergil :

" aeterna resonante Camena
laudetur, placeat, vivat, relegatur, ametur."

[46] DONAT., *Vit. Verg.*, p. 58 ; *Anth. Lat.*, No. 261 (RIESE). The epitaph of Bishop Mamertus, in which there is a reminiscence of the first line of this epigram, proves that it was already well known at the end of the 4th

more than one school-poet, and no less than six variations of it, evidently by different hands, have been interpolated into the verse-biography of Phocas.[47]   These productions were the work not merely of the pupils, but also of the masters.   In the later years of the decadence it was common for several writers to compose rival works on the same subject, and notable instances of this class of composition are the productions of the " Twelve Scholastic Poets," or " Twelve Scholars," [48] which occupy so large a part of the Anthology, and would appear, from the number of MSS. in which they are preserved, to have been much admired.   Their themes were various; a description, a mythological event, or the praises of some person would often serve; but as a rule they preferred a subject already treated by some well-known poet, such as Ovid,[49] or, oftener still, Vergil.

Thus the famous epitaph of Vergil, which, according to the biography, was composed by the poet himself,[50] was re-written as a distich and also expanded into two distichs by each of the Twelve.[51]   To this class of composition belong too the arguments in verse of the various Vergilian poems.[52]   The number and variety of these which have survived show that this too was a favourite subject for scholastic rivalry.   Some of these

---

century. Cp. L. MÜLLER, *Jahrbb. f. Philol.*, 1866, p. 865. There is also a resemblance between the second line and a couplet (v. 43) of the *Nux Elegia*, which RIESE has pointed out, drawing at the same time illegitimate conclusions as to the date of that Elegy. The epigram on Balista was very well known throughout the decadence and middle ages independently of the *Liber Epigrammaton* of Vergil to which it perhaps belonged.

[47] In two of these imitations the distich is reduced to a single line; PHOC., *Vit. Verg.*, v. 15 seqq.

[48] Cp. on these poets SCHENKL, *Zur Kritik späterer lateinischen Dichter* (*Sitzungsbericht. d. Wien. Akad.*, June, 1863, p. 52 seqq.

[49] *E.g.* the exercises on Ovid's four lines on the seasons (*Met.*, ii. 27 seqq.), *Anth. Lat.*, No. 566 seqq. (RIESE).

[50] "Mantua me genuit," etc., DONAT., *Vit. Verg.*, p. 63. An imitation of this line occurs in an epitaph of Lucan, quoted already by ALDHELM (7th cent.), "Corduba me genuit, rapuit Nero, proelia dixi." Cp. L. MÜLLER, *Jahrbb. f. Philol.*, xcv. (1867) p. 500; USENER, *Scholia in Lucani Bellum Civile*, p. 6.

[51] *Anth. Lat.*, 507–518, 555–566 (R.).

[52] *Vide* L. MÜLLER, *Ueber poetische Argumente zu Vergil's Werken*, in the *Rhein. Mus.*, xix. p. 114 seqq.

arguments refer to the Bucolics or the Georgics,[53] but the great mass of them belong to the Aeneid. We have arguments of all the books of the Aeneid consisting of a single line, of four lines, of five, of six and of ten.[54] A composition consisting of eleven hexameters, of uncertain date, gives the total number of verses in all the works of Vergil, and their contents.[55] The earliest instance of a composition of this kind, for the purposes of which Vergil's own words were very largely borrowed, is perhaps the hexastich attributed to Sulpicius Apollinarius, contained in a Vatican MS. of the 5th or 6th century. Of about the same date are the decastichs, preceded by five distichs, which bear the name of Ovid,[56] and show clearly the relations existing at that time between Vergil and Ovid as used in the schools. Similar compositions continued to be produced throughout the middle ages, and though Vergil was not the only poet to whom they were dedicated, yet a far larger number were devoted to him than to any other Latin writer. There are in the Anthology several epigrams in his praise, generally based on the commonplace comparisons of him with Homer in the Aeneid, with Hesiod in the Georgics, and with Theocritus in the Bucolics.[57] In one of these appears

---

[53] *Anth. Lat.*, No. 2 (R.), from MSS. of the 9th century. Cp. RIBBECK, *Prolegg.*, p. 379.

[54] *Anth. Lat.*, No. 1, 591, 634, 653, 654, 874.

[55] *Anth. Lat.*, No. 517 (R.).

[56] *Anth. Lat.*, No. 1 (R.) : *Vide* RIBBECK, *Prolegg.*, p. 369 seqq. ; L. MÜLLER, *op. cit.*, p. 115 seqq., the latter of whom suggests with reason that they may be the work of an African of the 5th or 6th century.

[57] *Anth. Lat.*, No. 713 (R.) (Vergil and Homer) ; the epigram, No. 777, " Vate Syracosio," etc. (Vergil, Theocritus, Hesiod and Homer), was perhaps prefixed to a collection of Vergil's minor poems (cp. L. MÜLLER, *Jahrbb. f. Philol.*, 1867, p. 803 seq.). It has not, I believe, been observed that No. 788—

> " Maeonium quisquis Romanus nescit Homerum
> me legat et lectum credat utrumque sibi,"

is evidently modelled on the first couplet of the *Ars Amatoria* :—

> " Si quis in hoc artem populo non novit amandi
> me legat et lecto carmine doctus amet."

Generally speaking, an account of Vergil's three chief models was always prefixed by the grammarians to their commentaries and biographies of him. As Vergil is compared with Homer, so Lucan is compared with Vergil in

a metrical version of the saying of Domitius Afer quoted by
Quintilian.[58] Some lines composed in a metaphorical and
obscure style profess to give counsel to those who venture in a
small boat upon the vast sea of Maro.[59]

Lastly, these poetical exercises drew their materials also
from passages in Vergil's more important works, just as we
have already noticed was the case with the prose declamations.
More than one poem in the Anthology is inspired by such a
passage,[60] and the school of rhetoric is particularly noticeable
in the so-called 'themata Vergiliana,' which are variations
upon verses of the poet, developed according to the pompous
and bombastic methods in favour at the time. Such are the
words of Dido to Aeneas (Aen., iv. 365 seqq.), of Aeneas to
Andromache (Aen., 3. 315 seqq.), of Saces to Turnus (Aen., xii.
653 seqq.).[61] We have besides an epistle of Dido to Aeneas,[62]

epigr. 233 (cp. SCHMITZ and L. MÜLLER in *Jahrbb. f. Philol.*, 1867, p. 799).
The epigram on Vergil, No. 855 (MEYER),—

> " Alter Homerus ero vel eodem maior Homero,
>   tot clades numero dicere si potero,"—

belongs to the latter part of the middle ages, and is therefore omitted by
RIESE. The lines have, as a matter of fact, nothing to do with Vergil, but
are part of a medieval poem on the Fall of Troy. Cp. DU MÉRIL, *Poésies
popul. lat. ant. au XII. sièc.*, p. 313.

[58] " De numero vatum si quis seponat Homerum,
>   proximus a primo tum Maro primus erit.
>   At si post primum Maro seponatur Homerum,
>   longe erit a primo, quisque secundus erit."
>   Attrib. to ALCIMUS AVITUS, *Anth. Lat.*, 740 (R.).

Cp. QUINTIL., x. 1. 86.

[59] " Qui modica pelagus transcurris lintre Maronis
>   bis senos Scyllae vulgo cave scopulos.
>   sed si more cupis nautae contingere portum
>   carbasus ut Zephiris desine detur ovans ;
>   tumque salis lustra reliquos ope remigis amnes ;
>   sic demum cymbam portus habebit opis."

Publ. from a MS. of the 10–11th century by L. MÜLLER in the *Rhein. Mus.*,
xxiii. p. 657 ; RIESE, *Anth. Lat.*, No. 788.
[60] *Vide* 46, *De Turno et Pallante*, 77, *De Niso et Euryalo*, 99, *De Laoco-
onte*, 924, *In Aeneam* (*Anth. Lat.*, ed. RIESE).
[61] *Anth. Lat.* (R.), 255, 223 (attrib. to CORONATUS), 244. The subject of
No. 223 is also treated in a prose declamation of ENNODIUS (Dist. 28, *Verba
Didonis*, etc.). For specimens of these verse declamations on other than
Vergilian subjects, *vide* 128 and 23, especially the latter.
[62] *Anth. Lat.*, No. 83 (R.).

in the style of Ovid, a lament on the fall of Troy, which its rhythm shows to belong to the latter part of the middle ages,[63] and other similar works of which it is needless to speak here.

These poetico-rhetorical productions cannot strictly be described as medieval; they belong rather to the last days of the empire and the period immediately following. The 5th and 6th centuries were especially fertile in this class of school versification, which was carefully preserved by men who were themselves evidently connected with the schools, and had no scruples in mixing these productions, which their degraded taste taught them to admire, with the minor poems of the great masters. Hence that strange confusion of names which makes the proper arrangment of the Latin Anthology a task of such difficulty. In the importance thus assigned to works of such base origin are clearly visible the dying struggles of classical poetry which, reduced to a miserable existence in the artificial atmosphere of rhetoric, had become emaciated to such a degree as to show the very skeleton that forms its framework. But though the character of this last phase of Latin poetry was such, we have preferred to regard it as medieval rather than classical, because it was through it alone that the ages of monastic asceticism were able to follow, however feebly, the footsteps of the masterpieces of the Roman literature which had come down to them in its company.

[63] Du Méril, *Poés. pop. lat. ant. au XII. sièc.*, p. 309 seqq. For a medieval version of the Aeneid in elegiac couplets, *vide* Hagen in *N. Jahrbb. f. Philol.*, cxi. 10, p. 696 sqq.

CHAPTER XI

It is impossible to imagine two things more utterly diverse the one from the other than paganism and Christianity. Nothing could be more different than their respective ways of regarding the world both within and without. Christianity is to a singular degree absorbing; it claims for itself all the being of a man and concentrates it upon one idea; all the feelings, the passions, the emotions, the instincts which play so great a part in artistic productions are reformed and regulated by it, and bidden to tend towards a single goal. All poetical inspirations meet at one point; one loves in God, one grieves in God, one rejoices in God, one lives in God; God is the basis of every formula which determines or satisfies the emotions, the passions, the enthusiasms, the hopes, and the fears of the human soul. The horizon of life is completely changed, and therewith its eschatological principles undergo a profound revolution. The eye is fixed anxiously on the problem of the life beyond the grave, and all the activity of mankind is concentrated on this one object. Life on earth is a burden, a pilgrimage, a hard and difficult trial; now for the first time one hears that there is a *worldly* life, that there is a *world* which is dangerous and harmful, from which a pious man must keep himself severely apart. A violent revolution must take place in the conscience of man to enable him to look upon himself and society and nature in this way. The poetical ideals conceived in an epoch of spontaneous expansion, when the spirit, as yet uncurbed and untormented, followed its natural impulses and claimed the whole world for itself, and with simple faith believed in it and loved it and deified it, recognising in it its own proper image, could not fail to be repugnant to minds which regarded in such a different manner the relations of human beings to one another, to nature and to God. The sentiment which produced hermits and monks could leave but little room in the mind for an appreciation of the artistic ideals of Homer and Vergil.

Had Christianity remained in the home of its birth and confined itself to being a religious reform among the Jews, its nature and origin would have tended to the production of a peculiar class of poetry which might well have been a second phase of the ancient Biblical poetry, with which it was by nature most intimately connected. It would have been a phase notably different, no doubt, from that which had gone before, for there was in the original idea of Christianity a humanitarian sentiment and a refinement of religious feeling which gives to Christ and His followers a type very distinct from that of David, or Isaiah, or any other of the fiery spirits of the old dispensation; but in any case it would have had this in common with the ancient Jewish poetry, that it would not have been the product of a school or of a course of study which had art for its sole aim. If there was one thing repugnant to the early Christian idea, it was artistic conventionality and affectation, with its tendency towards objects other than those of religion.

Partly because he was a poor Jew who was born and who lived in Palestine and was not affected in any way, like so many of his fellow-countrymen who travelled, by the Graeco-Roman civilization, partly because of the spiritual and mystical nature of his teaching, Christ remained throughout indifferent to every form of culture. Simplicity is the first external quality in the Christian ideal, which brings it into contrast with the ancient civilized world. Hence the highest Christian poetry was not a product of the field of art, from which the faithful followers of Christ held entirely aloof; it expressed itself not in forms but in ideas and sentiments, clothed for the most part in the simplest and humblest of language; and yet, without composing a verse, without so much as dreaming of poetry, merely following the impulses which the new idea suggested, it produced its ideal of Christ, which is without doubt the noblest of its poetical achievements, and which played no small part in inspiring that magical enthusiasm which counted by millions its converts and its martyrs. Of a similar nature, simple and regardless of the form, are the poetical effusions of Francis of Assisi and of the author of the *De Imitatione Christi*, which are late but faithful echoes of true and primitive Christianity.

In its diffusion through the Graeco-Roman world, Christianity found the soil well prepared alike by the positive and the negative qualities of the decadence; nor was it the only new element which gave to this epoch a character so different from that of the more splendid periods which were irrevocably gone. By a slow process, the stages of which can with sufficient study be clearly traced, it succeeded in percolating into Graeco-Roman society and modifying the latter, though not without itself undergoing the while considerable modification. The spirit of proselytism, which was as rooted in its nature as was the spirit of conquest in that of Rome, compelled it to make certain inevitable concessions. The first of these was that of being educated, of becoming cultured, of initiating itself into the Graeco-Roman civilisation, and, since the latter was too strong to be overthrown, of endeavouring to assimilate itself to it with a view of ultimately influencing and modifying it. And thus, strange as it seems with the ideal of Christ and his apostles before one, Christians could become painters and sculptors, poets and versifiers, and could find a vehicle for the expression of their religious sentiments where Christ would never have dreamt of seeking, nor indeed would have suffered any one to seek. And thus arose one of the first and chief of those thousand inconsistencies, which all the pious expedients suggested by faith have never been able to explain away, by virtue of which Christianity has survived to the present day.

Christianity was never at its ease when arrayed in the forms of ancient poetical art, and the ability of its various poets could never do more than slightly diminish the strangeness of its appearance. Not unfrequently indeed the contrast between the matter and the form would have been positively ridiculous to any one not blinded by the fervour of religious faith.

Christianity found a soil prepared for its reception in society, but it did not find artistic forms appropriate for its use. The mysticism and the new tendencies of thought which favoured the success of the new religion in the times of the decadence, just because they were the products of decay and not of regeneration, of a weak and senile decrepitude and not of a fervent and youthful energy, could not bring about that warmth of feeling necessary to remodel art in accordance with its new conditions; they could only serve to reduce the ancient forms of art to a yet lower level of degradation.

Such therefore was the condition in which Christianity found art; it seemed alive in the schools and the general civilisation, but it was dead in the brain and the heart. These empty forms then, which were the common property of the civilised world, Christianity undertook to withdraw from secular uses and make a vehicle for Christian religious expression. The employment of them had indeed become so purely mechanical that it seemed only natural to regard them as open to the first comer and capable of being adapted to any sentiment. Originated in Greece, it had been a task of no small difficulty, and one requiring the assistance of the most splendid representatives of the Latin genius, to transfer them to Rome; they were now to undergo a second transition yet more violent than the first, because in it was involved a negation of all those principles of art which Rome and Greece alike had observed. Indeed no such act of folly could have been attempted except in an epoch in which rhetoric exercised so tyrannous a sway over literature that all idea of the intimate connection which should exist between matter and form had long been entirely lost.

In fact, to copy Vergil like Prudentius, Sedulius, Arator, Juvencus and so many other Christian poets did,[1] by putting

---

[1] ZAPPERT (*op. cit.*, not. 58, p. 20 seqq.) has collected a large number of Vergilian reminiscences from various medieval Latin poets from the 5th to the 12th centuries. But this collection, large as it is, is yet quite inadequate, and a similar one might be made for Ovid or various other classical writers. A complete examination of the Vergilian elements in medieval poetry would be a colossal task, and would merely serve to confirm the already evident results of those fundamental facts of which they are but the natural consequence.

into hexameters the Life of Christ, or the Lives of the Saints, or events taken from the Bible, or to imitate Horace or Ovid by composing elegiac couplets or lyric odes on Christian subjects, was to produce work in which the convictions, the arguments, the moralisings might be sincere enough, but in which the real poetry of Christianity could have but little part. To versify the Gospels meant to christianise scholastic exercises, but it also meant to take away from the simple narrative its own proper poetry by tricking it out in a way repugnant to its nature. And yet men brought up amid the Roman culture, with the ancient models continually before them, could not but view with complacency any attempt, however feeble, to fill up what must have seemed to them a void in Christianity. The description of the storm in the hexameters of Juvencus might serve to recall the famous passage of Vergil; more than one ode of Prudentius could remind them of Horace. That there was nothing of the ancient poetry in these compositions beyond the form, and that true Christian poetry had equally little part in them, were matters of no great account in an age when poetry was merely looked upon as versified rhetoric. Hence the Christian poetry was Christian in subject and pagan in form, so that when a Christian poet, as for instance Ausonius, does not happen to write on Christian subjects, such is the influence of his classical models that it is well-nigh impossible to distinguish him from a pagan. This is particularly noticeable during the decadence and at the Renaissance, which are the two chief periods during which Christian Latin poetry was allowed to occupy itself with secular matters, and is one of the reasons which tended to confine poetry so rigorously to sacred themes during the dominion of asceticism. But even during the decadence, as long as paganism survived, the Christians were so concentrated by their struggles on the religious idea, that it was but seldom that their poetry treated of any other. And already at this period Christian culture is almost entirely represented by the clergy, even in poetry; the poems by laymen which have come down to us from these centuries are very few. Even at this early date one can foresee what will become of society and culture when paganism is finally extinct and

all the world is Christian. We are already in the middle ages;
religious authority and the religious idea have penetrated
in every act and ordinance of life to the very soul of things,
and Christianity, developing and adapting itself in accordance
with its successive triumphs, instead of being absorbed by
Roman society, has absorbed that society in itself. The spheres
of human activity have become widely separated from one
another in accordance with the various states and conditions
of men. The first great line of demarcation, finally fixed by
the triumph of Christianity over paganism, is that between
laity and clergy; the former are concerned with the material,
the latter with the intellectual life; it seems natural to the
laity that culture should have nothing to do with them, and
they are no more ashamed of not being educated than they are
of not being clergy. In the end the difference is reflected in
the very names, so that 'clericus' comes to mean a man of
education, 'laicus' the reverse; the former is respected, but
the latter is not therefore despised; each follows his own trade.
Thus culture and intellectual activity became the exclusive
property of a religious caste and became concentrated on religion; and every order of society felt the influence of this
caste, whose nature, mission and tradition was to concern itself
with the affairs of other people, and which held moreover in its
power the heart and the soul of every man from the loftiest
prince to the humblest villein.

All this defines clearly the direction which Latin poetry of
classical form is compelled to follow during the middle ages.
Being an artificial product, it is in the hands of the clergy and
occupies itself mainly with religion; with sentiments or emotions of any other character it is not concerned, for even when
its subject is secular, as for instance in the versified accounts of
historical events, the nature of the ideas and the moral reflections
shows clearly that the point of view is always strictly clerical
and religious. In the forms, the metres, and the general application of the classical machinery we regularly find the same
barbarism and the same ignorance as we have seen to prevail
in the contemporary schools of grammar and rhetoric, to which
this poetry may be said entirely to owe its existence. It was

M

not the expression of an emotion or a sentiment, it was not
even the intelligent imitation of a definite type of art; it was
merely an exercise in versification, a pastime, and nothing
more; it was a recreation to which an occasional hour might
be devoted, always, however, 'ad maiorem Dei gloriam.' A
professed poet, who was nothing but a poet, would have found
little enough encouragement among people of this kind. This
becomes clear when we see Lactantius, Aldhelm, Alcuin, Bede,
Rhabanus Maurus and others of their class writing Latin verses
in the same spirit as now-a-days one might play a game of
billiards, and amusing themselves by turning out enigmas, ana-
grams, acrostics, and similar puerilities by the hundred. The
character proper to the Latin poetry of the decadence is found
again in the metrical compositions of the middle ages, except
that the classical forms are even more rudely treated, and that
it is clear that, after the great change which has come over
everything, they have even less right than before to exist outside the schools.[2]   And it is further apparent that in clerical
literature the literary forms have become fixed, after that
manner of stereotyping which is peculiar to the church, on the
model of the literary taste which prevailed when the ecclesiastical system was first established in the Roman world.

Rhetoric and declamation, the eternal, illogical and incon-
clusive repetition of phrases and commonplaces, the conventional and exaggerated epithets, the regular purple patches
from this or that favourite author and other similar qualities
remained as constant and invariable in the ecclesiastical literature as the liturgy and the ritual. We find this in Augustine,
in Cassiodorus, in Gregory, in Thomas Aquinas, and we recognise it in more recent papal bulls and circulars, and in the
modern Catholic writers, who, inasmuch as they are still medi-

---

[2] LEYSER has vainly attempted to defend medieval Latin poetry in his
De ficta medii aevi barbarie, imprimis circa poesim Latinam. Helmst, 1719.
Somewhat more successful is WRIGHT in his *Anglo-Latin Poets of the Twelfth
Century (Essays on subjects connected with the Literature, Popular Supersti-
tions and History of England in the Middle Ages,* vol. i. pp. 176–217). But
the most one can admit is a very few unimportant exceptions. Cp. BAEHR,
Gesch. d. röm. Lit. im Karolingischen Zeitalter, cap. 11; EBERT, *Allgem.
Gesch. d. Litt. d. Mittelalters im Abendlande.* Leipz., 1874–87.

eval in their culture, their methods of thought and their dialectic, try in vain to measure themselves with modern science, which has no time to trouble about them.

The utter incompatibility that exists between Christianity and paganism could not fail to put Christian poetry to great inconvenience in its classical dress. Ancient poetry and ancient religion were so closely connected in their causes, their origin, and their development that they had become in great part actually identical. Mythology, itself a poetical creation, occupied so prominent a place in the expressions, the images, and the phraseology of poetry, to say nothing of its ideals, that it was impossible to employ the ancient forms to sing of Christ and the saints without at the same time introducing Apollo, the Muses, and the whole of the pagan Olympus. It is true that the purely poetical nature of this mythology enabled it, when brought face to face with the new ideas, entirely to throw off its religious character, and yet retain, as a collection of imaginary names and facts, its poetical value; it was thus that it gained a footing in Christian poetry and art, and managed to survive in modern European thought in a way which is at first sight surprising.[3] (Such a thing could of course only happen without detriment in an art the form of which was new, and which, while modifying what it preserved of the ancient idea, yet represented it, as far as it went, justly; in an art which was merely an imitation of ancient forms it could not happen without either a loss of the art itself, or, as we find in the Renaissance, a loss of the modern idea.) But the more Christianity absorbed the ideas of men the more did the original incompatibility between Christianity and the pagan mythology become apparent, and it was keenly felt by many an ascetic who would gladly have avoided it;[4] but these, in sparing their consciences, spoiled their art by the curious expedients to which they were driven, as when for the ordinary

---

[3] *Vide* PIPER, *Mythologie der christlichen Kunst, von der ältesten Zeit bis in 's sechszehnte Jahrhundert.* Weimar, 1847-1851.

[4] " Sed stylus ethnicus atque poeticus abjiciendus; dant sibi turpiter oscula Jupiter et schola Christi."
BERNARD. MORLAN., *De Contempt.*, p. 86.

invocation of the Muses they substituted a ' *Domine labia mea
aperies*,' or, worse still, asked inspiration of the God ' who had
made Balaam's ass to speak.' [5]

But this sentiment was too real not to succeed eventually in
finding the means of emancipation. Breaking down the barrier
of classical forms which imprisoned it, it found a vehicle of expression in that simple and vulgar Latin which had grown up
under the influence of the time and remained the regular organ
of the Christian liturgy and faith. Disregarding the quantity
and only following the stress, it associated itself with that popular poetry which was the natural outcome of the new rhythms
resulting from the intonation peculiar to the new spoken
languages. And thus there arose the many rhythmical forms
of Latin poetry, in which it is easy to see that the medieval
spirit feels far more at its ease and far better able to express
itself with freedom and sincerity. However well Prudentius
and those like him may occasionally have succeeded in their
compositions, none of them has ever been able to infuse into
his work one half of the true and fervent poetical feeling of
hymns like the *Dies Irae* and its fellows, so utterly foreign in
language and construction to the classical versification of the
schools. There one may feel how the soul fears and hopes,
there one may see its terrors and its longings, and one need be
no believer oneself to feel the charm of this beautiful poetry,
which comes straight from the heart. Among the rhetoricians
and the poetasters with their odes and hexameters it is often so
hard to believe that they are in earnest.

This new poetry, the most notable ancient monuments of
which belong to the ecclesiastical Latin and the religious
sentiment, arose from the same source as that from which the
new poetry of the laity, with its new thoughts and its new
language, was also one day to arise; and it was so in accordance with the spirit of the age that, existing during a long

---

[5] " Vix muttire queo, mutum, precor, os aperito,
　　ipse docens asinam quae doceat Balaam."

HERIGER (saec. x.), *Gest. Episc. Leodiens.* ap. PERTZ, *Mon. Germ.*, ix. 177.
Cp. the passages from PAULINUS NOLANUS, SIGEBERTUS and others collected
by ZAPPERT, *op. cit.*, not. 61.

period side by side with the classical poetry, it could not fail
to have its influence upon the latter.   And the influence was in
some measure mutual; for while the popular poetry led the
classical to neglect quantity and to adopt stress and rhyme, it
at the same time borrowed from it, or rather from those elements of culture among which it subsisted, not a few of its
facts, names and ideas.

These brief observations on medieval Latin poetry are intended to show how little the classical idea was present in the
minds of the caste which monopolised culture during the middle
ages, and this not alone in works of erudition, as we have
already pointed out, but also in those works of the imagination
which professed to be based upon ancient models; all which
only serves to explain and put in a yet clearer light the little
aptitude displayed by this class for the aesthetic appreciation
of the poetry of Vergil.   Hence this chapter may serve as the
corollary of those which have gone before, in that it has shown
that the deficiencies in the studies of these medieval ecclesiastics were accompanied by corresponding deficiencies in those
productions to which these studies led them.   Thus too we
have been brought in contact with the popular literature and
the new poetry, so that our next task will be to consider the
progress of our poet's fame in this new atmosphere.   But before entering upon a region so entirely different to that through
which we have hitherto been passing, it will be well to pause
and sum up the principal characteristics of that conception of
antiquity which was peculiar to the middle ages.

CHAPTER XII

THE disappearance from Western Europe during the middle ages of the study of Greek was a factor of no small importance in determining the medieval conception of antiquity and the position occupied in it by Vergil. That division of Europe into two parts, dominated by the two great centres of Rome and Constantinople, which appeared simultaneously with the fall of the empire and the rise of Christianity, which became so accentuated after the time of Justinian and which culminated in the schism of Photius and the separation of the two Churches, was no less marked in the world of culture and learning. Although Greek had been the language in which Christianity had first presented itself, and though it was the language of the Gospels, of Basil, of Chrysostom, of Dionysius the Areopagite and of so many other venerated Fathers, yet the centre of Christianity had become established at Rome and exercised from there that universal sway in religious matters which was proper to its seat; hence the Church was essentially Roman and Latin, and by adopting the most common organ of expression, which was Latin, it served to keep the Roman literature in some measure alive, notwithstanding its supreme indifference to everything connected with the secular side of the latter. The decadence was general, alike in the Latin and the Greek countries, and in both those connecting links which had bound the two together were in great measure destroyed, giving place to feelings of strangeness and distrust, and even of antipathy and hatred. Thus the civilisation of Western Europe lost that Greek element which had been so closely entwined with the Roman civilisation, and had had so great an influence upon Roman literature. Here and there one might be found who knew Greek, some dilettante who dabbled in the elements of the language, or some master who taught the rudiments of it to his pupils ;[1] but a knowledge of Greek was looked upon as a rarity, and even of those who professed to understand it, the great mass were unable to translate a line without falling into gross errors. The ignorance displayed in this respect by even the most distinguished men of the Latin Church is truly remarkable. The most obvious Greek words and those most indispensable in the language of Church and school were explained in the glossaries and encyclopædias, and this has misled certain modern writers by inducing them to suppose that the use by various medieval authors of occasional Greek words implies a knowledge of Greek on their part. No such knowledge existed. Except for a few books of Aristotle, which were known through Latin translations, the only acquaintance with Greece and Greek literature was that which could be obtained indirectly through the medium of the classical Latin writers. Homer was only known by the epitome of him in Latin verse, of which he himself, or, for some unaccountable reason, the Theban Pindar was not uncommonly supposed to be the author.[2]

---

[1] But few exceptions to what I have said can be found in the works devoted by various scholars to an examination of the study of Greek in the middle ages. *Vide* Cramer, *De Graecis medii aevi studiis*, Sundiae, 1849–1853 ; Le Glay, *Sur l'étude du grec dans les Pays Bas avant le quinzième siècle*, Cambrai, 1828 ; Egger, *L'Hellénisme en France*, Paris, 1869 ; Young, *On the history of Greek literature in England from the earliest times to the end of the reign of James I.*, Cambridge, 1862 ; Warton, *On the Introduction of Learning in England*, in vol. i. of his *History of English Poetry*, London, 1840, p. lxxxii. seqq. ; Gradenigo, *Intorno agli italiani che dal secolo xi. infin verso la fine del xiv. seppero di Greco*, in *Miscellanea di varie operette*, tom. viii., Venice, 1744 ; Tougard, *L'hellénisme dans les écrivains du moyen-âge du vii. au xi. siècle*, Paris, 1886 ; Traube, *Philol. Unters. aus d. Mittelalt.* (Abhandl. d. bayer. Akad. d. Wiss., xix. 2), Munich, 1891, pp. 52 seqq., 65. A history of the study of Greek in medieval Italy has yet to be written and would have a quite special interest, though the effects of the Byzantine dominion are in reality much less than one would at first sight be inclined to expect.

[2] The real author was a certain Italicus, who may also be the author of the *Punica*. The work certainly belongs to that period, and, whether actually written as a school-book or not, was for many centuries in common use in the schools. Hugo von Trimberg (13th cent.) places this Latin

Thus when the writers of the middle ages couple, as they frequently do in their allusions to the great men of antiquity, the names of Homer and Vergil, it is evident that they are simply copying mechanically the custom of the classical Latin writers and the tradition of the schools. Of the relations between Homer and Vergil they had themselves no idea, and any comparison between the two would have been for them an impossibility. Homer was a name and nothing more; the greatest poet of antiquity who was really known and studied was Vergil. And hence this writer assumed in the middle ages a position both in literature and education far higher than that which he had occupied among the ancients, who read and studied in their schools the Greek writers also. But on the other hand this more absolute supremacy of Vergil over the classical tradition was accompanied by a considerable decline in the importance of that tradition itself. The study of the classics was not allowed to employ more than a very small part of the intellectual activity; it had become an entirely secondary matter, and was regarded with suspicion and dislike. All the clergy who concerned themselves with secular studies were simultaneously preoccupied with other and weightier matters.

Homer after Statius, giving a reason for so doing which shows clearly that the original Homer was not at that time known in Western Europe :

" Sequitur in ordine Statium Homerus
qui nunc usitatus est, sed non ille verus ;
nam ille Graecus extitit Graececeque scribebat,
sequentemque Vergilium Aeneidos habebat,
qui principalis extitit poeta Latinorum ;
sic et Homerus claruit in studiis Graecorum.
Hic itaque Vergilium praecedere deberet,
si Latine quispiam hunc editum haberet.
Sed apud Graecos remanens nondum est translatus ;
hinc minori locus est hic Homero datus,
quem Pindarus philosophus fertur transtulisse
Latinisque doctoribus in metrum convertisse."

Vide HAUPT, *Monatsschrift d. Berl. Akad.*, 1854, p. 147. Cp. L. MÜLLER, *Homerus Latinus* in the *Philologus*, xv. p. 475 seqq., and the *Rhein. Mus.*, N. F., xxiv. p. 492 seq. ; DOERING, *Ueber d. Homerus Latinus*, Strassb., 1884. When medieval writers speak of Homer as being read and known in their time, they always mean this Latin Homer. Had WRIGHT considered this, he would not have said (*Biogr. Brit. lit.*, i. p. 40) that Homer was read in the schools of the West down to the 13th century, which is a grave error.

Cassiodorus, while recommending such studies to his monks, does not omit to express his opinion that it is quite possible to attain to *true knowledge* without them. 'None the less,' he adds, 'it may be well to take of them *soberly and with moderation*, not because there is in them any means of salvation, but because we hope that, as we pass lightly over them, it may please the Father of Lights to grant us the true and necessary knowledge.[3] These words serve to define exactly the position of the clergy with regard to secular studies during the middle ages. All the force of their intellects was directed towards theology and asceticism, and passed into the abstractions of dialectic and philosophy. In the face of these, every other literary study was regarded merely as an education for children or a pastime for adults, and to have occupied oneself exclusively or seriously with such things would have seemed frivolous and unworthy of the dignity of an ecclesiastic. Even those who did not go so far as to accuse Sylvester II. of magic because of his knowledge of mechanics and mathematics, yet confessed that he was 'too much given to secular studies.'[4] This way of looking at things was universal; it was not merely characteristic of those who tried to suppress secular studies as being founded on paganism; it was equally characteristic of those who affected, and in some measure strove to promote them. This may serve to explain certain contradictions which sometimes appear in writers contemporary with one another, of whom one may with justice deplore the decay of literary studies, while another speaks of them as being in an unduly flourishing condition.[5] That the various objections to secular

---

[3] "Sciamus tamen non in solis litteris positam esse prudentiam, sed sapientiam dare Deum unicuique prout vult . . . si tamen, divina gratia suffragante, notitia ipsarum rerum sobrie ac rationabiliter inquiratur, non ut in ipsis habeamus spem provectus nostri, sed per ipsa transeuntes desideremus nobis a Patre Luminum proficuam salutaremque sapientiam debere concedi." CASSIOD., *Instit. div.*, c. 28.

[4] "Studiis saecularibus nimium deditus." *Anon. Zwettling;* cp. HOCK, *Gerbertus*, c. 13.

[5] "Cum studia saecularium litterarum magno desiderio fervere cognoscerem, ita ut magna pars hominum per ipsa se mundi prudentiam crederet adipisci, gravissimo sum, fateor, dolore permotus, quod scripturis divinis magistri publici deessent, cum mundani auctores celeberrima procul dubio traditione pollerent." CASSIOD., *Praef. ad Div. Inst.*; "Unde miror satis

studies did not prevent them from continuing to exist, we have
already seen; but this existence was a sufficiently wretched
one, and any idea of· 'flourishing' under such circumstances
was out of the question. Their life at this time was like that
of an epileptic patient, with frequent fainting fits and a continual fear of a final fatal attack. The impression which this
period gives is such that the historian records as a wonderful
and well-nigh miraculous fact that classical studies survived
at all. It is one long story of their perpetual struggles for
existence and their feeble signs of life. Like beggars, they
slink from one monastery to another; seldom do they obtain
even temporary indulgence from a prince; Charlemagne, who
grudingly protects them, is followed by Louis the Good, who
detests them.[6]

It was not merely the pagan character of the ancient literature which made it distasteful; its general character of world-
liness was equally offensive. Aesthetic gratification was a
sensual sin; even recreation must be edifying. The aim of
culture, as dominated by monasticism, was not to embellish or
refine the spirit, but rather to edify and purify it with a view
to its future life and in accordance with the theological principles which constituted the essence of Christianity. The
ancient Latin works therefore, instead of having to compete
with the Greek, were compelled during the middle ages to
enter into a far more dangerous competition with the Sacred
Books. These last were the real classics of the time, according to which the mind moulded itself and in which it found

quod non velint mystica Dei sacramenta ea diligentia perscrutari qua tragoe-
diarum naenias et poetarum figmenta sudantes cupiunt investigare labore."
PASCH. RADBERT. (9th cent.), *in Math.*, p. 411 seq. (*Bibl. patr. max.*, xiv.);
" Alii autem studiis incitati carminum ad naeniarum garrulitates alta diver-
tunt ingenia, famam autem veritatis ergo, Dei sanctorum memorando gesta
. . . fabulis delectati, non pavent subcludere." GUMPOLD. ap. PERTZ,
Mon. Germ., iv. 213; "Cumque gentilium figmenta sive deliramenta cum
omni studio videamus . . . in gymnasiis et scholis publice celebrata et
cum laude recitata, dignum duximus ut sanctorum dicta et facta describantur,
et descripta ad laudem et honorem Christi referantur." *Histor. Eliensis*
ap. GALE, *Scriptores Hist. Brit.*, p. 468.

[6] "Poetica carmina gentilia quae in iuventute didicerat respuit, nec
legere, nec audire, nec docere voluit." THEGAN., *Vit. Ludovic. Pii*, § 19.

its most congenial nutriment. In these, especially in the Old
Testament, we find already that idea of the universality of
religion, penetrating and influencing every social organism
which is so essentially part of the Christian view of life.
They then, being in such harmony with the spirit of the time,
formed the first foundations of moral and religious education.
By their side stood Vergil and the other classical writers as
instruments of secular education, but separated from them by
that great gulf which separates the words of a man from the
words of God and literary esteem from religious veneration.
And though it would have been profanation to regard the
Sacred Books as literature and thus put them on a level with
the classical poetry, yet none the less they had a special
literary character of their own, and the continual employment
of them in the devotional books, the liturgies and the prayers
exercised a considerable influence, especially upon poetry, by
its suggestion of poetical forms and images of a peculiar type,
entirely different to the classical and withal more in harmony
with the fervent beliefs of the time.   This was one of the chief
of those causes which, as we have already seen, deprived such
classical studies as still survived in the schools of all real life,
and at the same time rendered it impossible for the medieval
mind to penetrate into the true nature of classical poetry or
to regard it without religious prejudice from a purely secular
point of view.   To understand a poetry essentially different
from that of the time in which one lives, it is necessary that
the mind should be able to rise to some higher region, from
which it may include within its horizon various phases and
forms of human productivity ; and there is further need of a
special aesthetic training to render the taste capable of appre-
ciating things to which it has not been used in ordinary life.
A bare act of will is not sufficient ; there must be present besides a degree of education and culture, alike individual and
universal, which it would be vain to look for among the monks
of the middle ages.   The culture of the middle ages, in everything concerned with secular matters, was too poor and feeble
a thing to raise the mind far above the common level.   Humanism was essentially foreign to this period ; the most worldly

monk, the most passionate admirer of the ancient writers, is
yet infinitely more Philistine than the worst Latinist of the
Renaissance could possibly be. Hence, where it is a question
of secular poetry at all, monk and layman alike understand
the new popular poetry far better than that of classical times.
Had this not been the case, it would be impossible to explain
the universal appearance in the monasteries of the popular
poetry, and the fact that the monks are its earliest representatives and editors, alike in Latin and the vernacular. No one
who fails to understand the nature and the causes of this decline from the ancient literary ideals, and the utter incapacity
of the medieval mind so much as to comprehend those ideals,
will be able properly to understand the fact of the Renaissance.

In fact, the medieval clergy were unable, through the nature
of their faith, to accept more than a small part of the learning of the ancients, and that part which they did accept they
were compelled, by their mental habit and the character
of their training, to regard merely from an external point of
view and in a false light ; but this must not be understood to
imply that such classical learning as they had did not to them
represent a great deal. The most bigoted and fanatical ascetic,
however much he might detest the ancients, yet did not hesitate
in ascribing to them the most profound wisdom, much in the
same way as he ascribed it to the Prince of Darkness, to whose
inspiration he would generally consider their works to be due.
This judgment was not, of course, the result of individual
examination ; it was due, rather, to that unalterable tradition
which continued to bring before them the names of Plato and
Aristotle, Caesar and Cicero, Homer and Vergil; nor was the
principle of *omne ignotum pro magnifico* without its weight
in assigning to the ancients an even greater reputation for
wisdom than they deserved. The tendency of Christianity was
not to deny the miracles of reason, but rather to exaggerate
them, thereby emphasising the merits of faith. The idea of a
necessary conflict between faith and reason, or of a continual
contradiction between them, was not one which the Christian
could accept ; he was therefore unwilling to condemn everything in antiquity, but, distinguishing the proper spheres of

faith and reason, and observing their points of contact and disjunction, he was able to harmonise them one with the other, and to show that they were divided rather by the limits of their activity than by any innate antipathy or incompatibility. Medieval asceticism might therefore regard antiquity as having accomplished wonderful things, but as having fallen into grave errors through the want of a higher light; hence its temptations were the more dangerous, in that they were the more seductive. Reason, according to Christianity, is not excluded, it is corrected and amplified by faith. But, naturally, the more important of the two is faith to those who take it seriously; and the more the mind becomes concentrated on this, the less liberty does it allow to the element of reason. Besides, there is the obvious dilemma: either reason says what is contrary to faith, and is therefore wrong; or it says the same, and then what is the use of it? Such was the state of thought in medieval monachism; the importance assigned to reason in that great philosophical movement which began with Scotus Erigena provoked the hostility of the Church, and it was certainly not with its blessing that reason began, timidly at first and then more energetically, to resume its activity, till it eventually succeeded in confining faith to its proper sphere of the conscience and the emotions and excluding it entirely from speculative investigation, and thereby rendered possible the science of the present day.

From all this there was generated an exaggerated and mistaken notion of the learning of the ancients. But, above all, since the moral idea was the only one which penetrated and influenced the productions of the Christians, so the moral and religious side of the classical works alone was considered, if apparent, or, if absent, imagined; the aesthetic side of antiquity was entirely disregarded.

Similarly, too, and for similar reasons, the historical conception of antiquity became greatly changed through the atmosphere of the middle ages. To those historical works which recorded the antecedents of that tradition of civilisation on which medieval society was based had been added the books of the Jews, which had for the faithful an irresistible authority,

and began history *ab ovo* with a cosmogony and an anthro-
pogony entirely in accordance with the monotheistic principles
of Christianity no less than of Judaism. And not only did
these books claim credence for a mythology entirely different
from that of the literary tradition, but they further demanded
that history as a whole should be regarded in a special and
peculiar manner of their own. Christianity, when it arose
from Judaism, had merely enlarged the limits of the latter by
putting every man into that relation with God which was
before claimed as the exclusive right of the Jew alone and
making the ' *In exitu Israel de Aegypto* ' the symbolical hymn
of ransomed humanity. As a whole, the idea of a divine Re-
deemer and the fruitful labours of his apostles led naturally
to that view of history which this idea suggested : the kingdom
of God, the fall of man, his various wanderings and his final
restoration to one fold under one shepherd, were the chapters
into which such a view would naturally divide the story of
mankind. And thus history was divided into two distinct
periods—a long period of error and darkness, and then a period
of purification and truth, while midway between the two stood
the cross of Calvary. The nearer and more sympathetic of
these two periods was that of the world as regenerated and
redeemed, with its moving and poetical stories of the sufferings of the martyrs and the triumphs of the Faith; all the
rest of history was but a negation, a preparation, a 'discord
rushing in that the harmony might be prized.' Two cities
loomed large through the atmosphere of this idea : Jerusalem,
the city of God and Christ, the city of the past; and Rome,
bathed in the blood of the martyrs, the seat of Peter and his
successors, the sanctuary and the centre of living Christianity.
For the Christian, the history of these two cities first meets
at the moment of the Nativity and the institution of the Apos-
tolate; and from that time onwards Jerusalem disappears and
Rome begins. But this Rome was the Rome of the Empire,
and no period of history was kept so vividly before the eyes of
the men of the middle ages as that of the Roman emperors.
The Papacy, the Fathers, the relations with the Empire of
Christianity in its beginnings, in its struggles and in its triumph,

the history of the organic development of the Church, the very elements of sacred and secular civilisation, all led back to this same period, the nearest in every respect to medievalism. As Christ stood at the fountain-head of the religious records of Christian history, so its political records began with the first emperor, Augustus, in whose reign Christ was born.[7] By a coincidence, on the miraculous nature of which the Christians were never tired of dilating, the beginning of Christianity had been contemporaneous with the beginning of the Empire, and Christ had been born at a moment when Rome was at the zenith of her power, when peace reigned throughout her vast dominions, and a new era was commencing under apparently the most favourable auspices. Christ stood at the very antipodes of all this splendour, and, if there is anything remarkable in the coincidence, it is that just at this moment there should have been born one who, whether willingly or no, was to drive mankind so far back and down from the height of civilisation to which they had then attained. But, all question of miracles apart, it is clear on historical grounds that the new religion would never have prevailed as it did had it not chanced upon a period disposed to a general renewal, and a society weary of itself and eager for something new ; the ideals of Christianity would have remained mere Utopian visions had they not found so many diverse peoples made homogeneous by the legions of Rome. The Christians themselves saw this, and it seemed to them, as it always appears to those who look on history with the eye of faith, that in it was to be recognised the agency of God preparing long beforehand the time most

---

[7] " Finis consummationis imperii Romani fuit tempore Octaviani imperatoris ; ante quem et post quem sub nullo imperatore Romanum imperium ad tantum culmen pervenit ; cuius anno 42 dominus noster J.C. natus fuit, toto orbe Romano sub uno principe pacato ; ad significandum quod ille rex caeli et terrae natus esset in mundo qui caelestia et terrestria ad invicem concordaret." ENGELBERT. ADMONT., *De ortu et fine Rom. Imp.*, 20. This idea is so constantly repeated by the medieval chroniclers that further instances of it need not be quoted. *Vide*, for these ideas and the Christian legends about Augustus, the numerous passages collected by MASSMANN, *Kaiserchronik*, iii. p. 547 seqq. ; GRAF, *Roma nella memoria e nelle immaginazioni del medio evo*, i. pp. 308–331.

suited for the Saviour's mission.[8] This is the view of all who
believe, like the Jews of Alexandria,[9] that the idea of Providence is the key of history. And, indeed, the achievements of
Rome herself contributed not a little to this view; for already
in ancient times they had suggested by their brilliancy the
idea of a special divine protection. It is a commonplace with
Roman writers, especially of the Augustan age,[10] upon which
Vergil frequently dwells, that an ancient destiny and a divine
purpose prepared and guided the events which were to lead to
the foundation of Rome and her subsequent proud position as
benefactress and centre of humanity; this idea was carried on
and reproduced in a Christian sense by the Christians, so that
the medieval writers, no less than the Fathers and Christian
poets of an earlier period, all firmly believe that God permitted
the conquests of Rome with the express object that that city
might, by its central position, serve as the seat of the Vicars
of Christ.[11]

When the political importance of Rome came to an end, her
influence was not lessened but only changed; the Papacy and
the Catholic Church had arisen in place of the Empire, and
were carrying on its traditions by the universality of their
nature, their institutions, and their aims. For the physical
force there had been substituted a moral one—a force not
entirely new, however, for they were not material means alone
which served to cement together the Roman Empire and to
give it that sense of cohesion which so long survived its political dismemberment. And thus, as heir of the great creation of

---

[8] *Vide* LASAULX, *Zur Philosophie der röm. Gesch.*, Munich, 1861 (in the
Acten der Baierischen Akademie), which is a useful work for the history of
this view.

[9] These too used to ascribe to divine agency the events of ancient history.
οἱ μὲν γὰρ ἐπὶ τῆς οἰκουμένης πάντες εἰσὶ ῾Ρωμαῖοι . . . δίχα γὰρ θεοῦ
συστῆναι τηλικαύτην ἡγεμονίαν ἀδύνατον. FL. JOSEPH., *B. I.*, 2, 16, 4.

[10] Among the many expressions of this idea which occur in Latin writers,
may be quoted the words put by LIVY (i. 16) into the mouth of Romulus:
" Abi nuntia Romanis, Caelestes ita velle, ut mea Roma caput orbis ter-
rarum sit; proinde rem militarem colant, sciantque et ita posteris tradant,
nullas spes humanas armis Romanis resistere posse."

[11] " Romanam urbem Deus praeviderat Christiani populi principalem
sedem futuram." THOM. AQUIN., *De regim. princ.*, i. 14. Cp. DANTE, *Inf.*,
2, 19, etc., etc.

Rome, the Church succeeded so entirely in taking the place of the Empire that the Pontifical power came to regard itself and to be regarded as the supreme power of the world, to which all others were subordinate. And in that the Church had inherited the abstract part of the Empire, this feature of her power could not fail to make its influence felt among the secular authorities also, who all gravitated towards the one great idea of the Empire—the idea which Charlemagne strove to realise, not as a novelty but as a restoration and a continuation, which therefore had its natural head at Rome. The rude German *Kunec* aspired to become *Caesar*, and boasted in the title, forgetting that the power which gave him this authority was a far higher than his own; and if the reins sometimes broke in the weak hands of this or that individual, yet many a prince felt on his neck a heavier weight than ever the ancient Empire had laid on its conquered provinces—the one poor consolation for us Italians in all this gloomy period of our history. And thus this idea of a universal empire became in the middle ages, particularly after Charlemagne,[12] so dominant, that the whole of history was looked upon merely as a succession of great monarchies, successively entrusted by the Divine Will with the sovereignty over many nations.[13] Hence, according to this view, the position occupied by Greece in history is insignificant—her one great man is Alexander— while of Rome before the Empire, notwithstanding her more edifying moral character, there is no mention whatever, except in connection with a few of the more important conquests. The middle ages did not concern themselves with any but the conception of the Empire already constituted and complete and fashioned on that gigantic scale which was their ideal of political society and imperial power; hence their historians pass generally with one step from the foundation of Rome to the times of Caesar and Augustus.

The principal part therefore of ancient history becomes the

[12] For the history of this view *vide* BRYCE, *The Holy Roman Empire.*

[13] *Vide*, for this and for the historical use made of the famous dreams of Daniel and Nebuchadnezzar, the numerous parallels collected by MASSMANN, *Kaiserchronik*, iii. p. 356–364.

N

history of the Empire as subordinated to and confused with that of Christianity and regarded from its point of view, and is full therefore of legends and misrepresentations. Rome always remained morally the head of the world, and no city in the West, notwithstanding the greatness of the new nations, was able to come near the splendour and importance of that venerable and majestic ruin, or even to equal the lustre which the Roman name had lent to Constantinople. The cities of the medieval princes, e.g., Charlemagne's Aquisgrana,[14] figure but slightly in history, and not proportionately to the achievements of their masters. Nationality was, it is true, growing up in the field of morals no less than in that of politics and in the new literatures as much as in the new political groups into which Europe was being divided, but its growth was gradual and for the most part unobserved. A system of reflection capable of reducing to a principle, as would be done now-a-days, that sentiment which slowly but surely was preparing for the birth of modern Europe, was not at this period in existence. Public rights did not rest in any way on a conception resulting from a feeling of nationality, but were based on the entirely opposite principles of feudalism and imperialism. Nor, indeed, had the nationalities themselves as yet become well-determined entities, however much their tendencies might be in that direction. Resulting from a combination of various elements, they were naturally unable to develop otherwise than gradually, and they had still much to experience and achieve before their respective individualities could be definitely fixed. And hence it arose that, in spite of national development, no real rebellion against certain ideas could take place, but these ideas continued to be accepted and followed. The Teutonic and Latin races were diametrically opposed to one another and separated by lively antipathies, for which there was every historical justification; the Germans, though quickly corrupted themselves, yet retained certain ideas which

[14] " Urbs aquensis, urbs regalis,
Sedes regni principalis,
Prima regum curia."
Cp. BRYCE, *The Holy Roman Empire* (ed. 1892), pp. 72, 318.

they had inherited from those barbarous ancestors of theirs
whom Tacitus had contrasted with the Romans—much as he
might have contrasted them with any other civilised nation—
and hence persisted in regarding the 'Wälschen,' or Latin
races, as dissolute and corrupt; but none the less they had
no hesitation in admitting their own barbarism,[15] and in recognising the intellectual and civil superiority of their rivals.
Hence that unanimous reverence, in intellectual if not in
material questions, which gave to all the nations of Europe so
lofty a conception of Rome that any idea of rivalry with her
was out of the question. This reverence shows itself in a
thousand ways, in words, in ideas, in the acts of the German
emperors who called themselves Roman, in the crowds of
pilgrims that flocked to the centre of civilisation and Christianity, in the naïve guide-books, written for their use, on
the 'Wonders of the Golden City of Rome,' in the emphatic
expressions in which a thousand writers of the middle ages
indulge,[16] and not least in the significant endeavours of so
many new nations and princely families to connect themselves
with Rome by legends of their origin, in which they traced
back their families, like Augustus and other Romans, to the
heroes of Troy and the great names of Roman history [17]—a

[15] "Auditoribus usus erat lacialiter fari neque ausus est quisquam coram
magistro lingua barbara loqui." BRUNO, *Vit. S. Adalberti*, 5 (ap. PERTZ,
Scriptt. rer. Germ., iv. p. 577). It is very common for medieval writers to
speak of themselves or their language as barbarous. One need only look at
the long notices under the word *barbarus* in the indices to the various
volumes of the *Scriptt. rer Germ. Vide* also my note on p. 122.

[16] The vast and complicated history of medieval Rome is an inspiring
theme alike for the Christian and the freethinker. GIBBON, PAPENCORDT,
GREGOROVIUS and REUMONT have studied it from diverse points of view, the
two last especially so. Gregorovius, in his work of unfailing delicacy and
acumen, has shown himself, as he was, at once scholar and poet, and has
produced a book which even those unacquainted with the subject may read
with pleasure. But by none has the fascination exercised by Rome over the
medieval mind been at once so fully and so vividly described as by ARTURO
GRAF in his *Roma nella memoria e nelle immaginazioni del medio evo*, Turin
(Loescher), 1882–3.

[17] Cp. GRAESSE, *Die grossen Sagenkreise des Mittelalters*, p. 66 ; BERGMANN,
La fascination de Gulfi, p. 27 seq., and REIFFENBERG, *Chron. rimée de
Philippes Mouskes*, i. p. ccxxxvi., the last of whom mentions also several
modern writers who have taken these medieval follies seriously. *Vide* also
ROTH, *Die Trojasage der Franken* in the *Germania* of PFEIFFER, i. 34, and,

tendency on which the greatness of the influence exercised by
so popular a work as the Aeneid will be readily understood.[18]

The imperfect and hitherto confused development of nationality, especially in matters of sentiment, rendered possible this
idea of the Empire, which resulted both from the traditional
elements of culture and also from the more obvious and
visible points of connection between the present and the past
in matters of politics and religion; but it could be no more
than an idea. The actual restoration of the ancient Empire
was an impracticable chimera; the conglomeration of various
peoples under one ruler was bound to be unnatural and pre-
carious. The secret of the old Roman cement had been lost,
and in any case the individualities of the separate nations had
become too highly developed for it to be possible to combine
them again into a single organism. Moreover, the German
races, whom the weakness of their superiors had suffered to
gain the upper hand, were incapable, as may still be seen at
the present day, of assimilation, and thus, so far from assimilating others, great masses of them were themselves assimilated
when brought into contact with various of the neo-Latin
nationalities. Yet the conditions of thought tended irresistibly
towards the idea of the Empire, which is always present to
the chosen spirits of the age, whether in the Utopia of a
thinker or in the deeds of an emperor; while here too is
apparent that lack of connection between the ideal and the
real which gives to the middle ages so peculiar a character.
It is an age which, while having its attention wholly fixed on
the ancient world, which it wished to continue or restore, was
yet throughout, without knowing or wishing it, preparing for
the developments of modern times; it resembles a man who,
by some strange hallucination, while walking forwards thinks

on the same subject, ZARNCKE, in the *Sitzungsbericht. d. sächs. Gesch. d.
Wiss.*, 1868, p. 257 seqq., 284; BRAUN, *Die Trojaner am Rhein*, Bonn, 1856;
CREUZENACH, *Die Aeneis etc. im Mittelalter*, p. 26 seqq.; G. PARIS, *Historia
Daretis Frigii de origine Francorum*, in Romania, iii. p. 129 seqq.; BUECHNER,
Les Troyens en Angleterre (Caen, 1867); GRAF, *Roma*, etc., i. p. 22 seqq.;
RYDBERG, *Undersokningar i germansk Mythologi* (Stockholm), i. p. 24 seqq.

[18] Cp. DUNGER, *Die Sage vom trojanischen Kriege inden Bearbeitungen
des Mittelalters und ihren antiken Quellen* (Leipz., 1869),p. 19.

that he is walking backwards and wishes to do so   Never was
there an age which, to judge by its thoughts and its writings,
was more opposed to the ideas of progress or social revolution ;
never an age which seemed more motionless and stereotyped ;
and yet there was never another in which thought and feeling
underwent such great changes or during which society was
so completely transformed. In this exceptional condition of
affairs is to be found the key to the many peculiarities and
eccentricities of this epoch in respect to matters in which
ancient and modern thought are in accord with one another.

Medieval ideas were of such a kind that Vergil was bound
to be, as in fact he was, the most popular of the Roman poets ;
for in him his readers found as it were an historical echo of
that Roman feeling which he had been so supremely able to
represent and interpret.[19] The historical epoch moreover to
which he belonged and in which he had been so prominent a
figure was the one which was best and most commonly known,
and formed the centre in every conception of antiquity. The
fact that he lived during the reign of Augustus, at the beginning of the Empire, and in such close proximity to the birth of
Christ, served to place Vergil in the most favourable light
possible for the medieval mind, and played no small part in
developing the historical side of his reputation. And together
with this went the religious and philosophical side, by virtue
of which he was regarded as a man who was 'not far from
the kingdom of God,' and was furnished besides with an unfathomable store of universal wisdom. All the ancients, whether
prose-writers or poets, were regarded as ' philosophers ' ; but
the schools of grammar and rhetoric kept chiefly the poets in
view, and here again Vergil occupied the first place. Hence
Vergil was the most widely known and, if one may use the

[19] " Ille (Homerus) in laudem Graecorum, hic autem (Vergilius) in gloriam
Romanorum conscripsit." Vergil. vit. (9th cent.), ap. HAGEN, Scholl. Bern.,
p. 997. Others express this differently, regarding him as the singer of
Octavian, who represented to the medieval mind the culminating point of
Roman greatness. "Aeneida conscriptam a Vergilio quis poterit infitiari
ubique laudibus respondere Octaviani ; cum paene nihil aut plane parum
eius mentio videatur nominatim interseri ? " Cnutonis regis gesta (11th
cent.) argum.

word, the most popular of the ancient writers, though he did
not really figure in the minds of enlightened men as the sole
representative of the wisdom of the ancients.   When the scientific ardour and the strong intellectual movement which arose
at the beginning of the 12th century had given to Aristotle
his well-known position in the schools of philosophy, he too
was looked upon as omniscient; but Vergil still remained at
the head, because his fame, though leading up to the idea of
the philosopher, yet was not properly an affair of the philo-
sophy-schools, but was connected with those more general and
elementary studies of Latin with which Aristotle had nothing
to do.   The central point of Vergil's fame was always the
school of grammar, which gives us a further and really the
fundamental side of his medieval celebrity.   The new tendencies and the new aims implied by scholasticism made themselves
felt, no doubt, even in the schools of grammar, and masters,
who were well-known in their own time and for generations
afterwards, composed poems expressly for school use, which
achieved great success; but the *Alexandreis* of Guatier de Lille,
with its many imitations of Vergil, though much read in the
schools, yet never acquired the authority of the ancient poet,
any more than the popular grammars of Villedieu or Petras
Elias were able to acquire the authority of Donatus.

To sum up then, the medieval reputation of Vergil has three
sides—the historical, the philosophical and religious, and the
grammatical; this last is the lowest and the most trivial, but
yet forms the base on which the others rest.   As for the
aesthetic or properly artistic side in this conception, it is reduced to nothing, and is supplied by the extent of the others,
which but for its absence could never have attained to such
striking proportions.

CHAPTER XIII

THE ordinary conception of the 'Middle Ages,' the conception which has given them their name, is that negative idea of them which results from the intimate relation between antiquity and the Renaissance. The Middle Ages seem a period of aberration, across which ancient and modern Europe hold out their hands and welcome one another. But this conception, based on the final results, must naturally be modified when one wishes to proceed from what is negative to what is positive, with a view to studying the true relations of the three great historical periods and the causes of the changes that led from the one to the other—changes which can never be sudden, but are always prepared beforehand and governed by strict physiological laws. An analysis of medieval thought in the matter of its conception of antiquity will show clearly a continuity on the one hand with that of antiquity itself, and on the other with that of the Renaissance. In the epoch immediately preceding the middle ages are to be found elements which may explain how many of the aberrations of that period came about, while in the middle ages themselves appear the tendencies which prepared the way for the Renaissance. Two parts of this great epoch of history may be distinguished, which, while during a certain period contemporaneous and parallel with one another, yet in the end serve to divide the middle ages into two distinct sections. There is the Latin middle age, with its closer connection with antiquity and its culture based on this, and the popular middle age, with its new elements and its emancipation from every tradition. The two classes of clergy and laity, the distinction between which formed, as we have seen, one of the chief characteristics of the middle ages, are found associated in both these movements, but not in equal proportions.   In the first the initiative and the preponderance is with the clergy, in the latter with the laity; the prevalence of the laity in culture and intellectual life comes out clearly in the Renaissance, which is all their doing, and had its psychological antecedents, as we shall see, in the secular and popular literature.[1]

Classical antiquity, with Vergil at its head, dragging itself along among the entirely unsympathetic and heterogeneous elements of medieval clericalism, may be compared to a sun which, shining through a fog, loses its power to illumine, to warm and to fertilise.   Nor could this great eclipse come to an end till the classical studies had been transferred to the laity— a change which could only be brought about gradually.   The supremacy of the clergy and the religious sentiment and the general preponderance of faith over reason in the middle ages were a necessary result of the recent conversion of Europe to Christianity.   Such an event could not possibly take place in such proportions, and with such intensity, without the accompaniment of a turmoil, the effects of which were of long duration.   Europe was bound to go through that period of enthusiastic illusion and fanatical concentration upon a single idea characteristic of every neophyte.   And this period, with its inevitable restriction of the intellectual movement to the sacerdotal caste, was bound to endure as long as reflection remained in abeyance and the laity were unable to reassume the initiative in matters of culture and intellect.

Certain personal tendencies of Charlemagne and certain measures of his on the subject of secular education have led many to regard this prince as the author of a sort of first Renaissance.   That he was indirectly useful to secular studies cannot be denied; but his only interest in them was with a

---

[1] The reawakened activity of the laity gave rise to a bitter animosity between the two classes, which occasionally found expression in violent language.   Thus, an inscription in the Church of St. Martin, at Worms, runs:

> "Cum mare siccatur et daemon ad astra levatur
> tunc primum laicus fit clero fidus amicus."

view to sacred studies, and nothing which he effected has anything whatever to do with the Renaissance. I do not know whether my judgment of this prince is prejudiced by that repugnance which an Italian cannot fail to feel towards one who was the cause of that temporal power of the Papacy which did such harm to all Europe and has been till recently the curse of our unfortunate country. It certainly seems to me as if about his historical personality of prince, legislator and warrior there hung an unpleasant odour of sanctity. He was the 'homo Papae' *par excellence*, and no other Christian monarch was ever such a favourite in the monasteries, which contributed not a little to the elaboration of the legend which originated that type of '*buon Carlone*' so justly ridiculed by the refined malice of Ariosto. Charlemagne's only conception of secular education was the clerical one, and all his measures, instead of stirring the laity to life, tended simply to leave them more and more under the barbarous and unprofitable dominion of the clergy, which he made still stronger by his new foundations. He strove mainly, and with reason, to raise the clergy from the unparalleled depth of barbarism and ignorance to which they had sunk in France; he wished the laity to be educated too, but this education was to be imparted by the clergy and its object was to enable them to understand the services in church.[2] He may perhaps have wished to make education compulsory,[3] but even so it was not to be secular in aim; parents were to send their children to the monastic or the parochial schools 'to learn correctly the Catholic Faith and the Prayers, so as to be able to teach them to those at home.'[4] Charlemagne was a great man by reason of his iron energy, and he displayed talents as an organiser uncommon in contemporary lay princes, but he was a thorough German, and lacked that refinement and imagination which distinguished the great Italian ecclesiastical organisers, who built up the marvellously solid fabric of the Roman Church; he lacked the

[2] *Vide* SPECHT, *Gesch. d. Unterrichtswes. in Deutschl.*, p. 26.
[3] *Vide* BUEDINGER, *Von den Anfangen des Schulzwangs* (Zürich, 1865), p. 17.
[4] *Vide* SPECHT, *op. cit.*, p. 29.

originality and the courage necessary for instituting what would have been the greatest and most fruitful reform of his time—a purifying of society from the clergy and a call to the laity to reclaim their intellectual ascendency. The age might not have permitted so entire a revolt, but a man of genius could have prepared the way for it; Charlemagne did just the reverse. Perhaps only an Italian could at this epoch have conceived of so happy a revolution, but unfortunately there were many causes to hinder an Italian from reaching as a layman such power as that which Charlemagne possessed.[5]

But the want of true impulse on the part of this prince serves only to render more striking the great phenomenon of the rekindling of an activity which seemed extinct, the re-awakening of so many feelings which seemed dead and the recommencement of a life which was to lead to Dante, to Michelangelo and to Galileo. Here however we have only to study this phenomenon in so far as it affected the conception of antiquity and of Vergil.

Like streams which flow for a distance under ground before breaking out into the light, the languages of Europe had long been living and moving unobserved beneath the cover of the Roman world with its Latin literature, till at last the influence became weakened and they were able without rebuke to come to the surface in all their native freshness and simplicity. The nature of their appearance was twofold, and in each case significant. On the one side they are found in the regions proper to ancient culture, and manifest themselves in glosses and in translations from the Latin writers; on the other they appear as the organs of living feelings, expressing national ideas and traditions as yet unembodied in literature, and tending to the formation of a literature of their own, independent of the

---

[5] The influence of Italy on Charlemagne was of course immense, for not only did he learn much of his imperial policy from the Papacy and derive strong support from its activity on his behalf, but it was his sojourn in Italy which gave him the idea of instituting reforms by means of education, and it was from thence that he obtained several of the masters who assisted him in this. Cp. SCHERER, *Ueber d. Ursprung d. deutschen Literatur*, Berl., 1864; WATTENBACH, *Deutschl. Geschichtsquell.* (6th edit.), i., p. 151 seq.

classical tradition.   Such a combination of two processes, apparently contradictory, in the spontaneous growth of the living languages, would have been incompatible with the culture and the ideas of the Renaissance, when humanism and classicism drove the popular element entirely out of literature; but we have seen how different it was in the middle ages.   This emancipation of the vernacular was so legitimate that it was even able to penetrate the walls of the monastery and prevail upon the monk to abandon now and then his strained attitude of mind and be a man again, if only for a moment.   There were conscience-pricks, no doubt, for the old pagan ideas of the various European peoples entered largely into their popular national poetry, and we hear many a voice raised against these 'vain and profitless' songs of the vulgar.   But if the conscience had found a way of adapting itself to the classical literature, which was after all but an artificial impost on the mind, it was compelled to admit these dear records of country, of mother-tongue, of early recollections, so natural in their growth, which it required an effort not to remember but to forget.   And here too was a fact of seemingly little moment, yet pregnant with grave consequences.   The popular poetry, with its indifference to culture, was secular in its very essence, and remained so in the middle ages even when the monks contributed to its production.   Through it the clergy came in contact with the people, and not only did the division between clergy and laity become less marked, but the laity began once more to take its proper place as intellectual leader.   And thus the clergy, without wishing or knowing it, were assisting in a movement which was destined eventually to deprive them of their undisputed sovereignty over the minds and hearts of men and to bring forth many an anathema from the Church.   But the march of events was irresistible, and a hundred other features, material or moral, of this very period show clearly enough that the absolute dominion of faith could not be more than transitory and that reason was imperiously demanding its proper rights.

The causes which produced popular poetry were so powerful that their influence even extended to Latin, producing that popular rhythmical Latin poetry which was essentially medieval,

had its own classics,[6] and kept living side by side with the vernacular literature to the end of the middle ages. This cannot
easily be explained if one does not consider the exceptional
state of half-life in which Latin was at this period; for while
it was not really a living language, it was yet a language in
use, and in use too to such an extent that a movement like that
in the vernacular was bound to appear to some degree in it also.
With the 12th century began that prodigious movement which
was to do so much in the spheres of science and art and to
mark the opening of a great epoch in the history of humanity.
In this movement the motive force comes from the laity;
among them took place that wellnigh paradoxical union, which
yet became so intimate, between the romantic and chivalrous
poetry of purely popular origin and culture, tradition and
learning, whereby the popular poetry was finally raised to the
level of an art.   Hence the apparently singular fact that the
Goliards, while composing rhythmical Latin poetry of an entirely unclassical and modern type, in form and feeling thoroughly in sympathy with the laity, yet, in that they write
Latin and are men of education and claim to be such in their
verses, look upon themselves as belonging to the clergy and
speak of the laity with the greatest contempt.[7]   Such a use of
Latin and its close connection with the vernacular as an organ
of thought and feeling made the names of the ancient tradition
very familiar to the popular literature, in fact more so than
would have been possible under more normal conditions; and

---

[6] TOMMASO DA CAPUA (12–13th cent.) distinguishes in his *Summa dictaminis*
(ap. HAHN, *Coll. mon.*, i. 280) three kinds of *dictamen*: "prosaicum ut Cas-
siodori, metricum ut Vergili, ritmicum ut Primatis." For this PRIMAS, who
is supposed to be the Primasso of Boccaccio (*Decam.*, i. 7), *vide* GRIMM, *Kl.
Schrift.*, iii., p. 41 seqq.; P. MEYER, *Documents manuscrits de l'anc. litt. de
la France conservés dans les bibl. de la Gr. Bret.*, i. p. 16 seqq.; SALIMBENE,
Cronica, p. 41 seqq.; STRACCALI, *I Goliardi*, Florence, 1888, p. 72 seqq.

[7] One writes:
> "Aestimetur autem laicus ut brutus,
>   nam ad artem surdus est et mutus."

Another:
> "Literatos convocat decus virginale,
>   laicorum execrat pectus bestiale."

Cp. HUBATSCH, *Die lateinischen Vagantenlieder des Mittelalters* (Görlitz,
1870), p. 22.

hence these names are found as it were in suspension in this heterogeneous medium, whether the new feeling finds expression in Latin or in the vernacular. Thus too it came about that antiquity, when brought into this new current, underwent a yet further change, new and different to that which it had undergone at the hands of the monks, so that we find it further curiously travestied according to the ideas of romanticism. Hence it may happen that an author, *e.g.* Ovid, is at the same time being 'moralised,' that is interpreted allegorically with a view to moral edification, and 'romanticised,' that is having the gallant adventures which he describes travestied according to the notions of contemporary chivalry. The current of the new popular poetry is so strong that it inundates the elements of culture and sweeps away with it the language, the forms and the facts of the ancient poetry, and makes them its own, without heeding that want of harmony which to a modern taste is so distressing.

The artistic and intellectual productivity of the time came thus to have two distinct directions, on the one hand learned or scholastic, on the other popular or romantic; and hence the conception of antiquity became in like manner two-fold and was divided into the scholastic and the romantic. The former coincided originally with the clerical conception of the early middle ages, and then went on gradually purifying and emending itself till it finally separated from the latter and culminated in the Renaissance; the latter, arising from secular ideas belonging to the later middle ages, remained peculiar to popular and romantic works and continued to find expression as long as the popular element was allowed any place in literature. Hence it is not surprising to find both conceptions present in one individual, and it was no uncommon thing for the same man to compose learned works and romantic poetry. The scholastic conception furnished little on the aesthetic or sentimental side and left this deficiency to be supplied by the romantic. We need not follow here the various vicissitudes of Vergil due to this romantic tendency; we shall speak of this in our second part.

But antiquity did not come equally under the influence of

romance in all countries of Western Europe; some were more
inclined to this form of travesty, others less; the tendency
varied, just as the date of the origin of the vernacular literature
is in some countries earlier, in others later.   These facts have
both the same obvious reason, namely, that in some countries
the classical studies were more truly indigenous and more vital
than in others.   Hence it will be readily understood that the
first to break away from the classical tradition were the non-
Latinised Germans and Celts; after these came France and
Provence, and lastly Italy, Spain and Portugal.   Italy was
naturally the home of the classics and was looked upon even
during the middle ages as classical *par excellence*.   Here Latin
and the vernacular were least at variance with one another;
not only was the latter the immediate and natural offspring of
the former, but although it had acquired a separate individuality, it yet bore such a likeness to its parent that it was better
adapted than any other vernacular to the classical forms.   And
thus it became, among the living languages, the classical language of the Renaissance, which had its origin, as it was bound
to do, in Italy, and spread thence, owing to Italian influence,
elsewhere.

Certain expressions by non-Italian medieval writers, and the
mention of schools held in Italy by laymen, have led some
modern scholars to suppose that already during that period of
the middle ages which was anterior to the growth of popular
literature the education of the laity in Italy was better than
elsewhere; and this fact has been brought into connection with
the Renaissance.[8]   That the Italian laity was in reality much
more cultured than that of the rest of Europe does not, however, seem to me probable, nor is it in any way proved by
these vague notices, which are all we have on the subject; and
while it is impossible to speak with certainty on the subject, it
is at least worthy of note that the Italian laity does not appear,
before the rise of the vernacular literature, to have been any
more productive than the laity of other countries.   However

---

[8] This is the subject of GIESEBRECHT's *De litterarum studiis apud Italos
primis medii aevi saeculis* (Berl., 1845).   Cp. BURCKHARDT, *Die Cultur der
Renaissance in Italien*, p. 173 seqq.

paradoxical it may sound, the true beginnings of the Renaissance must be sought, not in the elements of traditional culture, but in the new elements, not in the Latin literature, but in the vernacular. There is visible among the Italian laity a strong desire to be initiated in classical culture, but this desire appears contemporaneously with the development of the vernacular literature, and there are no striking traces of it at any earlier period.[9] The ideas too which we find among them, when this tendency appears, show clearly that in Italy, as elsewhere, the initiative in these studies was peculiar to the clergy; while even had the Italian laity been more highly educated than was the case in other countries, yet such education could not have been different in its aims and its limits to that of the clergy. The conception of antiquity and the position assigned to it in the history of humanity were the same for the Italian layman as they were for the monk, and it must therefore have required no little effort on the part of the laity, even in Italy, to throw off these medieval notions with which they were burdened and to arrive at that intelligent and appreciative study of the classics which is the characteristic of the Renaissance. To attain to this, it was necessary to free the mind entirely from that clerical influence which debarred it from a proper comprehension of antiquity; it was necessary to expand it, to elevate it and to exercise it in a school which should rouse to life again all its sleeping powers. And this school of exercise the layman found by devoting his energies to subjects untouched by tradition, whereby, in a fashion which was the more vigorous in proportion as it was more natural and spontaneous, he was gradually enabled to refine and purify himself, till he finally succeeded in elevating himself to the true level of ancient art. It was really only the agility of mind which the popular poetry and the new forms of art induced that made it possible to recover that feeling for antiquity which had long been lost or perverted. Latin, and its employment according to classical models, could only lead to stagnation, not to progress. This is clear enough

[9] For the literary culture and the Latin poetry of Italy during the 10th, 11th and 12th centuries, *vide* RONCA, *Cultura medievale e poesia latina in Italia*, etc. (Rome, 1892).

when we observe the difference in originality and artistic genius of the same man (*e.g.* Dante or others) when writing in Latin and in his mother-tongue.

The starting point then in the movement of modern life was the same for the Italians as for the other nations of Europe; the nature and the materials of their culture were identical; but for the reasons we have already mentioned, that elevation of mind which arose from the creation and the perfection of a new form of art was more vigorous and more rapid in Italy than elsewhere, so that though the Italians were the last to have a popular literature, this literature was greater, more noble and more monumental than any other, and was the first to free itself from plebeian influences and reach the level of an art.   In the region of purely popular poetry the Italian literature is poor as compared with that of other countries.[10]   Of national epic poetry of popular legendary origin there are no traces, nor indeed could there be, seeing that Italian thought and sentiment, even among the uneducated classes, was rooted in the actual history of the past—a fact incompatible with the production of epic poetry; and this was not merely the state of mind with which the Italians regarded themselves, but was also that with which other nations regarded them.   Nor was the store of popular lyric poetry so rich in medieval Italy as elsewhere,[11] while such of it as did exist soon freed itself from its purely popular character and reached artistic perfection more rapidly than was the case in other countries.

[10] Cp. WOLF, *Ueber die Lais, Sequenzen und Leiche*, pp. 112 and 223 seq.

[11] This cannot be maintained with absolute certainty, as the Italian libraries have not as yet been searched with any great care for literature of this kind.   Very few of the Latin poems of the Goliards hitherto published show signs of Italian origin; the view that the chief author of this class of compositions was an Italian has been too readily accepted by BURCKHARDT (*Die Cultur der Renaissance in Italien*, p. 174 seq.).   The MSS. of these poems at present known belong to non-Italian libraries.   In support of the contrary view BARTOLI (*I precursori del rinascimento*, Florence, 1877, p. 71 seq.) adduces several MSS. from Italian libraries; but he again is answered by STRACCALI (*I Goliardi*, Florence, 1880, p. 54 seqq.).   Cp. too WATTENBACH, *Deutschl. Geschichtsquell.* (6th edit.), i. p. 477.   Independently too of the Goliards, at an earlier period of the middle ages, Italy seems to have been poorer in this respect than other countries, as may be seen from DU MÉRIL, *Poésies populaires latines du moyen-âge*, Paris, 1847.

In fact, a careful consideration of the various popular literatures of the middle ages, whether Romance or Teutonic, will readily make it clear that not all of them had it in them to acquire a classical character, and thus become an element of culture for succeeding epochs.   In Germany, France and Provence they all reached about the same level, but that was not a very high one; they represented a merely transitory phase, a fact which further mirrors itself in the transitory nature of their various popular dialects, which were never able to attain to the dignity of a fixed literary form.   Hence the gap made by the Renaissance between them and the really modern literatures of their respective countries was very great, and they were for a long time entirely forgotten and even now can only be studied through the medium of grammar, dictionary and translation. The only nation which knew how to elevate the dialect and literature of the people to the proportions of classics and to create out of them a literary language of lasting qualities was the Italian, which more than any other had occasion and motive not to lose sight of classicism, and was already theoretically examining the 'volgare illustre' and the new poetry,[12] when the others were not so much as dreaming of anything of the kind.   This was the goal after which it strove from the first, quite independently of any direct reproduction or imitation of the antique, developing thereby a new form of art, which, like the art of ancient Rome, had for its inevitable and supreme condition 'la gloria della lingua' and 'il bel parlar gentile.'[13]

---

[12] Cp. BARTSCH, *Zu Dante's Poetik* in the *Jahrb. d. deutsch. Dantegesellschaft*, iii. p. 303 seqq.

[13] The artistic instinct of the Italians was given free play in this matter, and as everything was left to individual taste, the literary usage being as yet unformulated, it proved harder for many to write Italian than Latin. Noticeable in this connection are the following words from a Sienese MS. of the *Fior di Virtù*: "Poichè de' vocaboli volgari sono molto ignorante, però che io gli ho poco studiati; anche perchè le cose spirituali, oltre non si possono sì propriamente esprimere per paravole volgari come si sprimono per latino e per grammatica, per la penuria dei vocaboli volgari.   E perciò che ogni contrada et ogni terra ha i suoi propri vocaboli volgari diversi da quelli de l'altre terre et contrade; ma la grammatica et latina non è così, perchè è uno apo tutti e latini.   Però vi prego che mi perdoniate se non vi dichiaro perfettamente le sententie et le verità di questo libro." Ap. DE ANGELIS, *Capitoli dei Disciplinati*, etc. (Siena, 1813), p. 175.   Latin, however rude it

And thus it came about that the writers of the 14th century are and remain the true Italian classics, in that they have an intimate and organic connection with the subsequent literature and culture, and at the present day stand much closer to us than is the case with the other national poets of the period in their respective countries. It is a mere misuse of the word 'classic' to apply it, as is done in Germany, to Wolfram von Eschenbach, Gottfried von Strassburg and the other writers of the Mittel-Hoch-Deutsch, who hardly deserve such a title for that period of literature to which they belong; in spite of the patriotic exertions of various scholars, these authors will never succeed, owing to the wide gulf which separates them from the present, in gaining that position in the national culture which belongs in Italy to the group of writers that surrounds the lofty and essentially Italian name of Dante Alighieri.

might be, was called grammatical, as having regular rules which were not subject to the exigencies of artistic taste. It seems strange that POTT, who has succeeded in explaining so many things, should have failed to under-stand this simple medieval usage of the word "*grammaticus*"; vide *Zeitschr. f. vergl. Sprachforsch.*, i. p. 313.

CHAPTER XIV

AFTER all that has been said, it will be easy to understand
the historical reasons for the fact that the loftiest and noblest
synthesis of those medieval ideas of Vergil which we have examined should be found at the end of the middle ages in Italy,
and should be the work not of an ecclesiastic but of a layman.
Any one who has followed the course of our investigations and
noticed the connection between the evolutions of thought and
the vicissitudes of Virgil's fame will see clearly that it was no
result of chance that Dante felt himself so irresistibly drawn
towards Vergil, and that the greatest of the Latin poets exercised such an influence over the greatest of the Italians.

Dante, if we consider his knowledge or his tendencies, is seen
to belong entirely to the middle ages and to be widely separated
from the men of the Renaissance. He was no grammarian or
philologist or humanist by profession. His is a fervent and
enthusiastic soul, of eminently poetical fibre, open to every
great and noble sentiment, governed by a gigantic intellect
which felt an irresistible desire to exercise itself in vast and
lofty speculations. He embraced the whole encyclopaedia of
medieval scholasticism, but always with a special leaning towards its speculative side, introducing speculation even into
the popular literature, to which he thus gave a depth, not
only in his great poem, but also in his lyrics and his prose
writings, never before attained in Italian or any other modern
language. As a matter of fact, this speculative tendency was
the regular tendency of the studious minds of the period, to
which class Dante belonged. But what distinguishes Dante
from all the other scholars of his age was that he alone suc-

ceeded in mating speculation with poetry, and, what was more, with that popular poetry from which the other scholars held so far aloof, deeming it unfit for the expression of any but popular sentiments. Thus Dante, who by his studies and mental activity belongs nominally to the clergy, is yet a thorough layman, not merely in condition, but also in feeling, opinion and tendency, and in no previous medieval writer does learning become so entirely secular as it does with him. One feels at once that the works of the laity have risen from the humble sphere of merely popular productions to the levels of art and science worthy the name. The mere boldness of employing the vernacular for the purposes of so vast a work, so comprehensive in its historical and scientific notices and so profound in its philosophical and historical speculations, shows of itself how far Dante was able to soar above the level of contemporary thought, while at the same time making himself master of all its present elements and with an originality entirely his own bringing it into harmony with the past and the future.[1] There was at this time a growing anxiety for the dissemination of knowledge among the people at large as opposed to the caste of which it had hitherto been the special privilege; eminent men had observed this and had endeavoured, in spite of the prejudices of the time, to supply the general want. The need of this popularisation of learning was clear to the robust intellect and fervent spirit of Dante's contemporary, Raimundus Lullus; but all that he was able to do as poet and writer in the vernacular was little enough, and serves but to bring into greater prominence the creative power of Dante's miraculous genius.[2] It is this which connects Dante with the Renaissance, of which he was in reality a forerunner; but he is also connected there-

[1] " Questo (volgare) sarà quel pane orzato del quale si satolleranno migliaia e a me ne soverchieranno le sporte piene. Questo sarà luce nuova, sole nuovo il quale sorgerà ove l' usato tramonterà, e darà luce a coloro che sono in tenebre e oscurità, per lo usato sole che a loro non luce."   Convito, i. 13. In the face of this wonderful prophetic instinct, how ridiculous appear the sneers of the " perrucconi " of the period, with their contempt for the vernacular and their counsel, like that of Giovanni del Virgilio (Carm., v. 15) to Dante, to write in Latin because " clerus vulgaria temnit."
[2] With few words but just critical insight ERDMANN contrasts the two in his Grundriss der Geschichte der Philosoph., i. p. 367 (2nd edit.).

with at a point more specially characteristic of that period, viz.
his classical studies.

The great work of Dante is by nature encyclopaedic; such is
not its object, but it is the large basis on which it rests. The
two moving forces in the intellectual life of the period, reason
and religion, tend in his mind to reach a point of equilibrium,
and his poetry is derived, not from a separation, and still less
from an antagonism between them, but from their harmony.
For him, as for all the schoolmen, theology stands at the gate
of knowledge, and philosophy is but her handmaid; but yet
reason occupies with him a far higher place than in the philosophical schools of the time, for he does not merely regard it as
an instrument for present needs, but, looking into its noble
history, fires himself with an enthusiastic contemplation of its
triumphs in the past. These he recognises in antiquity, the
works of which he studies eagerly and at first hand, not merely
in the anthologies and dictionaries of quotations, as was the
case with so many eminent schoolmen[3] who, having their
thoughts concentrated on militant speculation, did not think of
looking for corroboration of their views in direct knowledge of
the history of philosophy and the great products of the human
intellect. Dante lifted the study of the classics to that same
lofty sphere to which he had lifted the vernacular and the
works of the laity; in the strength of the attraction they have
for him we feel already the approach of the Renaissance.[4]

Every one will of course understand that Dante was far from
having the same conception of antiquity as Politian, or studying
it as he did. Dante has, in his study of the classics, various
elements in common with the medieval clergy and is altogether
very much on the same footing as they. His studies are confined to the circle prescribed by the ordinary school tradition.

---

[3] ABELARD confesses that his quotations from the classics are made at
second hand (Opp., p. 1045): "quae enim superius ex philosophis collegi
testimonia, non ex eorum scriptis, quorum pauca novi, immo ex libris Sanctorum Patrum collegi."

[4] The connection of Dante with the Renaissance has been lightly touched
upon by BURCKHARDT (*Die Cultur der Renaissance in Italien*, p. 199 seq.) and
by VOIGT (*Die Wiederbelebung des classischen Humanismus*, p. 9 seqq.); more
has been said on the subject by WEGELE (*Dante Alighieri's Leben*, etc.,
p. 568 seqq.) and by SCHÜCK. (See below.)

He is ignorant of Greek,[5] and knows only a limited number of
Latin writers, not more than Rhabanus Maurus or John of
Salisbury knew, perhaps fewer.[6] His grammatical studies do
not rise above that very modest level which marks the limit of
medieval achievement in this field;[7] the usual defects of the
medieval schools are not unfrequently apparent in passages of
authors which he misunderstands, in etymologies, in definitions
and even in some of his literary theories.[8] As a Latinist too he
is far from being the equal of the humanists of a later period;
he writes the ordinary Latin of the period, and in this respect
not only does he not distinguish himself particularly from his
contemporaries, but is even, it must be admitted, inferior to
some of them.

Dante's classical culture moreover has this further in common
with the culture of the medieval clergy, that he too looks upon
antiquity through a medium which greatly distorts it.   His
learning is eminently scholastic, and the goal of his thoughts
is the discovery of truth by means of philosophico-theological
speculation, and this medieval tendency accompanies him in his
contemplation of antiquity; he is hence familiar with allegory,
and his mind is so prone to it that he even allegorises himself,
while in his poetry his philosophical and theological ideas present themselves to him in the form of images and symbols
which constitute no small part of the complicated fabric of his
creation. He is therefore ready to find allegories in the ancient

[5] That Dante knew no Greek is clear enough to any one who knows it
himself and has studied Dante and the middle ages. What there is to be
said on the subject has been said by CAVEDONI in his *Osservazioni critiche
intorno alla questione se Dante sapesse il greco*, Modena, 1860. *Vide* also
SCHÜCK, *op. citand.*

[6] For the classical studies of Dante *vide* SCHÜCK, *Dante's classische Studien
und Brunetto Latini*, in the *Neue Jahrbb. f. Philol. u. Paedag.*, 1865, Abth. 2,
pp. 253–289.

[7] Speaking of the *Laelius* of CICERO, he says: "E avvegnacchè duro mi
fosse prima entrare nella loro sentenza, finalmente v' entrai tant' entro
quanto l' arte di grammatica ch' io avea e un poco di mio ingegno potea
fare." *Convito*, ii. 13.

[8] Noteworthy, among others, are his ideas of comedy and tragedy. It
does not appear from any of his writings that he had ever read either
PLAUTUS, TERENCE, or SENECA, well known as they were in the middle ages.
The passage of TERENCE to which he refers (*Inf.*, xviii. 133) is doubtless
derived from the *Laelius* of CICERO.

authors, and this not only in Vergil, but also in Lucan, in Ovid
and others;[9] nor does he limit this method of interpretation to
poetical fictions, but sometimes applies it, after the fashion of
the middle ages, to historical facts, which thereby, without
losing any of their reality, yet come to be considered as oppor-
tune symbols of an idea which may, by the application of
allegory or anagogue, be found in them.

In all this Dante is at one with the ecclesiastical writers as
far as classical studies are concerned. And yet in the result he
differs greatly from them. As a layman, who, while pious, is
yet no ascetic, he has a high opinion of the human intellect, and
though he considers its powers as limited, yet he feels a great
respect for those of its representatives who were independent
of and anterior to the mission of Christ; hence he is not merely
acquainted with the ancients through the medium of the
schools of grammar, nor does he confine his study of them to
what is barely necessary, but he devotes himself directly to
them, not as a grammarian or philologist, still less as a humanist, but as a thinker and a poet. The scholastic and paedagogic
use of these writers disappears with him almost entirely from
sight; they are called instead to assist in the development of
his scientific activity. Of course Dante was not the first to do
such a thing, for the schoolmen had already brought Aristotle
to the front, but Dante was able to feel veneration for all the
writers of antiquity equally, regarding with respect not merely
the philosophers, but also all the others, whether prose-writers
or poets,[10] while for these last he shows a predilection, readily
intelligible in a man of his temperament and tendencies, which
is far higher and more liberal than anything of the kind one
is accustomed to meet with among the medieval ecclesiastics.
With him there is not only an absence of that hatred of the
pagans which inspired so many of the early monks and ascetics,
but also of that doubt and suspicion, that feeling of restriction
in dealing with secular studies, which characterises so many of
the more enlightened men of the Church. And in addition to

[9] *Convito*, ii. 1; iv. 25, 27, 28.
[10] Speaking of a passage of Juvenal, he says: " e in questo (con rever-
enzia il dico) mi discordo dal poeta." *Convito*, iv. 29.

the terms of familiarity on which he stands with the classical
poets, a further noteworthy point of difference between him
and his contemporaries—a point of difference almost surprising
in a man endowed with such strong Christian sentiments—lies
in the fact that he entirely ignores those Christian poets, such
as Prudentius, Sedulius, Juvencus and the like, who were so
popular among the ecclesiastics,[11] and does not so much as
mention their names, although he was by no means unacquainted
with theological literature and could rightly assess the poetical
value of the Church hymns, as is apparent from more than one
passage in his works.   Dante was able to express the Christian
idea in poetry far more successfully than they, in that, instead
of forcing it into forms unsuited to it, he created a form of his
own—a form moreover, it must be observed, peculiarly adapted
to that combination of Christian theology and philosophy which
is the special product of the Catholic Church, itself an offspring
of the union between Christianity and the Graeco-Latin civilisation.   During the thirteen centuries of its existence, Christianity had become inseparably interwoven with a thousand
elements of the ancient tradition.   Dante represents in the
highest possible degree the moment at which these two forms
were at equipoise and formed the exact complement one of the
other; the moment was transitory, but Dante did not consider
it as such, nor would he ever have wished it to be so.   Hence
he is in no respect a rebel against religion or what would in
modern times be called a free-thinker;[12] he did not foresee, he

---

[11] A great grammatical authority of the period, EBERHARD DE BETHUNE,
mentions in his *Laborintus* these poets among those who should be read in
schools. (Tractat. iii., *De Versificatione*). Another similar authority, ALEX-
ANDRE DE VILLEDIEU, maintains the advisability of reading the Christian
poets, especially himself, and abandoning the classical writers. Cp. THUROT,
op. cit., p. 98.

[12] SCARTAZZINI (*Dante Alighieri, seine Zeit*, etc. (Biel, 1869), p. 232 seqq.,
and *Zu Dante's innere Entwickelungsgeschichte* in the *Jahrb. d. deutsch.
Dantegesellsch.*, iii. 19 seqq.) maintains, basing his belief chiefly on the last
canto of the Purgatorio, that Dante was at one time troubled by grave
doubts, without, however, ever becoming an actual sceptic.   To me too it
has often seemed inconceivable that a man so much in advance of his time
should never have seen, at least momentarily, the weak points in the Christian religion.   But this could in any case only have been the result of some
passing and instinctive impulse, for it would have been impossible for any

could not foresee, that this development of the spirit of ratio-
cination, which was restoring to honour those ancient ideas
which had been discarded and despised, could not fail to lead
eventually, as in fact it did, to a weakening of the religious
sentiment and a real and continuous diminution of the influence
of Christianity upon the human conscience. The Church fore-
saw this clearly enough when it declared itself the enemy of
the whole movement and of Dante himself; and the result has
proved that, from the point of view of its own interests, if not
of ours, the Church was right.

Dante's esteem and predilection for antiquity stands in close
relation to his feeling with regard to ancient poetry. His soul
is essentially the soul of a poet, and poetry accompanies every
motion of his thoughts; Woman, Nature, Patriotism, Faith,
Science, he regards them all from a poetical point of view, and
feels deeply the poetry of them all. And hence, although, as
has been said, he views antiquity, like the monks, through the
medium of theology and philosophy, he is yet able to resuscitate
the ancient poetical spirit in a way that no monk had ever
been able to do. His mind, endowed to an extraordinary degree with speculative and synthetic powers, endeavours to
co-ordinate philosophically all the various objects of his poetical
fancy, and to combine Christianity with the ancient tradition,
the love of Woman and of Country with the love of Truth;
but the most essential fact is this, that his spirit is raised to
that elevation in which the poetical feeling ceases to be uni-
lateral and becomes universal, and does not concentrate itself
upon a single object but is susceptible to poetical impressions
of every kind—a fact which separates him immeasurably from
medieval monasticism and puts him on a level with the modern
man who can feel the poetry of Aeschylus and Vergil just as
he can feel that of David, Shakspeare or Goethe. Indeed, so
vigorous is this sympathy of his for ancient poetry, that he
has no need to express it in the Latin language or in Latin

one then to have arrived by a course of dispassionate reasoning at a firm
position of negation. The most robust intellect lacked the means of penetrating the leaden envelope of its religious environment, for the philosophy
of experience was as yet unborn.

verse, but finds Italian, in this as in all else, a more natural and a readier mode of utterance. When a poet could write

> ' Quale nei plenilunii sereni
> Trivia ride fra le ninfe eterne,'

or fashion a hundred other poetical images in a way that no Latin verse-maker had been able for centuries to do, it is needless to enquire whether he understood the spirit of ancient poetry. Dante is so familiar with the ancient poets and their works that they are always irresistibly present before him, and this too notwithstanding the fact that he cannot be called in any way an imitator of them. His images and his similes are often taken from nature or from recollections of his travels, but by far the greater part are taken from the history or the poetry of antiquity. No other medieval poet was able to do this to as great an extent as he, nor does any other show himself so familiar with the materials of classical poetry.[13]

Dante was governed by two predominant sentiments, a love of his country and a love of truth. All his emotions are summed up in that one word, ' Amore,' to which he gives the amplest significance, including in it too the love of the ideal woman, which he comes to understand in a lofty and mystical sense. And these two sentiments are so closely combined, both in his political and philosophical views, that it is often impossible to define the boundary between the two. We recognise both in the ardour with which he studied every branch of knowledge, finding his most congenial element in that antiquity which at one and the same time showed him the most purely human side of this knowledge and furnished the basis for his political and patriotic ideals. His love of Italy is of an extraordinary intensity, and is in close connection with his love of antiquity, for in his eyes the continuity between Romans and Italians is unbroken, and the history of the Latins begins with Aeneas and goes down to his own time; the glory of Rome he

---

[13] On the ancient elements in Dante, FAURIEL has written well in his *Dante et les origines de la langue et de la litt. ital.*, ii. p. 420 seqq.; but he has not sufficiently considered how far these elements are peculiar to Dante. For this part of the subject *vide* PIPER, *Mythologie der christlichen Kunst*, i. p. 255 seqq.

feels to be the glory of Italy, and his enthusiasm as poet and patriot is kindled by it.   His historical ideas were merely those which were common in medieval times; the conception of universal empire, based chiefly on an exclusive study of the history of Rome, was, as we have seen, the conception usual to the men of the middle ages.   But while this was to men of other countries a merely abstract idea without any connection with their own national history, Dante alone among the rest regarded it as essentially Italian, seeing in it a legitimate goal for Italian national aspirations.   The many passages of the *Divina Commedia* in which this view is expressed are too well known to need quoting here.

Now this strong national feeling was one of the chief reasons for Dante's sympathy with and predilection for Vergil.   In fact, it is clear that Dante regarded Vergil as an eminently national poet, 'la *nostra* maggior Musa,' 'il *nostro* maggior poeta,' as he calls him.   His soul as an Italian is deeply moved when he recognises in the poet's words the ancient history of Italy, and feels that is was for Italy that

'morì la vergine Camilla
Eurialo e Turno e Niso di ferute.'

And here we would remind the reader of what we have already said of Vergil's epic as the greatest poetical expression of Roman national feeling.   Many well-known passages in the *Divina Commedia*, among others the famous canto on the triumphal progress of the Roman eagles, as well as the *De Monarchia*, and the arguments there, based especially on Vergil, for the legitimacy of the Roman Empire, show how powerfully this feeling had taken possession of Dante and how perfect must have been the harmony between him and the author of the Aeneid.   The feeling therefore which led Dante to his political Utopia was based, strangely enough, on that idea which rendered its realisation impossible—the idea of national individuality.   However much he may say that he is a citizen of the world,[14] his patriotic utterances, the predilection he shows in

---

[14] "Nos autem cui mundus est patria velut piscibus aequor, quanquam Sarnum biberimus ante dentes et Florentiam adeo diligamus, ut quia dilexi-

all his writings for the Latins, whether ancient or modern, his
enthusiasm for that great Rome which is the glory of Italy, the
intense ardour with which by precept and example he affirms
the nobility of the Italian language, the terrible words in which
he denounces those 'abominable' ones who prefer other languages to their own,[15] and many other like things, mark him
out clearly as the greatest and the earliest representative of
Italian national feeling, and show that he felt himself to be
far more an Italian than a cosmopolitan. History showed the
position that Italy was to occupy in the empire of the world;
the predominance of Italy was, as we have seen, a view by no
means peculiar to Dante, and whatever the relations between
Kaiser and Pope might be, Italy was always regarded as the
centre of the imperial tradition. Thus Dante found in the
Aeneid not merely the basis for an abstract political theory but
also a medium entirely congenial to the intense patriotism
which animated him. Now-a-days it may be different, but
any one who can enter into the emotions of other periods of
history will understand what Vergil must have been to such an
Italian thinker and patriot in the 13th century. To arrive at
the conception of their own nationality without passing through
that of the ancient Romans would have been morally impossible
for the Italians. The influence which antiquity exercised upon
them at the time of their intellectual awakening was primarily
founded on their national feeling; the cosmopolitan and Utopian
ideas to which this influence led were in reality merely a
secondary development. Hence the tragi-comedy of Cola di
Rienzi, for all its absurdity, has a nobility and a grandeur in
the causes which brought it about that cannot fail to elicit
sympathy. The ideal empire was bound to be Italian, as the
actual empire had been.

Dante therefore is not an admirer of Vergil merely because

---

mus exilium patiamur iniuste," etc. *De vulg. eloq.*, i., c. 6. To the great
exile, wounded in his feelings of patriotism, it affords momentary comfort
to recur to the idea of the universal brotherhood of man.

[15] " .   .   .   e tutti questi cotali sono gli abominevoli cattivi d' Italia che
hanno a vile questo prezioso volgare, lo quale se è vile in alcuna cosa, non
è se non in quanto egli suona nella bocca meretrice di questi adulteri."
Convito, i. 11.

of the great fame which tradition allotted to him. He recognises that tradition is right in considering Vergil as the greatest
Latin poet, but he would have been able to see this for himself
without the aid of tradition, for he sees well enough how many
poets are dependent on Vergil and that he is their 'light' and
their 'glory,' and knows that they all 'do him honour,' and
that 'in doing this they do well.' He admits the position
which history assigns to Homer, and knows that Homer is one
'che le muse allatar più ch' altri mai'; but in reality he is
ignorant of Homer's works,[16] and for him the 'highest' poet,
to whom Homer himself does honour by coming to meet him, is
Vergil. The perfection of Vergil's work he feels as only a true
poet may; and he is proud as an Italian of this miracle of art,
for Latin and Italian are equally the national language of Italy,
and Vergil is the 'Glory of the Latins,' through whom

> 'Mostrò ciò che potea la lingua nostra.'

The vividness and depth of the impressions produced on him by
the Aeneid are clear from many passages in his works and show
how good a right he had to speak of the 'lungo studio e 'l
grande amore' with which he had perused the works of Vergil.
And how great was the power which he felt to be in the
utterances of Vergil is clear from the words with which Beatrice addresses the latter when about to commit her poet to
his charge:

> 'Venni quaggiù dal mio beato scanno
> Fidandomi nel tuo parlare onesto
> Ch' onora te e quei ch' udito l'hanno.' [17]

He tells us himself that he knows the Aeneid from beginning
to end,[18] but how different is this knowledge of his from that of
the cento-makers! He feels the fervour

---

[16] The story of Troy he only knows through the Latin writers, and this
too with an admixture of medieval ideas, as is seen in the fantastic end
which he gives to Ulysses (*Inf.*, xxvi. 91 seqq.). He does not even seem to
have known Dictys or Dares or the Latin Homer. Cp. *Convito*, i. 7. In
the few places where he quotes Homer, his immediate source is Aristotle or,
in one instance, Horace. Cp. Schück, *op. cit.*, p. 272 seqq.

[17] *Inf.*, i. 112.

[18] Vergil says to him:

' della divina fiamma,
Onde furo allumati più di mille;
Dell' Eneide dico.' [19]

The use which Dante makes of Vergil in his minor works
shows that the latter was really, as he says, his favourite
author, than whom no other was more sympathetic and whom
he had made the inseparable companion of his thoughts long
before making him the companion of his mystic journey. There
is nothing more striking in the history of Italian culture than
this sympathy which united by a secret and irresistible attraction the two greatest representatives of its two most brilliant
periods, and thus afforded an imposing proof of its wonderful
and unbroken continuity.[20]

As a poet, Dante is above all things original, and nothing
could be more foreign to him than imitation. This is shown
clearly by the fact that, in spite of his admiration for the classical
poets and for Vergil in particular, he has not been led by this
to imitate them in the nature of his artistic productions. A
man of his character cannot imitate; even when he tries to
imitate, he is original. It is apparent from Dante's poetry how
familiar he was with the ancients; reminiscences of his studies
of them encounter one at every turn; but yet the general
character of his art is entirely new and original, and essentially
different from that of ancient art. To convince oneself of this
one need but examine those passages in which he has obviously
followed some ancient model, as for instance in the celebrated
description of the punishment of Pier delle Vigne, which, he expressly states, was suggested to him by the Vergilian incident of
Polydorus. The only thing common to the two poets is the subject; the style and the art are entirely different. The ornate

" E così canta
L' alta mia tragedia in alcun loco;
Ben lo sai tu che la sai tutta quanta."
                                                    Inf., xx. 112.

[19] *Purg.*, xxi. 94.
[20] It seems incredible that HEEREN should have stated seriously that
Dante's knowledge of Vergil was second-hand. " Selbst die Rolle die Virgil
in Dante's Gedichte spielt zeigt wohl dass er ihn mehr aus Nachrichten
Anderer als aus eigener Einsicht kannte." *Gesch. d. klass. Litt. im Mittelalt.*, i. p. 320.

rhetoric and grandiloquent phraseology which the ancient Roman conception of the epic demanded are diametrically opposed to the natural and almost severe simplicity of Dante. When he says "e stetti come l'uom che teme," he knew well how far he was from reproducing the resonance and grandeur of the Vergilian "obstupui steteruntque comae et calor ossa reliquit." This profound difference he must have felt, and when he says to Vergil

'Tu se' solo colui da cu' io tolsi
Lo bello stile che m'ha fatto onore,'

there is no need to understand this literally, as if he had wished to write after Vergil's manner, which would not be true; the words must be understood in that sense which the reality justifies, like the words of Aeschylus when he describes his tragedies as crumbs gathered beneath the table of Homer. To the characteristic forms of the Dantesque poetry this passage cannot possibly refer; for if the *Divina Commedia* is not an imitation of any ancient work of art, still less are his earlier poems, to which alone these words refer, capable of being so described. The lyrics of Dante have absolutely nothing in common with ancient art, least of all with the art of Vergil; in form and sentiment alike they are entirely modern. Moreover, Dante explains elsewhere what he means by the 'stile che m'ha fatto onore.'[21] The fundamental characteristic of the 'dolce stil nuovo,' on the introduction of which he so prides himself, he defines thus:

'quando
Amor m'ispira, noto, ed in quel modo
Ch' ei detta dentro, vo significando.'[22]

To subordinate poetry to the influences of real emotions, to make it always follow 'dietro al dittatore'—this is the character-

---

[21] WITTE has wished to refer these words to the *De Monarchia*, and I too thought at one time that they should be referred to the prose writings. But Dante says clearly that it is his poetical style in which he glories, and knows that it is only in his poetry that he is truly original. WEGELE (*Dante Alighieri*, p. 348 seq.) argues against Witte, but he too has failed to grasp the true sense of the passage, referring the "stile" of which Dante speaks to the merely external imitation of Vergil's expressions.

[22] *Purg.*, xxiv. 52.

istic of the new style of which he is proud. Hence the word
'stile' comes to mean not so much the form of art as its subjective cause—a cause which may be identical in two poets
who differ greatly in the nature of their poetry and the manner
of their expression. And here it will be well to note in passing
that by the word 'Amore,' according to Dante's wont, are
chiefly understood the intellectual tendencies.

The poetical style of Dante is the product of harmonised
emotion and reflection; it is the product of a perfect originality which scorns every form of imitation or conventionality.
It is neither a tumultuarious improvisation nor a frigid versification of allegorised philosophical theories;[23] it is true poetry,
but poetry resulting from reflection, and as such its author
rightly contrasts it with the shallow and uninspired poetry of
Buonaggiunta, Jacopo Notaio and the rest, or with the works
of those 'grossi' of whom he speaks in his prose. And by
virtue alike of this artistic elaboration and this profound
thought clothed in poetical form, the noblest poetry of the
world is for him that of Vergil.

To sum up, the poetry of Dante is a product of individual
reflection, which rises high above the levels of popular and
conventional poetry; it is also classical, not by imitation of the
classics, but by the attainment of that artistic level which con-
stitutes a classic. Such is the 'bello stile' of Dante, and it
is only natural that Vergil, the greatest poet of antiquity then
known, should have been his chief model for poetical art so conceived.[24] Any one therefore who has succeeded in understanding

[23] This would be the result of the definition of Dante's style brought
forward by PEREZ, La Beatrice svelata, p. 65 seqq. To deny the allegory in
Dante is impossible, but allegory was to him merely a natural way of expressing those deep thoughts which he considered it the duty of the poet to
utter; he never looked upon it as an essential part of poetry.

[24] Dante's "primo amico," Guido Cavalcanti, was also a poet of the "stil
nuovo," and Dante himself says how well they agreed as to the true position
of the popular poetry. This could not have been the case, however, if, as
many commentators have supposed, the line in Inf., x. 63, "Forse cui Guido
vostro ebbe a disdegno," is to be understood of literature, as if Guido really
despised Vergil and the classical poets. But the context of this verse treats
clearly of the more profound ideas embodied in Dante's journey, and hence
the reason which Dante gives for his friend's absence is that they differed
on questions of philosophy, as we in fact know to have been the case. Cp.

the conception will perceive that, so far from enjoining an imitation of Vergil's actual artistic forms, it even rendered such imitation impossible; any imitation that there might be, must be in the spirit, not in the letter.

PEREZ, *op. cit.*, p. 382 seq.; or better, D'OVIDIO in the *Propugnatore*, iii. 2, p. 167 seqq. (*Saggi critici*, Naples, 1879, p. 312 seqq.) FINZI, however (*Saggi danteschi*, Turin, 1888, p. 60 seqq.), supports, though not very successfully, the other view.

CHAPTER XV

WHAT has just been said will enable us to understand the true position of Vergil in the *Divina Commedia*. A consideration of the foregoing remarks as to the general medieval conception of Vergil will show that the Vergil of Dante is on the whole in accord with this conception, and is certainly not the real Augustan Vergil, but that ideal Vergil which resulted from the views peculiar to the middle ages. At the same time it would be an error to suppose that Dante's reason for selecting Vergil for his guide was a purely external one, as if, when searching for some one suited for this office, he had been merely led to light upon Vergil by the halo which surrounded his name. Dante's great poem is of such a character, alike in its poetical framework and in the method of its treatment, that the personality and subjectivity of the author is kept continually in view. He has chosen to show us his ideal world, not outside of himself and without himself, but in himself and with himself. The choice therefore of his symbolical guides could not be a matter of chance or determined by merely external reasons, but was bound to be rigidly prescribed by the history of his thought. Had he wished to write a poem which should be purely didactic, in which he himself and his soul were but little considered, and in which his own personality merely figured artificially, like that of any other character, he might easily have chosen other personages, or even have adopted a common medieval practice, and introduced us to Pistis and Sophia, for example, instead of to Beatrice and Vergil. But the nature of his poem was such, and its connection with the history of himself and his emotions so intimate, that he could not fail to

choose as the guides of his ideal and psychological journey
those two who had been the actual companions of his thoughts
in all his vicissitudes.   And such were Beatrice and Vergil.

The name of Beatrice is the name of a real personage, and
recalls to the poet his earliest love, but the process of idealisa-
tion to which that love and its object are subjected is so
elaborate that it ends by giving to the name a mystical significance which, while always capable of awakening the deepest
emotions, is yet very far removed from that which it originally
possessed, so much so, in fact, that a reader of the *Divina
Commedia*, who was ignorant of the *Vita Nuova*, might at first
sight imagine that 'Beatrice' was a purely fanciful name.
Vergil, on the other hand, though subjected to the process of
Dante's thought, always remains a real and concrete personality, and never becomes a simple name significant of ideas or
emotions.   But in that he was Dante's favourite author, who
found in him food for many a cherished thought, he too is
carried along on the stream of Dante's imagination, following
its ideals and being himself idealised.   The ideals to which
Beatrice corresponds are not entirely of Dante's creation, but
are rather a synthesis of medieval thought; and the same is
true of Vergil, except in so far that while the one set of ideals
were associated with Beatrice by a process peculiarly Dante's
own, the other set had already been associated with Vergil by
the tendencies of medievalism, and thus the Vergil of Dante is
really nothing but a synthesis of the ideas already current
about him.   Not, however, that Dante is a compiler of medieval ideas; he is rather their interpreter and they come to life
in him; for his type of Vergil, whether personal or symbolic,
is far grander and more noble than what would have resulted
from a mere compilation of the ordinary conceptions of the
age.

Dante never refers in any of his various writings, in which
he makes such constant use of Vergil, to any authority relative
to that poet; of Macrobius and Fulgentius he seems to know
nothing; anyhow, he never mentions them, nor is there anything in his works to show that he has read them.   He knows
of an allegorical interpretation of the Aeneid, of which he does

not mention the author, speaking of it as of something generally
accepted; this however is not the interpretation of Fulgentius,
but that which, originally inspired perhaps by Fulgentius, was
current among schoolmen, such as Bernard de Chartres or
John of Salisbury. This work he may have met with in the
course of his philosophical studies in Paris. For the rest,
Dante could not have been otherwise than disgusted by Fulgentius, with his barbarous conceptions, so utterly opposed to
the Dantesque type of Vergil, and his clumsy and foolish ex-
positions of but a single side of the many that Dante saw and
felt in Vergil. In fact, the only work relative to Vergil which
Dante knew was the biography.[1]

We need not enter here into the discussions of the commentators as to what Dante precisely understood by the two guides
of his journey. The nature of our work only requires of us to
examine the connection between the Vergil of Dante and the
literary tradition, and to notice in what respects Dante's conception resembles that of the medieval clergy and in what it
differs from it.

Dante's journey is a pilgrimage, the object and the interest
of which is psychological. It is a graduated vision, in which
the soul, before arriving at the contemplation of that which is
highest, must first purify itself by passing through 'the temporal and the eternal fire,' and meditating upon everything in
the way of immorality and its eternal punishment that menaces
or destroys it. Being thus cleansed, it is permitted to plunge
itself in the waters of Lethe and Eunoe, and thereby become
capable of proceeding to the contemplation of the eternal idea.
Hence Dante needs two guides for this spiritual journey, the
one, more real and concrete, for the negative part in which the
soul has merely to purify itself in order to render itself worthy
of the beatific vision; the other, more mystical, ideal and
ethereal, for that part in which the soul is elevated to the
regions of perfection, where is 'la gloria di colui che tutto
move.' As this second part is the real object of the journey
and the first part is merely necessary as a means of attaining

---

[1] *Vide Inf.*, i. 67 seqq.; *Purg.*, iii. 25 seqq., vii. 4 seqq., xvi·i. 82 seqq.

to the second, the principal guide is Beatrice, on whom Vergil
is dependent; for it is she who has committed Dante to his
care, and it is to her that he appeals when any difficulty arises.
Thus Dante's guide, master and comforter in his meditation on
sad realities is a pagan of great celebrity and famous for wisdom ; in his contemplation of the supreme idea his guide is a
symbolical and ideal woman whose name recalls to the poet the
intense and pure passion of his earlier years, and this woman
is symbolical of those conditions of enlightenment to which the
soul can alone attain through the medium of Christianity. The
first guide is of such a kind that, though he has gone far on
the road towards purification and perfection, he can never come
to steep himself in the waters of Lethe and Eunoe, nor return
to that pure state which belonged to man before the Fall ; the
second guide has, on the other hand, been able to enjoy to the
full the benefits of the blood of Christ. Hence Beatrice knows
as much as Vergil, but Vergil does not know as much as Beatrice.

In the midst of all the various systems which have been
started to explain the symbolical meaning of Vergil and
Beatrice one fact is beyond question, and that is that Beatrice,
whether she be Theology or Philosophy, or whatever else it
pleases one to call her, has her essential *raison d'être* in Christianity, and that this is the main point of difference between
her and Vergil. This distinction is emphasised in more than
one passage by the poet himself, and notably so where he makes
Vergil say :

> ' quanto ragion qui vede
> Dir ti poss' io ; da indi in là t' aspetta
> A Beatrice, ch' è opra di fede.' [2]

There is no opposition between Vergil and Beatrice, for
Dante brings reason and faith into perfect harmony ; they
understand one another perfectly, and may be said to be fundamentally one and the same thing. But of this one thing they
represent two different moments and conditions, and hence it
will be possible for us, in following the course of our investi-

---

[2] *Purg.*, xviii. 46 seqq.

gations, to occupy ourselves exclusively with Vergil without further considering Beatrice.

The reasons which led Dante to choose Vergil for his guide were numerous; we have touched on some of them in speaking generally of what Vergil was to Dante, independently of the *Divina Commedia*; let us now briefly sum up these before we enter upon our examination of what Vergil is in this latter work.

In the first place Vergil was Dante's favourite author and the greatest poet with whom he was acquainted. Being a great poet himself, Dante appreciated the art of Vergil in a way which no other man of the middle ages had ever been able to do, and looked on him as his master in style in the sense we have explained above. He admired him further as the singer of the glories of Italy and as a poet of Italian feeling. It was through Vergil again that Dante had brought to maturity his lofty ideal of the Empire and all the elevated poetry which that implied; and in the formation of this ideal Vergil had served him not merely as theorist but also as actual historical witness both by the subject of his poem and by the period to which it belonged. Then, by following the system of allegorical interpretation which was in vogue in the middle ages, Dante found in the Aeneid just that account of the soul's progress towards perfection which was the subject of his own poem. Once more, in his conception of the relation between reason and faith and of the power of the intellect unenlightened by revelation to attain to certain great truths, Vergil stood out pre-eminently among the great names of antiquity as the one who, according to medieval ideas, appeared the purest and the nearest the Christ, of whom he had been, however unconsciously, a prophet. And finally, in the construction of his great poem, Dante derived the main idea and many of the details from Vergil, and made more use of him than of any other writer in the course of his work.[3]

All this will, I trust, make it clear that the office of guide assigned by Dante to Vergil is a thoroughly genuine one, and

[3] Cp. the numerous passages of the *Divina Commedia* quoted by GUIDO DA PISA in relating the deeds of Aeneas.

that the choice of Vergil for this purpose is not, as is generally
considered, a mere freak of the imagination determined by
external causes, but has just as true a psychological reason as
the choice of his other guide, Beatrice. And it is further
necessary to bear in mind the essential fact that Dante's is a
creative genius, not in the field of science, but in that of poetry,
and that therefore, while admiring intellectual greatness in
every form, if called upon to choose as his associate between a
philosopher and a poet, he could not fail to choose the latter.
Hence those with whom in his poem he spends much time are
always artists and poets, such as Vergil, Statius, Sordello,
Arnaldo and Casella, while the five men 'di cotanto senno,'
whom he meets in Limbo, are all poets. It is as poet that he
regards himself in the moments of his strongest emotions ; this
is his supreme merit, by which he hopes to obtain that return
from exile 'al bell' ovile ov' io dormii agnello '; and it is a
poet's crown which he aspires to take in his 'bel San Giovanni,'
where first he was admitted into the Christian communion :

> ' Con altra voce omai, con altro vello
> Ritornerò poeta, ed in sul fonte
> Di mio battesmo prenderò il cappello.' [4]

His nature and his predilections as poet, qualities in which
his guide shared, are all brought out in that passage where
both of them suddenly discover, to their great confusion, that
they have been forgetting the serious object of their journey in
listening to a fascinating song.[5]

Those scholars who have discussed the subject of the
Dantesque Vergil have generally found it quite natural that, in
searching for some character of antiquity who might be the
symbol of human reason as independent of revelation, Dante
should have lighted upon Vergil, owing to that general reputation for omniscience and semi-Christianity which the latter
enjoyed in the middle ages. No one has stopped to enquire
why Dante, as a schoolman, should not rather have chosen
Aristotle. In Dante's time, as he himself expressly states, the
' maestro di color che sanno,' was Aristotle, and not Vergil, and

---

[4] *Parad.*, xxv. 1 seq.   [5] *Purg.*, ii. 106 seqq.

omniscience was quite as generally attributed to him as to the
latter; Dante, like the rest, would regard Aristotle as the
supreme authority on philosophy and as the prince of human
reason,[6] and, as every one knows, in the region proper to
scholasticism his fame far surpassed that of Vergil.[7] Legends
as to his wisdom were not wanting; he too was believed to
have come as near being a Christian as was possible before
the coming of Christ, and his prospects of salvation were
seriously discussed;[8] Dante moreover, in the theoretical part
of his scheme of the empire, had not failed to make use of the
authority of Aristotle. But Aristotle was a Greek and no
Roman,[9] and entirely alien to Dante as poet, who never therefore felt that familiarity with him that he felt with Vergil, and

---

[6] " . . . in quella parte dove aperse la bocca la divina sentenzia
d' Aristotile da lasciare mi pare ogni altrui sentenzia." *Convito*, iv. 17.
For the authority of Aristotle and its reasons *vide Convito*, iv. 6.

[7] The most curious expression of this primacy of Aristotle in the times of
scholasticism is the *Fabliau* entitled *La bataille des VII. ars*. There among
others occur the following lines :

> " Aristote, qui fu a pié
> Si fist chéoir Gramaire enverse.
> Lors i a point mesire Perse,
> Dant Juvenal et dant Orasce,
> Virgile, Lucain et Etasce
> Et Sédule, Propre, Prudence,
> Aratur, Omer et Térence :
> Tuit chaplèrent sor Aristote
> Qui fu fers com chastel sor mote."

Vide JUBINAL, *Oeuvres compl. de Ruteboeuf*, ii. p. 426. " Propre " is not
Propertius, as Jubinal thinks, but the Christian poet Prosperus.

[8] *Vide* LAMBERTUS DE MONTE, *Quid probabilius dici possit de salvatione
Aristotelis Stagiritae*. Col. 1487. Tertullian at one time spoke of Aristotle
as " patriarcha haereticorum," while later Luther called him " hostis
Christi." In the French poem entitled " *Enseignements d'Aristote* " he
is made to speak of Christianity quite like a Christian. *Vide Hist. litt. de
la France*, xiii. p. 115–118. Cp. RUTH, *Studien über Dante Alighieri*, p. 258
seqq.

[9] Dante shows clearly in the *Divina Commedia* that his only acquaintance
with Greek was through Latin. Before Diomed and Ulysses (*Inf.*, xxvi. 73
seqq.) Vergil says to him :

> " Lascia parlare a me ; ch' io ho concetto
> Ciò che tu vuoi ; ch' e' sarebber schivi,
> Perchè ei fur Greci, forse del tuo detto."

Then before Guido di Montefeltro (*Inf.*, xxvii. 33) he says :

> " . . . parla tu, questi è Latino."

consequently could not, on such an occasion as this, have chosen him for his guide.

The Vergil of the *Divina Commedia* shows clearly, like every one of Dante's creations, how far Dante was at one with the middle ages and how far he was raised above them. We find here the medieval conception of Vergil, but the creative genius of the poet has enabled him to stamp upon it a character which is all his own, and to produce out of these rude elements, which have often provoked a smile, a type of an entirely original grandeur. Of the medieval ideas about Vergil, some are wisely eliminated, others are purified and elaborated.[10] At the time of Dante, in addition to the literary Vergilian tradition of which we have spoken, there were also current the popular legends which had grown up about his name and had by this time gained a footing in literature. Dante was doubtless acquainted with these legends, as was his 'dolcissimo Cino,' who had heard them from the people in the streets of Naples, but it is a great mistake to think of this, as has been done by one ancient commentator and nearly all the modern ones, in connection with the Dantesque type of Vergil. There is not a single passage in this poem in which Vergil appears as a magician, or indeed approaches that character in any way.[11] One need but reflect on the grandeur of Dante's conception

[10] Dante knew that his Vergil was above the level of the ordinary medieval type, and that he was better able to appreciate the poet than any of his contemporaries. This is what he means when he says of Vergil (*Inf.*, i. 9): "chi per lungo silenzio parea fioco." It cannot be interpreted to mean that Vergil had been for a long time forgotten, for this was not the case, as Dante knew when he spoke of him as "*famoso* saggio," whose fame "nel mondo dura."

[11] Some commentators have even wished to find an allusion to Vergil's magic in the lines (*Inf.*, ix. 22):

> "Ver' è che altra fiata quaggiù fui
> Congiurato da quella Eriton, cruda
> Che richiamava l' ombre a' corpi sui,"

as if coming under the influence of a witch were proof of being a magician! Dante, like all his contemporaries, believed in magic, but considered its practice as reprehensible.

FINZI none the less (*Saggi danteschi*, p. 157) supports the old view, with arguments however which show that he has little real acquaintance with what he calls "the popular tradition." The matter is ably discussed by D'OVIDIO, *Dante e la Magia*, in the *Nuova Antologia*, 1892, p. 213 seqq.

and on the serious and discriminating nature of his admiration
for Vergil, to see at once how distasteful these follies of the
Neapolitan populace, which others so eagerly collected, must
have been to him. And further, the way in which he treats
magicians and astrologers in his poem shows clearly that not
only would these acts have failed to constitute for him that
profound wisdom which the common people considered them to
imply, but that the possession of such wisdom as that with
which he credited Vergil would have actually excluded their
practice. Had Dante thought of Vergil as a magician, he
would have had to put him with Guido Bonatti, Asdente and
the rest, to whom Vergil shows himself by no means partial.[12]
But Dante has not looked for anything in Vergil foreign to

[12] Vergil when speaking of magicians, etc., says (*Inf.*, xx. 28) " Qui vive
la pietà quand' è ben morta " (*Ibid.*, 117) " Delle magiche frodi seppe il
giuoco " ; (*Ibid.* 121) " Vedi le triste che . . . fecer malie con erbe e con
imago."

D'OVIDIO (*op. cit.*), in defending this view, goes too far when he wishes to
prove by an ingenious line of argument (p. 216 seqq.) that the disdain manifested by Vergil in this canto for the magicians and soothsayers is meant
to be an indirect protest against the legends which described him as a magician. Of magicians proper Dante takes but little account ; they are only
mentioned here incidentally ; the sinners contemplated in this canto are,
as is clear from the nature of the punishment inflicted upon them, the
soothsayers, and Vergil's indignation against these is but a reflection of the
dislike felt by Dante to astrologers, like Michael Scott and others, who at
this time enjoyed great influence in the highest circles. But the legends
had never made Vergil a soothsayer ; they had merely made him a magician, and withal a beneficent one ; their naïve puerilities could not do more
than provoke a smile ; they were not of a kind to call forth such indignation. The two lines, so generally misunderstood,—

" Chi è più scellerato di colui
Che al giudizio divin passion porta,"—

refer exclusively to the soothsayers ; " passion " is here used in its philosophical sense as the converse of " action." God, being by nature essentially
active, and as such incapable of being rendered passive, it is the greatest of
all sins to look into His inscrutable judgments, as the soothsayers do, and
thus " vi portar passione " and endeavour to render them passive. Hence
Vergil rebukes those who; like Dante, feel pity for these lost souls, pointing
out that they do not appreciate the gravity of their sin, which offends God
in His very essence, so that in such a case as this it is impossible to indulge
in pity without a corresponding loss of piety. Thus the line—

" Qui vive la pietà quand' è ben morta "—

means, " Here piety (pietà) can only live when pity (pietà) is dead." This
play upon words (not an uncommon feature in Dante) will serve to explain
this passage, generally so maltreated by the commentators.

those ideals of his that were associated with the name of poet, and among those ideals magic had most assuredly no place.

The purely popular reputation of a literary man could not be of any account to one who held art so high as Dante did and had so lofty a conception of the ancient poets. In matters of art and intellect Dante is an intense aristocrat. But even in the literary tradition there were things connected with Vergil which were not in accord with the lofty conception which Dante had formed of him or the symbolical manner in which he wished to employ his name; and hence he has purified him from more than one stain which made him obnoxious to Christian eyes. Vergil is certainly not an obscene poet—indeed, he is distinguished among the rest for his refinement and reserve,[13] but yet the loves of which he sings in the Bucolics and even in the Aeneid had troubled the conscience of more than one medieval ascetic, who hence condemned his poetry as something sensual and lascivious; there were besides certain statements in his Biography, supported by various passages of the Bucolics, according to which Vergil should have been placed in the circle of those who sin contrary to nature,[14] among whom Dante had not hesitated to place both Priscian and his own master Brunetto. And again, when it came to be a question of the purity of Vergil's doctrine, though it was the general medieval view that the great Latin poet had come very near to adopting the principles of Christianity, yet it was felt that, as a pagan, he had fallen into certain unavoidable errors, chiefly Epicurean. This had been animadverted upon already, as we have seen, by Fulgentius, and agrees too with Vergil's biography, which describes him as the pupil of an Epicurean, and also with the fact that certain Epi-

---

[13] Cp. KLOTZ, *De verecundia Vergili*, in his *Opuscula varii argumenti*, p. 242 seqq.

[14] From this arose the anachronistic idea that when Christ was born all sodomites died, and among them Vergil. *Vide* SALICETUS ap. EMANUEL DE MAURA, *Lib. de Ensal.*, sect. 3, c. 4, num. 12 ; NAUDÉ, *Apologie pour tous les grands personnages soupçonnés de magie*, p. 628 seqq. HERDER has endeavoured to defend Vergil against these charges with little success, especially by giving an allegorical interpretation to the Fifth Eclogue ; vide *Ueber die Schamhaftigkeit Virgil's* in *Kritische Wälder*, ii. p. 188 ; cp. GENTHE, *Leben und Fortleben des P. Virgilius Maro*, p. 28 seqq.

curean principles do actually occur in his works, as was indeed
only natural in a poet living at a period when these principles
were in such favour among the Romans. All these matters
Dante has entirely ignored, either because he considered them
as unimportant blemishes on so great a reputation, or else
because his system of allegorical interpretation permitted him
to be blind to faults that others saw. In the circle of those
who sin against nature Vergil does not utter a word, and the
affection with which Dante there addresses his master Brunetto
shows that in such cases great merit could induce him to over-
look certain faults. Of the Epicurean philosophy, Dante has
no direct or adequate knowledge. He knows from Cicero's *De
Finibus* that Epicurus regarded pleasure as the highest good;
but he only knows this vaguely.[15] The principal fault for
which he condemns the Epicureans is that they 'l' anima col
corpo morta fanno,' but of this he could not accuse Vergil,
who had himself described the kingdom of the dead and who
speaks to him in this canto of the Epicureans without any
suggestion of sharing their errors. Such a method of idealisa-
tion is characteristic of Dante, and is not confined to his treatment of Vergil; for, regarding as he does everything on its
abstract side, he considers in each case merely what is truly
typical and essential, and is thus enabled to ignore those im-
perfections or deviations which would have troubled a smaller
mind. Thus the suicide Cato does not appear in the circle of
those who have sinned against themselves, but occupies that
lofty and exalted position which every one knows. And thus
too in the idea of Rome and the empire, which Dante follows
so assiduously throughout his poem, there appear the great
ideal types of Aeneas, Cæsar, Augustus, Trajan and Justinian,
but those brutal types of ancient Emperors, such as Nero,
whom historical tradition and medieval legend alike would not
have suffered to be placed anywhere but among the damned,
are not so much as mentioned.

Vergil appears in the *Divina Commedia* as far more definitely

---

[15] " Siccome pare Tullio recitare nel primo di *Fine de' beni*." *Convito*,
iv. 6. The *De natura deorum*, from which he might have learnt more about
Epicureanism, he did not know.

Christian than he does in the medieval tradition; but there is always a clear line drawn between what he was while alive and what he has become after death. Vergil speaks always as the soul of one dead, who has spent many centuries in the place which his deeds have deserved; at his death the veil fell from his eyes and the life beyond the grave revealed to him those truths which he had not known before and made him understand his error, which, though involuntary, was fatal, and the just consequences which it entailed. This is no special privilege of Vergil's; it is a knowledge which he shares with all the dead, not excluding the damned. This is the Christian view, not peculiar to Dante, and in that respect the Vergil of Dante agrees with the Vergil of Fulgentius. In Fulgentius too Vergil speaks as a shade brought up from among the dead; as he has another object in coming, he does not describe what is his condition there, but it is clear that he has learnt to know certain truths and to recognise certain errors, and that the subject is to him a painful and humiliating one, on which he does not care to dwell. But the Vergil of Dante, being different alike in character and intention, enlarges far more on what death has taught him; he knows that the gods whom he worshipped in his time are 'falsi e bugiardi'; he knows what is the nature of the Christian God of whom he was formerly ignorant, and when Dante adjures him

'Per quel Dio che tu non conoscesti,'

he knows that this God is 'una sustanzia in tre persone,' and knows the benefits of the 'partorir Maria.' These and similar things Vergil knows for the same reason that makes him acquainted with many facts subsequent to his life upon earth, even in matters relating to Dante's contemporaries, or that renders him familiar with various earlier facts with which he could not have been familiar in his lifetime, as when he speaks of Nimrod,[16] or quotes Genesis in the same breath as Aristotle.[17]

---

[16] "Questi è Nembrotto per lo cui mal coto
Pure un linguaggio nel mondo non s' usa."

Inf., xxxi. 78.

[17] "Se tu ti rechi a mente Lo Genesi," *Inf.*, xi. 106; "La tua Etica," *ib.*, 80; "La tua Fisica," *ib.*, 102.

All that he has learnt makes him reflect sadly on his own
condition and on that of Aristotle, Plato, and so many other
great men among the ancients, who have lost eternal bliss
because they did not know that which without revelation it
was impossible to know.[18] But if the Christian truths which
Vergil mentions or explains have been revealed to him by
death, this does not imply that his knowledge of them is like
that of any other dead man ; when Dante gave a symbolical
value to the name of a real personage of well-known characteristics, he could not represent the ultramundane wisdom of this
personage as entirely independent of or diverse from his wisdom during his life upon earth.   Hence between the two lives
of Vergil there is continuity, and never opposition.   What
Vergil has learnt after death does not induce him to disclaim
anything that his reason had taught him during his lifetime; a
good instance of this is when Dante raises a doubt, and Vergil
explains that his line,

> ‘Desine fata deum flecti sperare precando,’

if properly understood, in no way contradicts the Christian
doctrine of the efficacy of prayer for the souls in Purgatory.[19]
This harmony is always preserved as far as possible in that
ideal region to which the symbolical Vergil belongs, while certain inevitable deviations from it are deliberately passed over
in silence.   Thus, while Dante has taken from Vergil the main
idea of his journey among the dead, he has notably altered it
in matters of detail, to suit his own views and the exigencies
of Christian tradition; but no emphasis is ever laid on these
differences in any part of the poem.   Dante distinguishes
clearly in the work of the ancient poets between the idea expressed, whether literally or figuratively, and the poetical
expression in which it is clothed; and thus he too makes use

---

[18] “ E disiar vedeste senza frutto
    Tai, che sarebbe lor disio quetato,
    Ch’ eternalmente è dato lor per lutto.
  Io dico d’ Aristotele e di Plato,
    E di molti altri.—E qui chinò la fronte;
    E più non disse, e rimase turbato.”
                        Purg., iii. 40 seqq.

[19] *Purg.*, vi. 28 seqq.

of mythological names and images, not only as symbols, but also as purely poetical elements.[20] Of the journey of Aeneas to the shades he has adopted what he considers the fundamental idea, while of the merely formal and fanciful parts he has taken some and omitted or altered others, without however this method of treatment becoming in any way a subject of discussion between him and Vergil in the course of their entirely ideal association.[21]

The conception of a purification of the spirit and an intuition of great truths arrived at by sole force of character without external aid would necessarily, when applied to a man who already had a literary and learned reputation, of itself lead to a further conception of exceptional wisdom and vast and encyclopedic learning. And hence the Vergil of Dante is as learned as the Vergil of Macrobius, Fulgentius, or any other medieval writer. Dante's Vergil has only occasion to display certain sides of his universal knowledge, but it is none the less clear that this knowledge is virtually universal and only limited in the direction where that of Beatrice begins; moreover, what he knows as a shade harmonises with his previous knowledge as a man, for Vergil, it must not be forgotten, however much he may appear as idea or symbol, yet always retains his historical reality as man and as poet. Hence that omniscience which we

---

[20] Interesting as showing the way in which the Christian mind of Dante regarded the ancient poetical legends is the passage in *Purg.*, xxviii. 139, where Matelda says in the presence of Vergil and Statius:

> " Quelli ch' anticamente poetaro
> L' età dell' oro e suo stato felice
> Forse in Parnaso esto loco sognaro.
> Qui fu innocente l' umana radice,
> Qui primavera sempre, ed ogni frutto ;
> Nettare è questo di che ciascun dice.
> Io mi rivolsi addietro allora tutto
> A' miei Poeti, e vidi che *con riso*
> Udito avevan l' ultimo costrutto."

[21] *Vide* FAURIEL, *Dante et les origines*, etc., ii. p. 435 seqq. OZANAM (*Dante et la philosophie cathol. au treiz. siècle*, p. 324 seqq.) has devoted a lengthy work of research to Dante's predecessors in poetical journeys or visions in the unseen world. But this examination, though instructive in itself, is of little service in explaining Dante, whose work is essentially original and bears no real likeness to that of any of his so-called predecessors, except Vergil.

find attributed throughout the middle ages to Vergil appears
also in Dante, to whom this idea presented itself not merely in
connection with his poem, but also independently of it, as an
evident and perfectly reasonable fact; for in reality the nature
and the proportions of medieval knowledge were such that it was
possible, and even necessary, to conceive of the perfect scholar
as a man of encyclopedic learning, and the tendency, moreover,
of the scholars of the time, and of Dante among them, was
entirely towards polymathy. It was the habit of the middle
ages to look upon the ancient poets as scholars and philosophers; Dante too regards them as such,[22] but he differs from
his contemporaries in never forgetting that they are also, and
principally, poets. It is just the depth of thought in their
poetry which attracts him as a poet to the ancients, at the
head of whom is Vergil. Vergil therefore, as the greatest
ancient poet, is also the most learned, and the medieval idea
comes out strongly in such expressions as 'virtù somma,' 'quel
savio gentil che tutto seppe,' 'tu che onori ogni scienza ed
arte,' 'mar di tutto senno,' and the like. This reputation for
learning belongs to Vergil principally among the poets; in the
other classes of the great men of ancient times appear others
who are no less learned than he; for, as we have already
noticed, Dante is enthusiastic for every illustrious name of
antiquity, and shows great joy at finding himself in Limbo
with these 'spiriti magni,' of whom he says 'che di vederli in
me stesso m' esalto.' Dante was able to draw a distinction
where the medieval monks could not, and with him Vergil,
though not yet returned entirely to his true position, is yet
well on the way to return. If therefore the choice of Vergil as
representative of human reason corresponds to the position
which he occupied in the medieval tradition, yet the more
elevated conception of antiquity peculiar to Dante shows that
the true explanation of that choice lies in those personal and
subjective reasons of which we have already spoken.

The various souls with whom Vergil is in Limbo, and the

[22] This is the name which he gives to the poets he meets in Limbo (*Inf.*,
iv. 110) often to Vergil (*Inf.*, vii. 3; xii. 6; xiii. 47) and to Statius (*Purg.*,
xxiii. 8; xxxiii. 15).

reason for his presence among them, constitute already at the very beginning of the poem a general characteristic of that type which he preserves throughout. Vergil is one of those souls who are denied eternal bliss through no fault of their own. God has placed him 'fra color che son sospesi,' because he was 'rebellante alla sua legge,' 'non per fare, ma per non fare,' and 'per non aver fè,' among those who

> ' Se furon dinanzi al cristianesmo
> Non adorar debitamente Dio.'

With him are great men of every kind, poets, men of science, philosophers, heroes, historical personages, among them even Saladin, just as there had been, before Christ's descent to them, Moses, Rachel, and the other famous characters of the old dispensation. And together with these, who stand there

> ' con occhi tardi e gravi,
> Di grande autorità ne' lor sembianti,'

are the souls of all those infants who have died before baptism had purified them from their only sin.

Such was the company in which Vergil was:

> ' Quivi sto io co' parvoli innocenti
> Dai denti morsi della morte avante
> Che fosser dell' umana colpa esenti.
> Quivi sto io con quei che le tre sante
> Virtù non si vestiro e senza vizio
> Conobber l'altre e seguir tutte quante.'

The common condition of the various inhabitants of Limbo naturally establishes among them a certain community of feeling, but this does not in any way prevent each of them from having an individual character of his own, determined by what he had been in the life upon earth. The genius of Dante, with its aptitude for the portrayal of character, would never have confused diverse types; and had the guide chosen been Aristotle, Lucan or Ovid, he would doubtless have been represented with different features to those of Vergil. Here too we find the coarse and barbarous ideas of the middle ages refined to such a degree that the conception of Dante seems no longer based upon them, but rather upon the historical reality. When

Q

we consider the various requirements of the poem, which necessitated Vergil's appearing as at once an inhabitant of Limbo, a servant of Beatrice and a symbol, we may well feel surprise, not merely at the harmony brought about among these varied and apparently incongruous characteristics, but still more at the fact that after all the Vergil of Dante is far nearer the historical truth than any previous medieval conception of him had ever been. In fact, the Vergil of Dante is not merely the Vergil of the biography, but also the Vergil apparent to the reader of his poetry.

In the mild and gentle features of this Vergil, endowed with the most refined sensibility, just and reasonable even in anger, and, when vexed with himself, blushing like a girl,[23] it is impossible to fail to recognise the true author of the Vergilian poems, the 'anima candida' of Horace, and the 'Parthenias' of the Neapolitans. It cannot well be doubted that it was the intense and intelligent study of Vergil's poetry which led Dante to the formation of this noble and lofty ideal.

This character is furthermore in complete accord with all that Vergil symbolises. Dante regards genius and human knowledge with reverence and enthusiasm, but also with due intelligence; he does not regard them as something distant or mysterious, nor does he consider that he need abase himself before them. He is conscious of his own powers and does not endeavour to conceal that legitimate feeling of pride which must accompany such consciousness. In the presence of Vergil he feels perfectly at his ease, and there is evident sympathy and reciprocal esteem between the two poets. Dante treats Vergil with reverence and respect, but without any undue humility, as an elder member of the noble family to which he too belongs; and Vergil never adopts a haughty attitude, but behaves throughout in a friendly and almost paternal fashion.[24]

---

[23] " Ei mi parea da sè stesso rimorso;
 O dignitosa coscienza e netta
 Come t' è picciol fallo amaro morso ! "
 Purg., iii. 7 seqq.

[24] D'Ovidio (*Saggi critici*, p. 326) believes to have found certain traces of the pedagogue in Dante's Vergil, quoting as an instance the words " O creature sciocche, Quanta ignoranza è quella che v'offende ! " (*Inf.*, vii. 70).

A mind which really understood poetry and knew in what its true nobility consists could never have conceived of Vergil as the proud, gloomy and antipathetic wiseacre that we find in Fulgentius, and have regarded himself in his presence as merely a poor ' Homunculus.' The Vergil of Fulgentius was the offspring of that stolid and ignorant barbarism which degrades what it strives to ennoble; the Vergil of Dante sprang from a re-awakening of the human intellect which refined and elevated as much as barbarism had polluted and debased.

The delicacy of the touch with which Dante has delineated his figure of Vergil is brought out still more by certain light shadows which, without depriving Vergil of any characteristic essential to his purity, yet serve to show that he is farther from perfection than various others among the great men of antiquity. Not only does Dante admit that there were men before the coming of Christ more perfect than Vergil, but he even derives from the lines of the Aeneid itself the idea of contrasting its author with Cato and with that Ripheus, to whom, because he is described as ' iustissimus unus Qui fuit in Teucris et servantissimus aequi,' he assigns a place in Paradise. The type of Cato, delineated in a masterly manner and idealised after the traditional manner,[25] holy, majestic and venerable, but severe and Stoical, an ' atrox animus,' deprived of every human feeling, is higher in a noteworthy degree than that of Vergil, alike in its nature and its rewards. To such a height as this Vergil could not attain, and Dante therefore, with a skill all his own, not merely shows him as being on more equal terms with himself before his purification than Cato is, but also, without introducing any historical or realistic element from the biography, by merely developing his character, shows him to be susceptible to certain slight errors of judgment of which neither Cato nor still less Beatrice would have been capable. An instance of this is the passage in which Vergil

But here, though Vergil is speaking, the contempt for the vulgar expressed is all Dante's own, just as the fantastic theory of Fortune which Vergil subsequently expounds is purely medieval, and has nothing really to do with Vergil.

[25] Cp. WOLFF, *Cato der Jüngere bei Dante* in the *Jahrb. d. deutsch. Dante gesellschaft*, ii. 225 seqq.

suffers himself to be beguiled by the song of Casella, but a more characteristic example of the contrast between the two types is where Vergil, in speaking to Cato, thinks to move him by an appeal to his Marcia, an appeal which Cato quietly and severely puts aside, showing by the sole regard which he has for the 'Heavenly Lady who moves and rules' Vergil's movements how great is the difference in the degrees of purification to which their two souls have attained.

These various gradations in purification and perfection form the first principle which determines the behaviour of those who guide or encounter Dante on his journey. Thus Vergil, who is without the Christian Faith, leads him readily through the Inferno, but in Purgatory, where the more exclusively Christian element of grace comes into play, he feels uncertain and in many cases ignorant, and has to ask the way of others. This is that part of the road towards perfection which he could never traverse in its entirety or with security, lacking the escort of the 'tre sante virtù.' At a certain point therefore they are joined by Statius, who is represented as a sort of emanation of Vergil, seeing that he had become through the latter's agency not merely a poet but also a Christian, as Vergil himself would have been had he been born after Christ. And here there is introduced with great ingenuity for the first time the medieval idea of the prophecy of Christ contained in the Fourth Eclogue. Vergil, who was a prophet of Christ without knowing it, and does not so much as speak of Christ throughout the poem, finds as it were a supplement for this defect in Statius, who, having been born after Christ, was able to understand the meaning of the prophecy and to become by its means converted to Christianity. Statius, like Dante, is an enthusiastic admirer of Vergil's, and even goes the length of saying:

> 'E per esser vissuto di là quando
> Visse Virgilio assentirei un sole
> Più ch' io non deggio al mio uscir di bando.'

Then follows the fine passage in which he recognises the poet standing before him and expresses all his obligations to him:

' Tu prima m' inviasti
Verso Parnaso a ber delle sue grotte,
E prima appresso Dio m' alluminasti.
Facesti come quei che va di notte
E porta il lume dietro e a sè non giova,
Ma dopo sè fa le persone dotte,
Quando dicesti:—secol si rinnova,
Torna giustizia e primo tempo umano
E progenie scende dal ciel nuova.—
Per te poeta fui, per te cristiano, etc.'

But in spite of his conversion, a taint of impurity still clave to Statius, which prevented him from reaching the highest perfection, and from which he had to cleanse himself in Purgatory. Hence, when Beatrice comes, Vergil disappears; and though Statius follows Dante into Paradise, from that moment the poet forgets him, having no need of any other guide than Beatrice.

Such then is the principal idea which regulates the nature and the limits of the Vergil of the *Divina Commedia*. Dante has his one well-known idea for the better ordering of mankind; he aspires not merely to perfect himself, he aspires also to realise that ideal of human society which he considers to be most in harmony with the laws of justice, morality and religion, and hence most adapted for the development of the individual. The distinction between spiritual and temporal, between Pope and Emperor, forms the basis of this idea, which in its turn forms the basis of the *Divina Commedia*. Aeneas and Paul have been Dante's two predecessors on his journey, and at the bottom of the universe he finds associated, as the worst sinners of whom it is possible to conceive, the betrayers of Christ and of Caesar. This order of things is represented, not as a project of Dante's own, but as a fact determined by the will of God, made evident in great part by reason and by history, and confirmed by faith; it appears therefore as the ideal which Dante finds present to the minds of all the honest dead, and especially of his guides. It is evident that all that part of this ideal which referred to the Empire and the Temporal Power would be included in the knowledge of Vergil, and would appear in

his works literally as well as allegorically.[26] Vergil, historically, was a contemporary of the good Augustus and of the
peaceful beginnings of the empire, and withal near in time to
that great event whereby Providence was preparing Rome to
become

'lo loco santo
U' siede il successor del maggior Piero';

he was, besides, the singer of universal empire. But in addition
to this, he had also written allegorically of the contemplative
life and had in this respect too understood the most perfect
order of human society. It would be as unjust therefore to say
that Vergil represents in Dante only the imperial idea, as it
would be to maintain that the *Divina Commedia* contains
nothing but Dante's political views. The historical character
of Vergil could not fail to bring him into close connection with
the idea of the Empire, but this idea, which was in Dante's
case the outcome of profound speculation, was necessarily also
contained in the symbol of Vergil, because, according to Dante,
human reason was necessarily bound to acknowledge the legitimacy of the Roman empire and the perfection of his great ideal
for the regeneration of society.

An examination of medieval tradition, with the view of dis-
covering to what extent it had preceded Dante in associating
Vergil with the imperial idea, will show that here too the great
poet found nothing but the bare elements upon which to
work. The idea of the empire was, as we have seen, common
in the middle ages, and had been the aim of many princes, but
none of them had, like Dante, developed this idea into a political theory having its basis in a vast system of speculation
which included the whole history of mankind. It would be
vain to search in the middle ages for any other writer in whom
Vergil and the imperial idea are historically and philosophically so closely combined as is the case in Dante.[27]

---

[26] This aspect of the Vergil of Dante has been specially studied by RUTH
(*Studien über Dante Alighieri* (Tübing., 1855) p. 205 seqq.), who has also
written another special article on Dante's Vergil entitled *Ueber die Bedeu-
tung des Virgil in der Divina Commedia*, in the *Heidelberger Jahrbücher* for
1850.

[27] Before Dante, and before the middle ages, properly speaking, the writer

And here we must close our remarks on the Vergil of Dante, lest a too exclusive occupation of this ideal type should lead us to forget those points of contact between it and the Vergil of tradition which have led us to undertake its examination.

who has made most use of Vergil as a poet of the Roman Empire from a historico-philosophical point of view is St. Augustine.   But Augustine and his pupil Orosius, who regarded Rome as their persecutor and saw her falling and accusing Christianity of being the cause of her fall, could not arrive at the same ideas as the middle ages suggested to Dante.   Pagan Rome was still too near them, and they had not seen Christianity grown a persecutor in its turn and the history of the Church changed into a chronicle of obscenities.

CHAPTER XVI

It cannot be doubted that in all the varied expressions of
enthusiastic admiration which the universally recognised genius
of Vergil had called forth, from the time of Augustus onwards,
none was at once so magnificent and so true as that of Dante.
But in this, as in all the work of this privileged genius, it is
evident that, while his ideas rest on a medieval basis, they
ascend to a far higher level than was otherwise attained in
the middle ages. The *Divina Commedia* rises up before the
student of medieval thought with an abruptness which is quite
unexpected, and none of its surroundings can in any way equal
its proportions. The results which Dante was able to obtain
by a use of the ordinary materials of his age were entirely his
own and without any parallel. None of his contemporaries
had ever been able to conceive of Vergil as he did, and we have
seen clearly to what an extent this type of his is a refinement
of that generally current in medieval times. But if the Vergil
of Dante is in advance of the middle ages, another personification of Vergil, which belongs to the same century, may perhaps
serve as a corrective. This is the Vergil of the *Dolopathos*, a
romantic work by a monk, who would seem to have been neither
above nor below the ordinary level of his age in intellect and
culture. A brief examination of this work will serve to show
us Vergil as conceived during that last stage of the literary
tradition where the ideas derived from it are on the point of
becoming merged in those that have had their origin in the
popular imagination, just as the Vergil of Dante has brought
us into contact with that higher intellectual level in which the
dead medieval traditionalism is about to be transformed into
the real and living classical feeling of the Renaissance.

The *Dolopathos* was written in Latin in the 13th century by a certain John, a monk of the Abbey of Hauteseille in Lorraine and it was afterwards put into French verse by a certain Herbers.[1] The story of the work is briefly as follows.

Dolopathos, king of Sicily in the time of Augustus, has a son called Lucinian; this son he sends to Rome to be educated by Vergil, who instructs him in every branch of knowledge, and especially in astronomy. In the meantime the wife of Dolopathos dies, and the latter marries another woman and sends to recall his son. By means of astrology Vergil learns that Lucinian is menaced by some great danger, to avoid which he advises him to remain absolutely silent until he (Vergil) gives him permission to speak; so when Lucinian comes to his father, he refuses to answer any question and remains obstinately mute. Every other means having failed, the queen undertakes to make him speak, and, after employing every other artifice in vain, declares herself to be in love with him, but still without effect. Angered at his indifference and fearing the consequences of her declaration, she determines to have Lucinian killed, and so accuses him of having offered her violence. The king condemns his son to death, but a sage happens to arrive opportunely, and succeeds, by telling a story, in getting the execution postponed for a day. Other sages arrive in succession and do the same, till at last, on the seventh day, comes Vergil himself, tells a story in his turn, and gives Lucinian permission to speak. The latter declares everything, and the queen is burnt alive. The narrative then proceeds to describe the deaths of Dolopathos and of Vergil, the coming of

---

[1] *Li Romans de Dolopathos, publié pour la première fois en entier par* CH. BRUNET *et* ANAT. DE MONTAIGLON, Paris (Jannet), 1856. There exists in certain MSS. a Latin text of the *Dolopathos*, first brought to light by Prof. MUSSAFIA, who regarded it as the original text of the monk Jean de Hauteseille (*Ueber die Quelle des altfranzösischen Dolopathos*, Wien, 1865, and *Beiträge zur Litteratur der sieben weisen Meister*, Wien, 1868). The doubts which I and others felt at the time as to the correctness of this view have since been dispelled by the edition of this text made by OESTERLEY (*Ioh. de Alta Sylva Dolopathos sive De rege et septem sapientibus*, Strassb. and Lond., 1873). Cp. G. PARIS in *Romania*, ii., 1873, pp. 481–503 (for the dates *vide* p. 501); STUDEMUND in the *Zeitschr. f. deutsch. Alterth.*, N.F., viii. pp. 415–425.

Christ, the preaching of Christianity in Sicily and the conversion of Lucinian, who dies a saint.

This is, as anyone can see, merely a version of the popular story of the Seven Sages, which comes originally from India and occurs so frequently in various forms in the literature both of the East and West.[2] But while all the other Western versions resemble one another very closely, the *Dolopathos* has special characteristics which give it a place of its own in this family of popular stories. The principal of these characteristics from the point of view of the present work is the part played in it, and in it alone, by Vergil. In the Western versions the education of the prince is generally entrusted, not to one of the Sages, but to all seven; in the Eastern versions (in those at any rate as yet known, which all go back to an ancient Arabic text, now lost, called the *Book of Sindibâd*)[3] he is delivered over to Sindibâd, as the wisest man in the kingdom. It would appear therefore that the Hauteseille monk had before him a text, or, more probably, had heard a version, which kept to the Eastern form of the tale, and so, while retaining the idea of the prince's single tutor, had altered the details to suit his audience, and substituted Vergil for the Sindibâd of the original. In doing this he was guided or inspired by his monastic education; and his knowledge of Vergil is not merely popular, as was the case with the other authors of romances, but he gives evidence of a first-hand acquaintance with his poems and even quotes him in one passage of the work.[4] So real is this acquantance with Vergil that the whole chronology of the story is arranged to suit his appearance there. The events take place in the reign of Augustus and the wife which that emperor gives to Dolopathos[5] is a daughter of Agrippa. In other Western versions of the *Seven Sages*, in which Vergil does not take part, the Emperor is a Diocletian or a Pontian or some other belong-

---

[2] Cp. D'ANCONA, *Il libro dei sette savi di Roma*, Pisa (Nistri), 1864.

[3] I have endeavoured to trace the history of this book in my *Ricerche intorno al Libro di Sindibâd*, Milan, 1869 (transl. into English by H. C. Coote, London, 1882).

[4] v. 12369 seqq. (*Aen.*, viii. 40 seq.).

[5] Dolopathos was of Trojan origin;

"De Troie fu ses parentez." v. 162.

ing to an entirely imaginary period. The Greek name Dolopathos too, the meaning and significance of which is explained,[6]
is an invention of the author's, and gives proof of his culture,
though the clerical nature of that culture is shown by his
quoting St. Augustine[7] and giving to the story a religious
termination.

Although this poem is evidently the work of a man of education, yet by nature, conception and tendency it is entirely
romantic, and hence it would be vain to search for any rigid
historical sequence in the details which have been added to the
Oriental original. The author knows that Vergil comes from
Mantua, and thinks he ought to die there, but he puts Mantua
in Sicily. Still he does not call Sicily Naples, like some of
his contemporaries, and he knows that Palermo is the chief
city of the former. But his regard for history does not go
beyond a certain point. He refers to an Old Testament[8]
among the pagans before the coming of Christ and talks of
bishops, monks and abbots, just as he talks of dukes, counts
and barons, making Augustus Emperor of Rome and King of
Lombardy, and Dolopathos a feudal prince. The type of Vergil
too is entirely in keeping with his romantic environment; but
there is no need to have recourse for its explanation to the
purely popular legends of Vergil as magician, for though the
type approaches very closely to the popular one, yet it still
belongs distinctly to the literary tradition. Vergil appears as
the great master of secular learning; his only fault is that of
being a pagan and having no knowledge of the One God,
though even in this he comes as near to the truth as is possible before the birth of Christ; he is a man of high moral
character and a great philosopher; none is more celebrated
than he, or more honoured by Augustus;[9] his word is law to

---

[6] " Por ce ot nom Dolopathos
       Car il soufri trop en sa vie
       De doleur et de tricherie."
                                   v. 164 seqq.
[7] v. 12890 seq. (AUGUST., *De civit. Dei*, xviii. 17, 18).
[8] " Je sais tot le Viez Testament."   v. 4780.
[9] " César ot par toute la vile
       Commandé que tuit l'ennoraissent
       Et seignorie li portaissent."   v. 1652 seqq.

kings and emperors ; no man is more learned or a greater poet. In fact, Vergil is the ' clericus ' *par excellence.*

> ' A icel tans à Rome avoit
> I. philosophe, ki tenoit
> La renomée de clergie ;
> Sages fu et de bone vie ;
> D'une des citez de Sezile
> Fut néz ; on l'apeloit Virgile ;
> La citéz Mantue ot à non.
> Virgile fu de grant renom ;
> Nus clers plus de`lui ne savoit ;
> Par ce si grant renon avoit ;
> Onkes poëtes ne fu tex
> S'il créust qu'il ne fust c'uns Dex.' [10]

This king of wise men kept a school, but naturally his pupils belonged to the most aristocratic families. When Lucinian comes to Rome, his future master receives him with great politeness. On entering the school he finds Vergil seated in his chair ; he is dressed in a rich mantle lined with fur and without sleeves and wears on his head a cap of precious fur, while his hood is thrown back. Seated on the ground before him are the sons of various great barons, who, book in hand, are listening to his teaching :

> ' Assis estoit en sa chaière ;
> Une riche chape forrée
> Sans manches, avoit afublée,
> Et s'ot en son chief un chapel
> Qui fu d'une moult riche pel ;
> Tret ot arrier son chaperon.
> Li enfant di maint haut baron
> Devant lui à terre séoient,
> Qui ses paroles entendoient,
> Et chacun son livre tenoit
> Einssi comme il les enseignoit.' [11]

The course of instruction begins with the rudiments. Vergil teaches Lucinian to read and write, then instructs him in Latin and Greek, and finally introduces him to the study of the Seven Arts, beginning with grammar, the mother of all the rest, and

[10] v. 1257 seqq.   [11] v. 1318 seqq.

condensing them all, for his pupil's special benefit, into so small
a volume that it could be held inside the closed hand:

> ' Torne ses feuilles et retorne :
> Les vii. ars liberaus atorne
> En i. volume si petit
> Que, si con l'estoire me dit,
> Il le poïst bien tot de plain
> Enclorre et tenir en sa main.
>
> .   .   .   .   .
>
> Premier li enseigne Gramaire
> Qui mere est, et prevoste, et maire,
> De toutes les arts liberax etc.' [12]

It is easy to see that in this curious travesty is embodied the
Vergil of the medieval schools, the Vergil of the grammarians
and the authors of compendia. The character of astrologer,
distinct, as we shall see, from that of magician, enters merely
as an integral part of the romantic conception of a learned
man,[13] and is here moreover rendered necessary by the nature
of the story, as is often the case both in the East and the
West. The pious monk believes in the possibility of such
divination only in such cases as are permitted by God.[14] In
complete accordance with this is the author's attitude in respect
to the prophecy of Christ; in fact, after the deaths of Dolopathos and Vergil and the coming of Christ, the famous lines
of the Fourth Eclogue are among the arguments which serve
to convert Lucinian.[15] Beyond this it will not be necessary to
follow the *Dolopathos*, as its connection with the Vergil of
literary tradition goes no further.

With the Vergil of the *Divina Commedia* and the Vergil of
the *Dolopathos* this part of our work may end. These two
types represent the two extremes in the literary tradition of
the middle ages: on the one hand the noble creation of an
exceptional intellect, on the other the naïve and trivial concep-

---

[12] v. 1396 seqq.

[13] " La vii. est Astrenomie
Qui est fins de toute clergie."

Image du monde ap. JUBINAL, *Oeuvres compl. de Ruteboeuf*, ii. p. 424.

[14] He expounds this view at length, v. 1162 seqq.

[15] v. 12530.

tion of a common mind incapable of rising above the ordinary level of romanticism. They belong to two different streams of thought, distinct from that of the schools, yet capable none the less of being ultimately traced back to it; but what the one has added to its original in nobility and grandeur, the other has added in barbarism and triviality. After the time of Dante, whatever development took place in the regions of literary and learned thought belongs properly to the Renaissance, and the consideration of it would consequently be out of place in a work dealing professedly with the middle ages. But the Vergil of the *Dolopathos*, that final parody of the literary tradition, will serve, by the element of romanticism which it contains, to call us to the study of the views current as to our poet in a region different to that in which we have hitherto been, and may form therefore at once the conclusion of the present volume and the introduction to the next.

PART II

THE VERGIL OF POPULAR LEGEND

CHAPTER I

'Maint autres grant clerc ont esté
Au monde de grant poesté
Qui aprisrent tote lor vie
Des sept arts et d'astronomie ;
Dont aucuns i ot qui a leur tens
Firent merveille por lor sens ;
Mais cil qui plus s'en entremist
Fu Virgile qui mainte en fist,
Por ce si vos en conterons
Aucune dout oi avons.'

L'Image du Monde.

To the modern mind the popular poetry of the middle ages and classical poetry seem to differ so entirely from one another in form, in sentiment and in purpose, that the former can hardly fail to appear the outcome of a revolution directly and intentionally antagonistic to the latter. But that struggle between classicism and romanticism, which has actually taken place in modern times and on which this idea is based, never really occurred in the middle ages. Medieval popular literature did not arise from a rebellion or reaction against the classics any more than the medieval republics owed their origin to an anti-monarchical revolution. To render such a reaction possible there would have been necessary a critical and vigorous appreciation of antiquity, such as we have already seen did not at that time exist. The ideas of the clergy on the subject of ancient art were not much truer or more profound than those of the laity. Latin, which was still almost a living language, served as a connecting link between the ancient tradition and the new creations which were independent of it; for while on the one hand it tended to preserve various elements of antiquity, it was, on the other, the vehicle of living sentiments, and had, with a view to this amalgamation, adopted special forms in poetry, and generally undergone a series of changes which from the point of view of the classical ideal would be regarded as corruptions. It would be difficult to find a subject more exclusively medieval than that of the poem of Waltharius; and yet this subject is treated in Latin in hexameters moreover, and that too with such frequent Vergilian reminiscences that it is evident that the writer was a man of education, and, like every other 'clericus,' a diligent student of Vergil.[1] The same can be said of a quantity of medieval Latin literature, both prose and verse, which takes its subjects from the popular poetry. The popular poetry moreover never speaks slightingly of antiquity or of ancient poetry, but always treats it with great respect, and to a certain degree subordinates itself to it, invoking it by way of authority or at times even quoting its actual words.[2] In fact, it is quite the fashion for the romantic writer to cite some Latin work, real or imaginary, as the source from which his narrative is taken.[3]

There is, no doubt, in the popular poetry of some European peoples an earlier period, in which this poetry is exclusively national and admits of no admixture from extraneous sources.

---

[1] Vide GRIMM and SCHMELLER, Lateinische Gedichte des X. und XI. Jahrhunderts, p. 65 seqq. and CHOLEVIUS, Geschichte der deutschen Poesie nach ihren antiken Elementen, i. p. 20 seqq. In the rhythmical Latin song of the soldiers of Modena (10th cent.) is a reference to the story of Sinon, which is evidently derived from Vergil. Vide DU MÉRIL, Poés. pop. lat. ant. au XII. siècle, p. 268.

[2] ZAPPERT (Vergil's Fortleben im Mittelalt., p. 7 seqq. not., 64 seqq.) has devoted a large part of his work to a collection of Vergilian reminiscences in the popular poets of the middle ages, and has gathered together a large number of such passages from writers of various nationalities. But his references are of far too general a character; on these lines it might be proved that various Indian or Persian poets had read Vergil.

[3] Cp. REIFFENBERG, Cron. rimée de Philippes Mouskes, p. ccxxxv. seqq.

This is the period during which the Scandinavian, Teutonic and Celtic peoples preserved by means of their primitive epics the memory of a time in their history anterior to the influences of civilisation and Christianity. But as far as this period is represented by extant written documents it may be considered as of very brief duration. The very fact that these songs were committed to writing reveals the influence of external culture, especially when one considers that for this purpose *Latin* letters were used.

Far more numerous is that class of popular medieval poetry in which national characteristics are found combined with characteristics of a more universal nature—characteristics owing their origin to the elements which tend to consolidate various nationalities into a civil, intellectual and religious whole. But the most important group of all is that in which the specially national element has entirely disappeared, and there remain only the common and universal motives of sentiment, culture and religion. This class, which is less strictly epic than the other two, includes a number of fantastic narratives in verse and prose, and, above all, the romantic lyric poetry, which forms the mouthpiece of a subjectivity in no way peculiar to any one country. In the poetry belonging to these last two classes, and especially to the former of them, the great consolidating agency which tended to the fusion and transformation of national peculiarities both with one another and with universal ideas was the clergy. To them was due the translation of the popular literature into Latin, and the translation again of the Latin texts into the vernacular; to them belonged the civil and religious ideals, and it was in these ideals that the first assimilating elements were to be found.

In all this work of fusion, not to say confusion, the imagination played a striking part, and enjoyed an immoderate amount of liberty owing to the exceptional mental conditions of the time. There can be no doubt that the human mind in the middle ages worked on different principles to those which have guided it at more normal periods of history. The prevalence of allegory in the treatment of the most serious matters shows clearly that the association of incongruous ideas no longer

R

excited surprise and that any direct investigation of the real
causes of things, or any just appreciation of them, was not to
be expected. Hence the imagination, ever ready to break
bounds, failed to find in the influence of reflection those checks
and correctives which it encounters in an age accustomed to
critical investigation. And so the fact remains that while
among the phases of thought expressed in the phantastic productions of the middle ages a few may be found with a rational
and elevating tendency, there are others which have reached a
point at which they can only be regarded from the point of view
of the pathologist, and can hardly be explained at all without
reference to the laws of natural degradation. Any one who
considers carefully the diverse natures of ancient and medieval
poetry will at once see that the empty phantasies and conventional sentimentality which mark the close of the latter arose
ultimately from the same causes as the love of rhetoric and
declamation which brought about the downfall of the former.

In conjunction with this ascendency of the imagination we
find an extraordinary love of the marvellous, and that intense
and universal longing for stories of adventure which led to the
personification of a 'Lady of Adventure.' [4] The demand naturally regulated the supply, and not a stone was left unturned
in the attempt to satisfy the general craving for new stories.
Antiquity too had to furnish its quota, but the classical narratives were compelled to adopt romantic dress to suit the taste
of the time.

This fact, strange as it may appear to modern notions, appeared at the time to have nothing forced or ridiculous about
it ; what seems a travesty now did not seem so then, and was
in fact nothing more than a concise expression of the naïve
manner in which all matters connected with antiquity were
regarded. The same fact holds true of the medieval pictures
in which the characters, whatever nationality or historical
epoch they may belong to, all appear with the dress and surroundings of the painter's own country and time. All the
various themes of the romantic writers, whatever their origin,

---

[4] Cp. GRIMM, *Frau Aventiure*, in his *Kl. Schrift.*, i. 83 seqq.

came to have a common colour; and since the intelligence of the
time had little power of dissociating its ideas from its immediate surroundings, or which the fabric of its imagination
was based, all its characters became reduced to certain types,
which remained constant, however different might be their
names or their nationalites in the various narratives. Stories,
whether clerical, classical, Oriental, mythological or historical,
legends, whether Celtic, Scandinavian or Teutonic, all furnish
material for the romantic narrator. Ancient society comes to
be looked upon as if it were feudal: the ancient hero becomes a
Knight, the heroine a Lady; the heathen gods become magicians, each with his special attributes; the pagans of ancient
times come to be regarded much as any other non-Christian
peoples, and Nero passes as a worshipper of Mohammed just
as the Saracens pass for worshippers of Apollo. The love of
ancient fable and history becomes the romantic love of medieval sentiment; the classical poet or prose-writer becomes a
philosopher, a sage, a clerk, medieval in proportions and character, with all the peculiarities and exaggerations of the medieval scholastic tradition brought into special prominence, as one
would expect, in this free domain of the imagination.

One of the names of antiquity which remain most in evidence during this period of transformation is the name of
Vergil, which holds in the region of romance the same pre-
eminent position which was accorded it in scholastic circles.
Here however it was not only the personality of the poet, but
his work as well, which was subjected to these new influences—
results which, though brought about independently, are not
without connection the one with the other. The most attractive subjects which ancient poetry, legend or history had to
offer to the writers of romances were the warlike enterprises,
the marvellous adventures and the amours of its heroes.
Everything of this kind that ancient Latin literature or its
medieval imitations could supply was made use of for these
compositions, whether as subject or as incident. The story of
Troy, derived from Vergil, from pseudo-Dares and from other
Latin sources, the Thebaid of Statius, the marvellous legends
of Alexander, taken from Latin translations of the Greek

originals, the history of Caesar and the great Roman wars
taken from Lucan, and the various mythological stories of
which the Metamorphoses of Ovid were the chief storehouse[5]—
all these became the common property of the romantic literature, and formed moreover the subject of free translations or
adaptations in which the classical idea and conception were
entirely subordinated to the romantic. The original home of
this class of composition was France in the second half of the
12th century ; from there it spread, in the shape of translations, imitations, or adaptations, over the whole of Europe,
especially in Germany, which next to France was most distinguished in this field of literature. Benoît de Sainte-More,
Lambert li Cors, Heinrich von Veldeke, Albrecht von Halberstadt, Herbort von Fritzlar and others all produced works of
this kind, which enjoyed a widespread popularity.[6] But the
taste for ancient legends and stories and their imaginative
treatment was anterior to the birth of romanticism properly so
called. Previous to the development of the popular literature
or its amalgamation with the elements of culture and tradition, a similar style of composition had prevailed in medieval
scholastic literature among the clergy—similar notwithstanding the absence of certain characteristics and the prevalence in
it of the scholastic view of antiquity and a clerical tendency
towards moralising.

Of all the ancient legends, the one best known and most
frequently treated was the legend of Troy.[7] Vergil, who was
the prime authority for that mythical tradition which connected the origin of Rome with Troy, and who had, as we have

---

[5] King ALFONSO says, " El Ovidio mayor (Metamorphoses) non es àl entre
ellos (i.e. the ancients) sinon la theologia et la Biblia dellos entre los gentiles." Grande et general estoria, i. 8, c. 7. Cp. AMADOR DE LOS RIOS, Hist.
crit. de la lit. españ., iii. p. 603.

[6] An excellent critical history of this transformation of classical subjects
into romantic is to be found in the work of CHOLEVIUS already mentioned,
cap. 3-9. Cp. DERNEDDE, Ueber die den altfranz. Dichtern bekannten epischen Stoffe aus dem Alterthum, Erlangen, 1887 ; BIRCH-HIRSCHFELD, Ueber
die der provenzalischen Troubadours d. XII. u. XIII. Jahrh. bekannten
epischen Stoffe, Halle, 1878.

[7] Cp. DUNGER, Die Sage vom Trojanischen Kriege in den Bearbeitungen
des Mittelalters und ihren Quellen. Leipzig, 1869.

seen, made it fashionable among the various nationalities and
royal families of Europe to regard a Trojan origin as the chief
title to nobility, had contributed not a little to the great popularity of the legend of the Trojan war and of everything connected with it, and his influence is especially shown by the fact
that the sympathies of medieval readers were generally with
the Trojans rather than with the Greeks. This tendency is
already clearly marked in the preference manifested for the
account of the war attributed to Dares, which was regarded
as composed by a Trojan contemporary with the events and
written consequently from the Trojan point of view, over that
of Dictys, which was Greek in its sympathies ; in fact, even
Homer was accused of untruthfulness when his account differed
at all from that of Dares.[8]

But while the whole legend of Troy, which had been brought
into prominence by the celebrity of the Aeneid, was used by
romantic writers, it was naturally the Aeneid itself of which
most use was made in this connection. Thus Benoît de Sainte-
More, who composed the 'Romance of Troy,' is also the
probable author of the ' Romance of Aeneas.' [9]

In the Aeneid as considered from this point of view—a
point of view so different from that of the schools—everything
with any historical or even mythological significance which
would have tended to preserve the classical character of the
poem steps at once into the background. But there is in the
Aeneid one element more attractive than any other for the
writer of romance, which draws the attention to just that one

---

[8] So too the Italian GUIDO DELLE COLONNE. Cp. DUNGER, *op. cit.*, p. 19
seqq.
[9] The former work has been published by JOLY, *Benoît de Sainte-More et
le Roman de Troie, ou les métamorphoses d'Homère et l'épopée gréco-latine au
moyen-âge.* Paris, 1870. The latter has not yet been published. A fragment of the beginning was printed in 1856 by PAUL HEYSE in his *Romanische Inedita,* p. 31, from a Laurentian MS. An extract which gives a
sufficient idea of the whole appears in PEŸ, *Essai sur li Romans d'Eneas
d'après les MSS. de la biblioth. imp.* Paris, 1856. A critical edition of the
whole is promised by SALVERDA DE GRAVE, who in his *Introduction à une
édition critique du Roman d'Eneas* (La Haye, 1888) concludes from the
language that the *Eneas* is anterior to the *Roman de Troie* and not by
Benoît.

subject which is most needed in a work of this kind; this is
the erotic, the sentimental element, the characters of Dido and
Lavinia. And thus, out of the materials of the Aeneid, by
suppressing some and changing or developing others, was
formed a romance, in which the names indeed were classical,
but the incidents, the titles and the usages described, and the
general tone of the sentiment, were entirely medieval, and
corresponded to the contemporary idea of a chivalrous court.
And this work achieved a great success; but still more celebrated than the French 'Romance of Aeneas' was the German imitation by Heinrich von Veldeke, who became on the
strength of his *Eneit* the head of an important school of
German poets, who looked up to him as their master.[10]

This transformation of the ancient legends was not, properly
speaking, as it would appear at first sight to be, an effort of the
popular imagination as distinct from classical literary influences.
These romances were intended far more to find an audience
among the upper classes, and their authors, whether clergy or
laity, are men of culture, and treat their subjects in this way
of set purpose, having the Latin text before their eyes and not
infrequently citing it as their authority.[11] There was nothing
particularly original in their work: they merely collected and
formulated with a greater consciousness of aim and intention
the materials that were ready to their hand in the popular
literature. The names and facts of antiquity, which were re-

---

[10] Published separately by ETTMÜLLER, *Heinrich von Veldeke*, Leipzig,
1852; and by BEHAGEL, Leipzig, 1880; and compared with the French text
by PEŸ, *L'Enéide de Henri de Veldeke et le Roman d'Enéas* (in the *Jahrb. f.
roman. u. engl. Lit.*, ii. p. 1). The view of GERVINUS (*Gesch. d. deutsch.
Dicht.*, i. p. 272 seqq.) was expressed without any knowledge of the
French text. CHOLEVIUS, *op. cit.*, p. 102 seqq., has treated the subject
better, though he too was of course ignorant of the original. Gervinus has
been criticised by E. WÖRNER in his *Virgil und Heinrich von Veldeke* (in the
Zeitschr. f. deutsch. Philolog. von HÖPFNER *und* ZACKER, iii. 126). Gervinus' view as to the praises bestowed on Heinrich by Wolfram von Eschenbach and Gottfried von Strassburg is correct. On the curious miniatures
in the Berlin codex of this poem, *vide* PIPER, *Mythologie der christl. Kunst,*
i. p. 246, and KUGLER, *Kl. Schrift.*

[11] Thus HEINRICH VON VELDEKE often refers to Vergil : "Sô saget Virgiliûs
der mâre," "So zelt Virgiliûs der helt." Cp. tòo what he says on p. 26,
l. 18 seq.

garded by even the educated classes without any real historical appreciation, had passed, as regular elements of common
thought into the popular literature and had there come in
contact with and assimilated themselves to the dominant ideas
of the new art. Every popular poet knows and mentions,
among others, the names of Aeneas, Dido and Lavinia,[12] and
makes use of them in the interests of his poem; while, among
the narratives of the troubadours, classical subjects are found
associated indiscriminately with subjects purely romantic.[13]
Thus that productive writer, Chrestien de Troyes, speaks in
his romantic poem *Erec* of a saddle on which was em-
broidered the whole story of the Aeneid.[14] Of course in all
these cases, and equally so when the clergy took to writing
poetry of this kind, all true appreciation of antiquity is lost;
nor could it well be otherwise, seeing that every form of art
must have its own special point of view. On the other hand,

---

[12] A large number of examples of this are to be found in the learned
work of BARTSCH, *Albrecht von Halberstadt und Ovid im Mittelalter*. (Quedl.
u. Leipz., 1861), pp. xi.–cxxvii.

[13] " Qui volc auzir diverses contes
De reis, de marques e de comtes
Auzir ne poc tan can si volc.
    *   *   *   *

L'autre contava d'Eneas
E de Dido consi remas
Per lui dolenta e mesquina,
L'autre contava de Lavina
Con fes lo bren al cairel traire
A la gaita de l'auzor traire, etc."

Roman de Flamenca, pub. by PAUL MEYER, v. 609 seqq., p. 19. Cp. GUIRAUT
DE CALANSON, pub. by DIEZ, *Poesie der Troubadours*, p. 199, and similar
passages in GRAESSE, *Die grossen Sagenkreise des Mittelalters*, p. 7 seqq.

[14] " Si fu entaillée l'estoire
Coment Eneas mut de Troie,
Et com à Cartage à grant joie
Dido en son lit le reçut;
Coment Eneas la deçut,
Coment ele por lui s'ocist ;
Coment Eneas puis conquist
Laurente et tote Lombardie,
Et Lavine qui fu s'amie."

For other similar passages *vide* BARTSCH, *op. cit.*, p. xxi. seqq. and cxxii. seqq.
WACE's *Roman de Brut* begins with an epitome of the Aeneid, which gives
the genealogy of his hero.

however, the new art did not absorb the entire intellectual activity of the age, but grew up side by side with a traditional culture and an equally traditional literature, which was beginning to pass from the clergy to the laity just at the time that these romances were becoming numerous and well known. And thus it came about, surprising as it may seem, that while the classical texts themselves enjoyed as widespread a popularity as the romances, and while actual translations of them were made for the use of the laity, yet the romantic adaptations, even when viewed side by side with the originals, did not appear at all in the light of parodies or as having anything bizarre or ridiculous about them. Nor was this a solitary instance of the aptitude of the middle ages for associating things which seem to us incongruous.

This change in the manner of regarding the works of Vergil could not fail to have an effect on the manner of regarding his personality. For such an entirely new Aeneid a new Vergil was necessary, and we have in fact already encountered him, though not in any poetical capacity, in the Vergil of the *Dolopathos*. This type of the ideal ' clerc,' in the midst of surroundings essentially feudal, encircled by dukes, barons, bishops, abbots, courtiers, ladies and knights-errant, is also a poet,[15] as the author distinctly says, though no opportunity occurs in the poem of displaying his powers as such. Had the author wished him to appear as a poet, the Aeneid assigned to him would most assuredly not have been the classical one, but rather the ' Romance of Aeneas.' And, in fact, the story which in the *Dolopathos* Vergil is supposed to tell is thoroughly romantic both in form and character.[16]

We have seen that the figure of Vergil in the *Dolopathos* is the direct outcome of medieval literary and scholastic conceptions. The ' clerc ' and the ' discipline di clergie ' are the

---

[15] " Onkes poetes ne fu tex." v. 1267.

[16] It is the *Fabliau du Chevalier à la trappe*, combined with another story, which forms the novel of Tofano and Monna Ghita in the *Decameron* (viii. 4). For the history of these two stories *vide* D'ANCONA, *Il libro dei setti savi di Roma*, p. 112 seqq., 120; OESTERLEY in PAULI'S *Schimpf und Ernst*, p. 678, and BENFEY, *Pantschatantra*, i. 331.

monk and the school education of contemporary society. But in romantic poetry, which is entirely free from the influence of the school, everything connected with the latter acquires an extraordinary character, as of some wonderful thing seen from far or coming from another world, and the marvellous, which is so integral a part of this poetry, soon throws its halo over every name that has such an origin. And this was the more readily brought about in the case of Vergil since even in ordinary literary and scholastic circles his name was regarded with well-nigh superstitious reverence. Hence the Vergil of the schools was as certain to become in the region of romance the Vergil of the *Dolopathos*, as the Aeneid to become the 'Romance of Aeneas.' However much the author of the *Dolopathos* might belong by virtue of position and education to the clergy, there is yet something thoroughly characteristic of the laity in his conception of the learned man, whose nature seems at once to become phantastic and miraculous in consequence of the medium through which it is regarded. Like every other learned man, then, Vergil is an astrologer, or astronomer, as they called it, and by his knowledge of the stars he is able to be acquainted with future or distant events. No one at that time would have considered such knowledge impossible, though the more scrupulous might add, like the author of the *Dolopathos*, that such things could only be by God's permission. Thus far then was it possible for the scholastic conception of Vergil to trespass on the popular; so far, that is to say, as to ascribe to the ideal 'clerc' an acquaintance with astrology, as being the most striking of all forms of learning.

Moreover the marvellous, which was an essential element in romantic creation, placed in the foremost rank of its various characters the character of the magician,[17] which meets one in these romances at every turn, and which, though having little really poetical in it, was sure to find favour in an age which combined such a love of the phantastic and surprising with such great credulity. Every magician must of course be a man of learning, though every man of learning is not necessarily

---

[17] Cp. ROSENKRANZ, *Gesch. d. deutsch. Poes. im Mittelalter*, p. 67.

a magician; so far the two characters are quite independent of one another.

Magic is, properly speaking, an appendage of learning—in a certain sense too a parasite, from the moral point of view, though it can on the other hand also be regarded, when confined within certain limits, as belonging entirely to the realm of science, and hence as deserving of no blame. But it must not be forgotten that the idea of the magician arose entirely outside the circle of scholastic or scientific influences properly so called. There can be no doubt that, if left to itself, the scholastic conception of Vergil would never have changed into that of a magician such as we shall have occasion shortly to describe. The instances in which a classical man of learning has been transformed into a magician at all are very few, and these few instances are but partial and can generally be explained as arising from some such accident as a similarity of name; with none of them is there connected so complete a series of biographical legends as is the case with Vergil. It is true that there were cases in which students of mathematics, mechanics, astronomy, astrology, or physics, sciences which belonged to the domain of the so-called 'white' magic, came to be regarded as diabolical magicians; instances of this are furnished by Gerbert, Albertus Magnus and others; but the literary tradition, and even the literary legend, while making Vergil omniscient, had never forgotten his main characteristic of poet, and never actually described him, as we can learn from Dante, as a simple mathematician or astrologer, capable of working miracles, making talismans or the like. To establish the idea of Vergil as magician there must have been a peculiar conception of him already elaborated independently of literature among the people; and, in fact, our investigations will show that this idea of the magician is entirely popular in its origin, and only subsequently took a place in literature owing to the congenial soil which it found prepared for it there.

The original home of the idea was Italy.

One of the points in which the Italians, even in the middle ages, gave proof of their superiority to the other nations of Europe, was the small share which they took in the phantastic

productions of that period. Romanticism, as far as that displayed itself in the composition of romances, is hardly represented in Italy, and in this, no less than in the matter of the
' chivalry ' which was one of romanticism's chief products, the
position of Italy is, so to speak, a passive one ; a certain infiltra-
tion of these ideas was inevitable, but the small number of
such compositions to which Italian origin can be assigned
shows clearly how little they were in sympathy with the active
genius of the nation.   Among the various romances imported
were several French versions of the Story of Troy, but the
' Romance of Aeneas ' [18] never enjoyed any great popularity.
Vergil, Ovid and other ancient writers had been at an early
stage translated into Italian prose [19] with few alterations,
except for the addition, especially in the case of Ovid, of
certain moralising remarks.   Guido da Pisa, in describing the
adventures of Aeneas, shows, it is true, some of the influences
of the age, but he is very far from writing a romance, and only
leaves the Vergilian narrative to follow some other ancient
authority.   The imagination was kept more in due bounds
among the Italians than elsewhere, whether from the fact that
the power of reasoning is a national characteristic, or that the
traditional culture, degraded though it was, yet found a more
congenial home in Italy than in any other country of Europe.
The Italy of the middle ages, though conquered and dis-
membered, yet figures always as a centre of history and
civilisation, and the consciousness of this fact was never lost
by the Italians.[20]   It is vain then to look here for what may

---

[18] In the hitherto unpublished *Fiorità* of ARMANNINO, the *Roman d'Enéas*
has been used. Cp. MUSSAFIA, *Sulle versioni italiane della storia Troiana*,
p. 48 seqq.

[19] Cp. GAMBA. *Diceria bibliografica intorno ai volgarizzamenti italiani
delle opere di Virgilio*, Verona, 1838 ; BENCI, *Sui volgarizzamenti antichi
dell' Eneide di Virgilio*, in the *Antologia di Firenze*, vol. ii. (1821) p. 164
seqq.; *L'Eneide di Virgilio volgarizzata nel buon secolo della lingua da Ciam-
polo di Meo degli Ugurgieri*. Florence, 1858. This version was not certainly earlier than the *Divina Commedia*, as some have maintained.

[20] " During the gloomy and disastrous centuries which followed the downfall of the Roman empire Italy had preserved in a far greater degree than
any other part of Western Europe the traces of ancient civilisation. The
night which descended upon her was the night of an Arctic summer. The
dawn began to reappear before the last reflection of the preceding sunset
had faded from the horizon." MACAULAY, *Ess. on Macchiavelli*, p. 64.

be found among other nations which clung less closely to the recollection of a glorious past, a recollection so widespread and withal so historically accurate that it could never take an epic form. This does not, of course, imply that the Italians had not also their popular legends, referring to subjects of antiquity or the founding and history of various cities. There can be little doubt that when the study of history has made further advances in Italy, many of these hitherto despised legends will be brought to light, and thereby increase our at present somewhat insufficient knowledge of this subject. The fact however remains that the recollection of the old Roman empire assumed, as was indeed to be expected, a more phantastic shape to the barbarians than was the case with the Italians; and it could easily be proved that the number of legends referring to antiquity which had their origin in Italy was comparatively very small, and that not a few of those actually found there, especially in literature, are derived from foreign sources.

The native Italian legends have occasionally for their subject ancient historical or mythological incidents; more frequently however they are connected with ancient monuments, and still oftener only the names of the personages that figure in them are ancient. Many of the illustrious names of Roman history had remained floating in the memory of the people, disconnected from their historical surroundings, but preserving none the less certain characteristics which had their origin in history, however much this history might be perverted by the limited capacity of the popular intellect or the vagaries of the fireside gossips whom Dante describes:

> ' Traendo alla rocca la chioma,
> Favoleggiando colla sua famiglia
> De' Troiani, e di Fiesole, e di Roma.'

About these names the popular imagination had grouped a number of legends, which, whatever might be their origin, still preserved in each case such features as were popularly considered characteristic of their several subjects. Thus such names as Caesar, Catiline, Nero or Trajan retain in the legends distinct personalities. But since these legendary types were restricted in number by the limitations of the popular intelligence and took account only of the striking characteristics, there arose cases in which several names were grouped under a single head, such as that of sage, magician or tyrant, and consequently came to have a share in all legends referring to characters of this class, which are told indiscriminately, sometimes of one person and sometimes of another.

One of the most striking examples of what has just been said is the Vergilian legend, the course of which will be followed in the succeeding chapters, where it will be shown that this legend originated in Naples, and thence spread into European literature—in the first instance, however, outside Italy. Its origin in Italy was entirely the work of the lower classes, and had nothing to do with poetry or literature; it was a popular superstition, founded on local records connected with Vergil's long stay in Naples and the celebrity of his tomb in that city. It was connected with certain localities, statues and monuments in the neighbourhood of Naples itself, to which Vergil was supposed to have given a magical power. This belief had remained entirely confined to the common people and had found no artistic expression of any kind; it was little known outside Naples and little enough regarded in Naples itself; but foreigners who visited the place had heard of it and recorded it, and hence it passed not only into the popular romances, but even into Latin works of a learned nature, for in the one sphere no less than in the other the general conception of Vergil was quite in harmony with such a legend. From the 12th century onwards, therefore, that is to say from the commencement of romantic literature properly so called, one meets with a new phase in the conception of Vergil, the successive stages of which will be examined in the following chapters. This phase is so far distinct from that which we have already considered in that its origin and development are not, properly speaking, literary, but popular, even though the literary view in its last stages may have certain affinities with it. The word 'popular' does not, of course, mean to imply that this conception is in no way represented in learned literature, for it will be necessary to trace its history with the assistance of a num-

ber of literary works, most of which are in no way popular in
character, but rather that it originated among the people and
was augmented by the popular imagination. Were it otherwise, the literary tradition, however debased and barbarous,
would never have led up to this legend, nor indeed during the
period of the greatest barbarism is there any trace of it; it
was not till the 12th century that some one who happened to
hear it in the streets of Naples was attracted by it and introduced it into literature.

The medieval encyclopaedias, handbooks and similar works,
whether in Latin or the vernacular, are, in consequence of the
utter absence of the critical faculty with which they collect
together materials of every conceivable kind, quite as strange
and wonderful productions as the contemporary works of the
imagination to which allusion has already been made. In this
conglomerate of ideas classical, Christian and romantic, myth,
history, legend and romance all stood on an equal footing.
The *Novellino* which is meant to entertain, the *Gesta
Romanorum* with its moralisings intended to edify, Vincent
de Beauvais with his chaotic *Speculum historale*, and any
number of other authors of works of erudition, all speak of
Caesar, of Arthur, of Tristan, of Alexander, of Aristotle, of
Saladin, of Charlemagne, of Merlin without any sort of distinction and with equal gravity. Walter Burley, in a work
which was meant quite seriously, his 'Lives of the Philosophers,'
gives, among others, the life of Vergil, who ranks as a philosopher because he was a magician and knew the hidden secrets
of nature. Thus there is not a book of the period in which
one may not expect to find Vergilian legends. In an epoch
of universal credulity the lower classes were not alone in their
want of culture and literary impulse; and not only was the
number of educated people far smaller in the middle ages than
it has been from the time of the Renaissance onwards, but the
difference between the educated and uneducated was far less
marked than it is at the present day.

It is always of course difficult to point out the exact line
of demarcation between those creations of the imagination
which have their origin among the people and those that are

literary, and this is particularly the case in the middle ages; but most of all does this difficulty arise in treating of the transformations undergone at this epoch by the personages of ancient history in their passage from the educated classes, whose conception of them was already sufficiently phantastic to the common people, and in their return in still stranger guise from thence back into literature. Between the debased literary tradition, which was itself a fertile mother of legends, and the actual popular ideas, there is, of course, an unquestionable continuity, since it was only by means of these literary channels that the great names of history could possibly reach the minds of the lower classes. But at the same time it was equally inevitable that these names, on their arrival in an intellectual atmosphere so different from that in which they had hitherto resided, should acquire a new significance in consequence of the addition of novel traits of purely popular character, however much this addition may have been originally inspired by the imagination of more educated minds. A striking instance of this is furnished by the diverse characters of the two con- ceptions of Vergil treated in the two parts of this work which, in spite of their diverse titles, are yet in close connection with one another. It will here throughout be possible to observe that the facts brought forward in the second part are the result and development of those discussed in the first, and to mark the connection between the Vergil of the schools and the medieval literary tradition and the Vergil who is no longer a poet but a worker of magic, that Vergil whom we have found it necessary to call the Vergil of popular legend. But to avoid all possible misunderstandings, such as we have observed with surprise in the works of several students of this subject,[21]

---

[21] VIETOR, *Der Ursprung der Virgilsage* in the *Zeitschrift für romanische Philologie* of GROEBER, I. (1887), pp. 165–178, maintains, with well-reasoned arguments but not without prejudice, that the origin of the Vergilian legend is entirely literary. The same view is supported, but with crude and illogical reasoning, by TUNISON, *Master Virgil the author of the Aeneid as he seemed in the middle ages*, Cincinnati, 1890. With sounder logic GRAF, in his *Roma nella memoria*, etc., II. p. 22 seqq., while admitting the popular origin of this legend, yet claims that it was not unconnected with the literary legend, a fact which I should be quite willing to admit up to a certain point.

it may be well to observe that the popular is distinguished from the literary by its nature and by its character, whatever may be the actual condition of the person who cites it or believes it or even invents it. Thus, such a legend as that of Trajan and the widow, though idealised by no less a poet than Dante, is yet purely popular in character, even if it can be proved to have originated with a monk who wrote in Latin, just as those legends based on Roman monuments which one finds in the *Mirabilia* and elsewhere are purely popular, although they too are cited and believed by the educated classes and may very possibly have originated among them.

There are further some sound remarks on this same subject in STECHER, *La légende de Vergile en Belgique*, in the *Bull. de l'Acad. roy. de Belg.*, cl. de sciences 3me série, t. xix., 1890, p. 602 seqq.

CHAPTER II

AFTER all that has been said it will not appear strange that the earliest notices of the popular Vergilian legends are to be found in literary works which were in no way popular in origin or intention, but were written in Latin by persons of education and destined to be read by the highest classes of society. Thus, among the authors who will be most frequently cited in this connection are Conrad von Querfurt, Chancellor of the Emperor Henry VI., his vicegerent in Naples and Sicily and Bishop of Hildesheim, Gervasius of Tilbury, Professor at the University of Bologna and Marshal of the kingdom of Arles, Alexander Neckam, foster-brother of Richard Cœur de Lion, Professor at the University of Paris, Abbot of Cirencester, and one of the most passable Latin verse-writers of the time, and John of Salisbury, not to mention others. The most important of these for the purposes of the present enquiry are Conrad and Gervasius, who not only are the first to make detailed mention of the Vergilian legends, but also indicate their Neapolitan origin, a point which the subsequent evidence no less tends to confirm. In fact, these writers speak of the legends as current among the inhabitants of Naples, from whose lips they heard them in the first instance.

Conrad mentions them in a letter[1] written from Sicily in 1194 to an old friend of his, the prior of the monastery of Hildesheim, in which he narrates his impressions of his journey in Italy. This letter, besides containing much that bears on this subject, is in itself an interesting document, as showing the state of mind of the educated foreigner who then visited that

[1] Published by LEIBNITZ in the *Scriptores rerum brunsvicensium*, vol. ii. pp. 695-8.

country. The fame of Italy so excited the imagination that
even the present reality could not destroy the ideal that had
been formed of it from a distance. A thousand strange stories
that he had heard, a thousand school memories, not always
very lucid, of the classics floated in the mind of the traveller
in strange confusion, till, as it were in an enchanted country,
he seemed to himself to see things other and more than were
really before his eyes. It is impossible otherwise to account
for many of the absurdities which the worthy Chancellor
brings forward with the utmost earnestness. Such things as
he saw in Southern Italy! Olympus, Parnassus, Hippocrene
are all there, and he is not a little pleased to find them forming
part of the German dominions. Then, after passing with fear
and trembling between Scylla and Charybdis, he lights some-
where upon Scyros, where Thetis kept Achilles in hiding, and
is charmed to find at Taormina the Labyrinth of the Minotaur
(he meant the ancient theatre), and to meet the Saracens, a
race who have the enviable power, like St. Paul, of killing
serpents with their spittle. Any one who remembers how
Mandeville saw the rock to which ' the giant Andromeda ' was
tied and calls to mind other contemporary travellers' tales
will find nothing surprising in Conrad's letter. What, however, renders it singular is the personality of its author, who
had come to Italy, not as an antiquarian dilettante or as a
tourist, but as minister of the execrable Henry VI., from whom
he had orders to dismantle the city of Naples, which orders he
executed to the letter. Yet none the less he does not hesitate
to record with perfect faith the view of the Neapolitans, that
their walls and even the city itself were founded by Vergil,
and that Vergil had moreover deposited with them as palladium
a small model of the city in a narrow-necked bottle. This
palladium, which was to preserve Naples from all hostile
attacks, had not prevented it from falling into the hands of
the Imperialists, and if any one had a right to doubt its
efficacy, it was Conrad. But just as none is so deaf as he
who will not hear, so none is so credulous as he who will
believe. Conrad observes that the reason why this palladium
failed to act was that there was a crack in the glass, as was

discovered when it was examined. This one would suppose was a joke, did not the various other absurdities, all related with perfect gravity, put such an explanation out of the question.

The other marvels attributed, according to Conrad, by the Neapolitans to Vergil were a bronze horse, which, while it remained intact, prevented the horses there from breaking their backs; a bronze fly placed on one of the fortified gates, which while it lasted drove away flies from the city; and a butcher's block on which the meat kept fresh for six weeks. Besides, when Naples was infested, owing to the number of its crypts and subterranean dwellings, by multitudes of serpents, Vergil banished them all to beneath a gate known as the Porta Ferrea, and Conrad himself describes how the imperial soldiers, when demolishing the walls, hesitated long before this gate for fear of letting loose all the serpents it was supposed to contain.

Naples is troubled by the neighbourhood of Vesuvius, but Vergil proposed to remedy this by setting up against it a bronze statue of a man with a bent bow and an arrow ready on the string. This sufficed for a long time to keep the mountain quiet, till one fine day a countryman, not understanding why the figure should stand there for ever with its bow drawn, fired off the arrow for it and struck the edge of the crater, which thereupon straightway recommenced its eruptions.

In his anxiety moreover to provide in every possible way for the public good, Vergil had made near Baiae and Puteoli public baths, which were useful for every sort of illness, and adorned them moreover with plaster images representing the various diseases and indicating the bath proper for each special case.

In addition to all this, Conrad relates what was believed at Naples about the bones of Vergil. These, according to him, were buried in a castle surrounded by the sea, and if they were exposed to the air, it became suddenly dark, a noise as of a tempest was heard, and the waves of the sea became violently agitated. This, he adds, he had seen himself.

Gervasius of Tilbury, in his *Otia Imperialia*,[2] a sort of en-

---

[2] Published by LEIBNITZ in the *Scriptores rerum brunsvicensium*, vol. i. p. 881 seqq. Though the date of the work is 1212, several of Gervasius'

cyclopædia written in 1212 for the Emperor Otto IV., has
gathered together a collection of anecdotes of every degree of
absurdity, which form a veritable mine of popular superstitions.[3] His idea of the marvellous he explains in few words.
' We call those things marvellous,' he says, ' which we do not
understand, even though they be natural. Our ignorance of
their cause renders them marvellous.' He then cites the
examples of the salamander which lives in the fire, of the
chalk which blazes up when put in water, and so on, after
which he adds, ' Let no one doubt the veracity of what I
record. . . . These things exceed the powers of human
reason, and hence they are often disbelieved; and yet things
go on round us every day for which we are equally unable to
account.' It is clear that such principles as these will carry
one far, and assuredly the author makes no niggardly use of
them. A passage dealing with Vergil may well be quoted in
full, as it is thoroughly characteristic and takes one back to
Naples at the end of the 12th century, affording thereby an
opportunity of meeting with the legend in the place of its
origin.

After mentioning the butcher's block and the story of the
serpents, Gervasius proceeds as follows : ' A third marvel is
one which I have experienced myself, though I did not know
it at the time ; an accident gave me the proof of a fact so
extraordinary that I could hardly have believed it at second-
hand. In the year of the siege of S. Jean d'Acre (1190), while
I was at Salerno, I met an unexpected companion in the person of Philip, son of the Earl of Salisbury. . . . After
some days we decided to go to Naples, in the hope of finding
there the means of making our passage without great expendi-
ture of time or money. On arriving in the town we betook
ourselves to the house of Giovanni Pinatelli, Archdeacon of
Naples, who had been my pupil at Bologna, a man of noble

Neapolitan reminiscences belong to an earlier period, as is shown by various
passages in the work itself. Thus he mentions a fact which occurred in
1190, and another which occurred in 1175.

[3] The Vergilian part of the work has been published, with a learned
commentary, by LIEBRECHT, Des Gervasius von Tilbury Otia imperialia, in
einer Auswahl, etc. Hanover, 1856.

birth and illustrious for his learning. He received us gladly,
and on hearing the object of our visit, proceeded with us, while
dinner was being prepared, to the harbour. Within an hour
we had with little trouble succeeded in securing berths on the
terms we wished and in accelerating at our express desire the
day of the boat's departure. On our way home we were con-
gratulating ourselves on the ease with which we had obtained
everything we wanted, when our host, who remarked our
astonishment at our good success, asked us, "By what gate
did you enter the city?" When we had told him, he at once
exclaimed, "Ah, now I can understand how you came to be so
lucky; but tell me, through which part of the gate did you
come?" We answered, "We were intending to come in on the
left, when suddenly an ass laden with wood prevented us, and
to avoid him we had to come in on the right." "That you may
know," rejoined the archdeacon, "what wonderful things Vergil
has done in this city, come with me to the place, and I will
show you how striking a memorial he has left us of himself
there." On our arrival at the gate, he showed us, in a niche in
the right-hand wall, a bust of Parian marble with a laughing
face, while in the left-hand wall was a similar bust, only here
the face appeared distressed. On these two different figures
depended, according to him, the fortunes of all who entered,
provided that they turned to the left or right at haphazard,
and not of set purpose. "Every one," said he, "who enters the
city by the right-hand side will succeed in whatever business
he has in hand; every one on the contrary who enters on the
left will find and meet with nothing but disappointment. Since
therefore your meeting with the ass made you turn to the right,
you have been able to make arrangements for your journey with
ease and despatch."' This incident, which made a great impression on Gervasius, came near making him a fatalist; but
he expressly defends himself from this imputation by adding
at once, 'In Thy hands, O Lord, are all things, and there is
nothing that can resist Thy power.'

Several of the legends quoted by Gervasius are identical with
those of Conrad, except for such small differences in matters of
detail as would be only natural in the case of legends derived

from actual oral tradition current at the time.[4]   Thus the
butcher's block, according to Gervasius, owed its power to a
piece of meat let into one of its sides by Vergil, and had the
power of keeping meat fresh for an indefinite period, not for
six weeks only; the serpents were confined by Vergil beneath
a statue (*sigillum*) near the Porta Nolana.   On the subject of
the fly and the baths at Puteoli the two accounts agree.   In
the matter of the statue set up against Vesuvius, however,
the version of Gervasius shows a noticeable discrepancy.   His
statue was on Monte Vergine, and the figure did not have in
its hand a bent bow, but held to its mouth a trumpet, which
had the power of blowing back the wind which brought the
smoke and ashes of Vesuvius in the direction of Naples.   'Unfortunately, however,' he adds, 'whether it has got worn out
through age, or whether malicious people have damaged it, it
no longer has the desired effect, and the old trouble with Vesuvius is beginning again.'

Gervasius does not mention either the bronze horse or the
palladium of Naples, nor the walls which Vergil made, but,
besides describing the two marble heads at the Porta Nolana,
of which Conrad does not speak, he is the first to tell us that
Vergil was able, 'by his mathematical knowledge,' to bring
about that no conspiracy could ever take place in the cave at
Puteoli, and that he laid out a garden on Monte Vergine in
which grew every kind of medicinal plant.   Among these was
the herb *Lucia*, which could restore the sight of a blind sheep
that touched it.

As for Alexander Neckam, Roth maintains, in his interesting
article on 'Vergil as Magician,'[5] that he also visited Naples

[4] The doubts raised as to the authority of these writers by Vietor (*op.
cit.*, p. 171 seqq.) when he maintains that the Neapolitan populace knew
nothing of these legends or of Virgil, are wanting in all foundation and
rest on false conclusions drawn from false premises.   These writers were
no doubt credulous and may therefore have to some extent exaggerated the
stories which they cited and themselves believed; but no unprejudiced
critic could deduce from this that they invented these facts or introduced
the name of Vergil where their informants knew nothing of it.   Besides,
what they relate about the beliefs current at Naples is confirmed by other
writers and by the Neapolitans themselves, as we shall see presently.

[5] " *Ueber den Zauberer Virgilius* " in the *Germania* of Pfeiffer, vol. iv.
1859), pp. 257–298.   *Vide* p. 264.

and there heard Vergilian legends told by the inhabitants. But not only does Neckam not state that he had seen the marvellous bronze fly, as Roth asserts, but he does not so much as mention it at all. The fact is that at the time of Roth's article the *De naturis rerum* [6] had not yet been published, nor was he likely to have come across Michel's rare work,[7] in which the passage therefrom relating to Vergil is quoted at length.

The notices we have of the life of Neckham are so scanty,[8] that it is difficult to prove positively that he never was at Naples. In his poem *De laudibus divinae sapientiae*, written in old age, he speaks of his dislike of long journeys, of the snows of the Mont Cenis, and of the route followed by Hannibal, and says that he has no desire to visit Rome, for reasons which are not complimentary to the capital of Christendom.[9] From this it seems natural to conjecture that he was never in Italy. The date of his *De naturis rerum* is uncertain. Seeing that he was born in 1157 and died in 1217, that his work was already known at the end of the 12th century, and that in it he cites other considerable works of his own, it seems very probable that it was written between 1190 and 1200.[10] From this one may infer that the Vergilian legends were already at that time beginning to be known in Europe independently of Conrad and Gervasius. Nor is there anything remarkable in the fact that earlier travellers should have met with them and spread them, seeing that they were current at Naples, as we have observed, long before either Conrad or Gervasius visited that city.

---

[6] *Alexandri Neckam de naturis rerum libri duo*, with the poem of the same author, *De laudibus divinae sapientiae*. T. WRIGHT, London, 1863.

[7] *Quae vices quaeque mutationes et Virgilium ipsum et ejus carmina per mediam aetatem exceperint explanare tentavit* FRANCISCUS MICHEL. Paris, 1845. *Vide* p. 18 seqq.

[8] *Vide* WRIGHT, *Biographia Britannica literaria*, ii. 449 seqq., and the same writer's preface to the *De naturis rerum*. Cp. *Hist. lit. de la France*, xviii. 521 seqq.; DU MÉRIL, *Poésies inédites du moyen-âge*, p. 169 seqq.

[9] " Romae quid facerem? metiri nescio, libros
diligo, sed libras respuo. Roma, vale." p. 448.

[10] Thus argues WRIGHT with justice in his Preface, p. xiii. seqq.

CHAPTER III

HAVING thus excluded Neckam from the number of those
authors who came in contact with the Vergilian legends at
their actual source, it is time for us to enquire into the nature
of these legends themselves and to endeavour to ascertain
when they first arose and what was the reason of their origin.
We have already seen that, in the most ancient form of the
legend, Vergil appears as the protector of the city of Naples,
and that the chief works ascribed to him are talismans. Quite
apart from tradition and the ideas diffused in medieval Europe
by contact with Semitic races, the belief in talismans had unquestionably been stimulated in Southern Italy through the
influence of the Byzantine dominion. In fact, we find in
Constantinople, attributed to Apollonius of Tyana, many
works of this kind which are practically identical with
those attributed in Naples to Vergil. Thus, the famous
bronze tripod, part of which is still preserved in the hippo-
drome, was for many centuries looked upon as a talisman. A
legend stated[1] that at the time of Apollonius there was a
plague of serpents at Byzantium, and that he was summoned
for the purpose of getting rid of them. He erected a column
on which was an eagle with a serpent in its talons, and from
that time forth the serpents disappeared. At the time of
Nicetas Coniates († 1216)[2] this column with the eagle was
in existence, but it was destroyed, like so many other monuments of antiquity, when the city was taken by the Latins.

[1] Mentioned by Nicetas Coniates, Glycas, and Hesychius Milesius. Cp.
FRICK, *Das plataeische Weihgeschenk zu Constantinopel* in the *Jahrbb. f. Phil.
u. Paed.*, iii. Suppl., p. 554 seqq.
[2] *De signis Constant.*, cap. viii. p. 861, Bk.

The legend however lasted on and came to be applied to the fragment of the tripod, which, in fact, consists of three serpents intertwined. Furthermore, the Constantinopolitan legends related that Apollonius drove away the flies from that city with a bronze fly, the gnats with a bronze gnat, and the scorpions and other vermin in a similar manner.[3] The belief in such talismans was not by any means confined to Naples and Constantinople. At the time of Gregory of Tours (6th century) it existed also in Paris. 'It is said,' he relates, ' that the city was in ancient times consecrated so as to preserve it from fires, serpents and rats. When the sewer at the Pont-Neuf was being cleaned, a bronze serpent and rat[4] were found in the mud; and as soon as they were removed, great numbers of serpents and rats straightway appeared and the city began to suffer from fires.'[5]

Ancient pagan traditions spoke of flies and similar insects being driven away by supernatural agencies. Thus, flies were supposed to have been banished from the temple of Hercules in the Forum Boarium, and from a certain mountain in Crete.[6] ' The cicadas near Rhegium are mute,' says Solinus,[7] ' which is unique, and the more remarkable seeing that these insects are generally louder in the Locrian country than elsewhere. Granius furnishes the reason. One day they were making a noise when Hercules was asleep in this neighbourhood, so God commanded them to be silent, and they have preserved a perpetual silence ever since.' Christianity, which had to make so many concessions to old Pagan superstitions, had itself not only special saints, such as St. Bernard, St. Gottfried and

---

[3] CODIN., *De signis*, pp. 30 and 36 ; *De aedif. Const.*, p. 62 ; NIC. CALLIST., *Hist. eccles.*, iii. 18.

[4] Such talismans were often buried ; at one time live men were used in this way. *Vide* PLIN., *Nat. hist.*, 28 (3), and LIEBRECHT, *Eine alt-römische Sage*, in the *Philologus*, xxi. p. 687 seqq.

[5] *Hist. Fr.*, viii. 38. Cp. FOURNIER, *Hist. du Pont-Neuf*, i. p. 18 seqq. For other instances, see LIEBRECHT, *ad Gervas.*, p. 98 seqq., and NAUDÉ, *Apologie des gr. personn. acc. de magie*, p. 624. Albertus Magnus also was supposed to have made a golden fly which drove away all other flies. Cp. P. ANTON. DE TARSIA, *Hist. Cupersan.*, p. 26 (in the *Thes.* GRAEV. *et* BURMANN., tom. ix. p. v.).

[6] PLIN., *Nat. hist.*, x. 29 (45) ; xxi. 14 (46).

[7] *Collect. rer. memorab.*, p. 40 (ed. MOMMSEN).

St. Patricius, whose function it was to excommunicate flies
and the like, but had actual official forms of anathema suitable
for such occasions.[8]

It is not likely that the beliefs on the subject of talismans
current in Naples rested merely on oral tradition without some
material object to which to attach themselves.[9] Here too there
were works of art, whether classical or Byzantine, to which the
people, as at Constantinople, attributed a talismanic origin, and
when once such an idea had taken hold of the popular or literary
imagination, it could easily be expanded by the addition of any
number of objects, 'which were there once upon a time, but
now are no more.'

The chief and perhaps the most ancient of these talismans
seems to have been the bronze fly. An earlier writer than
either Conrad or Gervasius not only mentions it, but even
records at length the legend connected with it. This is John
of Salisbury, who knew Italy and Naples well, having in 1160,
as he himself says, already crossed the Alps ten times and
twice travelled through Southern Italy.[10]

This writer, a man of really superior intelligence, records
the following legend : ' It is said that one day when Marcellus
was going out on a fowling expedition, the Mantuan poet asked
him whether he would sooner have a bird with which to catch
all other birds, or a fly to exterminate all other flies. Marcellus,
after consulting with Augustus, chose, on the latter's advice,
the fly, which was to deliver Naples from its plague of flies.
His wish was fulfilled ; and from this we may learn that it is
right to prefer the general good to one's individual pleasure.' [11]

The names of Marcellus and Augustus brought in such close
connection with that of Vergil might at first sight seem to
throw doubt on the popular origin of the legend ; but it must

---

[8] Cp. LIEBRECHT, ad Gervas., 105 ; LALANNE, Curiosités des traditions, etc.,
p. 218 ; MENEBREA, De l'origine, de la forme et de l'esprit des jugements
rendus au moyen-âge contre les animaux, Chambéry, 1845.

[9] Cp. SPRINGER, Bilder aus der neueren Kunstgeschichte (Bonn, 1867), p.
18 seqq.

[10] Vide SCHAARSCHMIDT, Joh. Saresberiensis, p. 31.

[11] Polycraticus, i. 4. This work appeared in 1159. Vide SCHAARSCHMIDT,
op. cit., p. 143.

not be forgotten that the Neapolitan populace actually regarded Marcellus as Governor of Naples and Vergil as his minister. In the *Cronica di Partenope*, to which reference will be made in its proper place, the acts of Vergil are referred to the time when 'Octavian made Marcellus Duke of Naples.' This is the point at which the Neapolitan legend shows, as we shall see presently, a connection with the literary legend originating from the ancient biography of the poet. The anonymous author of a satire against the clergy, dated 1180, also alludes to Vergil's fly in the line :

'Formantem (video) aereas muscas Vergilium.' [12]

No other fly is ever referred to as having been made by Vergil besides the one at Naples, and it is clearly to this one that the anonymous writer refers, as does John of Salisbury. The latter is the only writer who relates the occasion on which the fly was made, but he must not therefore be supposed to be the author of this account, which is in its moralising tendency very suggestive of the *Gesta Romanorum* and similar works, and is in all probability due to some Neapolitan monk who wished to give the popular superstition an edifying turn.

This fly, which was as large as a frog, and, according to Conrad, existed on one of the fortified gates, was first of all removed to a window in the Castel Capuano and then to the Castel Cicala (afterwards called Castel St. Angelo, and destroyed by the priests of S. Chiara), where it lost its power. The *Cronica di Partenope* mentions a certain Alexander who professed to have actually seen it ; in the works of Alexander *Neckam*, as at present existing, there is, however, no mention of the fly.

The two marble faces at the Porta Nolana, which, according to Scoppa,[13] an old Neapolitan writer, was formerly called

---

[12] *Apocalypsis Goliae episcopi*, in WRIGHT, *Early poems attributed to Walter Mapes*, p. 4.

[13] Cp. *Io. Scoppae Parthenopei in diversos auctores collectanea ab ipso revisa*, etc. Naples, 1534, p. 20 seqq. The passages in this book relating to Vergil, which are not easy to find, were kindly communicated to me by my learned friend, Prof. De Blasis, of Naples, to whom I am indebted for assistance in various other parts of my work. Sig. MINIERI RICCIO in the

Porta di Forcella, also really existed, and Scoppa relates that as a boy he saw them there, before Alfonso II. of Aragon destroyed the gate and removed them to Poggio Reale.

Equally real was the bronze horse,[14] which in the year 1322 was still standing in the court of the principal church at Naples. It perished through the ravages of time and barbarism; but the people had a story that the farriers, finding their trade injured by it, knocked out its belly, in consequence of which it lost its power, and thereupon the priests, in the year 1322, had it melted into bells for the church. Others, however, stated that it was destroyed with a view to putting an end to the superstitions current with reference to it.[15] The head, which is still preserved in the National Museum at Naples, gives an idea of the colossal proportions of this remarkable work of art.[16]

The story of the statue which Vergil set up to counteract the wind coming from Vesuvius seems in like manner to have been founded on an actual object. Scoppa relates that it was at the Porta Reale, (formerly called Porta Ventosa,) ' where there are still some marble statues.' [17] As for the palladium

Catalogo dei libri rari in his library (Naples, 1864), vol. i. p. 110 seqq., makes the following note : " Scoppa, writing in June, 1507, disposes of the tradition adduced by SUMMONTE as to the origin of these heads. The latter relates that a young woman, who was a vassal of Isabel of Aragon, complained to her of the behaviour of one of her barons. Isabella thereupon compelled the baron to marry her and after the wedding had him executed. In memory of this were set up these two marble heads on the gate overlooking the square in which the baron had suffered punishment. This story I refuted in my ' *Memorie degli scrittori nati nel reame di Napoli* ' (1844) before seeing the book of Scoppa." Gervasius, who is much older than Scoppa, shows still more clearly that Sig. Minieri is right.

[14] It was mentioned by EUSTATHIUS MATERANUS at the end of the thirteenth century in his poem, now lost, entitled *Planctus Italiae. Vide* CAPASSO, *Hist. dipl. regni Sic.*, p. 50.

[15] DE STEFANO, *Luoghi sacri di Napoli*, f. 15 ; CAPASSO, *op. cit.*, p. 50.

[16] Cp. GALIANI, *Del dialetto napoletano.* Naples, 1779, p. 98 seqq. It must, however, be added that archæologists seem to doubt whether it ever formed part of a statue of a horse. *Vide* HELBIG, *Ann. d. Inst. arch.*, 1865, p. 271 ; CAPASSO, *op. cit.*, p. 51.

[17] Already in the fifth century occurs a Sicilian legend of a statue which kept back the fires of Etna as well as driving away all enemies from Sicily (OLYMPIODORUS in PHOTIUS, cod. 90). A similar statement in the eighth century is mentioned in the " Life of St. Leo, Bishop of Catania." *Vide Acta Sanct. Febr.*, iii. p. 224. Cp. LIEBRECHT, *ad Gervas.*, p. 106 seqq. and

of Naples, mentioned by Conrad, this was no doubt the object
which he describes himself as seeing and handling, viz. a model
of the city in a glass bottle. Even at the present day the
common people believe in such things, so that there is nothing
wonderful in the fact that in the middle ages these objects were
regarded as possessed of supernatural powers. This treasure
perhaps came to grief in the hands of the Imperialists; anyhow, later legends substituted for it an egg,[18] preserved in a
glass bottle, which was itself enclosed in an iron vessel. This
form of the legend, which is a much later one, supplanted
the former one at the time when the castle, built in 1154 by
William I. and enlarged by Frederick II., changed its name
from ' Castello marino ' or ' di mare '[19] to ' Castel dell' uovo.'
This latter name does not occur, as far as I know, in any document earlier than the 14th century. In the rules of the Order
of the Holy Spirit, founded in 1352 by Louis of Anjou, it is
called ' Castellum ovi incantati.'[20] In a Neapolitan MS. of the
end of the 14th century, the legend is quoted on the authority
of Alexander Neckam; but he does not, as a matter of fact,
anywhere allude to it.[21] To this name and legend refers also
the enigmatical inscription, likewise of the 14th century, preserved in Signorili's collection ;[22]

OVO MIRA NOVO SIC OVO NON TVBER OVO,
DORICA CASTRA CLVENS TVTOR TEMERARE TIMETO.

The same idea which represented Vergil as a benefactor and

262. As that illustrious scholar has observed, this Sicilian legend is not
without its connection with the classical legends of the Agrigentine Empe-
docles and his bronze statue at Girgenti.

[18] On the subject of this superstition see LIEBRECHT in the *Germania* of
PFEIFFER, v. p. 483 seqq. ; x. p. 408.

[19] This name is given to it by PIETRO D' EBOLI, FALCONE BENEVENTANO,
and others.

[20] MONTFAUCON, *Monumens de la monarchie française*, tom. ii. p. 329.

[21] Cod. ix., c. 24, f. 89. "Refert etiam (Alexander libro *de Naturis
Rerum*) quod in cratere quodam vitreo ovum Virgilius inclusit quo fata
civitatis Neapolis pendere dicebat." This is a MS. without title which contains comments on Vergil ; it is cited by CAPASSO, *Histor. dipl. regni Sic.*,
Naples, 1874, p. 354.

[22] DE ROSSI, *Prime raccolte d' antiche iscrizioni*, etc. (Rome, 1852), p. 92.
ROTH (*op. cit.*, p. 263) has tried to interpret it, but without any result worth
chronicling.

protector of Naples, as the builder of its walls and even as the founder of the city itself, caused also to be attributed to him the baths at Puteoli, which enjoyed a great reputation in the middle ages for their medicinal virtues.[23] The use in such baths of inscriptions,[24] denoting the maladies for which the treatment was intended, especially when several springs with different properties existed side by side, was not confined to Puteoli, but appears in the case of other baths celebrated at the time, as, for instance, those of Bourbon l'Archambault.[25] Benjamin of Tudela († 1173) speaks[26] of a petroleum well near Puteoli, and likewise of medicinal baths in that neighbourhood which were much frequented, but he makes no mention of Vergil. Richard Eudes,[27] in his poem composed in 1392, refers to the inscriptions, but likewise does not mention Vergil's name. Similarly La Sale, in a moral treatise quoted by Le Grand d'Aussi,[28] Burchard,[29] who visited this part in 1494, and others are silent on this point. This silence on their part, however, merely shows that the attribution of these baths to Vergil was a fact so exclusively popular that it had either never been brought before their notice or else had appeared to them too puerile to be worth recording. An instance of the latter case is furnished by Pietro da Eboli,[30] who could not have been ignorant of the legend and yet makes no mention

[23] *Vide* the various notices of these baths in the *Thes.* GRAEV. *et* BURM., tom. ix. part iv.

[24] Though Conrad speaks of statues, most of the notices on this subject only mention inscriptions.

> [25] " A Borbo avia risc bains;
> Quis volc, fos privatz o estrains,
> S' i pot mout ricamen bainar.
> En cascun bain pogras trobar
> Escrih a que avia obs."

Le Roman de Flamenca, publié par P. MAYER. Paris, 1865, p. 45. Cp. p. xiii.

[26] *Itinerarium*, i. p. 42 (ed. ASHER). *Vide* DU MÉRIL, *De Virgile l'enchanteur*, in his *Mélanges archéologiques et littéraires*, p. 436.

[27] Cp. MEYER, *Le Roman de Flamenca*, p. xiii.

[28] *Vide* DU MÉRIL, l.c.

[29] *Joh. Burchardi diarium ed.* ACH. GENNARELLI. Flor., 1854, p. 817.

[30] For this writer of the 12th century and his poem, *vide* E. PÈRCOPO, I *bagni di Pozzuoli, poemetto napoletano del sec. xiv.*, Naples, 1887, p. 11 seqq. (From the *Arch. stor. per le prov. napol.*, xi. pp. 597-750.)

of it in his poem on these baths, notwithstanding the fact that his more credulous patron, Conrad von Querfurt, had in all seriousness recorded it, as was also done by various other writers of a similar turn of mind, such as Gervasius, Elinandus, and the Neapolitan author of the *Cronica di Partenope*. The popular tradition had added to the actual facts the idea that the baths were due to Vergil and were serviceable for every disease. The Mantuan benefactor had wished especially to enable the poor by this means to dispense with the doctors, 'who, (to quote the *Cronica di Partenope*,[31]) 'in defiance of all feelings of charity, insist upon being paid.' But the doctors, who, as the old French poem says, 'ont fait maint mal et maint bien,'[32] did not find this suit them, and the heads of the school at Salerno especially found their business diminish to such a degree that they went secretly to the baths and destroyed the inscriptions, so that the poor invalids no longer knew where to go for their cure. 'But God punished them,' adds the legend, 'so that on their return they were caught by so furious a tempest that they were all drowned between Capri and La Minerva, except one who survived to tell the tale.'[33] This story is found not only in Conrad and Gervasius, but also in Burchard and others, who do not connect it with the name of Vergil. The legend even took to itself the form of history, and referred to an official document, supposed to date from the year 1409, in which there was stated to have been found at Puteoli, near the place known as the Tre Colonne, the following inscription: 'Sir Antonius Sulimela, Sir Philippus Capogrossus, Sir Hector de Procita, famosissimi medici Salernitani supra parvem navim ab ipsa civitate Salernae Puteolos transfretaverunt, cum ferreis instrumentis inscriptiones balneorum virtutum deleverunt et cum reverterunt, fuerunt cum navi miraculose submersi.'[34]

From what has gone before it will be seen that the Vergilian

---

[31] Cap. 29.
[32] *Vide* Du Méril, l.c.
[33] *Cron. di Partenope*, cap. 29.
[34] Cp. Panvinio, *Il forest. istr. alle antichità di Pozzuoli*, etc., p. 100; De Renzi, *Storia della medicina in Italia*, ii. p. 148; Mazza, *Urbis Salernitanae historia* (in the *Thes.* Graev. *et* Burm., tom. ix. p. iv.), p. 72.

legend in its original form was more or less the following.
Vergil not only lived at Naples, but was actually governor of
the city, or at any rate, through his connection with the court,
had some share in the government, and manifested great concern for the welfare of the Neapolitans.   There was moreover
at Naples a variety of monuments, classical or medieval, to
which the populace, as at other places, attributed magical
powers.   We have seen what a halo of wisdom surrounded the
name of Vergil among the literati of the middle ages.   The
inhabitants of Naples could not, in the face of the manner in
which their protector was universally regarded, attribute these
talismans to any one but him.

Of actual magic there has so far been no mention.   Though
Conrad speaks of the *ars magica* or the *magicae incantationes*
by which Vergil made these talismans, it is clear that he uses
these words in a good sense of natural magic or of a knowledge of the more recondite secrets of nature.[35]   Contemporary
belief held that it was possible by certain mechanical, astrolo-
gical or mathematical contrivances to produce objects endowed
with magical properties.   All this was looked upon as quite
independent of Satanic agency, and did not necessarily render
odious the trafficker in such arts, especially when they were
for the public good.   In fact, as we have seen, in the earliest
form of the legend Vergil appears not only as innocuous, but
also as a great benefactor, and none of the writers who record
the Neapolitan views concerning him makes any mention of
diabolical agency.   Gervasius attributes his achievements to an
ars mathematica or a *vis mathesis*.   Boccaccio, who lived at a

---

[35] The talismans of Apollonius of Tyana are attributed by Pseudo-Justin
(5th century) to his profound knowledge " of the forces of nature and their
sympathies and antipathies."   Cp. ROTH, *op. cit.*, p. 280.   It is certainly
not black magic to which Albertus Magnus is alluding when he says, " Cuius
veritatem nos ipsi sumus experti in magicis."   *Oper.*, t. iii. (Lugd., 1625),
p. 23.   Of the talking head attributed to him an old Italian writer says, " E
non fu per arte diabolica nè per negromanzia però chi gli grandi intelletti
non si dilettano di ciòe ; poichè è cosa da perdere l' anima e 'l corpo, che è
vietata tale arte dalla fede di Christo."   Above he had described him as
making it " per la sua grande sapienzia . . . a sì fatti corsi di pianeti
e calcola così di ragione ch' ella favellava."   *Rosario della vita di Matteo
Corsini*, in ZAMBRINI, *Libro di novelle antiche*, p. 74.

time when, as we shall see, the legend had already changed in character, had no fear of doing injury to the memory of the poet whom he so greatly revered by describing his works at Naples as done 'con l'aiuto della strologia,' or speaking of him as 'solennissimo strologo [36]—a view which has already met us in Servius and elsewhere. The populace then had done no more than develop in a materialistic manner the conception of Vergil held in the schools, and this conception was of such a nature that men of education found nothing incongruous in the popular legends. But while the scholastic conception was universal, the legends were exclusively Neapolitan, so that the question may well arise how the name of Vergil came to be so familiar to the people of Naples as to be connected with the talismans in which they believed. This, in fact, is the simplest form in which the problem of the origin of the legend presents itself. But before attempting to solve this problem it will be necessary to mention a fact which must not be passed over in this connection.

Gervasius of Tilbury relates the following : ' In the reign of Roger of Sicily, a certain scholar, an Englishman by birth, came before the king to ask a favour of him. And the king, generous of birth and nature, answered that he would grant him whatever he might wish. Now the Englishman was a famous writer, well versed in the Trivium and the Quadrivium and a devoted student of physics and astronomy ; he answered therefore that he would not ask for a mere ephemeral pleasure, but for something which in the eyes of men would seem but small, to wit, the bones of Vergil, wherever he should be able to find them in the king's dominions. The king consented, and the scholar, armed with letters from the king, betook himself to Naples, where Vergil had shown so many proofs of his power. When he presented the letters, the people were willing to obey, for, the position of the grave being unknown, they were ready to promise what seemed to them impossible to perform. Eventually however the scholar was able, by means of his art, to discover the bones in their grave in the centre of

---

[36] *Commento sopra Dante, Inf.,* i. 70.

T

a mountain, where not the slightest cleft or aperture betrayed
their presence. After lengthy excavations on the spot, a grave
was discovered, in which was found the body of Vergil perfectly
preserved, and under his head, among others, a book in which
was written the *Ars Notoria*.[37] The bones and the ashes were
removed and the Englishman took possession of the book. But
the inhabitants of Naples, calling to mind the great affection
which Vergil had shown their city, and fearing that if his
bones were taken away some terrible calamity might befall
them, preferred to disregard the king's command rather than
by obeying it to bring about the ruin of so great a city. For
this, they believed, was the reason why he had been buried in
a secret recess of the mountain, that the removal of his bones
might not deprive his various works of their power. The
Duke of Naples, therefore, with a number of the citizens,
collected the bones and put them in a sack and brought them
to the Castel di Mare, where they were shown, protected by
iron bars, to any one who wished to see them. When the
Englishman was asked what he had intended to do with the
bones, he answered that he would, by means of a spell, have
learnt from them all the art of Vergil, and that a period of
forty days would have sufficed him for this purpose. He con-
tented himself however with taking away the book, and, by the
kindness of the venerable Giovanni da Napoli,[38] cardinal under
Pope Alexander, I have seen some extracts from that book and
have made experiments satisfactorily establishing their value.'

This strange story of Gervasius is reproduced by Andrea
Dandolo [39] (*circa* 1339) and by the *Cronica di Partenope*, from
which latter work it is copied by Andrea Scoppa. Besides
Gervasius, the only contemporary writer who mentions a
similar incident is John of Salisbury, who, in his *Polycraticus*,
speaks of meeting a certain Louis, 'who spent many years in
Apulia, and, after many vigils, fastings and labours, succeeded

[37] The *Ars Notoria*, ridiculed by Erasmus, is not necromancy, but a form
of experimental science. Cornelius Agrippa wrote a work on the subject.
Vide LIEBRECHT, *ad Gervas.*, p. 161. Cp. ROTH, *op. cit.*, p. 294, and my
remarks on Vergilius Cordubensis in Chap. vii.

[38] Who died, according to LEIBNITZ, in 1175.

[39] MURATORI, *Scriptores rer. ital.*, xii. p. 283.

at last, as the reward of his useless sufferings and sad exile, in
bringing to Gaul the body, though unfortunately not the spirit,
of Vergil.'[40] It is very probable, as Roth also maintains, that
this is the same person as the one mentioned by Gervasius, for
John of Salisbury was at Naples in the reign of Roger, and the
expression 'in Gallias' with reference to a man whom Gervasius
describes as ' Anglus ' need cause no great difficulty.[41]

Roth is further of opinion that it was this circumstance
which set the Neapolitan imaginations working on the subject
of Vergil, but here I regret my inability to follow that able
scholar. The incident related by Gervasius presupposes the
existence of the legend. It is by no means impossible that an
eccentric Englishman should have got into his head the idea of
procuring the bones of Vergil and of extracting from them by
some magical means that treasure of hidden knowledge which
the world attributed to the poet. The fact that the Neapolitans refused to give them up and the reason of their refusal are
sufficient evidence that the poet was already celebrated at
Naples for the protection which his talismans and these very
bones themselves conferred on the city. The statement that on
this occasion the grave of Vergil was found, and that its discovery made a great impression on the Neapolitans, seems open
to question, notwithstanding the words of Gervasius that 'its
position was previously unknown to them.' To any one who
considers the immense authority and reputation enjoyed by
Vergil in the middle ages it will be abundantly clear that such
a discovery, brought about in so strange a manner, could not
have failed to impress not only the Neapolitans, but also the
whole literary world. We find, however, a general silence on
the subject, broken only by Gervasius. If we examine the
story more closely, it will, I think, appear that the incident of
the Englishman mentioned by John of Salisbury has become
combined with a legend explaining a sack of bones which was
shown behind an iron grating in the Castel di Mare, which
bones were supposed to be those of Vergil, while at the same
time this legend served to authenticate or accredit (a common

[40] *Polycraticus*, 2. 23.　　　　[41] Cp. ROTH, *op. cit.*, p. 295.

enough practice both then and afterwards) a certain book of
occult science, which Gervasius describes himself as having
seen, by giving out that it had come from the grave of Vergil.
Nor must we forget that John of Salisbury in speaking of this
Louis, whose acquaintance he had made, puts him in his true
light, that is, a ridiculous one, while Gervasius, who wrote a
few decades later, presents him with a number of evidently
legendary embellishments, and that, besides this, John of
Salisbury already knew of the story of the bronze fly, which
is equivalent to saying that the name of Vergil was at that
time already connected at Naples with talismans, quite independently of the vagaries of such madmen as this Louis. From
all this it appears to me clear that the fact related by Gervasius
cannot be regarded as the cause of the origin or development
of the Vergilian legends at Naples.[42]   It is moreover absolutely
certain that the idea of Vergil's protectorate over Naples and
of his rule there is anterior to the time of King Roger, since it
is expressly stated by Alexander of Telese that Vergil received
in fief, as a reward for his distich commencing ' Nocte pluit
tota,' the city of Naples and the province of Calabria.[43]

But though I do not draw from the narrative of Gervasius
the same conclusions as Roth, I have no hesitation in admitting
that the presence at Naples of the grave of Vergil played an
important part in keeping his name alive in the popular traditions.   Whatever doubts may be thrown on the grave which at
the present day is pointed to as Vergil's, or that which in the
middle ages may have passed for such,[44] it is an historical fact

---

[42] Of the same opinion is SCHAARSCHMIDT, *Joh. Saresberiensis*, p. 99.

[43] In MURATORI, *Scriptores rer. ital.*, v. pp. 637, 644. Cp. ROTH, *op. cit.*,
p. 288 seqq.

[44] It is much to be regretted that no serious archæological researches
should ever as yet have been made in the neighbourhood of the poet's grave.
The traditional site is generally discredited, but the unimportant work of
PEIGNOT, *Recherches sur le tombeau de Virgile* (Dijon, 1840), cannot be said
to have proved the point. COCCHIA, *La tomba di Virgilio, contributo alla
topografia dell' antica città di Napoli*, Turin (Loescher), 1889, maintains that
the grave is exactly at the spot where tradition places it, at the mouth of
the Grotto at Pozzuoli. The account in the ancient biography is precise
and perfectly worthy of credit, and might serve to point out the spot for the
excavations when the exact position of the second milestone on the Via
Puteolana has been ascertained by a careful study of the topography of

admitting of no reasonable doubt that Vergil wished to be buried at Naples, and that he actually was buried there.[45] The notice in the Life of Vergil ascribed to Donatus is probably derived from the biography of the poet written by Suetonius (98–138 A.D.) in his work *De Viris Illustribus*, and is confirmed by other notices which show that the grave of Vergil became the chief ornament of Naples and attracted visitors just as if it had been the shrine of some deity. Silius Italicus was accustomed, as we have already mentioned, to approach it as if it had been a temple (*adire ut templum*), while Statius actually calls it *templum*. In the 5th century still Sidonius Apollinaris speaks of the grave of Vergil as the boast of Naples.[46] It is clear therefore that the Neapolitans, seeing this species of worship going on, must at least have had the name of the poet impressed on their memories. If no notices to this effect have come down to us from the earlier part of the middle ages, that is merely because the writers who could have given such notices did not take interest in matters of this nature. From what we know however of the reverence with which Vergil continued to be regarded, we may conclude that the Neapolitans must have been for many centuries accustomed to enquiries from all educated foreigners as to the poet's grave. In the 10th century, that is to say at the time of the greatest barbarism, the author of the Life of St. Athanasius, when giving utterance to an enthusiastic eulogy on Naples, with which he was well acquainted, mentions Vergil and the epitaph which he had composed for his own tomb.[47] Later again, in the middle of the 12th century, the Provençal troubadour Guilhem

---

ancient Naples. Cocchia maintains that this condition is fulfilled by the grave in question, and it would certainly be difficult to prove positively that this was not Vergil's grave or to account for the ancient tradition which described it as such.

[45] "Ossa eius Neapolim translata sunt tumuloque condita, qui est via Puteolana intralapidem secundum." Donat, *Vit. Verg.*, p. 63.

[46] " Non quod Mantua contumax Homero
adiecit latialibus loquelis,
aequari sibimet subinde livens
busto Parthenopen Maroniano."
      Sid. Apoll., *Carm.*, ix.

[47] *Scriptores rerum longobardicarum* (in the *Mon. Germ. hist.*), p. 440.

Augier, when wishing to indicate Vergil, speaks of him merely as ' cel que jatz en la ribeira . . . lai a Napoli,' knowing that every one will understand his allusion.[48] It was certainly not left to the Normans to point out to the little republic of Parthenope, proud of its connection with ancient Rome, the existence of the grave of Vergil on its classic soil.[49] From this it follows that the popular notion that the grave of Vergil was intimately connected with the welfare of the city, and the cognate idea that, as Conrad says, his bones when exposed to the air produced storm and tempest, may very well have been of ancient date. And we have, in fact, already noticed that the grave of Vergil figures in the most ancient Vergilian legends, the most noticeable of which in the present connection is that of the inviolability of the cave at Puteoli, near the entrance of which is the actual grave assigned to him at the present day. Such legends were common enough even in pagan times. The value that the Athenians attached to the bones of Oedipus is well known, and similar beliefs were current elsewhere. Thus a legend, having reference to the hill which formed the grave of Antaeus, related that if a handful of earth were removed from that hill, rain immediately commenced to fall and continued till the earth was restored to its place.[50]

The poet who, while born near Mantua, wished to be buried at Naples must have had a great affection for that city in his lifetime. And, in fact, we gather from such authentic notices of him as remain that he did actually spend a great part of his life in this neighbourhood, enjoying the comforts provided by his exalted patron, and that in the midst of this inspiring scenery many of his immortal verses were composed. As we learn from a passage in his biography, his gentle and modest personality was well known to the Neapolitans, who gave him

---

[48] BARTSOH, *Chrestomathie Provençale* (4th edit.), p. 73, 2. For the date of this troubadour, *vide* SELBACH, *Das Streitgedicht in der altprovenzalischen Lyrik*, Marburg, 1886, p. 18 seq.

[49] Cp. SCHIPA, *Il Ducato di Napoli*, in the *Arch. st. delle prov. nap.*, xix. (1894) p. 445.

[50] POMPON. MELA, *De Chorographia*, iii. 106 (ed. PARTHEY). Cp. RAWLINSON, *ad Herod.*, i. 66.

the very characteristic nickname of *Parthenias*.[51] Nor does it seem open to reasonable doubt that his name must have lived on in connection with the estates which he held in this neighbourhood.

In proof of this, it is well to call to mind the garden which, according to the legend, Vergil had on Monte Vergine, of which Gervasius relates that it contained every kind of medicinal herb. The name of this mountain has undergone numerous variations. Its present name is Monte Vergine, but in Latin documents and writers it is called indiscriminately *Mons Virginis*, *Mons Virginum* and *Mons Vergilianus*. Giovanni Nusco, author of the Life of St. William of Vercelli,[52] founder of the church of Monte Vergine, states that the mountain was originally called Mons Vergilianus, which name he employs throughout. This assertion is denied by Roth,[53] who points out that in certain documents contemporary with the saint the mountain is spoken of as 'Mons qui Virginis vocatur,' and the church as 'S. Mariae Montis Virginis.' The fact, however, that when the name was changed some people should have continued to employ the earlier system of nomenclature is in no way remarkable. The author of the life of St. William was also contemporary with that saint, being received into the congregation of priests of Monte Virgine in 1132,[54] that is to say, ten years before the death of St. William and six after the consecration of the church. When he states that he is following local tradition in adopting the name Mons Vergilianus, it is doing violence to all probability to doubt his authority, especially since his character as ecclesiastic and member of the newly-founded congregation would undoubtedly have led him to prefer the name 'Mount of the Virgin Mary' to the pagan name of 'Vergil's Mount,' had he not come across a traditional usage which was too strong to be disregarded. And even if certain devotees were eager to adopt in their deeds of gift the name 'Mons Virginis,' the traditional name

[51] ". . . et ore et animo tam probum constat, ut Neapoli Parthenias *vulgo* appellatus sit." DONAT., *Vit. Verg.*, p. 57.
[52] *Acta Sanct. Iun.*, V. p. 114 seqq.
[53] *Op. cit.*, p. 287.
[54] *Acta Sanct. Iun.*, V. p. 112d.

continued none the less to be respected by the highest ecclesiastical authority, evidence of which fact is supplied by a bull of Pope Celestine III., in which this monastery is referred to more than once as 'Monasterium sacrosanctae Virginis Mariae de Monte Vergilii.'[55]   Nor is it impossible, since a place may well bear more names than one, that this Mons Vergilianus, before being called after the Virgin Mary, was actually known as *Mons Virginum*, which is the form of the name in Gervasius. The probable existence in pagan times of the worship of Vesta and Cybele in this neighbourhood would explain such a name perfectly well.[56]   Be this as it may, the unquestionable authentic name Mons Vergilianus and the legend, local[57] no less than Neapolitian, which placed Vergil's garden there, can but be explained by an actual estate belonging to Vergil situated in these parts. The existence of such an estate cannot now be positively proved, but it can be proved conclusively that within a century and a half of the poet's death, and perhaps earlier, estates were spoken of in this neighbourhood as having belonged to him.

Aulus Gellius[58] professes to have read 'in quodam commentario'[59] that the verses

[55] Costo, *La vera istoria dell' origine e delle cose notabili di Monte Vergine*, p. 123 seqq.

[56] The local tradition, mentioned by all the historians of the Monte Vergine, is that before being called *Mons Vergilianus* it was called *Mons Cybeles* from a temple of that goddess. Similarly, the name *Vesta*, which belongs to a spot on one of the slopes of the mountain, was derived from a temple of Vesta which had formerly stood there. *Vide* Giordano, *Croniche di Monte Vergine*, pp. 27, 38, 45.

[57] A 13th century MS. at Monte Vergine, containing the life of St. William, says as follows: "Nuncupatur Mons Vergilianus a quibusdam operibus et maleficiis Vergilii Mantuani poetae inter Latinos principis; construxerat enim hic maleficus daemonum cultor eorum ope hortulum quendam omnium genere herbarum cunctis diebus et temporibus, maxime vero aestatis, pollentem, quarum virtutes in foliis scriptas monachi quidam nostri fide digni fratres, qui praedictum montem inhabitant, apertis vocibus testantur, saepe [qui se] casu in praedictum hortum, non semel, dum peri uga montis solatii causa errarent incidisse, nihilominus intra hortum huiusmodi maleficii affectos esse, ut nec herbas tangere valuisse, nec qua via inde egressi sint cognovisse retulerunt. Deinde, mutato nomine Vergilii, Virgineus appellatur a semper Virgine Maria, cui templum positum est." Giordano, *Croniche di Monte Vergine*, p. 92.

[58] *Noct. Att.*, ii. 213. Cp. Serv. *ad Aen.*, vii. 740.

[59] Kretschmer (*De Aul. Gell. fontibus*, p. 77) and Mercklin (*N. Jahrb.*

'talem dives arat Capua et vicina Vesevo
ora iugo, etc.'

were originally recited and published by Vergil with the reading 'Nola iugo,' but that afterwards, when a request of his for
permission to bring water to a neighbouring piece of land had
been refused by the people of Nola, he was offended, and, not
wishing to contribute to the immortality of their city, altered
the verse to the form in which it now stands. Gellius does
not vouch for the truth of this story, nor would we, but it is
none the less a noticeable fact that a writer of the 2nd century
should, basing his statement on earlier authorities, expressly
refer to estates belonging to Vergil in the neighbourhood of
Nola; nor is it in itself improbable that Vergil should have
held such estates when we consider the length of time which
he spent in these parts.[60] Now the legend places the miraculous garden of Vergil at no great distance from Nola, at
Avella,[61] on the slopes of Monte Vergine, thus joining hands,
after a lapse of ten centuries, with the story we have cited
from Aulus Gellius, in which it finds a precedent which may
serve to explain it.[62] As for the special legendary attributes of
this garden, it is not impossible that the idea arose from an
actual garden of medicinal plants, such gardens being not uncommon in medieval times.[63]

---

für Philol., 1861, p. 722) fancy that this may have been a Vergilian commentary by Hyginus.

[60] This is also the opinion of RIBBECK, *Prolegg.*, p, 25.

[61] The *Cronica di Partenope* places it "above Avella and near Mercogliano."
But Mercogliano is nearer Avellino than Avella, whence ROTH (*op. cit.*, p.
226) would read Avellino in this passage of the *Cronica.* But SCOPPA says
clearly, " supra Abellam nunc Avellam quam Vergilius in *Georg.* maliferam
. . . nuncupat." PADRE GIORDANO (*Cron. di Monte Vergine*, p. 85 seqq.)
even asserts that Vergil had his summer residence at Avella. It is clear
that the legend could not indicate precisely the position of so marvellous a
garden. In the Monte Vergine MS. quoted above mention is made of
certain monks who professed to have actually seen it, having wandered into
it by chance, though they did not know how they had come in nor how they
got out. Other monks in the 17th century made a similar assertion ; PADRE
GIORDANO even records their names. *Cron. di Monte Vergine*, p. 92 seqq.

[62] It is worthy of note that two of the Neapolitan legends (that of the
serpents and that of the marble faces) are connected with the gate of Naples
which leads to Nola.

[63] Cp. Epig. 376 in the *Anthologia Latina* (MEYER), " De horto domini
Oageis, ubi omnes herbae medicinales plantatae sunt."

Some space has been devoted to the discussion of this fact, as it furnishes perhaps the best proof of any of the permanence of the name of Vergil in the local Neapolitan traditions during those periods when such permanence cannot be proved by actual historical documents. Many medieval legends present similar phenomena. Prepared and elaborated for a long time in obscurity, they appear suddenly in literature perfect and complete. The Vergilian legend is the more instructive, since history enables us firstly to observe the original impression produced on the Neapolitans by their actual contact with the poet, and afterwards to compare with this their conception of his personality as it reappears after the lapse of centuries, surrounded by the aureole of tradition, and transmuted by legendary influences as it were in a chemist's crucible. In this legend we are no longer, it is true, face to face with the Augustan poet, the brightest jewel of Roman poetry, but we encounter—a more interesting figure no doubt to the Neapolitans—the man of immortal renown who entertained so deep an affection for the city of Naples that he wished to be near it even in his grave. Hence the most ancient part of the legend must evidently be that which describes Vergil as extending a protectorate over the city, and it is in fact this idea which confronts us in the earliest notices that exist of a legendary Vergil, John of Salisbury's story of the bronze fly, and the statement by Alexander of Telese that Naples and Calabria were given to Vergil in fief by Augustus. With this, the fundamental idea of the legend, was coupled a curious fact in a manner well worthy of medieval erudition. Seneca, at the beginning of the Sixth Book of his *Quaestiones Naturales,* speaks of a violent earthquake which devastated Campania during the consulate of Regulus and *Verginius,* adding that, while the other cities of the province suffered severely, Naples escaped ' leniter ingenti malo perstricta.' In this passage some doubtless read *Vergilius,* and, not knowing what a consul at that time meant, interpreted it as ' when Vergil was consul of Naples.' In fact, Padre Giordano, Abbot of Monte Vergine, who in 1649 collected the traditions and chronicles of his monastery, actually states that when Vergil had gone to

Naples Augustus made him consul, and that his colleague was Regulus, mentioning further in this connection the eruption of Vesuvius, and citing the passage of Seneca to which we have referred.[64] Seeing that Alexander of Telese, a monk living in Samnium, some little distance from Naples, speaks of that city as belonging to Vergil, it seems reasonable to conjecture that this idea had some connection with the passage in Seneca, which, misunderstood by some monk in Southern Italy, would have served to strengthen the popular idea of a Vergilian protectorate of Naples.

Naples, which had succeeded, though not without severe struggles, in preserving its independence almost without interruption from the time of Justinian to the end of the 12th century, was thereby better able than other Italian cities to preserve the ancient traditions. The general intellectual level was not, however, during the centuries of barbarism any higher there than elsewhere, and consequently the conceptions of the famous names of antiquity which were kept alive in the memory of the Neapolitans underwent considerable transformations in the minds of men of every degree of culture, and tended inevitably to become associated with legendary surroundings. It is true that already at the end of the 9th century there were not wanting signs of a certain advance on the rude barbarism of the preceding ages; certain dukes, such as Sergius or Gregory III., and certain bishops, such as Athanasius I. and others, were unquestionably interested in secular studies as well as sacred, and it is not without surprise that, in the midst of the gloom of the 10th century, we encounter in this medieval Naples, of which we know so little, a duke such as John III., who, full of noble instincts, appears, like a miniature Charlemagne, as the patron of Latin letters, and even Greek, collecting together from every place, even from Constantinople, works both sacred and secular in both languages, such as Josephus, Dionysius, the history of Alexander the Great both in the original and in the translation, Livy, and other historians, chroniclers and the like, and summoning to his court and

---

[64] *Cron. di Monte Vergine*, p. 84.

rewarding liberally scholars and scribes who were able to translate and copy Greek works.[65] How strong was the Neapolitan sense of patriotism at the time, and how real their pride in their claim to be Romans and in the noble past of the ancient city which had been 'second to no city in Italy except Rome,' [66] is clearly shown by the enthusiastic eulogy of Naples into which the author of the *Life of St. Athanasius* breaks forth in the exordium of his work. It was this feeling, which is moreover so clear throughout the older Vergilian legends and is the strongest proof of the essentially Neapolitan origin of these, which acted as a lever to set in motion the rude intellects of clergy and laity alike to generate legends dealing with the ancient history of Naples under the Roman Empire; for even those who were to some extent imbued in secular studies had yet gained so little real profit from their education that they were quite as ready to misunderstand the names and facts of ancient history and the meanings of the ancient monuments and to view them through the medium of their own phantastic:imaginations as any of the most ignorant among the populace. A specimen of this is furnished by this very author of the Life of St. Athanasius when he writes, 'How excellent this city is, is shown by Maro the Mantuan in the famous verses which, when dying, he composed as his epitaph; for there he calls the city *Parthenope*, that is, *Virgin*, after a certain marriageable girl who once lived there. Eventually Octavianus Augustus ordered that it should be called *Neapolis*, that is, *Mistress of Nine Cities* (ἐννεάπολις), or, as some assert, *New City*, though the absurdity of the latter view is apparent, for how could a city be called 'new' when it was so old that the date of its foundation was not known?' [67] In this tissue of blunders it is instructive to observe the legend according to which Octavian gave the name of Naples to the city, since it shows that the Vergilian legend must have been in existence at

[65] Cp. SCHIPA, *Il Ducato di Napoli*, in the *Archivio st. per le prov. napol.*, v. xvii. p. 628 seqq.

[66] " Post Romanam urbem nulli inferior," *Vita Athanasii*, in the *Script. rer. Longobardicar*, p. 440.

[67] *Vita Athanas.*, loc. cit.

Naples already in the 10th century, anyhow as far as the legendary connection between Vergil, Octavian and Marcellus, which subsequently appears in Alexander of Telese, John of Salisbury, the *Cronica di Partenope*, etc., is concerned. In fact, the Abbot of the Monastery of San Salvatore, near Telese, who, though he lived at a later period, was no less barbarous in matters of classical culture than the anonymous Neapolitan hagiographer of the 10th century, in his dedication to King Roger wishes to *remind* the latter of the fact that Vergil received from Octavian as a reward for two verses Naples and Calabria, as of a fact well known ; and such it must also have been to the author of the Life of St. Athanasius, because the legendary interest of Octavian in Naples always goes hand in hand with his interest in Vergil and appears in the developed form of the legend as a consequence of the latter. Indeed, John of Salisbury actually states as much when he introduces with a *fertur* the Neapolitan legend of the miraculous fly, in which both Octavian and Marcellus appear—a legend which had surely been current from a very early period among the rude Neapolitan monks, since it must have been during the time of the ducal dominion that they conceived the idea of Marcellus made by Augustus ' Duke of Naples.'

All this part of the Vergilian legend, in which Naples, Octavian, Marcellus and Vergil appear together, though it is in spirit purely Neapolitan and hence *popular* at Naples, just as are the legends, which still exist there, in which Vergil appears as magician and benefactor of the city, yet shows by its connection with real historical facts, such as were the relations between Octavian, Marcellus and Vergil, that it originated among the educated populace, among the lower classes that frequented those monasteries and medieval monastic schools in Southern Italy which were under the influences of Neapolitan feeling.

For this part, therefore, and in this limited sense, may be admitted a *literary* origin of the *popular* Neapolitan legends concerning Vergil. In fact, as every legend referring to antiquity must have a point of departure and an original motive agency in the literary tradition of the schools and in surviving

monuments, thus the Vergilian legend was ultimately connected with the biography of the poet, which was read and
studied in the schools, and with his grave and its epitaph,
which were in existence at Naples. The notice in the biography
and the commentaries of the present made by Augustus to
Vergil for the famous lines, 'Tu Marcellus eris, etc.,' became
combined with the words of the epitaph, 'Calabri rapuere,
tenet nunc Parthenope,' understood with popular freedom and
from a Neapolitan point of view, and the two together were
taken to mean that Augustus had given Vergil for these verses,
in addition to a large sum of money, the sovereignty over
Naples and Calabria. Vergil, who, according to the biography
itself, was very fond of Naples and expressed the wish to be
buried there, becomes the patron of that city, which is furthermore held in high favour by Marcellus, who is made by the
will of Augustus joint-sovereign of it with him, while lastly
Augustus himself has such an affection for the place that he
gives it its name, and furnishes it also with a wall and towers.[68]

These ideas, the result partly of historical recollections derived from Vergil's biography and partly of the workings of
the imagination, are associated with and continued by the
popular ideas of the various benefits conferred on Naples by
Vergil the sage, who is no longer poet but magician. Midway
between the two is the superstition common alike to the educated and uneducated classes—the belief in the efficacy of the
grave of Vergil for the preservation of the city of Naples.
That this city, thanks to its powerful fortifications and still
more to its situation, was difficult or even impossible to capture, had been seen already by Belisarius,[69] and this idea is
repeated by more than one medieval writer. But a popular
superstition of unquestionable antiquity attributed the im-
pregnable character of Naples to the presence within it of a
palladium which preserved it—to the presence, in fact, of more
than one, for it was defended by pagan and Christian agency
alike, by the bones of Vergil and those of its patron saints
Agrippinus and Januarius. The medieval writers, who are

[68] Cp. SCHIPA, op. cit., p. 115.   [69] PROCOPIUS, De Bell. Goth., i. 9.

generally ecclesiastics, naturally record with greater readiness
the protectorate of the saints, but they are not ignorant of nor
do they always pass over in silence the protectorate which the
popular belief attributed to Vergil. The author of the Life
of St. Athanasius, owing to the religious character of his work,
only mentions the former; [70] but Alexander of Telese, though
also a monk, yet feels himself at liberty, since he is recording
the achievements of a lay prince, to confine himself to the
latter.[71] An offspring of this idea is the vessel, containing a
model of the city of Naples, which in the time of Conrad von
Querfurt was believed to have been made by Vergil to serve
as palladium. But at the same time the idea that the chief
palladium were the bones themselves still survived, as is shown
by the story of the Englishman Louis, who asked for them and
was refused them by the Neapolitans for fear lest some harm
might happen to their city if they gave them up.

All these popular ideas and legends, which had their origin
at an early period and continued to develop and spread during
the centuries of the dukedom, remained for a long time confined to the Neapolitans themselves and hardly made any
impression at all on the outside world. With the fall of the
dukedom and the rise of a completely new era under the
Norman kings, with the brutal invasion of the Imperialists,
who dismantled the ancient city of Vergil, the *operosum opus
Vergilii* as the Chancellor himself of Henry VI. calls it, the
spell was broken, the shrine of patriotic beliefs was violated,
and the sacred fire that had fed them was quenched for ever.
Foreigners, to whom the name of the wholly local St. Januarius
meant little, while the name of the world-famed Vergil meant
a great deal, being already convinced of the infinite nature of

---

[70] ". . . beati Agrippini ecclesia hactenus demonstratur . . . qui
etiam patronus et defensor est istius civitatis. Beatissimum quoque Ianu-
arium, Christi martyrem, postea Neapolites meruerunt habere tutorem,
quibus assistentibus faventibusque praefata urbs, Deo favente, tuta per-
mansit manebitque in aevum." *Vita Athanas.*, ed. cit., p. 440.

[71] " Quam ob rem adeo ipsa (Neapolis) inexpugnabilis constat ut, nisi
famis periculo coartata, nullatenus comprehendi queat. Nempe huiusmodi
urbis dominus olim, Octaviano Augusto annuente, Virgilius maximus poetarum extitit, in qua etiam ipse volumen ingens hexametris componit versibus."
De reb. gest. Roger, c. xix.

Vergil's knowledge, eagerly collected and disseminated these stories, and while in the new Naples, no longer Roman and hence no longer Vergilian, their production ceased and their very memory became faint, they began to be propagated in even stranger forms throughout the countries of Europe.

Having thus collected all the data which serve to throw light on the origin of these Neapolitan legends, it will be well to sum up the results of the investigation in a few words.

In its most ancient form this legend presents two distinct aspects : firstly, the name of Virgil connected with the idea of a special affection felt by him for Naples ; and secondly, the belief in certain public talismans attributed to him. The first of these two elements is exclusively Neapolitan ; founded, as we have seen, on real facts and on local traditions connected with them, it goes back without doubt to the time of Vergil's life at Naples and his burial there. The second is not exclusively Neapolitan, and is in any case distinct from and of later date than the first, being in fact one of the many similar legends which during the centuries of barbarism grew up round various ancient monuments. The point at which these two elements touch is this, that the medieval idea of the infinite wisdom of Vergil, combined with the ancient tradition among the Neapolitans of his affection for their city, caused to be attributed to him there all works for the public good which were looked upon as requiring for their production unusually profound knowledge, just as in other cities similar works were assigned to other authors. In this first form of the legend Vergil nowhere appears in a ridiculous aspect, nor is there any idea of maleficencᵉ or diabolical agency. The legend is in fine essentially *Neapolitan* in feeling and in origin, and is also *popular*, notwithstanding the fact that it is in some measure connected with the biography of the poet and shows signs of the influence of the rude Neapolitan monks.

In this examination of the origin of the legend it has been made abundantly clear that its nature in its earliest known form agrees well with that origin and with certain general principles already laid down. Vergil appears in it as possessed of a profound knowledge of the secrets of nature, and as making ise of this knowledge for the benefit of his favourite community. He appears less as a magician than as a scholar endowed with scientific knowledge which surpasses the range of ordinary intellects. Hence, in the changes which the conception of Vergil underwent, we shall be able to trace a law which is practically the same among the Neapolitan populace, who preserved the memory of their former benefactor, and the men of education, who read Vergil out of habit and admired him in deference to tradition. And so we shall find that the Neapolitan legends were no sooner transplanted into literature than they found, by reason of the conception of Vergil current in literary circles, the soil so well prepared for them that they straightway took root there and spread with a rapidity that is truly amazing.

CHAPTER IV.

THAT popular legends are liable to undergo modification in passing from mouth to mouth and from writer to writer is sufficiently well known. Small nuclei of legends are accustomed to attain to considerable proportions in two different ways, either by exaggeration or amplification of the legends themselves by the popular imagination, or by the attraction to them of other legends already existing either singly or as parts of another system. Legends are, however, generally subjected to the greatest modifications when they leave their native soil, especially when they owe their origin to some incident of local history or tradition. When such a legend passes from one country to another, it is very liable, in the absence of those local interests to which it appealed in the place of its origin, to be misunderstood and to be changed in consequence. In the first form of the Vergilian legend there could have been no allusion to diabolical agency; it would have been repugnant to the Neapolitans to think that their city owed anything to such questionable means. But though Vergil could not, as protector of Naples, appear in an unfavourable light, such a view was naturally no longer predominant when the legend had left Naples and spread over Europe. And we shall in fact observe that from this point onwards the Vergilian legend enters upon a second phase quite distinct from the first.

From *ars mathematica* and *astrologica* to *ars diabolica* was but a step, and though, for reasons already given, such a step was not to be expected of the Neapolitans, there was no reason why, as soon as the legend had left Naples, Vergil should not meet with the same fate as Gerbert and other famous students of astrology and mathematics and become a necromancer [1] in the blackest sense of the word; and such a transition was all the more likely in the case of a pagan, since many of the clergy, as has already been shown, were accustomed to discredit the famous writers of antiquity by describing them as worshippers of the devil and as owing their wisdom and talents chiefly to the infernal powers—a form of prejudice which, even if not universal, lasted on for a considerable time.

Bearing this in mind, it will not be difficult to understand the changes and amplifications to which the Vergilian legend was subjected when, on its rapid progress through Europe, it fell into the hands of the street singers and their fellows. This class of people, having above all things to interest the passers-by, so as to induce them to listen, were compelled not only to tell their stories in a way that engaged the attention, but also to have a large selection of stories at their disposal, so as to suit their audience and to be able to substitute one for another, if the first did not meet with approval.[2] Thus many of them, to show their superiority to their rivals, would recite a long string of the stories that they professed to be able to tell.[3] It is easy then to imagine with what eagerness they would seize on any novel subject. No sooner therefore had the Vergilian legend left Naples than they laid hold on it, and already at the beginning of the 13th century they were in full possession of it. In a long poem by the troubadour Giraud de Calançon, written some time between 1215 and 1220,[4] there is a lengthy account of the necessary stock-in-trade of a street minstrel. After enumerating the various instruments which he must

---

[1] According to the medieval etymology: "*mantia*, Graece divinatio dicitur, et *nigro*, quasi nigra, unde *Nigromantia*, nigra divinatio, quia ad atra daemoniorum vincula utentes se adducit." Therefore it is not a liberal art, for: "sciri libere potest, sed operari sine daemonum familiaritate nullatenus valet." Thus too a Vienna MS. in REIFFENBURG, *Chron. rim. de Philippe Mouskes*, i. p. 628.

[2] Thus GIRALDUS CAMBRENSIS (1197), in his *Gemma Ecclesiastica*, speaking of certain priests, says: "Similes sunt cantantibus fabulas et gesta qui videntes cantilenam *de Lauderico* non placere auditoribus, statim incipiunt cantare *de Wacherio;* quod si non placuerit, de alio." *Girald. Camb. op.*, ed. BREWER, vol. ii. (Lond., 1862), p. 290.

[3] GRAESSE, *Die grossen Sagenkreise des Mittelalters*, p. 6 seqq.

[4] *Hist. lit. de la France*, t. xvii. p. 580.

know how to play and the various tricks and acrobatic feats he must be able to perform, the writer gives a long list of the stories, whether prose or verse, that he must have by heart. Among these appear the Vergilian legends,[5] both the story of the miraculous garden and also others, not of Neapolitan origin, which will be discussed presently. Poets, mountebanks and buffoons, all in one, as were most of these *cantores francigenarum*, intent solely on interesting their audiences and enticing their money out of their pockets, it is easy to imagine with what liberty they treated the characters of their legends in the attempt to render them more interesting or amusing. What wonder that Vergil should have become in their hands a sorcerer of the first water?

But the fate which befell the legendary Vergil in the streets, befell him equally in literature. It is noticeable that in the *Dolopathos*, though Vergil has come to be, in consequence of the literary tradition, a quite ideal personage,[6] there is no suggestion of magic with reference to him. In the French 13th century version of it by Herbers the only allusion to Vergil as a magician is a passage relating to the little book in which he included, for the use of his pupil Lucinianus, all the seven liberal arts, of which it is stated that, when he was dead, he held it in his hand so firmly that it could not be removed, and that he was able to do this

" Par engin et par nigromance
Dont il sot tote la science." [7]

But this is a sufficiently innocent form of necromancy.[8] It

[5] " E de Virgili
Com de la conca a saup cobrir
E del vergier
E del pesquier
E del foc que saup escantir."

DIES, *Die Poesie der Troubadours*, p. 199 ; GRAESSE, *Die grossen Sagenkreise des Mittelalters*, p. 21 seqq. Cp. FAURIEL, *Hist. de la poésie prov.*, iii. p. 495.

[6] Cp. vol. i. chap. 16 of this work.

[7] *Li Romans de Dolopathos*, pub. par MM. C. BRUNET et A. DE MONTAIGLON. Paris (Jannet), p. 384.

[8] ROTH is wrong in confusing, like GRIMM (*Die Sage von Polyphem*, p. 4) and many others, the Latin text of the *Dolopathos* with the *Historia septem sapientum*. The latter is merely the Latin translation (not the original, as

would be interesting to know whether the author of the
Dolopathos omitted these stories on purpose or whether they
had not yet reached him at the date when his work was written.
It is certain however that they had already at this period,
anterior that is to both Gervasius and Conrad, been to some
extent, at any rate, disseminated in Europe, since Neckam,[9] who,
as we have seen, was never at Naples, speaks of the miraculous works of Vergil. Neckam indeed not only mentions the
butcher's block which kept meat fresh,[10] but also describes how
with a golden leech[11] Vergil freed Naples from a plague of
leeches which infested its waters, how he built a brazen bridge
by means of which he could travel whithersoever he would,
and how he surrounded his garden with a stratum of air as
impenetrable as a wall. He recounts besides another legend of
which mention will be made further on.

Another writer who, previous to the publication of Gervasius'
work, is acquainted with several of the Vergilian legends is
the monk Elinandus, the celebrated author of a Latin chronicle,[12] included by Vincent de. Beauvais in his *Speculum
Historiale* and much read in the middle ages. This chronicle,
which goes down to the year 1204, is noteworthy as containing
a number of details on the subject of the Vergilian legends not
recorded by any of the writers hitherto mentioned. In addition to the bronze fly, the baths, the butcher's block, and
the garden, in which, according to him, it never rained,
Elinandus attributes to Vergil a bell-tower, which, when its

is commonly supposed) of the *Roman des sept sages*. I can only mention
this fact here; the discussion of it would lead too far away.

[9] *De naturis rerum*, cap. 174. Neckam's Vergil-stories are quoted from
him by W. BURLEY, *De vita et moribus philosophorum*, cap. 103.

[10] PSEUDO-VILLANI gives a different account. NOBILE, *Descriz. della città
di Napoli*, ii. p. 781, writes as follows: "La cappella di S. Giovanni a Pozzo
bianco segue più innanzi al principio del vicolo dell' arcivescovado, anticamente detto *Gurgite*; ed era così denominato perchè l'altro vicolo che gli
sta dirimpetto, aveva fino ad un secolo fa un pubblico pozzo ornato di
marmor bianco, e sovr' esso sanguisughe scolpite, di cui il cronista nostro
Giovanni Villani, seguendo l'ignoranza del volgo, dice che Virgilio Marone
sotto la costellazione dell Aquario aveale fatte scolpire," etc.

[11] Published in tom. vii. of the *Bibliotheca patrum cistercensium* of
TISSIER.

[12] The only reason that Vincent de Beauvais has for doubting this story
is that the invention of bells was subsequent to Vergil.

bells were rung, moved in time with them,[13] and speaks besides, like Neckam, of the *Salvatio Romae*. The biographical notices preserved of Elinandus,[14] as well as the character of some of his legends, make it improbable that he was ever at Naples. In him, as in Neckam, appear traces of the changes that the legend had undergone in its passage from its native country. Nor must it be forgotten that Elinandus, before becoming a monk, had been a very popular troubadour; he himself, when looking back regretfully on the gaiety of his early life,[15] recounts how there had never been festival or tourney at which his voice had not been heard. To this is perhaps due the fact that, in the part of the chronicle relating to his own time, instead of describing events, he will speak of nothing but dreams, visions, apparitions, prodigies and legends, the Vergilian among others, which, though bearing very clearly on them the mark of the troubadour, were none the less carefully preserved by Vincent de Beauvais and Alberic de Trois-Fontaines.

It was no doubt from the poets of France that their German imitators first learned to look on Vergil as a magician. Wolfram von Eschenbach in his *Parzival*, composed between 1203 and 1215 and derived from French sources,[16] makes his magician Klinschor a descendant of Vergil, born in the 'Land of Labour'; other German poets of the same school, such as Boppo, Frauenlob, Rumeland, the author of *Reinfrit von Braunschweig*, etc., speak of Vergil in a similar manner throughout the 13th century. Thus, while on the one hand the Vergilian legend was being propagated by street-minstrels and poets of every sort, both orally and in writing, on the other hand it gained a great notoriety in the literary world by being included in learned works of popularity and authority, such as those of Gervasius, Neckam, Elinandus, Vincent de Beauvais and the like.

---

[13] *Vide Hist. lit. de la France*, tom. xviii. p. 87 seqq.

[14] "Non scena, non circus, non theatrum, non amphitheatrum, non forum, non platea, non gymnasium, non arena sine eo resonabat." *De reparat. lapsi*, p. 318.

[15] *Vide* Rochat in the *Germania* of Pfeiffer, iii. 81 seqq., and iv. 411 seqq

[16] Cp. v. d. Hagen, *Gesammtabenteuer*, iii. p. cxl. seqq.

CHAPTER V.

To any one who considers the conditions of the literary world in the middle ages it will be clear that the legendary Vergil of Naples presented an anomaly which was hard to reconcile with the pre-conceived notions of the poet. The Neapolitan legend, having originated at Naples, was the expression of purely Neapolitan feelings, and brought Vergil into connection with no other city; but this state of affairs could not last when the legend had left its native place. In the literary tradition, the connection of Vergil with Naples was only a secondary matter of no great importance. Vergil, one of the most eminent names of the ancient Roman world, could not remain altogether divorced from the great centre of that world. Vergil and Rome presented to the minds of that day such a homogeneous idea that to separate the legendary Vergil from legendary Rome must have seemed well nigh impossible. To think that Vergil should have made such use of his arts and knowledge for the sake of Naples, and yet have done nothing for Rome, that Rome that he called golden, that he called the head of the world, whose birth he had immortalised in an immortal poem! The idea was absurd. This lacuna in the Neapolitan legends had therefore to be filled in, and it was filled in as soon as these legends began to spread through Europe. In fact, already in Alexander Neckam and Elinandus are to be seen a Roman legend side by side with the Neapolitan. No great effort of the imagination was needed, for just as we have seen that at Naples the belief in certain talismans existed independently of Vergil and that therefore the Neapolitan populace had nothing to do but attach his name to them, so there had been similar stories for a long time current at Rome, to which it was equally easy to affix the poet's name. The only difference is this, that while the Neapolitan legends became Vergilian at Naples itself and through the agency of the people of Naples, the Roman legends became so outside Rome, through the agency of poets and literary men, and in imitation of the Neapolitan.

Alexander Neckam relates in his *De naturis rerum* that Vergil built at Rome a beautiful palace, in which were statues representative of the various provinces subject to the Roman empire, each with a bell in its hand. Whenever any of these provinces meditated revolt, its statue began to ring its bell. Thereupon a bronze warrior on the roof of the palace brandished his lance in the direction of the province in question, and the Romans, thus warned, were able to send troops to quell the revolt. It is however worthy of note that, while Neckam here attributes this marvel to Vergil, in his poem *De laudibus divinae sapientiae*,[1] in which he recapitulates his *De naturis rerum*, he tells the same story without mentioning Vergil's name. With certain variations, which, though slight, are yet sufficient to establish its independent origin, the story reappears in Elinandus, who does not however commit himself to the Vergilian authorship of the palace in question, but says merely 'creditur a quibusdam.'

That the people of Rome should, in the state of ignorance into which medieval barbarism and Christianity had plunged them, have been unaware of the true origin of the various monuments of antiquity that remained and have invented numerous legends to supply this deficiency in their knowledge, will be the more readily imagined when we consider that even during more enlightened periods of history similar processes may go on. The number of memorials accumulated in Rome was so great that a knowledge of the true origin and intention of every monument there would have required a far wider acquaintance with history than could be expected of the population of any city. The feeling that they were Romans

---

[1] Dist. 5, v. 290 seqq. (p. 447).

and the descendants of a great nation was not wanting to the inhabitants of Rome, and the magnificence of the surviving monuments tended to keep such sentiments alive, but the memory of special events could only survive in the form of certain names and certain legends. And however much the grandeur of Rome might influence its actual inhabitants, the impression it made on strangers must have been yet greater. Arriving at Rome, with that freshness of mind characteristic of peoples but recently emerged from barbarism, and entirely ignorant of the marvels which a civilised nation so powerful as the Romans were capable of producing, they were struck with amazement when brought face to face with the ruins of the fallen giant—ruins that even now have lost none of their imposing majesty. On returning home, these travellers unconsciously exaggerated what they had seen ; their hearers again exaggerated in their turn and so the legends grew.

In many stories, recorded for the most part by foreign writers, it is possible to recognise the product of strong impressions subsequently elaborated at a distance from the places to which they refer. The legends which originated in Rome itself are far simpler, referring mostly to some actual existing monument, which retains in the legend its proper form, merely its object and the name of its author being changed. Thus a certain votive vessel came to be regarded as the vessel in which Aeneas came to Italy.[2] The story of Trajan and the widow, immortalised by Dante, existed before it was referred to Trajan.[3] Probably a bas-relief on the triumphal arch in which the emperor is represented on horseback with a female

---

[2] PROCOP., *Bell. Goth.*, iv. 22. BECKER (*Handbuch d. röm. Alterth.*, i. p. 161) thinks it may have been a model, or a curiosity of some kind. According to WILLIAM OF MALMESBURY (ii. c. 13), in 1045 there was discovered at Rome the grave of Pallas : "tunc corpus Pallantis filii Euandri, de quo Vergilius narrat, Romae repertum est, ingenti stupore omnium. Hiatus vulneris quod in medio pectore Turnus fecerat quattuor pedibus et semis mensuratum est." I should doubt whether this legend, evidently not popular in origin, referred to any real discovery, as GREGOROVIUS maintains in his *Gesch. d. Stadt. Rom im Mittelalt.*, iv. p. 626.

[3] Cp. MASSMANN, *Kaiserchronik*, iii. p. 753 seqq. ; G. PARIS, *La légende de Trajan*, in Fasc. xxxv. of the *Bibl. de l'École des hautes études*, pp. 261-298 ; GRAF, *Roma nella memoria*, etc., ii. p. 6 seqq.

figure, symbolical of the conquered province, kneeling at his feet, was the original cause of its attribution to him.

In the marvellous palace attributed to Vergil by Neckam and Elinandus, and well known in the middle ages under the name of the *Salvatio Romae*,[4] there appears a strange medley of reminiscences of the Pantheon, the Colosseum, the Capitol, and the statues, symbolical of various nations, in the theatre of Pompey, by which Nero, in a moment of remorse, thought he was being attacked; while with all this was combined the inability to understand how ʾthe vigilance necessary for the preservation of so vast an empire could be maintained by any but supernatural means. This legend, which unquestionably arose outside Italy, was very common in the middle ages, and was told without reference to Vergil long before being attributed to him. It was originally applied to the Capitol, which thereby became one of the seven wonders of the world, as related by the Greek Cosmas[5] in the 8th century and other writers—a fact which suggests the idea that its original motive may have been the well-known story of the geese of the temple of Jupiter, which was one of the chief stories connected with the Capitol, and as such would doubtless have penetrated from Byzantium into the East. This theory receives further confirmation from the fact that a reminiscence of this story appears in several Arabic legends, in which, by a remarkable coincidence, occurs not only the idea of the *Salvatio Romae* (applied to Egypt) but also that of the miraculous mirror to which reference will be made further.[6] Later on the *Salvatio Romae*

---

[4] It is sometimes also called *Consecratio statuarum.*

[5] Mai, *Spicilegium Romanum*, ii. p. 221.

[6] King Sarcâf " made a bronze duck and put it on a pillar of green marble near the gate of the city. Whenever a stranger arrived, the duck flapped its wings and cried till the inhabitants came and arrested the stranger." Vide *Orient und Occident*, i. p. 331; cp. p. 335 and 340; *vide* also the article of Liebrecht, *ib.*, iii. p. 360, 363. Florus, in telling the story of Manlius, mentions only a single goose. Vergil in the shield of Aeneas likewise describes a single goose (of silver). *Aen.*, viii. 652 seqq. Dante, *De Monarch.*, says, "anserem ibi ante non visum cecinisse Gallos adesse." The song of the soldiers of Modena (10th cent.) runs:

" Vigili voce avis anser candida
fugavit Gallos ex arce Romulea

is referred by some to the Pantheon,[7] by others to the Colos
seum, and is described as one of the seven wonders of the
world, not only by Cosmas, as already stated, but also in a
work of the 8th century, ascribed to the Venerable Bede,[8] besides being mentioned in a Wessobrunn MS. of the same date,[9]
by the anonymous writer at Salerno in the 10th century [10]
and in an 11th century MS. in the Vatican.[11] It is further
mentioned in the *Mirabilia urbis Romae*,[12] a guide-book which
underwent various modifications at different times, but which
was certainly already known in the 12th century,[13] and by
Jacopo da Voragine [14] in the 13th century, who, like many
others, ascribes it to diabolical agency.[15] All these speak of it
without mentioning Vergil, as do also other writers subsequent

pro qua virtute facta est argentea
et a Romanis adorata ut dea."

Ap. Du Méril, *Poésies pop. lat. ant. au XII. siècle*, p. 269. Massmann wishes
to explain the legend as arising from the moving figures on certain clocks,
of which there was one in the Capitol. (*Kaiserchronik*, iii. p. 425.) He
considers it (p. 424) of Teutonic origin; I believe rather that it came from
Byzantium. Graf on the other hand (*op. cit.*, i. p. 201) believes that the
story arose at Rome in the 4th or 5th century through a transformation of
the ancient idea of the Capitol as the citadel of the Roman empire.

[7] So too Ludovico Dolce :

"Non la Ritonda or sacra, e gia profana,
La dove tante statue eran poste
Che avean legata al collo una campana."

Il primo vol. delle op. burl. del Berni, etc., part ii. p. 271.

[8] *Libellus de septem orbis miraculis*, in Bedae, *Op.*, i. 400.

[9] Massmann, *Kaiserchronik*, iii. p. 426.

[10] Muratori, *Scriptores rer. ital.*, ii. 2, p. 272.

[11] Preller in the *Philologus*, i. p. 103.

[12] Graesse, *Beiträge zur Liter, und Sage des Mittelalters*, p. 10.

[13] The first critical edition of the *Mirabilia* is that of Parthey: "*Mirabilia Romae ex codd. vatt. emendata.*" Berlin, 1865. The next that of Jordan in his *Topographie der Stadt Rom im Alterthum*, ii. (Berlin, 1871), p.
605 seqq., which contains also (p. 357 seqq.) an important contribution to
the history of the work. Finally, C. L. Ulrichs has published the *Mirabilia* in his *Codex urbis Romae topographicus*. Wurzburg, 1871, p. 126
seqq.

[14] *Legenda aurea*, clvii.

[15] In a MS. which we have already had occasion to cite it is attributed to
the art of astronomy or astrology. "Per hanc artem Romae senatores
necem virorum et bella in oris barbaris facta, regumque et regnorum detri-
mentum statum et stabilimentum noverunt." *Vide* Reiffenberg, *Chron.
rim. de Philippe Mouskes*, i. p. 628.

to Neckam and Elinandus.[16]   To bring this legend into connection with Vergil there was necessary the link which is supplied
by the last stage of the Vergilian legend, that namely in which
the poet assumes his well-known character of the Prophet of
Christ ; but this matter will be discussed in another chapter.
To explain why so interesting a monument was no longer to be
seen, the anonymous Salerno writer states that the statues
were taken to Byzantium, and that there the Emperor Alexander († 915), wishing to show them due respect, clothed them
in garments of silk, but on the following night St. Peter appeared to him and cried in an angry voice, ' I am the prince of
the Romans,' and on the following day the emperor died.

The legend of the *Salvatio Romae* is the earliest occasion on
which Vergil is brought by legend into contact with Rome. We
know that he possessed a house on the Esquiline,[17] but he does
not seem to have resided there habitually ; [18] and even had he
done so, his presence could not have had so great an effect on
the popular imagination at Rome as was the case at Naples
The inhabitants of the capital of the greatest empire the world
has ever known, accustomed as they were to greatness of every
sort, could not have received any deep or lasting impression of
the personality of Vergil, however much they might be able to
distinguish and appreciate him among the crowd of notabili-
ties passing perpetually before their eyes.   If therefore we

[16] The largest collection of notices of this subject is in MASSMANN, *Kaiserchronik*, iii. p. 421 seqq. We may add the following hitherto unpublished
one : " Una porta artificiata era in Roma sotto il monte Gianicolo dove
anticamente abitò il re Giano primo re d' Italia da cui è nominata il monte
Gianicolo. La detta porta era di metallo ornata maravigliosamente e con
grande artificio, perocchè quando Roma, quella nobilissima città, aveva pace,
stava la detta porta sempre serrata, e quando si ribellava alcuna provincia,
la porta per se stessa si apriva. Allora li Romani correvano al Pantheon,
cioè Santa Maria Rotonda, dove erano in luogo alto statue le quali rappres-
sentavano le provincie del mondo. E quando alcuna si ribellava, quella
cotale statua voltava le spalle e però li Romani quando vedevano la statua
volta, s' armavano le milizie, e prestamente andavano in quella parte a
riacquistare." *Libro imperiale*, 3, 8 (cod. saec. xv., Magliab. xxii. 9).
[17] " Habuitque domum Romae Esquiliis iuxta hortos Maecenatis, quanquam secessu Campaniae Siciliaeque plurimum uteretur." DONAT., *Vit. Verg.*,
p. 57.
[18] " Si quando Romae, *quo rarissime commeabat*, viseretur in publico,"
etc. DONAT., *Vit. Verg.*, p. 57.

find at Rome certain monuments connected by legends with the name of Vergil, such legends have assuredly not grown out of popular recollections of the poet, but are of much later date, being a reflection of Vergilian legends originated elsewhere, fused and confused by outside agencies with legends connected with the city.

CHAPTER VI

IN the 13th century, when the Vergilian legend was already
widely spread through Europe, we find it in process of undergoing considerable changes and amplifications at the hands of
various popular poets, and this chiefly in certain largely read
French works.   Such are the *Image du Monde*, a sort of
Encyclopedia,[1] written in 1245, and attributed, with no very
good reason, to Walter of Metz, the *Roman des Sept Sages*,[2]
written both in prose and verse, translated into many languages
and one of the most popular books in Europe, and the romance
in verse entitled *Cleomadès*, written by Adénès towards the
end of the 13th century.[3]

In 1319 the Vergil legends occur in the hitherto unpublished
Renart contrefait,[4] and in this same 14th century certain of
them appear in various collections of anecdotes formed specially
for the use of ascetics, moralists and preachers, in which case
they are, according to the usage of the time, interpreted allegorically for the edification of the faithful.   Among these may
be mentioned certain redactions of the *Gesta Romanorum*,[5] and

---

[1] Cp. *Hist. lit. de la France*, t. xxiii. p. 309; DU MÉRIL, *Mélanges*, p. 427
seqq.

[2] KELLER, *Li Romans des Sept Sages*, p. cciii. seqq., 153 seqq.; ID., *Dyo-
cletianus Leben von Hans von Bühel*, p. 57 seqq.; LOISELEUR DESLONGCHAMPS,
Essai sur les fables indiennes, p. 150 seqq.; D'ANCONA, *Il libro dei sette Savi
di Roma*, p. 50 seqq., 115 seqq.

[3] *Hist. lit. de la France*, t. xx. p. 712 seqq.; DU MÉRIL, *Mél. arch.*, p. 435
seqq.; *Li Roumans de Cleomadès, par* ADÉNÈS LI ROIS, *publ. pour la prem.
fois par* ANDRÉ VAN HASSELT, Brux., 1865-6, vol. i. pp. 52-8.

[4] DU MÉRIL, *Mélanges*, p. 440 seqq.

[5] *Gesta Romanorum*, ed. AD. KELLER, Stuttg. and Tübing. 1842; *id.*
(Germ. trans.) GRAESSE, Dresd. and Leip., 1847. Cp. WARTON, *Dissert. on
the Gesta Romanorum* in his *History of English Poetry*, i. p. cxxxix. seqq.;

the *Violier des histoires romaines,*[6] based on that work. To the 13th century belongs the 'Universal Chronicle,' written in German verse by Ians Enenkel (1250), a citizen of Vienna, in which work occur several of the Vergilian legends.[7]

In these versions of the story it is Rome, naturally enough, which appears as the chief field of Vergil's activity. The Neapolitan legends remained stationary, being sometimes transferred to Rome, while the Roman legends went on increasing. The legend of the *Castel dell' Ovo* had assumed formidable proportions; it was no longer a question of a simple talisman preserved in this castle, but, according to the *Image du Monde,* the whole city was balanced on an egg, and began to tremble as soon as the egg moved :

> " Que quant ancuns l' uef remuait
> Toute la cité en crolait."

The *Cleomadès* in its turn states that there were two castles in the sea, each built on an egg, and when once some one tried breaking one of the eggs, the castle at once sank; but the other is still to be seen at Naples floating on its egg.

> " Encor est là l'autres chastiaus
> Qui en mer siet et bons et biaus :
> Si est li oes, c'est vérités,
> Seur quoi li chastiaus est fondés."

The idea of the *Salvatio Romae* was moreover coupled with the idea, long current in the East, of a mirror in which one could see everything which happened at a distance. One such mirror there used to be, according to Benjamin of Tudela,[8] at the top of the lighthouse at Alexandria; it had been placed

---

DOUCE, *Dissert. on the Gesta Romanorum* in his *Illustrations of Shakespeare.* (London, 1836), p. 519 seqq. ; *Gesta Romanorum,* ed. H. OESTERLEY, Berl., 1871.

[6] *Le Violier des histoires romaines, nouv. éd. par* M. G. BRUNET, Paris (Jannet), 1858.

[7] All this part is published in v. D. HAGEN, *Gesammtabenteuer,* ii. p. 513 seqq.

[8] *Itinerario,* i. p. 155 seqq. (ASHER). Cp. DE GUIGNES in *Mémoires et extraits des MSS.,* etc., i. p. 26 ; REINAUD, *Monumens arabes, persans et turcs,* t. ii. p. 418 ; LOISELEUR, *Essai sur les fables indiennes,* p. 153 ; NORDEN, *Voyage,* t. iii. p. 163 seqq.

there by Alexander, and with it one could see any vessel of
war that was coming against Egypt at a distance of 500 para-
sangs.[9]   The *Salvatio Romae* changed into such a mirror, which
is ascribed to Vergil in the *Roman des Sept Sages*, the *Cleomadès*
and the *Renart contrefait*.[10]   But unfortunately, like all things
mortal, the mirror perished at last; the *Roman des Sept Sages*
tells us how.   A foreign king,—Hungarian, Carthaginian,
German or Apulian,—the accounts differ,—unable to bear any
longer this constant surveillance on the part of the Romans
accepted the offer of three knights to go and break the mirror.
These, when they were come to Rome, buried gold in various
places and gave themselves out as finders of hidden treasure.
The emperor, being of an avaricious disposition, wished to
make trial of their powers, whereupon they gained his confidence by digging up the gold they had themselves hidden.
When they found that the emperor believed in them, they said
that a great treasure was to be found under the column that
supported the mirror, and they were accordingly commissioned

---

[9] Two such mirrors appear in the Arab legends published by WÜSTENFELD,
Orient und Occident, i. pp. 331-5.   In the *Titurel* a similar mirror is attributed to Prester John.   Cp. v. D. HAGEN, *Briefe in die Heimath*, iv. p. 119;
OPPERT, *Der Presbyter Johannes in Sage und Geschichte*, p. 175 seqq.
Catherine de Medici was supposed to have one.   Cp. REINAUD, *Monumens
arabes, persans et turcs*, ii. p. 418.   G. BATT. PORTA in his *Magia naturalis*
(lib. xvii. cap. 2) even discloses the secret for causing "ut speculis planis ea
cernantur quae longe et in aliis locis geruntur."   According to a medieval
version of the story of Troy, the Palladium was such a mirror.   *Vide* CAX-
TON, *Troye-Boke*, ii. cap. 22, ap. DU MÉRIL, *Mélanges*, p. 470.
   In modern popular tales such mirrors are common enough.   *Vide e.g.*
AFANASIEFF, *Narodnyia russkiia skazki*, vii. 2, 41; viii. 18 (and note); SCHOTT,
Walachische Märchen, 5, 13 ; HALTRICH, *Deutsche Volksmärchen*, 30, etc.
They are generally described as small and portable ; Vergil too has such a
one as this in the *Gesta Romanorum* (cap. 102, ed. KELLER) by means of
which he shows a man the infidelity of his wife and her plots against his
life.   *Vide* v. D. HAGEN, *Erzählungen und Märchen*; SCHEIBLE, *Das Kloster*,
ii. p. 126 seqq.; SIMROCK, *Die deutschen Volksbücher*, vi. p. 380 seqq.   It is
to this legend perhaps that the "Vergil-mirrors" preserved in several
museums refer.
   For the medieval superstitions on the subject of magic mirrors, *vide*
PAPENCORDT, *Cola da Rienzo*, chap. vii.; ORIOLI in the *Biblioteca italiana*,
fasc. i., 1841, pp. 67-90 ; DU MÉRIL, *Mélanges*, p. 469 seqq.; DUNLOP-
LIEBRECHT, p. 201.
   [10] Cp. too GOWER, *Confessio Amantis*, i. 5 ; FROISSART, *Poésies*, p. 270.
To this too refer the *Castiaus-Miréours* of Rome in the French poem *Balan*;
vide G. PARIS, *Hist. poét. de Charlemagne*, p. 251.

to search for this.   After removing the column, they propped
up the mirror with wooden supports, to which, as soon as it
was night, they set fire, and straightway fled.   So the mirror
was broken into a thousand pieces, while the Romans, out of
anger at its loss, forced their emperor to drink molten gold as a
punishment for his avarice.   This story, the end of which recalls a well-known incident of Roman history, existed independently of Vergil and the magical mirror.   We meet it again in
the *Pecorone*, in the novel with the heading: ' *Chello and Ianni
di Velletri give themselves out as soothsayers to do harm to the
state of Rome.   They are received at the court of Crassus, and, to
gain his favour, dig out certain treasures which they had themselves previously buried.   They then state that there is a great
treasure hidden under the Tribune's Tower.   Crassus puts wooden
supports to the tower, to which they set fire and then escape in
the night.   On the following morning the tower falls and causes
great slaughter among the Romans.*" [11]   Vergil therefore and the
magical mirror do not occur in this version of the story, which
deals only with a building called the Tribune's Tower, ' on the
walls of which were fastened portraits, in metal, of all Romans
who had ever been distinguished, so that this tower was looked
upon as the noblest monument in Rome.'   This novel is closely
parallel to a curious anecdote told by Flaminius Vacca,[12] an
archaeologist of the 16th century, who however attributes the
work of destruction to a Goth.

When once Vergil had gained the reputation of being a
magician, not only were various marvels at Rome attributed to

---

[11] *Pecorone*, Day 5, Nov. 1.   According to BENJAMIN OF TUDELA, the mirror at Alexandria was similarly destroyed by the treachery of a Greek who
was an enemy of Egypt.

[12] " I remember that in the time of Pius IV. there came to Rome a Goth
with a very ancient book which described a hidden treasure as marked by a
serpent and a figure in bas-relief, holding in one hand a cornucopia and
with the other pointing to the ground.   He searched till he found this sign
on the side of an arch, and then asked permission of the pope to dig for
the treasure, which he said belonged to the Romans.   But when the excavations extended to under the arch, the people feared that it would fall, and
began to suspect malice on the part of the Goth, thinking that a desire to
destroy the Roman monuments might still prevail in that nation.   So they
rose against him and compelled him to take to flight, and the work was
abandoned."   Ap. NARDINI, *Roma antica*, ed. NIBBY, i. p. 40.

him, but there came to be assigned to him all sorts of stories of other men who had gained a like reputation also. One of these men, as is well known, was the pope Sylvester II., or Gerbert, who earned his name as a magician by a knowledge of mechanics and mathematics which, in an ecclesiastic of that period and above all a pope, was a simple scandal. It was the easier to confound the two names seeing that many writers, such as Gervasius of Tilbury, Elinandus, Alberigo and others, who mentioned the legends about Vergil, mentioned those connected with Gerbert also. An instance of such confusion is to be found in the poems mentioned above.

It is stated in the *Mirabilia* that where the church of St. Balbina in Rome now stands there stood formerly the *Mutatorium Caesaris*, and that in it was a candelabrum made of the mineral called *asbestos*, which, when once lighted and exposed to the air, could never be extinguished, as the etymology of the word implied. Exactly the same legend is found in the *Image du Monde* connected with the name of Vergil, the sole difference being that, instead of a candelabrum, there appear two tapers and a torch which could not be extinguished. In the *Cleomadès* and the *Sette Savi*[13] it is a constantly burning fire, before which is the statue of an archer with an arrow ready strung pointing towards the fire and bearing an inscription in Hebrew, 'If any one touches me, I shall shoot.' One day an idler, who probably did not understand Hebrew, touched the figure; the arrow flew into the fire and put it out, and it could never again be lighted. This legend, applied here to Vergil,[14] had already been told of Gerbert. Similar is the story that, in the Campus Martius at Rome, there was a statue, pointing

---

[13] So too in the *Fleur des Histoires* of JEAN MANSEL. *Vide* DU MÉRIL, *Mélanges*, p. 438.

[14] In the *Eneide* of HEINRICH VON VELDEKE it is ascribed to a magician called *Geometras*. In the *Romans d'Alixandre* (ed. MICHELANT, p. 46) an ever-burning lamp is attributed to Plato:

> "En miliu de la vile ont drecié un piler.
> C. pies avoit de haut; Platons le fist lever;
> Deseure ot une lampe, en sou I. candeler
> Qui par jor et par nuit art et reluist si cler
> Que partout en peut-on et venir et aler,
> Et tous voient les gaites qui le doivent garder."

with the first finger of its right hand and bearing on its fore-
head the inscription, ' *Hic percute*.' No one before Gerbert
had been able to guess the meaning of these words. When the
sun was in the zenith, he observed where the shadow of the
finger fell, and, having marked the place, returned there at
night with a single servant. After various incantations the
earth opened, and gave access to a subterranean cavern full of
all sorts of treasure. In this cavern was a chamber with a
carbuncle set above a shield and emitting a miraculous light.
A number of knights, all of gold, stood in the passages, and
opposite the carbuncle was the figure of a child with a bent
bow. As soon as one touched any of these treasures all the
knights shook their weapons. Gerbert's servant however
could not resist the temptation of the many beautiful things all
round him, and so took up a little knife and put it in his
pocket, whereupon the figure of the child immediately let fly
its arrow, which struck the carbuncle and extinguished it, nor
could they find the way out till the knife was restored.[15] The
first part of this story, that is to say the part relating to the
statue and the treasure, is also attributed to Vergil, with a few
variations, by Ians Enenkel.[16] Others tell the story without
mentioning either Gerbert or Vergil, but speak merely of a
certain *clericus*.[17] Finally it may be remarked that this legend
is merely a variation on Zobeid's story in the Arabian Nights.[18]

In like manner, just as Gerbert is said to have made a head
which spoke [19] and foretold the future, his own death being

---

[15] WILL. MALMESBURY, *De gest. reg. ang.*, lib. ii. cap. 10; ALBERIC DE
TROIS FONT., *Chron.* par. ii. pp. 37–41; VINCENT DE BEAUVAIS, *Speculum historiale*, lib. 24, cap. 98 seqq.; HOCK, *Gerbertus*, cap. 15.

[16] V. D. HAGEN, *Gesammtabenteuer*, ii. p. 525 seqq.; MASSMANN, *Kaiserchronik*, iii. p. 450.

[17] *Gesta Romanorum*, cap. 107 (ed. KELLER).

[18] Page 100 of LOISELEUR'S edition. (*Pantheon lit.*). Cp. too the *Thousand
and One Days*, p. 346 (same edition).

[19] The story of the talking head, which Albertus Magnus made and St.
Thomas Aquinas destroyed, is well-known. A similar head was attributed to
the Marquis of Villena. TOSTADO (*Sup. num.*, cap. xxi.) speaks of a bronze
head which prophesied in the village of Tabara. Its chief use was to tell
when there was a Jew in the place, which it did by crying out "Iudaeus
adest" till the Jew was removed. Thus too, in Northern mythology, Odin
learns the future from the head of the giant Mimir. Cp. THORPE, *Northern
mythology*, i. p. 15; SIMROCK, *Edda*, p. 392.

caused through a misunderstanding of one of its predictions,[20] so a similar story is told in the *Image du Monde* and *Renart contrefait*[21] of Vergil. One day, when about to start on a journey, he consulted this head, which answered that if he took care of *his head*, all would be well. He thought that this referred to the prophetic head, but while on his journey he was not sufficiently careful to keep the sun off his own head, and died in consequence of sunstroke. Now here we have a fact which is one of many others that prove that the attribution of these legends to Vergil could only have taken place among more or less educated people; for while it is an historical fact, mentioned in the chief biography of the poet, that he died from the effects of a sunstroke while on a journey,[22] no such incident finds a place in any of the popular Neapolitan legends.

The reader has perhaps already been wearied by the long succession of puerile stories which it has been necessary to tell, and I must make the more claim on his indulgence seeing that the series of them is by no means yet complete. But however tedious may appear the dissection of these phantastic triviali-ties, I trust that the prospect of being thereby enabled to explain a most singular phenomenon will induce him, as it has induced me, to persevere.

[20] ALBERIC DE TROIS-FONTAINES, *Chron.* l. c.; HOOK, *Gerbertus*, l. c.

[21] Cp. too BART. SIBYLLA (end of 15th cent.) *Peregrin. quaest.*, dec. iii., quaest. 2.

[22] "Dum Megara vicinum oppidum ferventissimo sole cognoscit languorem nactus est eumque non intermissa navigatione auxit, ita ut gravior aliquanto Brundusium appelleret, ubi paucis diebus obiit." DONAT., *Vit. Verg.*, p. 62 seq.

CHAPTER VII

DURING the same period as that to which the legends describing Vergil as a magician belong, the view that the Sibyl had foretold the coming of Christ was growing popular among the lower classes. This idea, originally started in the times of controversy with the pagans, had spread among the Fathers and other ecclesiastical writers and was firmly fixed in the medieval mind; issuing from theological literature, it had become part of the popular religious notions, and in the 12th century we meet with it repeatedly among laity and clergy alike. Hence the mention of the Sibyl in romantic literature becomes from this time onward as common as is the representation of her in works of art down to the 16th century.[1] It was an idea intelligible to every one, being derived from the more obvious part of the Christian doctrine as elaborated by the medieval theologians; it was moreover a very favourite idea with these theologians, one which they were continually bringing forward and on which they laid much stress, so that every one was familiar with the purport of the Franciscan poet's well-known line, 'teste David cum Sibylla.'[2] This great notoriety achieved by the Sibyl, or rather the Sibyls, was the result of the Church's method of communicating with the faithful and spreading the doctrines of her religion. The religious instruction, the preaching, and still more the Miracle Plays, standing as it were halfway between the liturgies and the popular poetry,

---

[1] Cp. PIPER, *Mythologie der christ. Kunst*, i. p. 472 seqq.

[2] Already in the 5th century the verses of the Sibyl were recited in churches on Christmas Day. Cp. DU MÉRIL, *Origines latines du théâtre moderne*, p. 185 seqq., where there are other notices of the Sibyl in the middle ages.

were all calculated to assist in the dissemination of such ideas
as these. These naïve dramatisations of religious beliefs,
thoroughly popular in character and without any pretence at
literary merit, gave the Church a great hold over the minds of
the people, and both of themselves and also by their influence
on the development of the modern theatre contributed not a
little to the spread of these ideas in the new literature which
was at that time growing up.

We have already seen how closely the name of Vergil was in
this connection associated with that of the Sibyl, and how
familiar the Fourth Eclogue, with its Sibylline prophecy of
Christ, was to the ecclesiastics of the middle ages. Vergil
therefore followed the Sibyl on the road to popularity, and all
the more readily seeing that his name was already familiar for
other reasons.[3] In sermons, especially at Christmas, he would
be mentioned in connection with the Sibyl; when she was
represented in Christian art, he was usually by her side, or
there were at least quoted the famous lines from the Fourth
Eclogue;[4] in more than one Miracle Play, Vergil and the Sibyl
appear in the list of characters.[5] Already in the 11th century,
in the celebrated Latin Mystery of the Nativity performed in
the Abbey of St. Martial at Limoges, Vergil appears among
the other prophets of Christ;[6] and, similarly, in that performed

[3] " Evvi Femonoè, quella Sibilla
　　　Che ridicea li risponsi d'Apollo,
　　　Che delle x. Sibille fu quella
　　　E Virgilio il su' dire versificollo;
　　　Di Cristo disse la prima novella
　　　E del die del giudicio e profetollo."

L'Intelligenza ap. OZANAM, Documents inédits, p. 364 seq. Cp. too the ancient
German poem Die Erlösung (ed. BARTSCH, Quedl. u. Leip., 1858) p. 56 seqq.
v. 1903–1980.

[4] Cp. Supra, p. 102.

[5] Cp. REIDT, Das geistliche Schauspiel des Mittelalters in Deutschland, Fr.
a. M., 1868, p. 27. For the bibliography of this important part of the history
of the modern theatre vide HANUS, Lat. böhm. Oster-spiele des 14–15 Jahrh.,
Prague, 1863, p. 17 seqq.

[6] In MONMERQUÉ et MICHEL, Théâtre français au moyen-âge, p. 9; DU
MÉRIL, Orig. lat. du théât. mod., p. 184; WEINHOLD, Weihnachtspiele, p. 70
seq. On the origin of these Mysteries and their connection with a sermon
of St. Augustine on the Nativity, vide SEPET, Les prophètes du Christ; étude
sur les origines du théâtre au moyen-âge, in the Bibl. de l'école des Chartes,
1867 (tom. iii. sér. 6), p. 1 seqq., 210 seqq.

at Rheims.[7] After Moses, Isaiah, Jeremiah, Daniel, Habakkuk, David, Simeon, Elizabeth, and John the Baptist, the procentor calls upon Vergil in these words:

> ' Vates Maro gentilium
> Da Christo testimonium,'

whereupon Vergil comes forward in the character and dress of a young man and says:

> ' Ecce polo, demissa solo, nova progenies est.'

Then, after Nebuchadnezzar and the Sibyl have been called upon to give evidence, the procentor turns to the Jews with the words:

> ' Iudaea incredula
> Cur manes adhuc, inverecunda?'

Vergil plays a similar part in the Mystery of the Foolish Virgins,[8] and in other Mysteries written in the vernacular, in German, Dutch, etc.[9] In a great dramatic work by Arnold Immessen (15th century), by a curious inversion of ideas, the Cumaean Sibyl cites Vergil as an authority.[10]

[7] Cp. Du Cange, *Gloss. med. et. inf. lat.* (ed. Henschel) s. v. *festum asinorum.*

[8] Wright, *Early Mysteries*, p. 62.

[9] Cp. Weinhold, *Weihnachtspiele*, p. 74; Du Méril, *Mél. arch.*, p. 456; *Mittelniederländisches Osterspiel*, ed. Zacher in Haupt's *Zeitschr. f. deutsch. Alterth.*, ii. p. 310; Piper, *Virgil als Theolog und Prophet* in the *Evan. Kalend.*, 1862; Stecher, *La lég. de Vergile en Belg.*, p. 598, seq., p. 72. In a French Mystery on the "Vengeance of Jesus" there speak before Tiberius in favour of Christ Terence, Boccaccio and Juvenal, the last of whom mentions that in the forty-second year of Octavius there was a rumour that a virgin was about to bear a son;

> " Le noble poete Virgille
> Qui lors étoit en ceste ville
> Composa aucuns mots notables
> Lesquels on a vu véritables
> Et plurieurs grands choses en dict
> Naguaires avant son trespas."

V. L. Paris, *Toiles peintes de Reims*, p. 680.

[10] Sibilla Cumaea
> (*quae fuit tempore Tarquinii Prisci.*)
> " Ik finde ok van dussen saken
> dat de meister Virgilius
> versch gemaket hebbe, de ludet alsus:
> Magnus ab integro," etc.

Der Sündenfall und die Marienklage, ed. Schönemann (Han., 1855), p. 97; Piper, *Virgil*, etc., p. 78.

Vergil does not, however, always take part in the Mysteries; sometimes the Sibyl is the sole representative of the Gentile prophets. In a Latin Mystery of the Nativity the Sibyl recognises the coming of Christ by the star which guides the Magi.[11] This star, according to an old Spanish poet, was also seen by Vergil.[12]

The dissemination of this idea among the people led to the production of a number of legends which, after going through various phases, eventually became connected with those that described Vergil as a magician. The poet's tendencies towards Christianity are referred to in the Latin verses sung at Mantua, which have already been quoted;[13] these speak of St. Paul's visit to his grave, a legend which is not exclusively Mantuan, but appears, with additional details, in the *Image du Monde*.[14] According to this, St. Paul, who was a man of great learning, was grieved to find on his arrival at Rome that Vergil was just dead, and his grief was the greater owing to the fact of the poet's having written verses so clearly referring to the coming of Christ. He saw that he had had a soul inclined to Christianity and regretted that he had come too late to convert him :

> 'Ah ! si ge t'éusse trouvé .
> Que ge t'éusse à Dieu donné ! '

he exclaims, which is exactly the sentiment expressed by the Latin verses. Such interest, however, did he take in Vergil's death that he eventually discovered the subterranean chamber in which the poet was buried. The access to it was most difficult; a furious wind blew, and terrible sounds were heard.

---

[11] " Tertio loco Sibylla gesticulose procedat, quae inspiciendo stellam cum gestu nobili cantet :

" Haec stellae novitas fert novum nuntium," etc.

Carmina burana, ed. SCHMELLER, Stuttg., i. 47, p. 81.

[12] " Virgilio de Mantua fué sabio poeta
ca fué el primero que vido cometa
à partes de Grecia sus vrayos lançando."

FRAY DIEGO DE VALENCIA, in the *Cancionero de Baena; vide* DU MÉRIL, *Mél. arch.* p. 460.

[13] Supra, p. 98.

[14] This passage appears in DU MÉRIL, *Mél. arch.*, p. 456 seqq.

The apostle, however, was able to see Vergil seated between two lighted tapers, surrounded by books thrown in confusion on the floor; above him hung a lamp, and before him stood an archer with drawn bow. This St. Paul saw from outside, but entry was difficult, for at the door stood two bronze men who kept plying two steel hammers with such persistency that it would have fared ill with any who dared to cross the threshold. The two hammerers the apostle was able to stop, but no sooner had he done so than the archer's arrow flew against the lamp and everything fell into dust, and St. Paul, who had wished to bring away Vergil's books, was compelled to return empty-handed.

Among the legends of miracles, immediately preceding the birth of Christ, which foretold his coming to the heathen, a celebrated one is that of the church of *S. Maria in Ara Caeli* at Rome. According to this legend, Augustus summoned the Sibyl to enquire of her concerning the divine honours decreed him by the Senate. The Sibyl answered him that the king who was to reign eternally should come from heaven; and straightway the heavens opened and Augustus saw a virgin of marvellous beauty seated on an altar with a child in her arms, and heard a voice saying, 'This is the altar of the Son of God.' The emperor fell on his face in adoration, and afterwards declared the vision to the Senate. On the spot on the Capitol where the vision was seen was subsequently built the church which still bears the name of *S. Maria in Ara Caeli*. This legend occurs already in the 8th century, in Byzantine writers, and subsequently finds its way into the *Golden Legend*, the *Gesta Romanorum*, the *Mirabilia* and other widely-read works; [15] it is more than once represented in art, and notices of it in writers of the 12th century are especially frequent. Even Petrarch mentions it in one of his letters.[16] The *Mirabilia* relates, in addition, a similar legend, which is also found in other contemporary works.[17] 'In his palace, where stood the temples

---

[15] Cp. MASSMANN, *Kaiserchronik*, iii. p. 553 seqq.; PIPER, *Myth. de christ. Kunst*, i. p. 480 seqq.

[16] Cp. PIPER, *op. cit.*, i. p. 485 seqq.

[17] Cp. MASSMANN, *Kaiserchronik*, iii. p. 554 seqq.

of Piety and Concord, Romulus had set up a golden statue, with
the words, "I shall not fall till a virgin shall bear a son."
When Christ was born, the statue fell to the ground.'[18] Others
refer this to the temple of Pallas, others to the temple of Peace,
others again to the *Salvatio Romae*, and ascribe the prediction
to Vergil. Thus, Alexander Neckam, after speaking of the
Salvatio Romae, adds, 'When the poet was asked how long the
gods would allow this noble edifice to stand, he answered, "Till
a virgin shall bear a son." On hearing this the people clapped
their hands and exclaimed, "Then it will stand for ever." But
on the day that the Saviour was born the building immediately
fell into ruins.' [19] The original significance of the legend was
thus altered by the introduction of the name of Vergil. The
words as coming from Romulus are a boast which time proved
vain ; as coming from Vergil, with his legendary connection
with the Sibyl and his position as prophet of Christ, they are a
prophecy.

A development of this legend, as applied to Vergil, occurs in
a French poem, as yet unpublished, of which there is a MS. in
the Turin library.[20] This work is a curious combination of
several poems, two of which, the one entitled *Vespasian, or the
Revenge of Jesus on the Jews*, the other *The Deeds of the Lorrai-
ners*,[21] are already known. To connect these two poems, there

[18] The signs of the coming of Christ are enumerated as follows in the
Flores Temporum of HERMANNUS GIGAS : "Fons olei Romae erupit ; vineae
Engaddi balsamum protulerunt ; omnes sodomitae obierunt ; bos et asinus
ante praesepe genua flexerunt ; idola Aegypti corruerunt ; imago Romuli
cecidit ; templum pacis corruit ; mane tres soles oriebantur et in unum
paulatim jungebantur ; meridie circulus aureus in caelo apparuit in quo
virginem cum puero Caesar vidit, et mox insonuit : hic est arcus caeli."
For the variants *vide* MASSMANN, *op. cit.*, p. 557 seq.
[19] *De naturis rerum* (ed. WRIGHT), p. 310. A version of this legend occurs
in the poem by GUILLAUME LE CLERC DE NORMANDIE entitled *De Notre Dame*;
this was partly published by MARTIN, *Le Besant le Dieu* (Halle, 1869), p.
xxxvii.–xl., and in full by STENGEL, *op. citand.*, p. 14 seq.
[20] Cod. gall. xxxvi. ; *v.* PASINI, *Catal.*, etc., ii. p. 472. On fol. 583 is the
date, "Ces livres fu escris en l'an de l'incarnation MCCC. et XI. au mois
de joing."
[21] This MS. was unknown to both PAULIN PARIS and DU MÉRIL. There
is some account of this part of it by PROST in the *Revue de l'Est*, 1864, pp.
5–9. Since then it has been described at greater length and more correctly
by STENGEL, *Mittheilungen aux franz. Handschriften der Turiner Universi-*

is inserted, by way of introduction to the second of them, a third, narrating the history of St. Severin, who is related on the one side to Vespasian, on the other to Hervis and Garin of Lorraine. But this is not enough. As the romance of Vespasian recounted the vengeance taken for the death of Jesus, it was necessary to describe the antecedents to that event; first, therefore, comes a long poem which begins with the Creation and narrates the whole story of the Old and New Testament down to the Crucifixion. Not content, however, with taking his account direct from the Bible, the author has been pleased to develope the legend mentioned above, and to introduce Vergil as relating the whole story in question. In the only MS. of this poem with which I am acquainted the beginning is wanting; enough however remains to enable one to form an idea of the treatment of the subject. Instead of a good Octavian or Romulus, we have here *Noirons li arabis*, a gloomy tyrant corresponding to the medieval idea of Nero, a worshipper of the Devil and of Mohammed, an entirely imaginary character, who builds, in honour of his gods, a palace resplendent with gold and gems, then summons Vergil and says to him, 'You who know all things, tell me how long my palace will last.' Vergil answers, 'It will last till a virgin bears a son.' 'Then it will last for ever, for what you say can never be.' 'Yet such a day will come,' replies Vergil. And in fact thirty years later Christ is born and the palace falls to the ground. Nero sends angrily for Vergil and says to him, 'You knew then that a virgin should bear a son; why did you not tell me?' Vergil then proceeds to expound the new faith, to which Nero will not listen, and an altercation begins. At last the emperor declares that he and Vergil will have a duel, and that the victor shall cut off his opponent's head. Vergil agrees, but wishes, before entering the lists, to go home once more to visit his parents and Hippocrates and his other learned friends. He goes, calls them all together and expounds to them the situation. Hippocrates sets to work to search in his books, and finds there everything concerning the coming of Jesus,

täts-Bibliothek, p. 12 seqq. The part that concerns us has no title of its own, being merely a long preamble to the *Romans de Vespasien*.

which he communicates to Vergil; the latter, strong in this invincible armour, goes off confident of success. Nero perceives that his enemy carries weapons which will overpower him, and, seeing his end approaching, declares to Vergil who he really is. He tells the old story of *Lucibel* or *Lucifer*, and of the rebellious angels who were changed into demons, one of whom he professes to be; he discourses further of their mission on earth, of the building of Babylon and similar subjects. Vergil thereupon proceeds to relate the whole of sacred history, beginning with the creation of the world. The author having thus reached the point at which he was aiming, embarks upon a boundless sea of words, entirely losing sight of Vergil, and even forgetting to mention the result of the duel; a scene however, at the end, in which Nero and Mohammed are found talking to one another in hell, leads one to infer that the former was decapitated by Vergil. This poem, in treatment no less than subject-matter, may probably take rank as a masterpiece of imbecility.

With this phantastic production of a French troubadour may be compared, in so far as the connection of Vergil with Christianity is concerned, the works of two German writers, the almost contemporary *Reinfrit von Braunschweig* [22] and the *Wartburgkrieg*.[23] The legend, as it appears in these two German productions, is as follows. On the Mountain of Sorrows (the *Magnetberg* or *Agetstein*, to which medieval German poetry makes frequent reference [24]) lived a great magician, a Greek or Babylonian prince, called Zabulon (*i.e.* Devil); he had read in the stars of the Saviour's birth 1,200 years before that event, and employed all his arts to frustrate or postpone it. He was the inventor of necromancy and astrology, and wrote numerous books on these subjects with the above-mentioned object.

---

[22] *Vide* the extract from *Reinfrit* given by GÖDEKE in the *Archiv. des hist. Vereins für Niedersachsen*, N.F., 1849, p. 270, and the edition of it by BARTSCH in the collection of the *Liter. Verein.*, 109. *Vide* v. 21023–54, 21314–713, 24252–69.

[23] SIMROCK, *Wartburgkrieg*, p. 195 seqq., 303. Cp. v. D. HAGEN, *Briefe in die Heimath*, iii. p. 169 seq.; GENTHE, *Leben und Fortleben*, etc., p. 68 seq.

[24] Cp. CHOLEVIUS, *Gesch. d. deutsch. Poesie nach ihren antiken Elementen*, i. 96; BARTSCH, *Herzog Ernst*, p. cxlviii. seqq.

When the 1,200 years were nearly passed, there was living
a very virtuous man named Vergil, who, having given
everything away to others, was reduced to a state of great
poverty. Vergil knew of this Zabulon, of his arts and his
malevolence, so he embarked on board ship and sailed for the
Mount of Sorrows. Thanks to the assistance of a spirit enclosed in a ruby of the form of a fly set in a ring, he succeeded
in obtaining possession of the books and treasures of the
magician, while in the meantime the 1,200 years were expired
and the Virgin gave birth to Christ.

Thus the primitive idea of Vergil as prophet of Christ, after
passing through various stages, comes to be connected with
one of the legends describing Vergil as a magician—that one,
namely, that relates how he obtained the book from which he
learnt the black arts.[25] In this we recognise the book on the
Ars Notoria, which, according to Gervasius, the Englishman
found in Vergil's grave; this book has here become the book
of Zabulon, and in other accounts becomes Solomon's book on
necromancy, which, as is well-known, was a standard work on
the subject. In the *Wartburgkrieg*, Vergil is described as
having only obtained this book with great difficulty.[26] But the
legend appears also in other forms, without any connection
with the coming of Christ.

Enenkel also, a more or less contemporary writer, describes in
his *Weltbuch* how Vergil, ' that child of hell,' [27] as he calls him,
acquired his extraordinary proficiency in magic. While working
one day in his vineyard, he happened to dig up a bottle containing twelve devils, a discovery which gave him great pleasure.
One of these devils promised, if set at liberty, to initiate him in
every secret art. ' Initiate me first,' answered Vergil; ' then I
will let you out.' So the devils taught him magic and there-

[25] There are similar legends related of the magicians Heliodorus and Pietro Barliario.

[26] " Wer gab dir Zabulones buch, sage fürwert, wiser man
          Das Virgilius ûf den Agetsteine
          mit grossen nôten gewan. "

[27] " Er was gar der helle kint." Ap. v. d. HAGEN, *Gesammtabenteuer*, ii.
p. 513 seqq.

upon he broke the bottle and set them at liberty. Heinrich
von Müglin (circa 1350) relates in verse this same story in a
form approaching nearer to that of the *Reinfrit*, but without
any mention of the coming of Christ.[28] According to him,
Vergil leaves Venice in company with others to seek his fortune and sets sail for the Mount of Sorrows.[29] There he finds
a spirit shut up in a bottle, which, in return for its liberty,
shows him the place where, under the head of a corpse, lies a
book of magic. He has hardly opened the book when 80,000
devils appear and place themselves at his disposal; he thereupon sets them to work to pave a long street. Later, in the
15th century, Felix Hemmerlin[30] too relates that a devil put
Vergil in possession of the book of Solomon on condition of
being set at liberty. Vergil accordingly opened the bottle in
which it was; but seeing it begin to assume enormous proportions, did not think it wise to leave such a creature at large
and bethought him of a stratagem. 'I am sure you cannot
get back into that bottle,' he said to the devil; the devil said
he could, and to prove his point did so, whereupon Vergil at
once put on the stopper, sealed it with the seal of Solomon,
and left the devil imprisoned for good. Thus, in this story of
the imprisoned spirit putting its supernatural powers at the
service of its liberator, we find applied to Vergil a well-known
legend of Rabbinical or Mohammedan origin, which is familiar
to every one from the Arabian Nights and forms moreover the
basis of the famous *Diable boiteux*. The same story is told
too of Paracelsus, and appears moreover in various popular
legends of the present day.[31]

---

[28] This poem was published by ZINGERLE in the *Germania* of PFEIFFER, v.
p. 369 seqq.
[29] Vergil starts on his voyage with a prayer to the Madonna:

" Mariâ muter, reine meit,
  bhut uns vor leit !
wir sweben ûf wildes meeres vlut, got der soll uns bewarn."

[30] *De nobilitate*, cap. ii. fol. viii. Cp. ROTH, *op. cit.*, p. 298.
[31] Cp. DUNLOP-LIEBRECHT, pp. 185–483; GRIMM, *Kinder- und Hausmärchen*,
xcix.; DU MÉRIL, *Études d'Arch.*, p. 463; JÜLG, *Arji-Borji*, p. 70; BENFEY,
Pantschatantra, i. p. 115 seqq.; VERNALECKEN, *Mythen und Bräuche des
Volkes in Oesterreich*, p. 262.

In this way was the conception of Vergil as magician spread through every country Latin or Germanic; there was not a writer of any sort or kind who was not familiar with it; and the richer in improvements and additions the legend grew, the richer was it likely to grow, for the proverb *on ne prête qu'aux riches* holds very true of legends. A similar though somewhat more abstract conception of Vergil, arising out of these various stories, appears in a curious Latin work entitled *Virgilii Cordubensis philosophia*,[32] which, though it does not actually relate any Vergilian legends, yet belongs to this phase of thought by reason both of its title and subject matter. This Vergil of Cordova is described as an Arabian philosopher, whose work was translated into Latin at Toledo in 1290.[33] But the *translator* was certainly no Moor, nor did he know much about Arabic, or he would not have called an Arabian philosopher Vergil and made him a contemporary at Cordova of Seneca, Avicenna, Averroes and Algazel! He appears to have been a charlatan who wished to give himself authority by taking the name of Vergil and making a profession of Arabian learning. With striking effrontery he asserts, at the beginning of his work, that all the scholars and students who came from various parts to Toledo found it necessary, when discussing any difficult problem, to have recourse to him, knowing how thorough was his acquaintance with everything abstruse, thanks to that science 'which some call necromancy, but we *Refulgentia*.' They sent to ask him to come to Toledo, but he did not wish to leave Cordova, and told them to come to him, which they accordingly did. Then follows in the book an account of the learned discussions which ensued on such subjects as First Causes, the World and the Human Soul, and the important revelations made by the spirits which he summoned for this purpose. He speaks further of these spirits, and also of the *ars notoria*, which

---

[32] Published by HEINE in his *Bibliotheca anecdotorum seu veterum monumentorum ecclesiasticorum collectio novissima*. Pars i., Lips., 1848, p. 211 seqq.

[33] My friend, Dr. STEINSCHNEIDER, has communicated to me his doubts as to this date; he does not believe the work to be earlier than Raimond de Pennaforte.

he describes as a sacred science, which only he who is free
from sin can learn; and states that the authors of it were the
good angels, who committed it to Solomon.[34]   The latter thereupon shut up in a bottle all the evil spirits, except one lame
one, which subsequently succeeded in liberating all the others.
When Alexander came to Jerusalem, his master Aristotle, who
up to that time was a quite insignificant person, managed to
find out where Solomon's books were stored, and, having obtained possession of them, gained by their means his world-
wide celebrity for wisdom.   The Latin of this work is very
peculiar; no less so is the philosophy, which is a strange
medley of Jewish and Rabbinic ideas, with occasional Christian
doctrines, such as that of the Trinity and Unity.   Of Vergil
there is really nothing in all this but the name, but it is clear
that the author's idea in adopting this name was his conception
of Vergil as magician, just as the connection of Vergil with
the study of grammar led the equally remarkable grammarian,
to whom reference has already been made, to adopt the name
of Vergil for his grammatical work.   Thus two most different
forms of the conception of Vergil lead to the same result, a
phenomenon which is well worthy of note as demonstrating not
only the vicissitudes to which this conception was subjected in
the course of its association with various phases of thought, but
also the fact that this association was in many cases so close
that the mere name of Vergil became symbolical of the branch
of learning with which it was connected.

Nor was anything which seemed to the popular mind characteristic of a magician omitted in the case of Vergil.   This view
of him once firmly established, the rest came easily of itself.
No good magician had ever failed to study at Toledo, so Vergil,
like Gerbert and others, had to go through a course of studies
at that city.   'Men go to Paris,' says Elinandus, 'to study

[34] "Et unus magister legebat de arte notoria quae est scientia sancta et
ita debet esse sanctus qui eam voluerit legere; similiter et audientes sancti
et immaculati et sine peccato debent esse," etc., p. 242.   The fabulous
notices of this writer as to the various professors of the *ars notoria*, of
pyromancy, of necromancy, and of geomancy at Cordova have all been
solemnly accepted as facts by AMADOR DE LOS RIOS, *Hist. crit. de la lit.
esp.*, ii. p. 159

the liberal arts, to Bologna for law, to Salerno for medicine, to
Toledo for necromancy, and nowhere to learn honesty.'[35] The
renown of Vergil as a magician and his connection with Naples
led to that city's sharing with Toledo the honour of originating
the black arts.[36] It was inevitable that in the world of
romance, where Vergil would meet so many other magicians,
he should come to be connected with some of them. In the
Parzival of Wolfram von Eschenbach the magician Klinsor is
a native of the Land of Labour and Vergil is one of his ancestors;[37] nor is a connection with Merlin wanting.[38] Thus
the legend was no longer a simple catalogue of wonders worked
by Vergil, but came to contain a series of personal details,
furnishing all the materials for a biography. We have already
seen how, in the *Image du Monde* and *Renart contrefait*, the
story closes with the death of Vergil. His personal appearance,
further, is described in the first of these two poems:

> ' Il fu de petite estature
> Maigres et corbes par nature,
> Et aloit la teste baissant,
> Toz jors vers terre resgardant:
> Car coustume est de soutil sage
> C'à terre esgarde par usage.'

So too in the *Dolopathos*:

> ' Virgile de poure estature
> Et petite personne estoit;
> Com philosophe se vestoit.'

There is further a class of legends into which the name of
Vergil is only introduced occasionally, and which do not appear

---

[35] *Vide* TISSIER, *Biblioth. cisterc.*, vii. p. 257.

[36] " De Toulete vint et de Naples
qui des batailles sont les chapes
à une nuit la Nigromance."

La bataille des VII. arts, ap. JUBINAL, *Oeuvres de Ruteboeuf*, ii. p. 423.

[37] " Sin lant heizt *Terre de Labûr.*
Von des nachkomm er ist erborn,
der ouch vil wunder het erkorn
von Napels Virgilius."

Parzival, ed. LACHMANN, p. 309.

[38] In BONAMENTE ALIPRANDO, of whom we shall speak lower down.

in any collection of legends having reference to his magical powers; their association with him is quite arbitrary, and arises merely from a momentary confusion of ideas on the part of the narrator or compiler. This is the cause in the *Gesta Romanorum*, a work which had a most varied career. The author was doubtless thinking of the *Salvatio Romae* and the magic mirror when he ascribed to Vergil a statue which used to denounce all breakers of the law.[39] The mirror seems likewise to have been in his mind when he gives, in Story 102, the name of Vergil to the *clericus* who showed a man how his wife and her paramour were performing an incantation to kill him, and caused the incantation to kill the adulterer instead. Similarly the name of Vergil appears in other places, especially in the German and English versions of the *Gesta*, where it did not stand in the original,[40] *e.g.* in the story of the Merchant of Venice. Such liberties are not unusual, and only show how familiar the name of Vergil the Magician was to writers of every class. Thus, the romance writers, knowing the legend which made Vergil the founder of Naples, ascribed to him a number of other buildings and cities,[41] chiefly in Italy; in southern Italy itself, outside Naples, various buildings were attributed to him, as, for instance, those on the island of Ponza

---

[39] Cap. 57 ed. KELLER. Cp. BRUNET's note in the *Violier des hist. rom.*, p. 129 seq.   To this story alludes a Latin poem pub. by FRANCOWITZ (FLACIUS ILLYRICUS) in his collection *De corrupto ecclesiae statu*, Basilea, 1557; Justice speaks:

> " En sic meum opus ago
> ut Romae fecit imago
> quam sculpsit Vergilius,
> quae manifestare suevit
> fures, sed caesa quievit
> et os clausit digito;
> nunquam ultra dixit verbum
> de perditione rerum
> palam nec in abdito."

[40] Cp. WRIGHT, *The Political Songs of England from the reign of John to that of Edward II.*, p. 388.

[41] ALARDE DE CAMBRAI says in his *Diz des Philosophes :*

> " Virgiles fu aprés li sages ;
> bien fu emploiés ses aages ;
> grant science en lui habonda;
> mainte riche cité fonda "

near Gaeta;[42] while the author of a Franco-Italian poem, as yet unpublished, describes him as the founder of Brescia.[43]

We may close our account of this sporadic class of Vergilian legends by a somewhat more detailed notice of the legend which connects the poet with Julius Caesar.

The Romans believed in the middle ages that the golden ball on the top of the Vatican obelisk contained the ashes of Julius Caesar.[44] Hence the medieval inscription attributed to Marbod, Bishop of Rennes, which appears, with the legend to which it refers, in the *Mirabilia* :

> ' Caesar, tantus eras quantus et orbis,
> et nunc in modico clauderis antro.' [45]

This inscription, with the two additional verses,—

> ' post hunc quisque sciat se ruiturum
> et iam nulla mori gloria tollat,'

is attributed by Elinandus to Vergil.[46] According to a legend quoted in the *Victorial* of Gutierre Diaz de Games (15th century), this obelisk was made by Solomon, who wished the ball on it to contain his bones. When Julius Caesar died, Vergil went to Jerusalem and treated with the Jews for the purchase of this obelisk. The Jews, thinking to make a good business of the matter, offered it him on condition of receiving a certain sum for every day it was on the road between Jerusalem and

---

[42] Ruy Gonzales de Clavijo († 1412), speaking of the island of Ponza, says, " hay en ella grandes edificios de muy grande obra que fizo Virgilio." V. Ticknor, *Hist. of Span. Lit.*, i. p. 185.

[43] This poem occurs in a 13th century MS. of the Marciana of Venice. Speaking of Uggieri, it says :

> " El albergò a un bon oster ;
> qel fo Virgilio qi la fondò primer,"

i.e., the city of Besgora, which, from the Tuscan translation, we learn is Brescia. I owe this note to my learned pupil and friend Prof. Rajna.

[44] Cp. Gregorovius, *Gesch. d. St. Rom im Mittelalter*, iii. 557, and Massmann, *Kaiserchronik*, iii. p. 537 seqq. Dolce (*Il primo vol. delle op. burl. del Berni*, etc., part ii. p. 271), alluding to this, says :

> " Non la Guglia, ov' è il pomo che accogliea
> Il cener di chi senza Durlindana
> *Orbem terrarum* si sottomettea."

[45] V. l. : At nunc exigua clauderis urna.

[46] Ap. Tissier, *Biblioth. patr. cisterc.*, vii. p. 222.

Rome; but Vergil had the laugh of them, for, by his magical powers, he made the obelisk pass from the one city to the other in a single night, and so the bones of Julius Cæsar took the place of those of Solomon.[47]

These isolated legends do not add much to the portrait we have already drawn of Vergil as magician, and might be multiplied almost indefinitely without increasing our knowledge; they were the mere outcome of the conception of him derived from those legends of which he is a more constant factor. But the picture of the legendary Vergil cannot be said to be yet complete. It was not to be expected that a character so well and universally known should not be brought into some connection with the fair sex; to the romantic mind such a thing would have seemed little short of an anomaly. The relations therefore, of Vergil to women are those which must now engage our attention.

[47] Vide *Bruchstücke aus den noch ungedruckten Theilen des Victorial von Gutierre Diaz de Games*, ed. L. G. LEMCKE, Marburg, 1865, p. 17 seqq.; *Le Victorial par Gutierre Diaz de Games*, trad. *de l'espagnol par le Comte* A. DE CIRCOURT *et le Comte* DE PUYMAIGRE, Paris, 1867, p. 39 seq., 542 seq. The same fact is related by JEAN D'OUTREMEUSE, *Le Myreur des Hist.*, i. p. 243 (ed. BORGNET, Brux., 1864). RABELAIS alludes to this when he says (ii. c. 33): "Pour ce l'on feit dixsept grosses pommes de cuivre plus grosses que celle qui est à Rome à l'aiguille de Virgile."

CHAPTER VIII

THOSE who maintain that Woman owes a deep debt of gratitude to Christianity and Chivalry, maintain what is contrary
to the facts. The romantic ideal of the Saint, no less than
that of the Lady, is an ideal irreconcileable with the well-being
of society. What, one may ask, would become of the human
race, if every woman were either a St. Theresa or an Isolde?
for these two characters, opposite as they are, are both equally
subversive to society in that they ignore its principal foundation, the family. Human nature in the middle ages had need
of all its strength to combat these two powerful principles, of
which the one wished to turn the world into a desert, where
every man should be for himself alone, while the other strove
to make of it a lunatic asylum, from which morality and
common sense were to be alike rigorously banished. On the
one side were the Fathers and the ecclesiastical writers, unanimous in their praises of celibacy as the only state which could
lead man to perfection—a doctrine not only absurd, but also
immoral, in that it is egotistical, is contrary to the first principles of human society, and places human perfection in direct
opposition to natural laws and the continued existence of the
human race. The sacred character given by the Christian
Church to marriage, which to many appears one of the chief
merits of Christianity, must seem a simple mockery to any one
acquainted with the history of the middle ages, when he considers this vast army of men in authority who on every occasion, both by precept and example, were doing their best to
bring woman and marriage into contempt. On the other side
was Chivalry, in a different manner, but with equally deadly

effect, loosening the bonds of married life and depriving woman
of those foundations on which her dignity, her purity and her
self-respect are based. In spite therefore of certain ideals of
chastity presented by the Christian hagiographies, in spite of
the incense burnt at the altar of Woman in romances, at
tourneys and in the Courts of Love, there never was a time in
the world's history in which women were more grossly insulted,
more shamefully reviled or more basely defamed than they
were in the middle ages, by men of every class, beginning with
the most serious writers of theology and going down to the
mountebanks of the street-plays. The number of anecdotes,
trivial or obscene, that drag women in the dirt is simply
infinite, and, incredible as it may seem, such anecdotes figure
not only in the repertories of buffoons, whose only object is to
amuse, but also in the collections of preachers, who used to
quote them in the pulpit with the professed object of drawing
a moral from them, though often enough they too were merely
anxious to raise a laugh.[1] Anyone who knows these collections
will understand the contemptuous indignation of the poet when
he cries :

> ' Ora si va con motti e con iscede
> A predicare, e pur che ben si rida,
> Gonfia il capuccio, e più non si richiede.

To this class of story belong all the more ancient of the
legends which connect Vergil with women. In the earliest
and most common of these, Vergil appears as in love with a
daughter of the Emperor of Rome ; his passion however is not
only not returned, but receives most cruel treatment at the
hands of its object, who cannot resist the temptation of making
a fool of the great man. Pretending to fall in with his views,
the lady proposes to introduce him secretly into her room by
drawing him up in a box to the window of the tower in which
she lives. Full of joy, Vergil agrees, and, arriving at the appointed hour, finds the box all ready for him ; he gets into it,
and with great satisfaction feels it moving upwards. For a

---

[1] Cp. GRAESSE, *Gesta Romanorum*, ii. p. 289 ; DU MÉRIL, *Poésies populaires latines du moyen-âge*, p. 315. For the literature of this subject *vide*
TOBLER, *Zeitschr. f. roman. Philol.*, ix. pp 288-290.

time all goes well; then suddenly, when half way, the box
stops, and remains suspended there till morning. Great is the
amusement of the Romans, who knew Vergil well, when they
see such a celebrated and serious person in such a situation.
Nor is this all; for the Emperor, informed of the matter,
threatens Vergil with all sorts of punishments as soon as he
is let down again. These his arts enable him to avert; but
the outrage is unpardonable, and he determines on a terrible
revenge. He causes all the fires in Rome to be suddenly extinguished and declares that the only means of rekindling them
is from the person of the Emperor's daughter, and that the fire
so obtained cannot be communicated from one to another but
that each person must fetch it for himself. After some hesitation, his commands have eventually to be obeyed; the Emperor's daughter is brought into the public square, the Romans
get fire from her in a way better left undescribed, and Vergil is
avenged.

This story consists of two distinct parts, which are here
united, but which also occur separately—the incident of the
outrage and the incident of the revenge. It is only in the
second that Vergil appears as a magician. The first belongs to
the vast cycle of stories which describe feminine cunning, and
expresses the common idea that no man, however great, is safe
from woman's wiles—an idea which found very frequent expression in the middle ages, and used to be illustrated by
numberless examples, some derived from history or tradition,
others purely legendary. David, Samson, Hercules, Hippocrates, Aristotle, are but a few in the long list of those who
followed their father Adam in falling victims to a woman; and
when Aristotle and Hippocrates had lent their names to such
stories, it was inevitable that Vergil should follow. We may
cite, for instance, the following lines of an anonymous French
poet:

> 'Par femme fut Adam deceu
> Et Virgile moqué en fu,
> David en fist faulx jugement
> Et Salemon faulx testament;
> Ypocras en fu enerbé;
> Sanson le fort deshonnoré;

> Femme chevaucha Aristote,
> Il n'est rien que femme n'assote.' [2]

Thus too Eustace Deschamps (14th cent.) writes:

> ' Par femme fu mis à destruction
> Sanxes le fort et Hercules en rage,
> Ly roy Davis à redargucion,
> Si fut Merlins soubz le tombel en caige;
> Nul ne se puet garder de leur langaige.
> Par femme fut en la corbeille à Romme
> Virgile mis, dont ot moult de hontaige.
> Il n'est chose que femme ne consumme.' [3]

Then later, in his *Rosier des Dames*, Bertrand Desmoulins makes Truth say:

> ' Que fist à Sanson Dalida
> Quant le livra aux Philistins,
> N'à Hercules Dejanira
> Quant le fict mourir par venins?
> Une femme par ses engins
> Ne trompa-elle aussi Virgile
> Quant à uns panier il fut prins
> Et puis pendu emmy la ville?' [4]

This idea and these instances illustrative of it are commonplaces in poetry, alike satirical, burlesque and moral, throughout the 13th and 14th centuries, and innumerable passages similar to those above might be quoted.[5] Of Aristotle there

---

[2] From a Berne MS. quoted in CHABAILLE, *Li Livres dou Tresor par Brunetto Latini*, p. xvi. It is noteworthy that BRUNETTO in the above work (lib. ii. p. 2, cap. 39), when speaking of the evil influence of women, mentions Adam, David, Solomon, Samson, Aristotle and Merlin, but not Vergil.

[3] Similar are the verses by PAU DE BELLVIURE, quoted by MILÀ Y FONTANALS, *De los trovatores en España*, p. 435:

> " Por fembre fo Salamó enganat
> lo rey Daviu e Samssó examen,
> lo payra Adam ne trencá 'l mandament
> Aristotil ne fou com ancantat,
> e Virgili fou pendut en la tor,
> e sent Ioan perdé lo cap per llor
> e Ypocras morì per llur barat."

[4] Vide *Récueil de Poésies franc. des XV. et XVI. siècles réunies et annotées par* ANAT. DE MONTAIGLON, vol. v. p. 195. Montaiglon quotes here other French verses of the same date, referring to Vergil's adventure, from GRACIAN DUPONT, the *Nef des princes* and the *Débat de l'homme et de la femme*.

[5] Among these we may yet mention the well-known German poet HEIN-

was told a story, of oriental origin, which made the philosopher wear a saddle at the command of his lady.[6] The adventure of the chest, which in later times was always referred to Vergil, is told of Hippocrates [7] in a *Fabliau*.[8] It forms too, without mention of either Vergil or Hippocrates, the subject of a novel of Fortini,[9] of a German popular song,[10] and of a French one which is still current.[11]

The second part of the story, without the first, is found in European literature some centuries before being assigned to Vergil. Thus it occurs in an old MS. of the *Acts of S. Leo*,[12]

RICH VON MEISSEN, called FRAUENLOB, who also in one of his poems gives a list of women's victims, beginning with Adam :

> " Adam den ersten menschen betroug ein wip
> Samsones lip
> wart durch ein wip geblendet, etc."

and not forgetting Vergil :

> " Virgilius
> wart betrogen mit valschen sitten."

But, as may be gathered from his name, this gallant poet only finds in all these examples an encouragement to put up with the caprices of his own lady. *Vide* v. D. HAGEN, *Minnesinger*, iii. p. 355.

[6] BARBASAN-MÉON, *Fabliaux*, iii. p. 96; LE GRAND D'AUSSY, *Fabliaux*, i. p. 214. Cp. v. D. HAGEN, *Gesammtabenteuer*, i. p. lxxxv. seqq. ; BENFEY, *Pantschatantra*, i. p. 461 seqq. This anecdote occurs also in the *Promptuarium exemplorum*, compiled for the use of preachers. Cp. DU MÉRIL, *Mélanges*, p. 474.

[7] LE GRAND D'AUSSY, *Fabliaux*, i. p. 232 seqq. He believes that the name of Hippocrates was applied to this story before that of Vergil. In the French romance of the Holy Graal the story is told of Hippocrates, and there is also an account of the revenge, only it takes a different form. Hippocrates there makes the lady fall in love with a hideous dwarf. V. P. PARIS, *Les rom. de la table ronde*, i. p. 246 seqq.

[8] This story is probably also of Oriental origin, but a parallel to it has not yet been discovered in Oriental literature. Its likeness to the Tartar story of Gueulette is very slight.

[9] " Un pedante credendosi andare a giacere con una gentildonna si lega nel mezzo perchè ella lo tiri su per una finestra, resta appiccato a mezza via ; di poi messolo in terra con sassi e randelli gli fu data la corsa." FORTINI, *Nov.*, 5. Some, such as v. d. Hagen and Roth, wish to connect this with the Nov. viii. 7 of the *Decameron* and with a passage in the *Filocopo* (p. 283, ed. SANSOVINO). But the parallel fails at the essential point.

[10] Called *Der Schreiber im Korb* ; current in the 15th and 16th centuries. *Vide* SIMROCK, *Die deutschen Volksbücher*, viii. p. 396. Cp. v. D. HAGEN, *Gesammtabenteuer*, iii. p. cxliii.; UHLAND, *Schriften*, iv. p. 512 seqq.

[11] DE PUYMAIGRE, *Chants pop. rec. dans le pays messin*, p. 151 seq.

[12] *Acta Sanct. Feb.*, iii. p. 225. It is noteworthy that in the English version of the popular book on Vergil, of which we shall presently speak, he

where it is told of a magician Heliodorus, who lived in Sicily in the 8th century. These *Acts of S. Leo* are translated from the Greek, and the legend is clearly of oriental origin. In fact it occurs practically in this form in a Persian history of the Mongol Khans of Turkestan and Transoxiana, translated by Defrémery,[13] and in an anecdote on which an Arab proverb is based.[14] From the East the legend came, like many others, to Byzantium; indeed, in a modern Greek work of last century, the two parts of the story are told together of the Emperor Leo Philosophus.[15] And before the two parts came to be united, the second alone was related of Vergil. The earliest instance of this that I know is in the poem by the troubadour Giraud de Calançon, which I have already mentioned, which cannot be later than the year 1220. In this, among the other acts of Vergil with which the street singer must be acquainted, occurs also 'the fire which he knew how to extinguish' ('del foc que saup escantir.') Again, in the *Image du Monde*, the whole of the second part is told without the first.—This latter may well have been ascribed, independently of the former, to Vergil before he had come to be looked upon as a magician; for in this he appears merely as the man of great learning, whose reputation only serves to make him the more ridiculous in the hands of the novelist or a more warning example in those of the moralist. The second part, though at first sight appropriate enough, yet appears clearly on examination as a subsequent addition, for while in this Vergil figures as a most powerful magician, he is certainly nothing of the kind in the

is made to play another trick on the Emperor's daughter. He there causes her, while in the middle of the street, to think that she is crossing a river and to lift up her dress accordingly. Cp. GENTHE, *Leben und Fortleben*, etc , p. 56. A similar story is told of the magician Heliodorus (p. 224) : " alias (mulieres) iter facientes falsa fluminis specie obiecta, indecore nudari compulit, et per siccum pulverem quasi aquam inambulare." Cp. LIEBRECHT in *Orient und Occident*, i. p. 131. Prof. Liebrecht has also kindly pointed out to me a similar Arabic legend in DE HAMMER, *Rosenöl*, i. 162. Cp. also WEIL, *Biblische Legenden der Muselmänner*, p. 267.

[13] *Journ. asiat.*, iv. sér. 19, 85 seqq. ; LIEBRECHT in the *Germania*, x. p. 414 seqq.

[14] FREYTAG, *Arabum proverbia*, ii. p. 445, no. 124.

[15] Cp. LIEBRECHT, *Neugriechische Sagen* in the *Zeitschr. f. deutsche Philologie*, ed. HÖPFNER and ZACHER, ii. p. 183.

other, where he is neither able to foresee his awkward position nor to escape from it.

The two parts appear together in a Latin MS. of the 13th century [16] and in the 'Universal Chronicle' of Jans Enenkel; [17] then in the *Renart Contrefait* and in a large number of works of the 14th, 15th and 16th centuries, chiefly French and German, but occasionally also English, Spanish and Italian. In the Icelandic *Rímur* too appears a version [18] of the insult and the revenge, only there the insult is doubled, for the lady, after having made a fool of Vergil with the box, makes him take her for a ride in the way that is elsewhere recorded of Aristotle. Independently moreover of those who mention the story in connection with other Vergilian legends, there are many who record it, and especially the first part of it, when declaiming, whether in jest or earnest, against women and the sin of sensuality. Thus the Spanish poet Juan Ruiz de Hita (1313) mentions it *apropos* of the *Pecado de Luxuria*, while later, in the times of Ferdinand and Isabella, when Diego de Santo Pedro was saying, on behalf of women, in his *Carcel de Amor* that 'women furnish us with the theological virtues no less than the cardinal, and make us better Catholics than the Apostles,' the adventure of Vergil was cited in an opposite sense in a Spanish poem of which not even the title can be quoted.[19]   Indeed, in its aspect as a moral example this story

[16] Du Méril, *Mél. arch.*, p. 430.

[17] V. D. Hagen, *Gesammtabenteuer*, ii. p. 515 seqq.; Massmann, *Kaiser-chronik*, iii. p. 455 seqq.

[18] The gist of this story is given in Koelbing, *Beiträge zur vergleich. Gesch. d. Poesie u. Prosa d. Mittelalters* (Breslau, 1876), p. 220 seqq.

[19] *Cancionero de obras de burlas provocantes a risa,* p. 152.   The following also, in addition to those already cited, allude to this adventure of Vergil's. The French poem, *Le bâtard de Bouillon* (cp. *Hist. lit. de la France*, xxv. p. 613) ; an anonymous chronicle of the Bishops of Liège (*vide* De Sinner, *Cat. cod. bibl. bern.*, ii. 149) ; Symphorien Champier, *De claris medicinae scriptoribus*, tract. 2 ; Martin Franc, *Champion des Dames*, fol. 104 ; a MS. and the ancient edition of the *Lancillotto* in prose (*vide* v. D. Hagen, *Ges.*, iii. p. cxl.) ; Reinfrit von Braunschweig (*vide* id., *op. cit.*, l.c. ; the lady is there called *Athanata*) ; an old German song beginning "Her Vilius von Astronomey ze schule gie" (id., *op. cit.*, p. cxli.) ; Hawes, *Pastime of Pleasure*, c. xxix. ; Gower, *Confessio amantis*, i. viii. fol. 189 ; the Spanish tragi-comedy *La Celestina*, act vii. ; the *Corbacho* of Talavera ; Diego Martinez in the *Cancionero de Baena*, ed. Michel, ii. p. 29 ; Diego de Valencia, *ib.*, p. 87 ; the *Romance de don Tristà*, in Michel, *Tristan*, ii. p. 302, etc.

was not only repeated in literature *ad nauseam*,[20] but was frequently figured in art, and representations of it in marble, wood or ivory were even set before the eyes of the faithful in the churches.[21] It also furnished a subject to numerous painters and engravers, among whom may be mentioned Lucas van Leyden, George Pencz, Sadeler, Hopfer, Sprengel and others.[22]

The earliest Italian writer (as far as I know) who connects this story with Vergil, is (with the exception of Aliprando, to whom allusion will be subsequently made) Sercambi (1347–1424), who relates it in his Chronicle.[23] After a time however the story became so well known that a certain tower at Rome was pointed to as the scene of the occurrence; at least this seems the most natural explanation of the name *Torre di Virgilio* as applied at Rome to the *Torre dei Frangipani*,[24] and of the appearance of the anecdote in the German 15th century version of the *Mirabilia*, as well as in another German work of the same date on the Seven Principal Churches of Rome.[25] Berni[26] again mentions as one of the objects which people went to see at Rome

---

[20] A chronicler of Metz, PHILIPPE DE VIGNEULLES, speaks of a festival in that city, in the course of which various illustrious personages, such as David, Alexander, Charlemagne, etc., figured on horses or in carriages. He adds, " Pareillement estoit en l'ung d'iceux chariots le saige Virgile qui pour femme pendoit à une corbeille." *Vide* PUYMAIGRE, *Chants populaires recueillis dans le pays messin*, p. 153, and *Les vieux auteurs castillans* of the same writer, tom. ii. p. 79.

[21] *Vide* LANGLOIS, *Stalles de la cathédrale de Rouen*, p. 173 ; DE LA RUE, *Essais hist. sur la ville de Caen*, p. 97 seqq. ; MONTFAUCON, *Antiquité expliquée*, tom. iii. p. 111, pag. 356.

[22] Cp. BARTSCH, *Peintre graveur*, n. 16, 51, 87, 88, 136 ; GRAESSE, *Beiträge*, p. 35 ; BEKKER and VON HEFNER, *Kunstwerke und Geräthschaften des Mittelalters und Renaissance* ; WOLFF, *Niederländische Sagen*, p. 492 seqq. A picture by Malpicci in the *Iconographie des estampes à sujets galants*, etc., par M. LE COMTE D'I. (Geneva, 1868), p. 507, has been supposed without good reason to represent the extinction of the fire ; but this is unquestionably the subject of a work by I. Steen described by STECHER, *La lég. de Virg. en Belgique*, p. 625. The incident of Aristotle and Phyllis is also represented in several works of art ; cp. BENFEY, *Pantschatantra*, i. p. 462.

[23] *Novella inedita di Giovanni Sercambi*. Lucca, 1865. (Only 30 copies printed.) It was republished by Prof. D'ANCONA in the *Novelle di Giovanni Sercambi*, Bologna, 1871, p. 265 seqq.

[24] MARANGONI, *Memorie dell' anfiteatro romano*, p. 51.

[25] MASSMANN, *Kaiserchronik*, iii.p. 454.

[26] *Il primo libro delle opere di M. Francesco Berni e di altri.* (Leyden,

'La torre ove stette in due cestoni
Virgilio spenzolato da colei.'

Aeneas Sylvius in his *De Euryalo et Lucretia* (1440) tells the
first part of the story with moral observations. As an impre-
cation again it occurs amongst the others in the *Murtoleide*:

'Possa come Virgilio in una cistola
Dalla fenestra in giù restar pendente.'

Similarly in the old Italian '*Padiglione di Carlomagno*' is the
following octave:

Ancora si vede Aristotil storiare
E quella femmina che l'ingannò,
Che come femmina lo facea filare
E come bestia ancor lo cavalcò,
E 'l morso in bocca gli facea portare,
E tutto lo suo senno gli mancò;
Da l'altra parte Virgilio si mirava
Che nel cestone a mezza notte stava.' [27]

Many other passages might be cited from Italian works of the
15th and 16th century to show that this adventure of Vergil's
had by that time become as well known in Italy as elsewhere.
A few instances will suffice. Thus in an unpublished *Canzone
morale in disprezzo d'amore*,[28] which occurs in a 15th century
MS. in the Magliabecchiana at Florence, after the instances of
Jupiter, Aristotle, Solomon, etc., comes that of Vergil:

'Lett 'hai d'una donzella che ingannava
Virgilio collocato in una cesta,
E fuor della finestra
Attaccato lasciollo infino a giorno.'

Again, in another unpublished poem of the same period we
read:

1823), part i. p. 147. The incident is also alluded to in the *Carte Parlanti*
of PIETRO ARETINO (Ven. ed. 1650, p. 44) in the words: "che Virgilio nella
cesta non ebbe tanto concorso di popolo."

[27] This stanza occurs in all the printed editions of the poem, but Prof.
Rajna informs me that it and some dozen others are wanting in all the
MSS. which he has seen. The oldest edition known belongs to the first
part of the 16th century.

[28] Cod. 40, pal. ii., f. 140b–141b; communicated to me by Prof. Rajna.
The preceding poem bears the name of GUIDO DA SIENA erased and that of
MESSER BARTOLOMEO DA CASTELLO DELLA PIEVE substituted for it.

'E tu Virgilio parasti le botte
Che sanno dar le donne a' loro amanti,
Tu ti pensasti rimetter le dotte
Con colei che ti fea inganni tanti.
A casa sua tu andasti una notte

.   .   .

Fatto lo 'mposto cenno, ella fu presta,
E pianamente aperse la finestra.
Con una fune una cesta legoe,
Per dimostrare di farti contento,
E fuor della finestra la mandoe
Dove tu eri e tu v' entrasti drento;
Tirotti a mezza via e poi t' appiccoe
A un arpion per tuo maggior tormento
E fino al giorno istesti appiccato,
Dal popolo e da lei fosti beffato.' [29]

Nicolò Malpiglio, in a canzone addressed to Nicolò d' Este,[30]
speaking of Love, says:

'El Mantuan poeta nel canestro
Pose quest' altra cui tu lusingasti
E non ti vergognasti
Dar di tanta virzù solazzo al volgo.'

In the *Contrasto delle Donne* of Antonio Pucci,[31] after various
other anecdotes comes that of Vergil:

'Diss' una che Virgilio avia 'n balìa:
—Vieni stasera, ed entra nella cesta
E collerotti a la camera mia.—
Ed ei v' entrò, ed ella molto presta
Il tirò su; quando fu a mezza via
Il canape attaccò, e quivi resta;
E la mattina quando apparve il giorno
Il pose in terra con suo grande scorno.
Risp. Virgilio avea costei tanto costretta
Per molti modi con sua vanitade

---

[29] This poem, which begins " Or mi posso doler di te Tubbia," and ends
" E tu te goderai col tuo marito," is found in a codex belonging to Sig. C.
Guasti. These verses were transcribed for me by Prof. d'Ancona. The
sixth verse of the first stanza is wanting in the MS.

[30] Cod. Ambros. D. 524 inf. ; according to Prof. Rajna, who brought it to
my notice, its date is about 1440.

[31] Published by Prof. D'ANCONA in the *Propugnatore*, 1870, i. p. 417 seq.
I say "published" because the old edition mentioned by BRUNET (iv. p. 121)
is of great rarity and does not bear the author's name.

> Ch' ella pensò di farli una beffetta
> A ciò che correggiesse sua retade ;
> E fe' quel che tu dì non per vendetta
> Ma per difender la sua castitade ;
> Ver' è che poi, con sua grande scïenza,
> Fece andar sopra lei aspra sentenza.'

In another, considerably earlier poem, belonging perhaps to the 13th century, entitled *Proverbs concerning the Nature of Woman*,[32] the same story is told of the philosopher Antipater :

> ' D' Antipatol filosofo udisti una rasone
> Con la putana en Roma ne fe derisone
> Q' entr' un canestro l'apese ad un balcone
> Ogni Roman vardavalo con el fose un briccone.'

Similarly contemporary Italian art often took this legend for its subject. A wood-cut by an unknown artist of the early Italian school, representing the insult and the revenge, bears the following quotations from the passage of Pucci just cited :

> ' Essendo la mattina chiaro il giorno
> Il pose in terra con suo grande scorno.—
> Ver' è che poi, con sua grande scienza,
> Contr' a costei mandò aspra sentenza.' [33]

A picture of the revenge by Perin del Vaga was reproduced by E. Vico in an engraving bearing the date ' Roma 1542 ' and the legend ' *Virgilium eludens meritas dat foemina poenas*.' [34] In a MS. of the *Trionfi* of Petrarch in the Laurentian library there is a miniature illustrating the Triumph of Love, which contains representations of four of Cupid's most illustrious victims—Hercules spinning, Samson shaved, Aristotle with a saddle and Vergil in a chest.[35] A similar story is still at the present day current among the people at Sulmo, but there the victim is Ovid, who in truth is far more in his element here than Vergil.[36]

---

[32] Publ. by TOBLER in the *Zeitschrift f. roman. Philol.*, **ix.** p. 289 seqq. (*vide* p. 301, n. 31) ; *Monaci Chrestomaz. ital. dei primi secoli*, p. 142.

[33] In the Dresden collection ; described by GRAESSE, *Beiträge*, p. 35 seq.

[34] *Vide* BARTSCH, 46, and *Iconographie*, etc., par M. LE CTE. D'I., p. 733.

[35] Cod. Strozz. no. 174. The tower does not appear ; Vergil is hanging in the chest, while the lady stands before him.

[36] *Vide* DE NINO, *Ovidio nella trad. pop. di Sulmona*, Casalbordino, 1886, p. 38 seq.

The second part of the legend appears in one of those many Italian collections of popular tales which are still eagerly read by the lower classes. Here however it is told, not of Vergil, but of another magician, Pietro Barliario (confounded by some with Pietro Abelardo), who has, like Vergil, inherited not a few of the marvels of the ancient magician Heliodorus :

> ' Adirato si parte indi comanda
>   A' demoni che tosto abbiano spento
>   Tutto il fuoco che fosse in ogni banda,
>   Fosse da loro estinto in un momento.
>   Onde per compir l'opera nefanda
>   La donna fè pigliar con gran tormento,
>   E in piazza fu portata di repente,
>   Nuda, parea che ardesse in fiamme ardente.
> Correa il popol tutto in folta schiera
>   A provveder di fuoco le lor case.
>   Fra le piante di quella in tal maniera
>   Sorger la fiamma, onde ciascun rimase.
>   E l'uno a l'altro darlo invano spera
>   Chè presto si smorzava; intento sparse
>   La Dea ch' ha cento bocche un gran romore
>   E l'avviso n'andò al governatore.—'

This story, which had, as we have seen, its origin outside Italy, was not the only one which brought the magician Vergil in contact with women. Fragmentary recollections of certain customs of the ancient world, and still more the national usages of the barbarian invaders, had brought it about that, even in the more civilised parts of Europe, Trial by Ordeal was a matter of common occurrence, the principle underlying such trial being the idea that God would indicate the right by means of a miracle. The low estimation in which women were held at this period led to such ordeals [37] being regularly employed whenever a wife's conduct was called in question. But however fertile might be the invention of jealous husbands in providing formidable methods of proof, still more fertile was the imagination of the romance-writers and the moralists, who, in the course of their persecutions, jesting or serious, of the

[37] A great many of them are enumerated in DU MÉRIL's learned introduction to *Floire et Blanceflor*, p. clxv. seqq.

female sex, endeavoured to show that there was no ordeal, however terrible, which woman's wit could not frustrate; and innumerable were the anecdotes of every kind which they invented in proof of this. And here medieval Europe, being thoroughly in sympathy with the East, where the position of women was then, and still is, a very low one, was able to borrow from Eastern sources any number of anecdotes derogatory to woman's dignity.

To one of these, which was sufficiently common both in the East and the West, was attached the name of Vergil; and here too the fundamental idea was similar to that in the story of the chest, viz., that the highest wisdom of man is unavailing against a woman's cunning. Vergil,[38] so it was said, constructed at Rome a marble head with the mouth open. Women whose chastity was called in question were required to put their hand into this mouth and swear to their innocence, when, if they swore falsely, the mouth shut and not much remained of the hand. One day, however, a woman who was suspected, not without good reason, by her husband, and required to undergo this ordeal, found means to frustrate it. She directed her gallant to dress up as a madman and stand near the place of trial, and then, as soon as she came, to run up to her and embrace her. This he accordingly did; but while she professed the greatest indignation at his behaviour, her husband, thinking he was only a poor madman, let the matter pass. Thereupon the woman, putting her hand into the terrible mouth, swore that no man had ever embraced her except her husband and the madman who had just been seen to do so; and as this was the absolute truth, her hand came out of the figure's mouth unharmed. Thereupon Vergil, who in his omniscience was aware of the deception, was forced to confess that even he was no match for a woman.

This story, with merely the names and localities changed,

---

[38] *Vide* the *Fleur. des histoires* of JEAN MANSEL in DU MÉRIL's *Mélanges*, p. 444 seqq.; the *Faits merveilleux de Virgile*, of which we shall speak presently; *Kurzweilige Gespräch*, Francf. 1563 (also in GENTHE, *Leben und Fortleben*, etc., p. 75). Cp. MASSMANN, *Kaiserchronik*, iii. p. 449; SCHMIDT, *Beiträge*, 139–141 seq.

occurs in the *Çukasaptati*, a collection of Indian romances, and in the history of *Arji Borji Khan*, a Mongolian work of Indian origin (*Sinhâsanadvâtrinçat*).[39] In Europe too it had been known from very early times; in Macrobius [40] occurs an anecdote (doubtless derived from some old Latin author), which, except for the absence of the erotic element, is practically the same. As a specimen of woman's wit the story made the round of Europe independently of the name of Vergil, even after that name had been attached to it by certain writers. Instances of this are to be found in the French romance of Tristan,[41] in the novels of Straparola, in those of Celio Malispini, in the *Mambriano* of Cieco da Ferrara,[42] in the *Patrañuelo* of Timoneda, etc., etc.[43] The most ancient work, as far as I know, in which it is applied to Vergil is an anonymous German poem, dating from the first part of the 14th century, entitled 'An account of the statue at Rome which bit off the fingers of adulterous women.'[44] The story thus told of Vergil and

---

[39] Cp. BENFEY, *Pantschatantra*, i. p. 457; BARTSCH in the *Germania* of PFEIFFER, v. 94 seq. The Mongolian version of this story in the *Arji Borji* has been published by JÜLG under the title *Erzählung aus der Sammlung Ardschi Bordschi, ein Seitenstück zum Gottesgericht in Tristan und Isolde*, Innsbruck, 1867; and again by the same in his learned work *Mongolische Märchen* (Innsbruck, 1867) p. 111 seqq. Cp. my article in the *Revue critique*, 1867, i. p. 185 seqq.

[40] "Tremellius vero Scrofa cognominatus est eventu tali. Is Tremellius cum familia atque liberis in villa erat. Servi eius, cum de vicino scrofa erraret, subreptam conficiunt; vicinus advocatis custodibus omnia circumvenit, ne qua efferri possit; isque ad dominum appellat restitui sibi pecudem. Tremellius qui ex vilico rem comperisset, scrofae cadaver sub centonibus collocat super quos uxor cubabat; quaestionem vicino permittit. Cum ventum est ad cubiculum, verba iurationis concipit; nullam esse in villa sua scrofam nisi istam, inquit, quae in centonibus iacet; lectulum monstrat. Ea facetissima iuratio Tremellio Scrofae cognomentum dedit." MACROB., *Sat.*, i. 6. 30.

[41] MICHEL, *Tristan*, i. p. 199 seqq.

[42] Vide *Novelle del Mambriano del Cieco da Ferrara esposte ed illustrate da* GIUSEPPE RUA (Turin, 1888) pp. 65–83.—In a *Novella del geloso* (communicated to me by Prof. D'ANCONA) which occurs in Cod. Perug. C. 43, p. 120v. and begins "Per cortesia ciascun geloso," the authorship of the "pietrone della verità" is attributed to Merlin:

"Però quel pedron ha vertù tale
Che vi lassò il bon Merlin perfetto
Qualunque omo o dona fesse male, etc."

[43] Vide DUNLOP-LIEBRECHT, p. 500.

[44] Published by BARTSCH in the *Germania* of PFEIFFER, iv. p. 237 seqq.

localised at Rome was connected with a monument which still exists there at S. Maria in Cosmedin and is called the ' *Bocca della Verità.*' It is, in reality, an ancient gargoyle, but it is described in the *Mirabilia* as a mouth gifted with oracular powers. An inscription placed on the spot in 1632 states that this mouth was formerly used for oaths by putting the hand between its teeth, a fact confirmed by its name of *Bocca della Verità*—a name which belongs also to the neighbouring square and which certainly goes back to the middle ages.[45] All this explains how the story of the woman came to be regarded as happening in Rome at the *Bocca della Verità* and how this latter came to be associated with Vergil. And indeed, in the German 15th century version of the *Mirabilia*, the name of Vergil is actually introduced *apropos* of this marble head, and this story is then told to explain how the mouth lost its power.[46]

[45] V. D. HAGEN (*Briefe in die Heimath*, iv. p. 106) states that the ancient temple of Chastity used to stand on what is now the site of Maria in Cosmedin, and derives the legend from this fact. This temple was certainly near the Forum Boarium, but modern archaeologists (cp. BEKKER-MARQUARDT, *Handbuch der röm. Alterthümer*, i. 480 seqq.) do not place it on the site of the church, which they believe was occupied by the temple of Ceres. Moreover, the earliest mention of the legend (in the *Mirabilia*) speaks of oracles without any special reference to chastity. Cp. also PLATNER, *Beschreibung der Stadt Rom*, iii. 1. p. 381 ; CRESCIMBENI, *Storia della Basilica di Santa Maria in Cosmedin*, Rome, 1715.

[46] Cp. MASSMANN, *Kaiserchronik*, iii. 449. This story, too, like that of the chest, appears in works of art. It occurs, for instance, in Lucas van Leyden's series of engravings illustrative of the wiles of women. Cp. (besides BARTSCH) PASSAVANT, *Le peintre graveur*, iii. p. 9. PLATNER (*op. cit.*, iii. 1. p. 382), speaks of a picture on this subject in a house at Rome. The German poet HANS SACHS (16th cent.) ascribes to Vergil a bridge where, at the sound of a bell, all who had been unfaithful to their marriage-vows had to take to flight. With this he shows King Arthur how common is the latter's lot. Cp. V. D. HAGEN, *Gesammtab.*, iii. 136.

CHAPTER IX

THE various anecdotes which had by this time come to be associated with Vergil were, as we have seen, sufficiently numerous, and it only needed a certain amount of arrangement, or, where gaps occurred, of imagination, to produce a complete biography of the famous magician. Nor, in fact, are such biographies wanting. But, before reaching this last stage of the Vergilian legend, it may be worth while first to glance at the course of its progress in the place of its origin, that is to say, in Italy, and particularly Naples. It has already been shown that, with the exception of a few stories heard at Naples itself by Gervasius and Conrad, all the Vergilian legends had their origin outside Italy, and that, though they were recorded in works which were at that time widely known, only a very few of them found their way into Italian literature. The most noteworthy Neapolitan document in the matter of the Vergilian legends that we possess is the *Cronica di Partenope*,[1] wrongly attributed in the first edition to Giovanni Villani, and subse-

---

[1] We have adopted the title *Cronica di Partenope* as the shortest, but the title differs both in the MSS. and the editions. A frequent one is *Chroniche de la inclita città de Napole con li bagni di Puzzolo et Ischia*. For the two earliest editions (the first without date, the second of the year 1526), see BRUNET, *Manuel*, v. 1226 seq. The MSS. are very numerous. The part of the work which refers to Vergil has been published by GRAESSE (*Beiträge*, p. 27 seqq.) and by Prof. VILLARI in the *Annali delle università toscane*, viii. p. 162 seqq.,—in the latter case from a Neapolitan MS. of the year 1471. A few chapters are also published in GALIANI, *Del dialetto napoletano*, p. 95 seqq. B. CAPASSO, in his charming work *Le fonti della storia delle prov. napoletane dal 560 al 1500* (*Arch. st. per le prov. nap.*, I. (1876) p. 592 seqq.) has not only made a special study of the MSS., which differ greatly from the printed editions, but has also corrected various erroneous views previously current as to the authorship, the nature and the composition of the *Cronica*, and pointed out the real character of the work.

quently to 'Bartolomeo Caraczolo dicto Carafa, cavaliere di Napoli,' though the latter neither was nor professed to be any-thing more than the author of the second of the three docu-ments of which this curious contribution to Neapolitan history consists. The whole chronicle belongs to the 14th century; the earliest part is the work of an unknown Neapolitan, who probably wrote it soon after the year 1326, and consists of a collection of stories, derived from various sources (including oral tradition), relative to the antiquities, both sacred and secular, of the city of Naples, and including not a few legends, among which appear also those referring to Vergil.[2] Though himself a Neapolitan, the author by no means confines himself to the stories current in Naples in his day, but relates in addition all that he can find in Gervasius and in the works of a certain Alexander. If by the latter he means Alexander Neckam, we can only infer that his text of that author was a very mutilated and interpolated one, or that he had only read him in some very incomplete and inaccurate series of extracts.[3]

The stories found in Gervasius are substantially reproduced by the *Cronica,* and, except for a few small additions in har-mony with the original, the legend at Naples retains the form which we have seen belonged to it in the 12th century. Vergil appears as the great benefactor of Naples, at the time when he was 'consiliario et quasi rectore o vero maistro di Marcello,' and was appointed by Octavian 'duca de li napolitani.' It was Vergil who made the aqueducts, the fountains and the cloacae of Naples; it was Vergil who instituted the *Gioco di Carbo-nara,*[4] similar to the *Gioco del Ponte* at Pisa, which began as a military exercise and ended in a free fight. In addition to the usual talismans appear a copper grasshopper, which drove away all grasshoppers from Naples, and a little marble fish, known as the 'preta de lo pesce,' which attracted fish in abundance.[5]

---

[2] "Di questa parte della Cronica, che corrisponde ai primi 57 capitoli della edizione comunementa nota, o piuttosto del raffazonomento fatto nel 1526, non si conoscono finora codici speciali ed esclusivi." Capasso, *op. cit.*

[3] Cp. the similar fact already noted above, p. 269.

[4] Cp. Petrarch, *Epist. de rebus fam.,* lib. v. ep. 6.

[5] Cp. Sacchetti, nov. 216: "Maestro Alberto della Magna giungendo a

The legend too of the *Castello dell' Ovo*, which had, as we have
seen, undergone such modifications outside Italy, appears here
in its original form of a palladium protecting the city. Similarly Gervasius' story of the eccentric Englishman reappears
in the *Cronica* with only a few alterations of no great moment.
There, however, it is added that, 'secondo che se legge ad un
chronica antiqua' (what this chronicle can have been we do
not know, but it was certainly a Neapolitan one), just as the
scholar found the book beneath Vergil's head, so had Vergil
himself found it under the head of Chiron in a cave on the
Monte Barbaro, whither he had gone to fetch it in company
with a certain Philomenus or Philomelus.[6] But though this
book is called a book on *necromancy*, and though the *Cronica*
speaks at times of Vergil's works as being due to magic, yet
the author gives it clearly to be understood, in more places
than one, that by such magic he merely means a knowledge of
the 'mirabile influenza de la pianeta'; no diabolical powers
whatever are anywhere attributed to Vergil, who is always
spoken of with the greatest respect and regularly described as
'esimio poeta.' As for the fact that the cave at Puteoli was
protected from all sorts of crime, this had been brought about
not, as is elsewhere asserted, by diabolical means, but by means
of 'geometry.'

It is only natural, since the grave of Vergil was on the road
to Puteoli just at the mouth of the cave, that this locality
should have become a centre of Vergilian traditions. Some

uno oste sul Po gli fa uno pesce di legno col quale pigliava quanti pesci
volea.''

[6] Chiron is evidently the Centaur Chiron, who figures in the mythical
history of medicine and hence also in that of magic. The *Herbarium Apulei
Platonici traditum a Chirone Centauro magistro Achillis* was much used in
the middle ages. *Philomelus* (in the MSS. also spelt *Philomenus*) may be
the ancient physician *Philoumenos*, who gave his name to some popular
remedies which are strongly suggestive of magic. (*Vide* BEKKER-MARQUARDT,
Handbuch der röm. Alterth., iv. p. 117 seqq.). It seems probable that this
story, which the writer in the *Cronica* says he read in an old chronicle, was
not popular in origin but invented to accredit a work by some forerunner of
Cardanus and Paracelsus. It is well known that, according to Neapolitan
legend, Monte Barbaro contains all sorts of treasures and similar marvels,
and this belief goes back to the times of Conrad von Querfurt, who mentions
it in the letter of which we have already spoken.

time later Scoppa, after repeating the Vergilian legends found in the *Cronica di Partenope*, adds the following remark on the subject of the cave at Puteoli : ' I know that some maintain, on the authority of Pliny, that this cave was the work of Lucullus and not of Vergil. But I prefer to follow our chronicles, considering that in matters relating to antiquity the most ancient documents are, especially when local, of the greatest value.' And how common was this view at Naples is shown not only by the name *Grotta di Virgilio*, but also by the story, which Petrarch himself tells, of how he was solemnly questioned on the subject by King Robert and answered that ' he did not remember having read anywhere that Vergil was a stone-mason.' [7]

From this we may gather that even in the 14th and 15th centuries the original Vergilian legends were still current at Naples and that no trace was to be found in them of the foreign conception of Vergil as necromancer or lover. The only legend of apparently extraneous origin which appears in the *Cronica* is that of the four skulls, set up by Vergil at Naples, which informed the Duke of everything that went on in the world. This legend is, of course, based on the idea of the *Salvatio Romae* and the marvellous mirror combined with that of the talking head, which was, as we have seen, attributed to Vergil as well as to Gerbert; it seems, therefore, to be of foreign extraction.

The author of the *Cronica* has been careful not to add anything of his own to the legends he records ; he has not striven to render them either more phantastic or more plausible. Barbarous as he is, he is yet a literary man, and possesses a certain culture which distinguishes him from the uneducated masses;

---

[7] " Nusquam nemini me legisse marmorarium fuisse Vergilium." *Itin. Syr.*, i. p. 560 (ed. Basil., 1581); THEOD. A NIEM, *De Schismate*, ii. 22. Among the others who speak of the cave at Puteoli as the work of Vergil may be mentioned THERSANDER, *Schauplatz viel. ungereimt. Meyn.*, ii. 308, 554; JEAN D'AUTUN, *Chroniques*, i. p. 321 etc., and MARLOWE, who, in his *Doctor Faustus*, Act I. sc. 26, says :

> " There saw we learned Maro's golden tombe,
> The way he cut an English mile in length
> Thorough a rock of stone, in one night's space."

he wishes to appear as an historian, and so, when he comes to record the Vergilian legends, he not only speaks of the real Vergil as he knew him from his works and from the literary tradition, but also, when applying these legends to this Vergil, he regularly cites, or professes to cite, from books, and never refers to the contemporary local traditions, though these were doubtless well known to him. Alexander Neckam, as we have seen, he quotes at secondhand, and hence even describes him as saying what, as a matter of fact, was said by another writer; Gervasius of Tilbury, also only known indirectly, becomes, either at the hands of the original author or at those of one of the various interpolators of this chronicle, *Santo Gervasio Pontefice*, while his *Otia Imperialia* become the *Responsi* (i.e. *Riposi*) *Imperiali*. The chief authorities however, whether acknowledged or not, are always local Neapolitan ones, such as an anonymous *Cronica antica*, the *Planctus Italiae* of Eustazio da Matera (now lost), the *Life of St. Athanasius*, and perhaps others, of which we are now ignorant, from which were derived the stories connecting Vergil with Octavian and Marcellus and the passage in praise of Naples, ' Signora di nove città, etc.' [8]

But whether previously registered or not by ancient writers, the legends here referred to were still living, anyhow in great part, in the popular Neapolitan tradition at the time when the *Cronica* was first written down, and even when it was subsequently transcribed by various hands or so freely reconstructed for the purposes of the printed edition. The living nature of the legend is clear enough in the passages where the author wishes to criticise it and to correct the errors *della gente grossa*, as he feels himself justified, without perhaps too much reason, in calling them. Thus, the legend of the cave at Puteoli, which

---

[8] *Vide supra*, p. 284. Vietor is quite mistaken when he describes (*op. cit.*, p. 177 seq.) this Chronicle as a collection of legends entirely derived from literary sources and in no wise connected with local Neapolitan traditions, and wishes to maintain that the Neapolitans themselves, if they knew anything of these legends, must have got to know them through some Italian translation of Gervasius ! Apart from the fact that Gervasius himself, whatever Vietor may say, expressly asserts that he was merely recording legends that he heard at Naples, the Chronicle registers legends which are not found in Gervasius or any other of the foreign writers, but in Neapolitan writers anterior in date to all these.

he cites, was unquestionably current at the time; the people, however, maintained that Vergil finished this prodigious piece of work in a single day, and this is too much for the writer, who, while conscientiously chronicling all the rest, makes an exception here, observing that 'the common people believe that Vergil made the aforesaid cave in a single day; but this would be impossible, except by divine agency, *quae de nihilo cuncta creavit.*'[9] Similarly we see that the legend of the *Castel dell' Uovo* was still current among the people, though the belief that this talisman protected the city from capture could not have continued to exist after the events of the 12th century; and hence, with reference to this belief, the author confines himself to stating that it was held by 'gli antiqui napoletani.' When the *Cronica* was printed (at the end of the 15th century) with the promising title of 'nobilissima et *vera* antica cronica,' (that too in spite of the false attribution of the work, on the title-page itself, to Giovanni Villani,) and afterwards too, when it was reprinted in 1526, various passages were suppressed and others added, while the whole work was freely remodelled; but that the Vergilian legends continued current, and that many other stories about Vergil were in existence among the populace besides those recorded in the *Cronica*, is clear from the following passage, so creditable to Italian common-sense, which was added, in the name of the ancient author, by Astrino, when he prepared the work for the press in 1526:[10] 'I could have recorded many other things which I have heard told of this Vergil, only they seemed to me for the most part to be fabulous or false, so that I did not wish to burden the reader with them. And seeing that I have already recorded many such stories, which I myself in no wise believe to be true, I must ask the reader's pardon for this; for I did not wish to diminish the fame, whether true or false, of this great poet and of his benevolence towards the famous city of Naples. But the

---

[9] This passage is omitted from the printed editions, but occurs in the MSS.

[10] It used always to be believed that the credit of these words belonged to the ancient author of the *Cronica*; Capasso, however, has shown that they are not found in any MS., but are an addition of Astrino's. *Vide* CAPASSO, *op. cit.*, p. 596 note.

truth of these things is known to God alone. And this I have said, because I never record anything false or fabulous without informing the reader of the fact.'

The Neapolitan legends spread very little in upper Italy; they were however well known in southern Italy outside Naples. The earliest mention of them in our popular poets with which I am acquainted is in a composition by Ruggieri Pugliese, which is probably not later than the first part of the 13th century :

> ' Aggio poco senno alla stagione,
> E saccio tutte l'arti di Virgilio.' [11]

In the rest of Italy the Vergilian legend does not appear in literature till the 14th century, and then, owing to the close connection between contemporary Italian and foreign literature, the native element appears in combination with the exotic. A few Tuscan writers, however, had heard it at first hand from the people of Naples. Thus Boccaccio, who knew Naples well, when speaking in his Dante Commentary (1373) of Vergil's marvellous works in that city, mentions only the three well-known ones, the fly, the bronze horse and the marble faces at the Porta Nolana. He adds that Vergil lived much more at Naples than at Rome, and came there from Milan,[12] having a taste for poetry and knowing that Octavian befriended poets. Before him Cino da Pistoria [13] alludes to the marvellous fly in some satirical verses aimed at the city of Naples :

> ' O sommo vate, quanto mal facesti
> A venir qui ; non t'era me' morire
> A Pietola colà dove nascesti ?
> Quando la mosca, per l'altre fuggire,

---

[11] *Le Rime antiche volgari secondo la lezione del cod. vaticano* 3793 *publ. per cura di* A. D'ANCONA e D. COMPARETTI. (Bologna), I. p. 430.

[12] This occurs in the interpolated text of the life attributed to Donatus. The genuine text makes Vergil pass direct from Milan to Rome (cp. REIF-FERSCHEID, *Suetoni*, etc., p. 401), as Francesco da Buti remarks in his commentary.

[13] *Poesie di Messer Cino da Pistoia racc. da* SEB. CIAMPI, t. ii. p. 157 (ed. 3). Ciampi's idea that this satire is directed against Rome, not Naples, is refuted by the passage we have quoted as well as by the whole sense of the poem. The " *animal si vile* " which " *anticamente* " gave its name to the district where " *ogni senso è bugiardo e fallace* " is the Siren Parthenope.

> In tal loco ponesti
> Ov' ogni vespa doveria venire
> A punger quei che su ne' boschi stanno.'

The popular 14th century Florentine poet Antonio Pucci, in a common-place book of his (of which there are two MSS. at Florence),[14] records, among numerous other jottings of every kind, various stories relating to Vergil, viz. the fly, the horse, the castle balanced on an egg, the garden, the two tapers and the lamp which never went out, the two incidents of the emperor's daughter, the head that talked, the account of the poet's death and the powers supposed to be possessed by his bones. Pucci however speaks of Vergil's grave as situated at Rome, an error very probably derived from one of the foreign writers whose works he was in the habit of imitating; [15] at the same time he says nothing about diabolical agency, but ascribes the Vergilian marvels to 'Astronomy.' In the same century Gidino da Sommacampagna, in a sonnet addressed to Francesco Vannozzo,[16] attributes them to his knowledge of the secrets of nature, citing the authority

> ' Dell' eccellente fisico Marone
> Che circa il natural pose sua cura.'

In a curious sonnet of his,[17] of the kind afterwards known under the name of *Burchiello*, Andrea Orcagna, the great artist of the 14th century, says :

> ' E l'ampolla di Napoli s'è rotta.'

unquestionably alluding to the famous *ampolla* in the Castel dell' Uovo, which, as we learn from Conrad von Querfurt, lost its power *quia modicum fissa est*.[18]

---

[14] *Vide* the notice of them by Prof. D'ANCONA in the *Propugnatore*, 1870, i. p. 397 seqq.

[15] Cp. WESSELOFSKY, *Le tradizioni popolari nei poemi di Antonio Pucci*, in the *Ateneo italiano*, Ann. i.

[16] Pub. by ZANELLA, Verona, 1858.

[17] TRUCCHI, *Poesie inedite di dugento autori*, Prato, 1846, ii. p. 29.

[18] This line of Orcagna's cannot refer to the vessel containing the blood of St. Januarius, for Orcagna died about 1368, and the first mention of that famous relic belongs to the 15th century. *Vide* VILLARI, *Legg. e. trad. che illustrano la Div. Com.* in the *Ann. delle Univ. Tosc.*, viii. p. 219 ; GIOV.

But if Vergil's early connection with Naples had prevented his legendary figure from assuming in that city those ridiculous or odious features which belonged to it elsewhere, no such influences were at work in the rest of Italy. Hence an echo of the foreign legends may be found at Rome in the fact that Vergil's name was associated with various monuments or localities in that city.[19] Thus we know that the *Meta sudans* was called *Torre di Virgilio*,[20] a name also given to the ruins of the Torre dei Frangipani,[21] and that the Septizonium was called the *Scuola di Virgilio*.[22] This last is mentioned in the curious little poem, of the 15th or 16th century, entitled *Prospettiva milanese*:

SCHERILLO, *Di San Gennaro protettore della città di Napoli e della reliquia del suo sangue* in the *Strenna della scuola cattolica per l'anno* 1875 (Naples), p. 147 seqq.

[19] That the name *Tor de' specchi*, still borne by a street in Rome, is connected with the magic mirror of Vergil is a mistaken notion of Keller, v. d. Hagen, Massmann and others. GREGOROVIUS (*Gesch. d. Stadt Rom im Mittelalter*, iv. p. 629) is right in believing that the name of the street comes from the family *De Speculo* or *De' Specchi*, which had its castle there. Visitors to Rome, however, remembering the Vergil-legend, would naturally explain the name of the locality by reference to that, and perhaps the *Spiegelburg*, which in a German version of the *Mirabilia* is the scene of Vergil's adventure, is really nothing but the *Tor de' Specchi*. Cp. MASSMANN, *Kaiserchronik*, iii. p. 454.

[20] GIORG. FABRICIO, *Roma* (1587), p. 21.

[21] Pulled down in the 13th century by Gregory IX. *Vide* MARANGONI, *Memorie dell' anfiteatro romano*, p. 51.

[22] *Vide* v. D. HAGEN, *Briefe in die Heimath*, iv. p. 118. The Septizonium, which was finally destroyed by order of Sixtus V., is frequently referred to as the "School of Vergil" in documents of the period. Cp. HUELSEN, *Das Septizonium des Septimius Severus* (xlvi. Winkelmannsprogr.), Berlin, 1886, p. 30; STEVENSON, *Il Settizonio Severiano* in the *Bull. della Comm. arch. comun. di Roma*, 1888, p. 272. The name *Scuola di Virgilio* is now given at Naples to a spot on the sea-shore, where a temple of Fortune or Venus Euplea is supposed to have stood. I have searched in vain for any instance of this nomenclature in the middle ages. It is not found in any Vergilian legends which occur in literature. In the *Faits merveilleux de Virgile*, a work of French origin, of which we shall speak presently, there is a notice of a school of necromancy founded at Naples by Vergil, and some have connected the name with this. I believe rather that the passage in the book has given the name to the locality. A Neapolitan fisherman, living near the *Scuola di Virgilio*, told a foreigner (*vide* p. 373) that it was here that Vergil used to give lessons to Marcellus; and this agrees with the *Cronica di Partenope*, which describes Vergil as Marcellus' tutor. This is sufficient to explain the name without having recourse, as some have done, to a derivation of *scuola* from *scoglio*.

‘ Eravi di Virgilio un’ academia
edificata nel più bel di Roma
et hor dintorno a lei vi si vendemia ;
erano septe scole, etc.’ [23]

If we compare these names with the notices we have of the
troubles which Petrarch suffered at the hands of the Roman
Court in consequence of his Vergilian studies, it will be sufficiently clear that the name of Vergil was at that time associated in Rome with the idea of magic in its worst form. But
all this is certainly not earlier in date than the foreign legends
which have this tendency, and is in fact merely an outcome of
them. If one considers how closely the name of Vergil was
connected with that of Rome, and how frequently it was introduced into the guide-books to that city which the foreign
visitors used, it will be easily understood how the idea of
Vergil as magician became familiar to the Romans, and how
his name came to be applied to monuments and localities in the
city. But the date when this came about may be gathered
from the fact that in the earliest MSS. of the *Mirabilia Urbis
Romae*, which belong to the 12th century, though the *Martiro-
logium* (i.e. *Fasti*) of Ovid is cited, there is no mention whatever of Vergil, even in connection with the legend of Octavian
and the Sibyl. Had his name been at this time already associated with any monument in the city, the *Mirabilia* could not
have failed to notice it. Only after the spread of the legend
in Europe did the name find its way into the *Mirabilia*, and
thence to Rome; for it was an essentially non-Italian notion
that Rome was the scene of Vergil’s magic exercises, and that
he kept a school there. Thus, in the 14th century, Hans Folz,
the barber-poet of Nuremberg, writes in one of his burlesques
that ‘ once upon a time it was said that there lived at Rome a
scholar learned in necromancy, called Vergil, who used to be
able to answer any question that might be put to him,’ and then
goes on to mention three curious answers which he once gave
to three curious questions.[24]

[23] Vide *Atti della R. Accademia dei Lincei*, ser. 2, vol. iii., v. 96 seqq.

[24] “ Nun gingen umb die zeit die mer
wie das zu Rom ein meyster wer

In a 13th century MS. of the *Mirabilia* there occurs, under
the heading of the *Mons Viminalis*, the following note: ' From
this place Vergil, when attacked by the Romans, fled, after
making himself invisible, to Naples; hence the expression,
" *Vado ad Napulum.*" ' This rough and ready etymology was
used to explain the name of a street which led to the Viminal,
and was then called *Magnanapoli* (really a corruption of *Balnea
Pauli*). The legend on which it was based was one recounting
the sequel to the incidents of the chest and the extinction of
the fire; and just as this latter was an old story applied first
to Heliodorus, then to Vergil and finally to Pietro Barliario,
whose name is still sometimes heard in the South of Italy,
so the sequel to that adventure had also originally belonged
to Heliodorus. Heliodorus, so ran the legend, to escape the
punishment he deserved, drew on the wall a picture of a ship
with its sails and sailors, and then, by his diabolical art,
changed the picture into a real ship, in which he escaped to
Sicily.[25] In like manner it was related of Vergil that, when
put in prison for his outrage on the lady who had played the
practical joke on him, he was able to escape by drawing on the
wall the figure of a vessel, which then became real and, rising
into the air, carried him and all his fellow-prisoners to Naples.[26]

in der nigromancey erkant
der was Virgilius genant,
eim yden er beschidung melt
wes man in vraget in der welt."

Vide ZARNCKE, *Vier Sprüche von Hans Folz*, in the *Zeitschrift f. deutsch.
Alterth.*, viii. (1851), p. 517 seqq.

[25] *Acta Sanct. febr.*, iii. p. 255. According to a Latin 13th century MS.,
published by DU MÉRIL (*Mélanges arch.*, p. 430), Vergil liberates himself
from prison by having brought to him a tub of water, into which he plunges
and straightway disappears. Perhaps this is what Giraud de Calançon means
by his "Com de la conca s saup cobrir." The same incident occurs twice
in the legend of the magician Heliodorus: " ut autem allata est (pelvis cum
aqua) continuo in eam se conicit et ex oculis abit cum hoc dicto: salvus
sis, imperator, quaere me Catanae." The same story is also told of Pietro
Barliario. The " Quaere me Catanae " of Heliodorus and the " A Napoli
vi aspetto " of Barliario explain the " Vado ad Napulum " of Vergil. It is
also related in the " *Forty Vizirs* " (Behrnauer's transl., p. 23) how a certain
sheikh saved himself from death by plunging into water and being promptly
conveyed to Damascus.

[26] The idea of a magic ship which flies through the air is common in
modern popular tales. Cp. the Russian story called " The flying ship "

This story, which is told also of Barliario, is attributed to Vergil, not only in the *Mirabilia*, but also in the *Aliprandina* (a Mantuan chronicle so called because written in verse by Bonamente Aliprando in 1414), of which it will now be necessary to speak further.

The only one of the three cities with which Vergil was connected where his personality made any really deep impression was Naples. Mantua is quite barren of legends concerning him, a circumstance which may perhaps be explained by the fact that, though it was his birthplace, he does not seem ever to have made any long stay there. Of course the Mantuans were not likely, in the middle ages, to forget that Vergil had been born in their country, and, as we learn from Donizo,[27] several places in that neighbourhood bore the poet's name or were pointed to as having been frequented by him. But all these identifications referred, rightly or wrongly, to actual incidents in his life; there was no suggestion in any of them of attributing to him any supernatural powers. If Mantua coined money bearing his effigy[28] and raised a statue to him,[29] this

(*letucii korabl*) in AFANASIEFF'S collection, vol. vi. p. 137 seqq., and the numerous parallels adduced in his note in vol. viii. p. 484 seqq.

[27] " Haec tibi sint nota, Maronis dicitur aula
    hactenus et sylva, per quam pascebat ovillas,
    ast et Balista mons nascitur hanc prope sylvam
    in quo Virgilius titulum fecit hoc modo scriptum :
    monte sub hoc lapidum, etc."

DONIZ., *Vit. Mathild.* ap. MURATORI, *Scriptt. rer. it.*, v. 360. Of the *Mons Balista* Muratori says, "nunc appellatur *Monte di Vilestra* . . . sed longe ante Vergilium Balistae monti nomen fuit."

[28] *Vide* ZANETTI, *Nuova raccolta delle monete e zecche d' Italia*, vol. iii. p. 249 seqq., pl. xvii.

[29] In the 16th century. Carlo Malatesta threw the statue into the Mincio, but was afterwards compelled to restore it to its place. I do not know when the popular tradition, mentioned by a recent traveller, arose, according to which there is pointed out, at a spot two miles from Mantua, the cave into which Vergil used to retire to meditate. *Vide* KEYSSLER, *Neueste Reisen*, p. 1,016; cp. BURKHARDT, *Die Cultur der Renaissance in Italien*, p. 148. Aeneas Silvius, on his journey to the congress of Mantua (1459), visited the so-called villa of Vergil on the Mincio. Cp. BURKHARDT, *op. cit.*, p. 181. In the last century DE BROSSES, after a visit to Pietola to see the house in which Vergil was born, writes : " Je n'y vis autre chose qu'une maison de campagne assez propre ou il n'est pas la plus petite question de Virgile. Je demandai aux gens du lieu pourquoi cette maison portait le nom de Virgiliana. Ils me répondirent que ce nom lui venait d'un ancien duc de Man-

was merely a tribute paid him by the upper classes of the country, and are no indication of the existence of any local popular traditions. A proof of this is the poem of Aliprando, to which reference has been made above.[30] The absurdity and *naïveté* of the composition show clearly that, had there been any special local traditions current about Vergil, the author would have been just the man to avail himself of them. But there is nothing of the kind apparent; Aliprando speaks of Vergil as one of the glories of Mantua, but he compiles his biography partly from Donatus and partly from the ordinary series of Vergilian legends, without any special reference to Mantua. He begins by referring, like the ancient biographer, to Vergil's father and mother, and to the latter's prophetic dream, in consequence of which

> ' La donna fece l'animo giocondo,
> E quando venne lei a partorire
> Nacque il figlio maschio tutto e tondo.'

He goes on to speak of Vergil's personal appearance, of his studies and works, and of the lands he lost, but recovered through gaining Octavian's favour by his celebrated '*Nocte pluit tota*' distich.

Then, after mentioning the prophecy of Christ, Aliprando comes to tell the stories of the basket, the revenge, the poet's imprisonment and his escape in the manner already described. Here, however, he adds that Vergil, in order to procure provisions for his journey, sent a spirit to fetch the dishes from Octavian's table, who, when he saw his dinner suddenly disappearing,

> ' Senza mancamente,
> Disse : Virgilio questo ha fatto fare ;
> E della beffa rallegrò la mente. '

Similar stories are told of other magicians, as, for instance, of

toue qui était roi d'une nation qu'on appelle les Poètes et qui avait écrit beaucoup de livres qu'on avait envoyé en France." Colomb, *Le président De Brosses en Italie.* Paris, 1869, p. 117.

[30] *Aliprandina, osia Chronica della città di Mantova di* Buonamente Aliprando, *cittadino Mantuano ;* in Muratori, *Antiquit. Ital. med. aevi,* t. v., p. 1,061 seqq. Cp. Cantù, *St. univers,* ii. p. 658 seqq.

Pietro Barliario. Of Vergil's wonderful works Aliprando is
acquainted with but few; in fact, he only knows of the magic
fly, which according to him was kept in a glass bottle, and of
the *Castel' dell' Ovo*, which he describes Vergil as building in
the sea. To these, however, he adds a fountain of oil,[31] made
for the use of the Neapolitans. In describing Vergil's death,
he follows Donatus, and, after adding a few notices as to his
grave, he concludes with the following eloquent funeral oration,
which he puts into the mouth of Octavian:

> ' Di scienza è morto lo più valente;
> Non credo che nel mondo il simil sia.
> Prego Dio che grazia gli consente,
> Che l'anima sua debba accettare;
> Le sue virtudi non m'usciran di mente.
> Ben mi dolgo. Non posso io altro fare.'

But in spite of this funeral oration and in spite of his prophecy
of Christ, Aliprando's Vergil is a full-blown magician, on terms
of the fullest intimacy with Satan and accompanied by the
inevitable book of magic. On the occasion of his flight to
Naples he had left this book behind; so he sent his disciple
Milino [32] to Rome to fetch it, with particular instructions not
to open it—instructions which Milino of course promptly dis-
obeyed. A crowd of devils immediately surrounded him, howl-
ing for his orders, so to get rid of them he set them to work
to pave the road from Rome to Naples. This legend is simply
an amplification of the one, already mentioned, referring to the
cave at Puteoli; in fact, Felix Hemmerlin, who visited Naples
in 1426, tells the devil-story of this very cave.[33] It recurs

[31] According to the legend, the statue in Sicily mentioned by Olympiodorus (*vide* p. 268) used to emit on the one side ever-flowing water, on the
other inextinguishable fire. It used to be believed of the famous tripod at
Constantinople that its three serpents' heads had at one time been in the
habit of sending forth on festival-days streams of water, wine and milk.
Vide BONDELMONTI, *Liber insularum* (ed. DE SINNER), p. 123.

[32] A form of the name Merlin, which appears also as Mellino, Merilino,
Meriliano, Merleg, etc. *Vide* KELLER, *Romans des Sept Sages*, cxcvii. seqq.
The name of Vergil was similarly corrupted, especially in Germany, becom-
ing Filius, Filias, Filigus, etc. JAKOB VON KÖNIGSHOFEN speaks of the
"great master Virgilius whom the people call Filius." Cp. v. D. HAGEN,
Gesammtabenteuer, ii. p. cxliii.

[33] *De nobilitate*, cap. ii. Cp. ROTH, *op. cit.*, p. 262.

with slight variations in the poem of Heinrich von Müglin (14th century) which has already been cited,[34] and it is undoubtedly to it that Fazio degli Uberti alludes when, on describing his journey from Rome to Naples, he mentions, in the *Dittamondo*,[35]

'Quella fabricata e lunga strada
Che di Virgilio fa parlare assai.'

The manner in which Aliprando mixes together legend and history in his account of Vergil naturally leads us to the consideration of the Vergilian biography which bears the name of Donatus. As has already been shown,[36] this work contains interpolations of different kinds, most of them literary in origin, but some few popular. The only one of these, however, which removes the poet out of his proper sphere of action as a man of letters is a story that relates how Vergil was brought under Augustus' notice by his skill as a veterinary surgeon. His only ward however for these services used to consist of bread, or the Emperor regarded him merely as a plain stable-man. Onf day though, after Vergil had guessed quite accurately the sire and dam of a certain horse, Augustus, who had some doubts as to his own origin, asked him, to prove his skill, if he could tell him from whom he was descended. 'You are the son of a baker,' was the prompt reply, 'for you give me nothing but bread.' Here it is clear that Vergil simply appears as the author of a more or less witty remark, and not in any way as a magician; the fundamental idea of the story is rather that of the supernatural wisdom which enabled Vergil, even in matters of veterinary surgery, to know more than other people. From this Roth argues that the interpolation may be due to some Neapolitan at the beginning of the 12th century, but in all probability it is of much later origin. Roth himself remarks

[34] *Germania*, v. p. 371. Vergil has scarcely opened the book when he finds himself surrounded by 80,000 devils asking for orders.

"Er sprach : Vart in den grûnen walt,
Und macht mir palt
Eine gute strâz, das man dar nâch muge varen und ouch rîten,"

[35] Lib. iii., cap. i. v. 5.
[36] *Vide* supra, p. 141 seqq.

that the story is not found in any text of Donatus earlier than the 15th century ; while, in the *Novellino* [37] (second half of the 13th century) the same story is told of a Greek scholar, and it occurs besides in the Arabian Nights. To this may be added the fact that Aliprando, who made such constant use of this biography, altogether ignores the anecdote, and that it is not found attributed to Vergil in any writer earlier than the 15th century. Were there, however, any such connection, as Roth attempts to show, between it and the bronze horse of the Neapolitan legend, it would surely have been mentioned by some of the writers who record the Vergilian legends. Hence it seems almost certain that this interpolation is not earlier than the 15th century.[38] But be this as it may, there can be no doubt that in the biography this legend stands alone, and that the biography of Donatus, however many stories of literary origin may have been interpolated into it, has been very little influenced by the popular legends. In fact, as we have already seen, it has rather served to supply the authors of Vergilian legends with materials than taken such legends into itself. In certain other Latin biographies of Vergil, indeed, written at a late period of the middle ages, chiefly for the use of schools, the ideas of magician and astrologer come out more clearly, though they are nowhere greatly developed. Thus, in an unpublished Latin biography to which reference has already been made,[39] Vergil is described as a great magician, doctor and

[37] Cp. also the novel published by PAPANTI, *Cat. dei nov. in prosa*, i p. xv. seqq.

[38] AMPÈRE (*L'empire romain à Rome*, i. p. 351 seqq.) maintains that this story was attributed to Vergil because of the grave of the baker, M. Vergilius Eurysaces, which is now to be seen at Rome near the Porta Maggiore, decorated with bas-reliefs illustrative of the art of baking, and was discovered in the year 1838, after having for many centuries been covered by buildings as old as the time of Honorius. But, besides the many other objections which might be urged against this view, Ampère has failed to perceive the absurdity of supposing this late interpolation to belong to the times of Donatus himself, who lived only a little before the reign of Honorius.

[39] Cp. supra, p. 147. The legends of Vergil as magician, which were well known to the author of this biography, who believed them to be true, find a confirmation, according to him, in Vergil's poems, for the 8th eclogue shows that he was versed in magic. But this does not mean, as VIETOR (*op. cit.*, p. 169) asserts and GRAF (*Roma*, etc., ii. p. 238) admits that, according to this writer, the scene in the 8th Eclogue was the origin of

astrologer, and an account is given of the *Salvatio Romae* which he made.

This brief glance at the progress of the Vergilian legend in Italy will have served to show that it never attained in that country to such startling proportions as it did elsewhere. The only story which seems to have been really well known in Italy was that of the chest, which had already, under the guidance of moralists or satirists, made the round of Europe, but which was, as we have already seen, quite distinct in origin from the rest of the legends. Of Vergil as magician in league with the devil there appears in Italy but a faint reflection of the foreign extravagances. In the 14th century, notwithstanding the extensive development the legend had already undergone in Germany and France, the author of the *Cronica* knows little more of it than was current at Naples before ever it spread into Europe; Boccaccio knows merely two or three of the Neapolitan legends; while Aliprando, at the beginning of the 15th century, has only the roughest and most inconsistent conception of Vergil as magician, and is ignorant of the greater part of the legends connected with him, Neapolitan as well as foreign. Neither in the legendary accounts of the *Cronica* nor in those of Aliprando do we ever entirely lose sight of Vergil the poet; how far different is the case with the foreign legends, we have already seen. In the 16th century again one comes across a fact which shows how little the Italians were inclined to associate the name of the poet with these fables. The anonymous writer of the *Compassionevoli avvenimenti di Erasto*, while paraphrasing the *Roman des Sept Sages* and referring to the inextinguishable fire and the marvellous mirror, yet makes no mention of Vergil and transfers the scene of the story from Rome to Rhodes. It is easy to understand the little headway made by these legends in Italy, when one considers that just

these legends, and in no way proves that their origin was literary. As every one knows, the 8th Eclogue of Vergil is merely an imitation of Theocritus, and Theocritus was never supposed to be a magician. In a Vergil MS. of the 14th century (now in the Laurentian Library; Sta. Maria Novella, 180) there is a biography of the poet which describes his works of necromancy; this biography is, however, wholly derived from the *Lives of the Philosophers* of WALTER BURLEY.

about this time the Renaissance was beginning. That serious
and regular study of classical authors which was taking the
place of the former indiscriminating traditional admiration
was eminently calculated to dissipate the legendary haloes with
which the ignorance of the middle ages had decorated the great
names of Latin literature. Italy was the first to raise again
the torch of knowledge, and such legends as came within the
brightness of that torch could only venture there furtively and
under the shadow of jest or superstition.

CHAPTER X

WE are now in a position to examine the ultimate phase through which the Vergilian legend passed. This phase, as we have seen, was bound to be a sort of synthesis of all preceding ones— a legendary biography, in fact. Such a conglomeration and development of the Vergilian legends into a biography is to be found in the Liège Chronicle of Jean d'Outremeuse, entitled the *Myreur des Histors*.[1] This Chronicle is a compilation from all sorts of writers down to the 14th century, and presents, especially in the part which treats of ancient history, an extraordinary farrago of legends and absurdities of every sort. The biography of Vergil appears in combination with various other stories, which interrupt it from time to time, for the writer never forgets that it is the duty of a chronicler to respect chronology; indeed, so impressed is he with the paramount importance of this duty, that, when he does not know a date, he invents it, a process which is, not unnaturally, often necessary in the case of the legends. But, apart from the imaginary dates which serve to connect it with the rest of the history, the biography of Vergil seems to have been composed by its author separately before being assigned its place in the Chronicle; and it is a remarkable work in more ways than one.

The author had before him, in the first place, the *Image du Monde*, and, in addition to this, several other French and Latin texts treating of Vergilian miracles. His aim is to unite as many of these legends as possible, and so he occasionally records

---

[1] *Ly myreur des histors, chronique de Jean des Preis dit d'Outremeuse pub. par* AD. BORGNET, Brux., 1864. Cp. LIEBRECHT in the *Germania* of PFEIFFER, x. p. 408 seqq.; STECHER, *La légende de Virgile en Belgique*, p, 621 seqq.

as different incidents two or three versions of the same story.[2] Some incidents again he has invented, while others he has developed with an imaginative power worthy of a better cause. In all this he has striven as far as possible to exclude all reference to the real personality of Vergil, and has carefully avoided mixing the notices of biographers, such as Donatus, with the legends. His Vergil has three different aspects, all of them legendary — the magician, the gallant, and the prophet of Christ. The exclusion of all historical facts is the more noteworthy, since it is evidently done of set purpose, for the author was doubtless acquainted with Vergil's poetry and with his ancient biographies, and has not failed in the rest of his work to accumulate as many authorities as possible. His portrait moreover of the legendary Vergil is, in the three aspects already noticed, far more highly coloured than that of any of his predecessors.

The scenes of Vergil's activity are still Rome and Naples, but he is no longer an Italian by birth, but the son of Gorgilius, King of Bugia in Libya. He leaves his home in search of adventures and, arriving at the kingdom of the Latins, is so impressed by the account given by the king (an uncle of Julius Caesar) of the city of Rome, that he decides to go there. It would be tedious and unprofitable to follow his adventures at Rome in detail; it will suffice to point out generally the connection between his history as told in this work and the legends with which we are already familiar. The stories previously enumerated were enough, one would have thought, to characterise Vergil as a magician of sufficiently deep dye, without requiring the help of more; yet Jean d'Outremeuse does not fail to add several, chiefly with a view of emphasising the magnificent way of life which Vergil's magic enabled him to adopt. Among

[2] Thus, for instance, in the *Cleomadès* it is stated that Vergil set up in Rome four statues, representing the four seasons, which used to hand on an apple from one to the other as the seasons changed. The *Romans des Sept Sages*, on the other hand, speaks of two such statues, which indicated in this way the passage of the weeks. Jean d'Outremeuse attributes to Vergil the four statues of the seasons, the two of the weeks, and twelve more besides for the twelve months of the year. These last are also mentioned in JEAN MANSEL'S *Fleur des Histoires*. Cp. DU MÉRIL, *Mélanges*, p. 440.

such additions is the account of the entertainments given by
Vergil, at which, to amuse his guests, he caused the spirits
under his control to perform all sorts of tricks and buffooneries.[3]

More noteworthy than this however is the development
which Jean d'Outremeuse has given to the idea of Vergil as
prophet of Christ. We have already seen that this idea was
not in its origin popular, but that it subsequently became so,
and that it had not hitherto been associated to any great extent
with the idea of Vergil as magician, though there had been,
as already noted, certain points of contact between the two
legends;[4] but Jean d'Outremeuse, thinking all is fish that
comes to his net, has no hesitation in mixing them thoroughly
together. Some had maintained that Vergil, in quoting the
words of the Sibyl, had borne witness to the faith without
knowing it, while others asserted that the famous lines of the
Fourth Eclogue were a deliberate and intentional prophecy of
Christ; Jean d'Outremeuse however goes farther, and, though
his dislike for historical facts prevents him from mentioning
the Sibyl or quoting the verses, yet he introduces Vergil as
delivering long discourses, not only to the Romans but also to
the Egyptians—discourses in which, not content with the mere
prediction of Christ's coming, he enters into full particulars of
His life and death, and expounds the doctrine of the Trinity
and all the other articles of the Creed, thereby converting
large numbers of persons to the Faith that was to be. All this
does not prevent Vergil from continuing to be a magician;
only when the famous speaking head had foretold his approaching death, then at last he sends to the devil all the
spirits that had served him, and humbles himself before God
by making a confession of his faith. After this he writes a
book on Christianity, gives a final banquet, at which he incul-
cates its doctrines, has himself provisionally baptised and finally

[3] It is well known how Albertus Magnus used to entertain his guests by
making spring appear in mid-winter and the like. Similar stories were told
of the great magician Pases. Cp. SUIDAS, s. v. Πάσης, and FRIEDLÄNDER,
Darst. d. Sittengeschichte Roms, i. p. 364.

[4] It is entirely foreign to the Neapolitan legend, which is the more remarkable seeing that in the neighbourhood of Cumae the name of the Sibyl
is preserved by the Neapolitans in connection with the famous cave.

settles himself to die, holding in his hand a work on theology
and being seated in an arm-chair on which he had with his
own hand depicted all the events of the New Testament, from
the Annunciation to the Assumption. And there he remained
sitting till St. Paul came in search of him and pulled his mantle,
whereupon he fell into dust. The apostle was grieved, thinking
that he had died a pagan, but consoled himself on reading the
work he had left behind him.

Equally liberal has the author been in his development of
the story of the chest, which, duly amplified, forms the foundation of the whole series of gallant adventures in this biography.
Though she had never seen him, the beautiful Phoebilla,
daughter of Julius Caesar, heard so much about Vergil that
she got to be in love with him as few women have ever been.
So ardent was this passion that, putting aside every consideration, the imperial lady sent for Vergil and made him the following ingenuous declaration: 'Sire Virgile, dites-moy se vos
aveis amie; car se vos me voleis avoir, je suis vostre pour
prendre a femme ou estre votre amie; s'il vos plaiste.' Vergil
answered that, as for marrying, that was not in his line, but
that otherwise he was at her disposal; and so began an intrigue
that lasted a long while. As time went on, however, and the
fame of Vergil grew greater and greater by reason of the various
wonders that he did, Phoebilla began to grow more and more
anxious to be recognised as his wife. But every time that she
broached the subject, which occurred pretty often, Vergil answered her that just then he had something else to think
about, 'ilh moy convient penser à outres chouses,' and that his
studies would not allow him to marry; if, however, one day he
were able to do so, she should be the favoured one. But the one
day never came, and Phoebilla, sick at last of being put off to the
Greek calends, suddenly came out with a story that her father
had discovered everything and was threatening terrible punishment. Vergil however, being omniscient, promptly told her to
try that on some one else, and said that, as to marrying, he could
not think of it, but that, if she liked, he was willing to go on
as they were. Phoebilla, thus slighted, pretended to agree, but
meditated revenge; she said that her father, to prevent her

from having any intercourse with Vergil, had determined to shut her up in a tower, but that she proposed drawing him up through the window in a chest. And here comes in the incident with which we are already familiar, only it is told in a very different manner.   Jean d'Outremeuse has noticed that the Vergil of the first part of this story does not agree with the Vergil of the second, and has accordingly introduced a variation which does away with the contradiction.   Vergil, according to him, was well aware of the trap which had been set for him, but pretended not to be, and therefore put into the chest a spirit which he caused to resemble himself in appearance.   The spirit played its part to perfection, and, as soon as it was day, the emperor hastened to the spot to punish the vile seducer, but was greatly disconcerted when, on cutting open the head of the supposed Vergil with his sword, there came out, instead of blood, a pestilent smoke which filled the air to such an extent that it became as dark as night.

Not content with this, Vergil left Rome, taking with him all the fire; but, moved by the prayers of the emperor and the Romans, he consented to make peace,—not however before playing another trick on poor Phoebilla, for one day he caused by his enchantments all the women who were in a certain temple to begin to tell in a loud voice all their secrets, and among them was Phoebilla, who seems to have had some particularly interesting ones to tell.   Shortly afterwards occurred the death of Julius Caesar, who was succeeded by Octavian; Caesar's widow however, who laid claim to the throne, entered into a conspiracy with her daughter Phoebilla to get rid of Octavian and of Vergil, who was his great ally.   But Vergil, who knew all about their intentions, arranged with the aid of his demons a new trick, too complicated to be described briefly, by means of which the two women killed two dogs in the belief that they were their two enemies.   Vergil, who had expected that the conspirators, thus discovered, would be punished, was so incensed when they escaped through the influence of the Senate, that he left Rome for ever, once more taking the fire with him and letting the Romans know that the only way to recover it was from the person of Phoebilla; the latter. being

constrained to undergo this further disgrace, died shortly afterwards of shame and mortification.　And here, according to the
Mireur des Histors, Vergil's connection with the female sex
comes to an end, for though Jean d'Outremeuse mentions the
Bocca della Verità, he does not relate the anecdote connected
with it.

As the reader will have observed, what Jean d'Outremeuse
has done is merely to amplify as far as he can the various
legends already current and to reduce them to order by occasionally modifying or retouching them.　But this version of his
was buried in a voluminous and little read chronicle, so that,
although interesting to us as furnishing in a brief compass a
view of the whole legend at a certain stage of its development,
it can merely be regarded as the work of an individual and
could have had little or no influence on the spread of the Vergilian legends themselves.　In fact, the work on Vergil which
was most popular in Europe from the 16th century onwards is
entirely different in character to this version, and has nothing
in common with it except a few stories derived from the same
sources.　A brief examination will make it sufficiently clear
that this work originated in France.[5]　No MS. of it is known,
and in any case its composition does not seem anterior to the
invention of printing.　The earliest printed version known is
the French, entitled *Les faits merveilleux de Virgille*, of which
there are several very rare editions, dating from the beginning
of the 16th century, and two modern ones, which are also hard
to procure.[6]　The popularity of this work was so great that it
was translated into various languages ; three such translations,

---

[5] Görres (*Die teutschen Volksbücher*, p. 228) confounds the origin of the
book with that of the legend when he maintains that the former first appeared in Italy.　From what we have seen of the state of the legend in Italy
this is manifestly impossible.

[6] Brunet (*Manuel*, ii. 1167 seq.) describes five editions, the latest of
which dates from the year 1530.　The edition of Guillaume Nyverd has
been reproduced in facsimile by Techener (Paris, 1831) and by Pinard in
the same year.　A more recent reprint, of 100 copies, bears the title *Les
faits merveilleux de Virgille, réimpression textuelle de l'édition sans date,
publiée à Paris, chez Guillaume Nyverd: suivie d'une notice bibliographique
par* Philomneste Junior, Genève, chez I. Gay et fils, éditeurs.　1867.

in English,[7] Dutch[8] and German,[9] were published; a fourth, in
Icelandic, remains in manuscript.[10] As is generally the case
in the translation of popular books, the versions furnish variants; but these are of small moment, consisting merely of
occasional additions or substitutions which do not in any way
influence the character of the work as a whole.

The idea of the prophet, which attains to such great proportions in the account of Jean d'Outremeuse, is entirely wanting
in this work. In the treatment of the marvels of Vergil's
doing, again, there is a complete absence of the erudition which
characterises d'Outremeuse, who did not fail to include in
his account whatever he could find in literature dealing with
the subject. Thus, in the *Faits merveilleux* a number of the
talismans, such as the fly, the horse, and so on, are omitted.
On the other hand, other parts of the legend are treated with
much greater freedom than in the *Mireur des Histors*.

The book begins with a legend about the founding of Rome
and of the city of Rheims, a legend which exists independently
of this work and appears also in the *Roman d'Atis et Profilias*.[11]

[7] *This boke treatethe of the lyfe of Virgilius and of his death, and many
maravayles that he did in his lyfe tyme by witchcraft and nigromansy, thorough
the help of the devylls of hell. Emprynted in the cytie of Anwarpe by me
Jokn Doesborcke* (s. d.) 4°, 30 pp. with woodcuts. This book, of which only
one copy is known, was reprinted by UTTERSON (London, 1812; 60 copies).
This edition was reproduced by THOMS in his collection, *Early English prose
romances*, Lond., 1828 (2nd ed., Lond., 1858), No. 2. This was translated into
German by SPAZIER (Brunswick, 1830). An extensive extract from this
English version appears in WRIGHT, *Narratives of sorcery and magic*, Lond.,
1851, i. p. 103 seqq.

[8] *Een schone Historie van Virgilius van zijn Leuen, Doot, ende van zijn
wonderlijke werken, di hy deede by Nigromantien, ende by dat behulpe des
Duyvels.* T' Amsterdam by H. S. Muller, 1552. For this version, which is
based on the English, *vide* GÖRRES, *Die teutschen Volksbücher*, p. 225 seqq.,
and VAN DEN BERGH, *De Nederlandsche volksromans.* (Amst., 1837), p. 84 seqq.
The German translation of v. D. HAGEN, *Erzählungen und Märchen*, i. p. 153
seqq. has been reproduced by SCHEIBLE, *Das Kloster*, ii. p. 129 seqq.

[9] Pub. by SIMROCK in his *Deutschen Volksbücher*, Fr. a. M., vol. vi. (1847),
p. 323 seqq., but no ancient editions of this version, which is based on the
Dutch, seem to be known. A free version of this German text has been
published as the second volume in the series *Medieval Legends* (D. Nutt,
1893).

[10] This translation was made in 1676 from the Dutch; the MS. is at
Copenhagen. *Vide* HALFDAN EINARSSON, *Hist. lit. isl.*, 108; NYERUP, *Dan.
Volksbücher*, p. 203; MÜLLER, *Sagabibl.*, iii. p. 484.

[11] DU MÉRIL, *Mélanges*, p. 426.

Vergil is the son of a knight in the Ardennes and is born not long after the foundation of Rome; on the day of his birth the whole city trembles. While studying at Toledo, he learns that his mother has been robbed of her property, and hastens at her request to Rome. Failing to obtain justice from the Emperor,[12] he persecutes his enemies with his spells and, when attacked in his castle by the Emperor himself, compels the latter by his magic arts to make peace with him and restore his property. The fundamental idea of this story is of course the actual incident in Vergil's life familiar to every reader of the First Eclogue. The adventure of the chest, which had in Jean d'Outremeuse's hands undergone such changes, here keeps its primitive form. To this however, and also to the story of the *Bocca della Verità*, (here described as the mouth of a bronze serpent,) certain additions are made which give the book all the features of a romance. Vergil was married, and among the various articles of general utility which he made was a figure suspended in the air and visible from every part of Rome, which had the property of curbing all unchaste desires on the part of every woman that saw it.[13] This did not please the

---

[12] The Roman Emperor of Vergil's time is, according to this book, a certain Persis, who figures also in the *Mirabilia*. According to the *Roman des Sept Sages* Vergil lived under Servius; the *Gesta Romanorum* in one chapter puts him in the time of Titus, in another in that of Darius. Hans Sachs locates him in Britain at the court of King Arthur.

[13] In a *History of Pisa* written in French in the 15th century, a MS. of which is at Berne, mention is made of two pillars set up by Vergil, which are still in the cathedral at Pisa, on which used to appear the portraits of all who were guilty of flagrant offences. *Vide* De Sinner, *Cat. codd. mss. bibl. Bernensis*, ii. p. 129; Du Méril, *Mélanges*, p. 472. In contradiction to this story, in which Vergil appears as the guardian of public morals, is another, according to which he made an artificial prostitute for the use of the Romans. This is related by Enenkel in his *Weltbuch*; cp. v. D. Hagen, *Gesammtabenteuer*, ii. p. 515; Massmann, *Kaiserchronik*, iii. p. 451. A Rabbinic legend also speaks of such a statue as existing at Rome; *vide* Praetorius, *Anthropodemus pluton.*, i. p. 150, and Liebrecht in the *Germania* of Pfeiffer, x. p. 414. We may notice a curious fact which perhaps gave rise to this strange legend. The *Mirabilia*, in describing a fountain ornamented by a Medusa, says: "femina circumdata serpentibus sedens et habens concham ante se significat Ecclesiam multis scripturarum voluminibus circumdatam, quam quicunque audire voluerit non poterit nisi prius lavetur in concha illa." In many MSS. this is corrupted as follows: "femina circumdata serpentibus sedens habens concham ante se (signat) pudicatores qui pudicabant eam, ut quicunque ad eam ire voluerit non poterit nisi prius

Roman ladies, who accordingly asked Vergil's wife to remove
the nuisance, whereupon she, in her husband's absence, climbed
up to the figure by means of a magical bridge of his and threw
it to the ground.   Vergil on his return was very angry, and·
replaced the figure; his wife again attempted to throw it down,
but this time he caught her in the act and threw her down
after it.   Discouraged however by his ill-success, he gave up
trying to contend with the evil passions of women; 'pour bien
je l'avoye faite,' he exclaims, 'mais plus ne m'en meslerai et
facent les dames à leur voulenté.'[14]

   But if in this anecdote a spirit of misogyny prevails, such is
not the case in the gallant adventures that follow.   Disgusted
with his wife, Vergil remembers to have heard of the beauty of
the daughter of the Sultan of Babylon; quick as lightning he
visits her and persuades her to accompany him through the air
to Rome.   As soon as the lady wishes to return to her father,
he carries her back instantaneously and then returns himself
to Rome.   When the Sultan asks his daughter where she has
been, she tells him everything except Vergil's name, which
she did not know.   'When he returns,' says the Sultan, 'ask
him to give you some of the fruit of his native country.'   This
she does, and so the Sultan learns from what country he comes.
But that is not enough.   'When he returns,' says the Sultan
again, 'make him drink a sleeping-draught, which I will give
you; in that way we shall find out who he is,'—his real object
being to take vengeance on the seducer of his daughter.   The
plan succeeds; Vergil and his paramour are seized and thrown
into prison, and condemned to be burnt alive.   But when the
day of execution arrives, Vergil utters a spell, which makes it
appear as if the river were overflowing its banks; the Sultan
and his court, imagining themselves in the water, begin to
make desperate efforts to swim, while Vergil, rising into the
air before their eyes, carries off his lady to Rome.   Arrived

lavetur in concha illa."   GRAESSE, *Beiträge*, p. 8 and p. viii.; cp. too the
Graphia aureae urbis Romae, in OZANAM, *Documents inédits*, p. 170.
   [14] In the French *Romance of the Holy Graal*, Hippocrates has a wife who
causes him much trouble and eventually brings about his death.   There is
thus a noteworthy parallel between this legend and that of Vergil.   *Vide*
P. PARIS, *Les romans de la table ronde*, i. 267 seqq.

there, he wishes to give her a husband and to provide her with a suitable dowry, so he founds for her the city of Naples, which is so beautiful that the Emperor of Rome becomes jealous and besieges it; but Vergil with his spells puts him to flight, and the Sultan's daughter is married to a Spanish nobleman who had helped Vergil in the defence of the city.[15] At Naples Vergil founds a school of necromancy, builds a bridge for the use of merchants, embellishes the city in various other ways, and continues to live there till the day of his death.

The earlier legends had, as we have seen, accepted, with certain modifications, the historical account of Vergil's death; but to the author of the *Faits merveilleux* it seemed unworthy of such a man to die of a simple inflammation of the brain brought on by a sunstroke. In the French version, accordingly, of this popular work Vergil goes out to sea one day and is surprised by a furious tempest in which he disappears without leaving a trace; while in the other versions the manner of his death is still more striking and dignified. Vergil, perceiving that he was growing old, wished to make himself young again; so, after giving all the necessary instructions to his faithful slave, he had himself cut in pieces and salted. Everything went satisfactorily and the rejuvenescence began; only unfortunately the emperor, who had become a great friend of Vergil's and felt anxious at not having seen him for some days, came in suddenly and by this means inadvertently broke the charm. Thereupon appeared the naked figure of a child, which flew three times round the cauldron which contained the body, crying out, 'Cursed be the hour in which you came'; then it vanished and Vergil remained dead. This story, which suggests the classical legend of Pelias and Medea, is not uncommon in medieval writers,[16] but its application to Vergil is of very late date. By a curious coincidence, it is told also of Paracelsus, who speaks in his works of the magician Vergil.

---

[15] ROTH sees in this an allusion to the Spanish conquest of Naples and maintains therefore that the book cannot be earlier than 1435. *Op. cit.*, p. 283.

[16] GRAESSE, *Die Sage d. ewig. Jude*, p. 44; SIMROCK, *Handb. d. deutschen Mythologie* (ed. ii.), p. 260.

The adventure with the Sultan's daughter, so different in character to the other stories which bring Vergil into connection with women, has undoubtedly, like the other novel features in the account, found its way into this work from some pre-, vious collection of popular legends, possibly from a romance of Spanish origin.[17] At any rate, it is with this legend and no other that the *Romance de Virgilio* in the *Romancero* of 1550 must be connected, slight though that connection is. Here even the legendary Vergil is hardly recognisable; the powerful magician has disappeared, though he has not given place to the prophet or the grammarian, and still less to the poet. The only characteristic which recalls the legendary Vergil is the fact that he is in love. In this romance Vergil appears as a gallant *hidalgo*, who, when punished for an indiscreet amour, bears his punishment with saintly patience and, as a reward, obtains at length the object of his affections, to whom he is married with the sanction of the king and the blessing of the archbishop.[19]

The following is a condensed version of the romance:—

'The king commanded that Vergil should be arrested and put in prison, as punishment for the violence he had offered in the palace to a lady called Donna Isabella. Seven years he kept him in prison without thinking of him, till one Sunday at dinner[20] he remembered him. 'Where is Vergil?' he asked his knights. Then answered a knight, who was Vergil's friend, 'Your highness has caused him to be put in prison.' 'Well then,' said the king, 'let us eat, and after dinner we will go and see Vergil.' 'No,' answered the queen, 'without him I will not eat.' 'What are you doing, Vergil; what are you

---

[17] Cp. Nov. 5, of Book i. of the *Pantschatantra* in BENFEY, i. p. 159 seqq.

[18] *Romancero castellano publ. por* G. B. DEPPING, tom. ii., No. 82, p. 202 seq. Cp. TICKNOR, *History of Spanish literature*, i. p. 114 seq.

[19] BRAGA, in his *Historia da poesia popular portugueza* (Oporto, 1867), p. 176 seqq., finds a parallel to this legend in the Portuguese legend of Reginaldo (ALMEIDA GARRET, *Romanceiro*, ii. p. 163 seqq.), in which a page is condemned to death for seducing the king's daughter, but the king, hearing him sing in his prison, pardons him and gives him his daughter in marriage.

[20] HINARD (*Romancero espagnol*, ii. p. 242) translates "at mass," and DURAN, OCHOA and others read "*en misa*"; but DEPPING's reading "*en mesa*" is certainly the right one.

doing?' asked the king, when they were come to the place. 'My lord, I am combing my beard and my hair, for here must they grow and grow grey, for to-day it is seven years since you imprisoned me.' 'Be patient, be patient, Vergil; but three years more are needed to make ten.' 'My lord, if your highness bids me, I will pass all my life in this place.' 'Vergil, as reward of your patience, to-day you shall dine with me.' 'My clothes are torn, I cannot show myself.' 'I will give you clothes, Vergil; I will bid them bring you them.' This pleased the knights and the ladies, and most of all did it please a lady called Donna Isabella; so they called an archbishop and married her to Vergil. Then he took her by the hand and led her out into the garden.'

Herewith the long list of strange stories to which the fame of Vergil gave rise throughout the middle ages may come to a close. After the 16th century the Vergilian legends disappear and become known only to scholars. The age of credulity was past and the phantasies which it had generated were dissipated before the clear light of critical reason and empirical philosophy. The highest regions of human activity were freed from the intrusion of the uncultured, and works of science and art were no longer under the influence of the aberrations of ignorance. So great a change could not, of course, come about suddenly; its progress was gradual; and thus the Vergilian legends, though their treatment has become scientific, have left clear traces in various learned works which deal with the occult sciences. In the 15th and 16th centuries Trithemius, Paracelsus, Vigenère, Le Loyer and others mention the legends of Vergil's magical powers, believe them and even augment them.[21] Even in the 17th century, when the question as to whether magic and witchcraft had any real existence,[22]—a question earnest enough when the stake was so often called upon to

[21] BL. DE VIGENÈRE, in his *Traité des chiffres et secrètes manières d'écrire*, speaks of a Vergilian alphabet; TRITHEMIUS (*Antipal.* i. cap. 3) of tables made by Vergil to determine the characters of persons; PARACELSUS (*De imaginibus*, cap. xi.) attributes to him magic images; LE LOYER (*Des spectres*, etc., cap. vi.) an echo.

[22] Cp. ROSKOFF, *Gesch. des Teufels* (Leipz. 1869), ii. p. 359 seqq.

B B

solve it,—was eagerly discussed, the magic of Vergil was from
time to time referred to as an historical fact. Men who in
their temperament and modes of thought belonged still to the
middle ages could not bring themselves to believe that a man
of Gervasius of Tilbury's position should have recorded what
was not true.[23]   At length however the learned and clear-
headed Gabriel Naudé finally overthrew these and similar
legends in a work which gained a great celebrity at the time,[24]
and which, obvious though its arguments may now seem, did
not fail to meet with opposition. But the progress of the intellectual regeneration soon brought forgetfulness of the middle
ages, which came to be regarded as a distant epoch, little
deserving of serious attention. When the Vergilian legends
were alluded to, as they were from time to time by scholars,
they were treated as curiosities, just as in several collections of
antiquities there were preserved 'magic' mirrors which bore
the name of Vergil.[25]   And so in more recent times, when the
study of the middle ages was recommenced, the conception of
the great Latin poet had become so far removed from that
current in medieval times, that it seemed quite unintelligible
how such legends could have arisen, and more than one scholar
refused to believe that they really referred to the author of
the Aeneid, and preferred to assign them to Vergil, Bishop of

---

[23] "Gervasium quod attinet . . .   haud quidem eum fabulosum et
vanum auctorem existimaverim; fuit enim Cancellarius Aulae Othonis Im-
perialis, cui etiam aliud opus, *Ocia imperialia* inscriptum, dedicavit . . .
Fatendum quidem est fabulosa nonnunquam a principibus legi, sed a *Can-
cellariis* non proficiscuntur." Iac. Gaffarelli, *Curiositates inauditae*, p. 160.
L'Ancre too, in his work *L'incrédulité et mescréane du sortilège plainement
convaincue*, cites (p. 280 seq.) the instance of Vergil; cp. Bodin, *Daemonom.*,
lib. ii. c. 2.

[24] *Apologie pour tous les grands personnages qui ont esté faussement soupçonnés de magie.*   The whole of chap. xxi. is devoted to Vergil. Of Gervasius and his work he says : " qui est à la vérité si rempli de choses absurdes
fabuleuses et du tout impossibles, que difficilement me pourrois je persuader
qu'il fust en son bon sens quand il le composoit " (p. 611).

[25] There was one at Florence in the 17th century; *vide* Naudé, *op. cit.*,
p. 627. Another, which was last century still in the treasury of St. Denis
at Paris, was described in the ancient inventory thus: " Le miroir du prince
des poètes Virgile, qui est de jaiet." Fougeroux de Boudaroy read a paper
on it to the Academy of Sciences in 1787. The mirror was accidentally
broken by Mabillon while he was examining it. *Vide* Du Méril, *Mél.*,
p. 447.

Salzburg, or some other medieval Vergil.[26] This idea was erroneous and devoid of all evidence in its favour, as may be easily gathered from what has gone before; but at least it had the advantage of simplicity over the long and tortuous course which we have been compelled to follow in our endeavour to trace to its source the conception of Vergil as it presented itself to the medieval intellect.

As for the oral popular traditions, they only remained alive after the middle ages in Naples and Southern Italy, the home of their birth.[27] At Monte Vergine they were still flourishing

[26] This was the view of COLLIN DE PLANCY, LE GRAND D'AUSSY; cp. too *Mélanges tirés d'une grande biblioth.*, v. p. 182.

[27] The fame of Vergil could only of course extend to countries of Latin culture and belonging to the Latin Church; among the Byzantines, the modern Greeks and the Slavs his influence was naturally but small; at the same time however there are unquestionable traces of the legendary Vergil in modern Sclavonic popular tradition. Thus there is a game played by Polish children (brought to my notice by the late Prof. DE SCHIEFNER; cp. *Ehstnische Märchen aufgez. v.* KREUTZWALD, *übers. v.* LOEWE, Halle, 1869, p. 357 seq.) in which the name of Vergil occurs. Vergil stands in the middle of his comrades, who dance round him, holding hands and singing:

" Ojcice Wirgiliusz uczyl dzieci swoje
Hejże, dzieci, hejże ha,
Róbcie wszystko, co i ja."

(Father Vergil taught his boys: "Attention, boys, attention; do everything that I do.") Then the dancers stop and have to imitate whatever Vergil does; any one who fails to imitate him must become Vergil in his stead. It might perhaps be doubted whether there is here any allusion to the magician Vergil; but De Schiefner instances as a parallel an English game in which the central figure is called Simon, by which Simon Magus must be meant.

Among the Servians and Croatians there exists a belief in a mysterious locality known as *vrzino kolo* (cp. VUK STEPH. KARADSCHITSCH, *Lex. Serbic.* s.v.), which is the *Thirteenth School*, i.e. that in which necromancy is learnt; and in a Sclavonic index (not later than the 14th century) of apocryphal and proscribed books it is said of the heretical Bulgarian priest Ieremias (10th century) that he *byw w nawieh na werzilowie kolou.* This obscure expression was ingeniously interpreted by IAGIČ, who recognised in the words *vrzino* and *werzilowie* the name of Vergil the magician. The heretic Ieremias, who was also accused of sorcery, is here described as "going among the dead in the circle of Vergil" in search of the wisdom with which to produce his heretical works, and this "circle of Vergil" is the *Thirteenth School* from which, according to a superstition still current in Servia and Croatia, necromancy proceeds. Vide *Archiv. f. slav. Philol.*, ii. (1877) p. 465 seqq.; PYPIN Y SPASOWIČ, *Istorija Slavianskih Literatur* (2nd edit., St. Petersburg, 1879) i. p. 84 seqq.; *Archivio per lo studio delle trad. pop.*, vi., 1887, p. 266 seqq.

A Sclavonic version of the *Faits merveilleux* does not, to my knowledge,

in the 17th century. Padre Giordano, the Abbot of the
monastery there, who accepted them all as facts, compiled with
their assistance a curious biography of the poet, a work of
much learning, in which, besides the historical and legendary
authorities with which we are already familiar, we find also
references to oral tradition, and not a little, it must be said,
which is clearly due to the author's own invention.[28] In Naples
itself the legends continued to exist in a modified form among
the people, and even at the beginning of the present century
several travellers mention them.[29]   One of these speaks of a
visit which he paid to the *School of Vergil*[30] and relates,—with
how much accuracy we do not know,—part of a conversation
he had with an old fisherman who lived on the spot.

exist; a popular Servian tale presents some of the features of the death of
Vergil as recorded in some forms of that work, and also alludes to the extinction of the fire; but the name of Vergil does not occur (vide *Archiv f.
slav. Philol.*, i. (1876, p. 286 seq.). The only popular work, as far as I know,
which could have brought the conception of Vergil as magician before the
Sclavs is the *Book of the Seven Sages*, which was translated in the 14th
century already into Bohemian, and subsequently into Polish and Russian,
and in this form enjoyed a wide popularity in Russia itself. BUSLAIEFF has
published (*Istoričeskaja Christomatija*, Moscow, 1861, pp. 1393–5), from a
17th century MS. in his possession, the part of the story which refers to
Vergil. Cp. MURKO, *Die Gesch. d. Sieben Weisen bei den Slaven*, Vienna,
1890 (*Sitzungsber. d. k. k. Akad.*).

[28] *Croniche di Montevergine*, pp. 66–95. According to Padre Giordano
Vergil was very anxious to learn the meaning of the Sibylline books, which
contained a prophecy of the birth of Christ. He took the verses of the
Fourth Eclogue from this passage, but without understanding their real
meaning. He studied this subject so earnestly that at last he got ill and
had to go for his health to Naples, Octavian making him consul of that city.
To rest from the cares of office he went to spend a few days at Avella, where
he heard of the famous oracle of Cybele, which was on the hill known afterwards as Montevergine. He went to consult this as to the meaning of the
Sibylline books, but at first received no answer. When he asked again, the
Oracle answered, "Satis est; discedite," and, on his consulting it a third
time, "Satis est; nondum tempus." Hoping therefore for an answer before
long, Vergil built a villa on the hill and planted there his famous garden.
But no answer ever came, and at last he abandoned the Sibylline books in
despair and decided to compose the Aeneid, undertaking with this object
the journey to Greece which proved fatal to him. In this account historical
and legendary matter are found in connection with details which are evidently due to the author himself, for P. Giordano does not defend them by
reference to any authority, as he always does when he can.

[29] Cp. v. d. HAGEN, *Briefe in die Heimath*, iii. p. 180; DUNLOP-LIEBRECHT,
p. 187; ROTH, *op. cit.*, p. 280.

[30] *Vide* supra, p. 348 seq.

'Sit on that wall,' the old man said to him; 'that is where Vergil used to sit. One often saw him there with his book in his hand. He was a handsome, fresh-looking man; he knew how with his magic to preserve his youth. These walls were covered with circles and lines. He used to come here with Prince Marcellus and teach him the secrets of the spirit-world. Often in the wildest storms, when no fisherman would have dared to go out, they used to put to sea in a boat. No rower was ever afraid when Vergil was with him; the fiercer the storm, the better he liked to be here. Often he sat up there on the mountain and looked out towards the gulf. Many of his books he wrote there. No doubt they were prophecies which he wrote, for there was never a storm but he foretold its coming. Then he visited the gardeners and field-labourers and gave them good advice and taught them when to sow their corn. Often when cloud and storm were coming down from Vesuvius he would turn them back with a powerful spell, and often he would spend whole nights with his face towards the mountain when the lightnings were beginning to flash about its head, perhaps in silent converse with its spirits. There had long been talk of making a road from Naples over the Posilipo; he came to our aid, and in one night his spirits had built the road through the cave. . . . Another time he helped us in a wonderful way. The gnats had become as great a plague here as they were in Egypt in the days of Moses. So he made a great golden fly, which rose at his command into the air and drove all the gnats away. So too once all the wells and fountains had become infested with leeches; he made a golden leech, threw it into a well and the plague was stayed.'

'The old man would have gone on,' adds the traveller, 'but it had grown quite dark already; so I thanked him for his story and rowed back.'[31]

At the present day the legends may be said to have well-nigh died out at Naples; but a few still linger in the neighbourhood of the cave at Puteoli, where a native once described to me the

[31] *Italienische Miscellen* (Tübingen, 1803), vol. iii. p. 150 seqq. Cp. DOBENECK, *Des deutschen Mittelalters Volksglauben und Heroensagen*, i. p. 195.

house which had belonged to Vergil on the mountain there and
how the cave had gone through it, while another explained that
a cleft in the rock was the window through which Vergil used to
speak to his lady. Nor is the memory of the great magician quite
extinct in other parts of Italy. At Borghetto, in Sicily, a strange
story [32] was current two or three decades ago about 'Virgillu
magu putenti e putirusu che cummannava l'arti arbolica megghiu
di qualunqui magu,' in which we find recollections of Vergilian
magic combined with reminiscences of the popular romances of
the *Rinaldi*, so dear to these islanders, and Vergil brought into
contact with Malagigi, their great magician. The story relates
that Vergil was married to a wife who caused him infinite
trouble. In despair he applied to Malagigi, who was his friend
and a past master in the arts of necromancy, and confided his
griefs to him. Malagigi took pity on him, and proceeded to
initiate him in magic as the only way of freeing him from the
tyranny of this Xanthippe, for ' senza forza di magarìa la mug-
ghieri cummanna e duminia.' Vergil used and abused this power
of his to such an extent in tormenting his wife that even the devils
whom he employed, though forced to obey his orders, felt sorry
for her ; so true is it that ' cu' havi virga 'n manu, si jetta allura
a l'abusa di potiri.' When however Vergil died and his lost
soul presented itself at the gates of hell, it found its entrance
barred, for the devils were so afraid of his power that they
refused to admit him. This was displeasing to Malagigi, who
accordingly sought a remedy. He collected the bones and the
soul of Vergil and carried them to a desert island where he
deposited them in a stone sepulchre, as big as a house, without
a cover, and left them there, after binding them with potent
spells. Whenever any one came to the grave and looked at
the bones, the sky at once became dark with clouds and a tre-
mendous storm arose, which lashed the sea to fury and engulfed
vessels and their freights.—In this story, therefore, besides the
non-Neapolitan feature which brings Vergil into contact with
women, it is interesting to observe the reference to the legend,

[32] Publ. by PITRÈ, *Fiabe, novelle e raconti populari siciliani*, Palermo,
1875. Vol. ii. p. 13 seqq. (No. 53).

which is unquestionably Neapolitan and of ancient origin, according to which it was believed at Naples in the 12th century, as we learn from Conrad von Querfurt,[33] that the bones of Vergil were preserved in a castle surrounded by the sea and that, if they were exposed to the air, it suddenly became dark and the waves began to beat against the castle.

That marvellous wisdom, by which it was believed at Naples that Vergil made the cave of Puteoli and other works for the public good and which was developed into sorcery and applied, as we have seen, in similar legends at Rome and elsewhere, still finds a memorial in the popular tradition at Taranto, where the Triglio aqueduct is attributed to Vergil. It is there related that 'the wizard Vergil was contending with the witches for the dominion of Taranto, and consequently wished to gain the affections of the people by producing some work that should be acceptable to them. The Tarentines were at that time much troubled by drought, and nothing could have been more acceptable to them than a plentiful supply of water. Vergil therefore began to construct an aqueduct from the direction of Triglio, and completed it in a single night, to the extreme satisfaction of the Tarentines. The witches, for their part, not wishing to be beaten, had commenced to build an aqueduct from Saturo; but in the morning they had only half finished it, when the news came that Vergil had already brought water to the city and had been received with acclamation by the inhabitants.'[34]

It is interesting to find the fame of Vergil the magician still living in this distant corner of Italy, as it had been already in the 13th century, when Ruggieri Pugliese alluded to the 'arts of Vergil.'[35] But a still more pleasing reminiscence of these 'arts' is to be found in the really poetical little love-song, the work of some poet of the Siculo-Provençal school, which a country-woman was heard to sing not long ago in a small village

[33] *Vide* supra, p. 259.
[34] This legend is recorded by Prof. L. VIOLA in a notice of his on the excavations made at Taranto, published in the *Notizie degli Scavi di antichità*, edited by the R. Accademia dei Lincei, 1881, p. 411 seqq. note. Viola observes that the legend arose out of the fact that the Saturo aqueduct does not reach the city.
[35] *Vide* supra, p. 346.

near Lecce, within a short distance of the place where Vergil died : [36]

> 'Diu! ci tanissi l'arte da Vargillu!
> 'Nnanti le porte to' 'nducìa lu mare,
> Ca da li pisci me facìa pupillu
> 'Mmienzu le riti to' enìa 'ncappare;
> Ca di l'acelli me facìa cardillu,
> 'Mmienzu lu piettu to' lu nitu a fare;
> E suttu l'umbra de li to' capilli
> Enìa de menzugiurnu a rrepusare.'

[36] Brought to my notice by the late Prof. Morosi.